VW Owners Workshop Manual

by J H Haynes

Member of the Guild of Motoring Writers

Bruce Gilmour
and A K Legg T Eng (CEI), AMIMI

Models covered
VW Golf Diesel C, D & LD, 1471 cc & 1588 cc
VW Jetta Diesel C, D & LD, 1588 cc

*Does not cover petrol engine models or 'Mk 2' models introduced during 1984
Covers most features of the Golf Diesel Van and Caddy*

ISBN 0 85696 992 3

Printed in England *(451-9N3)*

Haynes

THE BOOK

Haynes Publishing Group
Sparkford Nr Yeovil
Somerset BA22 7JJ England

Haynes Publications, Inc
861 Lawrence Drive
Newbury Park
California 91320 USA

British Library Cataloguing in Publication Data
Gilmour, Bruce
VW Golf & Jetta Diesel owners workshop manual.
– 2nd ed. – (Owners Workshop Manual/Haynes)
1. Golf automobile   2.Jetta automobile
I. Title   II. Legg, A. K.   III. Haynes, J. H.
VW owners workshop manual   IV. Series
629.28'722   TL215.G6
ISBN 0–85696–992–3

Acknowledgements

Thanks are due to the VW organisation for the supply of technical information and certain illustrations. Castrol Limited provided lubrication details, and Lucas CAV Limited supplied information on the testing and servicing of the CAV fuel injection pump and injectors.

Lastly thanks are due to all of those people at Sparkford who helped in the production of this manual.

About this manual

Its aim

The aim of this manual is to help you get the best value from your vehicle. It can do so in several ways. It can help you decide what work must be done (even should you choose to get it done by a garage), provide information on routine maintenance and servicing, and give a logical course of action and diagnosis when random faults occur. However, it is hoped that you will use the manual by tackling the work yourself. On simpler jobs it may even be quicker than booking the car into a garage and going there twice, to leave and collect it. Perhaps most important, a lot of money can be saved by avoiding the costs a garage must charge to cover its labour and overheads.

The manual has drawings and descriptions to show the function of the various components so that their layout can be understood. Then the tasks are described and photographed in a step-by-step sequence so that even a novice can do the work.

Its arrangement

The manual is divided into eleven Chapters, each covering a logical sub-division of the vehicle. The Chapters are each divided into Sections, numbered with single figures, eg 5; and the Sections into paragraphs (or sub-sections), with decimal numbers following on from the Section they are in, eg 5.1, 5.2, 5.3 etc.

It is freely illustrated, especially in those parts where there is a detailed sequence of operations to be carried out. There are two forms of illustration: figures and photographs. The figures are numbered in sequence with decimal numbers, according to their position in the Chapter – eg Fig. 6.4 is the fourth drawing/illustration in Chapter 6. Photographs carry the same number (either individually or in related groups) as the Section or sub-section to which they relate.

There is an alphabetical index at the back of the manual as well as a contents list at the front. Each Chapter is also preceded by its own individual contents list.

References to the 'left' or 'right' of the vehicle are in the sense of a person in the driver's seat facing forwards.

Unless otherwise stated, nuts and bolts are removed by turning anti-clockwise, and tightened by turning clockwise.

Vehicle manufacturers continually make changes to specifications and recommendations, and these, when notified, are incorporated into our manuals at the earliest opportunity.

Whilst every care is taken to ensure that the information in this manual is correct, no liability can be accepted by the authors or publishers for loss, damage or injury caused by any errors in, or omissions from, the information given.

Introduction to the
VW Golf/Rabbit Diesel

The Golf (UK) or Rabbit (USA) Diesel is the first small family car to be released by a major manufacturer with a diesel engine which can compete with a similar sized petrol engine. Its greatest asset is the fact that it can average 50 mpg, which is an obvious advantage in times of fuel shortage. In fact, this diesel engine is most economical in town traffic where its petrol counterpart is least economical.

The hatchback body is designed with safety cell zones and the brakes and steering also incorporate safety features. The engine and transmission unit is mounted transversely at the front of the car, and drive is through the front wheels.

Independent suspension all round and a well-appointed interior make the car very comfortable to ride in.

Since its introduction, the Golf/Rabbit has undergone a number of modifications, all aimed at improving some technical aspect. With the backing of the VW organisation, this car appears to be all set for a successful production run over many years.

Contents

VW Diesel Golf

General dimensions, weights and capacities

Dimensions
Overall length:
    1471 cc .... 3.705 m (145.9 in) standard, 3.725 m (146.6 in) with rubber strips
    1588 cc:
        Golf .... 3.815 m (150.3 in)
        Jetta .... 4.195 m (165.3 in)
Overall width .... 1·610 m (63·4 in)
Overall height (unladen) .... 1·410 m (55·5 in)
Wheelbase .... 2·400 m (94·5 in)
Track:
    Front .... 1·390 m (54·7 in)
    Rear .... 1·350 m (53·1 in)
Ground clearance .... 0·122 m (4·8 in)
Turning circle .... 10.0 m (32.8 ft), between kerbs

Weights
Kerb weight:
    1471 .... 830 kg (1830 lb)
    1588 cc:
        Golf .... 870 kg (1918 lb)
        Jetta .... 845 kg (1863 lb)
Payload (maximum) .... 420 kg (925 lb)
Trailer weight (maximum) up to 12% gradient:
    Trailer without brakes .... 400 kg (885 lb)
    Trailer with brakes .... 800 kg (1765 lb)
Roof rack load (maximum) .... 75 kg (165 lb)

Capacities
Engine oil .... 3·5 litres (6 Imp pints, 7·4 US pints)
Transmission oil .... 1·25 litres (2·2 Imp pints, 2·65 US pints)
Coolant .... 6·5 litres (11·0 Imp pints, 13·6 US pints)
Fuel tank .... 45 litres (9·9 Imp gal, 11·8 US gal)

Use of English

As this book has been written in England, it uses the appropriate English component names, phrases, and spelling. Some of these differ from those used in America. Normally, these cause no difficulty, but to make sure, a glossary is printed below. In ordering spare parts remember the parts list may use some of these words:

English	American	English	American
Accelerator	Gas pedal	Locks	Latches
Aerial	Antenna	Methylated spirit	Denatured alcohol
Anti-roll bar	Stabiliser or sway bar	Motorway	Freeway, turnpike etc
Big-end bearing	Rod bearing	Number plate	License plate
Bonnet (engine cover)	Hood	Paraffin	Kerosene
Boot (luggage compartment)	Trunk	Petrol	Gasoline (gas)
Bulkhead	Firewall	Petrol tank	Gas tank
Bush	Bushing	'Pinking'	'Pinging'
Cam follower or tappet	Valve lifter or tappet	Prise (force apart)	Pry
Carburettor	Carburetor	Propeller shaft	Driveshaft
Catch	Latch	Quarterlight	Quarter window
Choke/venturi	Barrel	Retread	Recap
Circlip	Snap-ring	Reverse	Back-up
Clearance	Lash	Rocker cover	Valve cover
Crownwheel	Ring gear (of differential)	Saloon	Sedan
Damper	Shock absorber, shock	Seized	Frozen
Disc (brake)	Rotor/disk	Sidelight	Parking light
Distance piece	Spacer	Silencer	Muffler
Drop arm	Pitman arm	Sill panel (beneath doors)	Rocker panel
Drop head coupe	Convertible	Small end, little end	Piston pin or wrist pin
Dynamo	Generator (DC)	Spanner	Wrench
Earth (electrical)	Ground	Split cotter (for valve spring cap)	Lock (for valve spring retainer)
Engineer's blue	Prussian blue	Split pin	Cotter pin
Estate car	Station wagon	Steering arm	Spindle arm
Exhaust manifold	Header	Sump	Oil pan
Fault finding/diagnosis	Troubleshooting	Swarf	Metal chips or debris
Float chamber	Float bowl	Tab washer	Tang or lock
Free-play	Lash	Tappet	Valve lifter
Freewheel	Coast	Thrust bearing	Throw-out bearing
Gearbox	Transmission	Top gear	High
Gearchange	Shift	Torch	Flashlight
Grub screw	Setscrew, Allen screw	Trackrod (of steering)	Tie-rod (or connecting rod)
Gudgeon pin	Piston pin or wrist pin	Trailing shoe (of brake)	Secondary shoe
Halfshaft	Axleshaft	Transmission	Whole drive line
Handbrake	Parking brake	Tyre	Tire
Hood	Soft top	Van	Panel wagon/van
Hot spot	Heat riser	Vice	Vise
Indicator	Turn signal	Wheel nut	Lug nut
Interior light	Dome lamp	Windscreen	Windshield
Layshaft (of gearbox)	Countershaft	Wing/mudguard	Fender
Leading shoe (of brake)	Primary shoe		

Buying spare parts
and vehicle identification numbers

Buying spare parts

Spare parts are available from many sources, for example: VW garages, other garages and accessory shops, and motor factors. Our advice regarding spare part sources is as follows:

Officially appointed VW garages – This is the best source of parts which are peculiar to your vehicle and are otherwise not generally

Vehicle identification plate (Golf)

Chassis number (Golf)

available (eg complete cylinder heads, internal gearbox components, badges, interior trim etc). It is also the only place at which you should buy parts if your car is still under warranty – non-VW components may invalidate the warranty. To be sure of obtaining the correct parts it will always be necessary to give the storeman your car's engine and chassis number, and if possible, to take the old part along for positive identification. Remember that many parts are available on a factory exchange scheme – any parts returned should always be clean! It obviously makes good sense to go straight to the specialists on your car for this type of part for they are best equipped to supply you.

Other garages and accessory shops – These are often very good places to buy materials and components needed for the maintenance of your car (eg oil filters, bulbs, fan belts, oils and greases, touch-up paint, filler paste etc). They also sell general accessories, usually have convenient opening hours, charge lower prices and can often be found not far from home.

Motor factors – Good factors will stock all of the more important components which wear out relatively quickly (eg clutch components, pistons, valves, exhaust system, brake cylinders/pipes/hoses/seals/ shoes and pads etc). Motor factors will often provide new or reconditioned components on a part exchange basis – this can save a considerable amount of money.

Vehicle identification numbers

It is most important to identify the vehicle accurately when ordering spare parts or asking for information, since modifications are constantly being made.

The vehicle identification plate is located on the front crossmember by the bonnet lock on Golf models, and on the left-hand side door-jamb on Rabbit models.

The chassis number is located in the engine compartment on the right-hand side suspension strut mounting on Golf models, and in the passenger compartment on the left-hand side of the instrument panel on Rabbit models.

Chassis number (Rabbit)

Engine number is stamped on the side of the block

Transmission code and date of manufacture (ie 4-12-78)

The engine number is located on the front of the cylinder block, just below the cylinder head (photo).

The transmission type number is stamped on the gear housing below the left-hand driveshaft. The code letters and date of manufacture are stamped on the bottom of the bellhousing (photo).

These numbers should be identified and recorded by the owner, they are required when ordering spares, going through the customs, and regrettably, by the police, if the vehicle is stolen.

When ordering spares remember that VW output is such that inevitably spares vary, are duplicated, and are held on a usage basis. If the storeman does not have the correct identification, he cannot produce the correct item. It is a good idea to take the old part if possible to compare it with a new one. The storeman has many customers to satisfy, so be accurate and patient. In some cases, particularly in the brake system, more than one manufacturer supplies an assembly, eg both Teves and Girling supply front calipers. The assemblies are interchangeable but the integral parts are not, although both use the same brake pads. This is only one of the pitfalls in the buying of spares, so be careful to make an ally of the storeman. When fitting accessories it is best to fit VW recommended ones. They are designed specifically for the vehicle.

Tools and working facilities

Introduction

A selection of good tools is a fundamental requirement for anyone contemplating the maintenance and repair of a motor vehicle. For the owner who does not possess any, their purchase will prove a considerable expense, offsetting some of the savings made by doing-it-yourself. However, provided that the tools purchased meet the relevant national safety standards and are of good quality, they will last for many years and prove an extremely worthwhile investment.

To help the average owner to decide which tools are needed to carry out the various tasks detailed in this manual, we have compiled three lists of tools under the following headings: *Maintenance and minor repair, Repair and overhaul,* a *Special.* The newcomer to practical mechanics should start off with the *Maintenance and minor repair* tool kit and confine himself to the simpler jobs around the vehicle. Then, as his confidence and experience grows, he can undertake more difficult tasks, buying extra tools as, and when, they are needed. In this way, a *Maintenance and minor repair* tool kit can be built-up into a *Repair and overhaul* tool kit over a considerable period of time without any major cash outlays. The experienced do-it-yourselfer will have a tool kit good enough for most repair and over-haul procedures and will add tools from the *Special* category when he feels the expense is justified by the amount of use these tools will be put to.

It is obviously not possible to cover the subject of tools fully here. For those who wish to learn more about tools and their use there is a book entitled *How to Choose and Use Car Tools* available from the publishers of this manual.

Maintenance and minor repair tool kit

The tools given in this list should be considered as a minimum requirement if routine maintenance, servicing and minor repair operations are to be undertaken. We recommend the purchase of combination spanners (ring one end, open-ended the other); although more expensive than open-ended ones, they do give the advantages of both types of spanner.

Combination spanners - 6 to 19 mm
Adjustable spanner - 9 inch
Transmission drain plug key
Set of metric feeler gauges
Brake bleed nipple spanner
Screwdriver - 4 in long x $\frac{1}{4}$ in dia (flat blade)
Screwdriver - 4 in long x $\frac{1}{4}$ in dia (cross blade)
Combination pliers - 6 inch
Hacksaw, junior
Tyre pump
Tyre pressure gauge
Oil can
Fine emery cloth (1 sheet)
Wire brush (small)
Funnel (medium size)

Repair and overhaul tool kit

These tools are virtually essential for anyone undertaking any major repairs to a motor vehicle, and are additional to those given in the *Maintenance and minor repair* list. Included in this list is a comprehensive set of sockets. Although these are expensive they will be found invaluable as they are so versatile - particularly if various drives are included in the set. We recommend the $\frac{1}{2}$ in square-drive type, as this can be used with most proprietary torque wrenches. If you cannot afford a socket set, even bought piecemeal, then inexpensive tubular box spanners are a useful alternative.

The tools in this list will occasionally need to be supplemented by tools from the *Special* list.

27mm ring spanner (for fuel injectors)
Sockets (or box spanners) to cover range in previous list
Reversible ratchet drive (for use with sockets)
Extension piece, 10 inch (for use with sockets)
Universal joint (for use with sockets)
Torque wrench (for use with sockets)
'Mole' wrench - 8 inch
Ball pein hammer
Soft-faced hammer, plastic or rubber
Screwdriver - 6 in long x $\frac{5}{16}$ in dia (flat blade)
Screwdriver - 2 in long x $\frac{5}{16}$ in square (flat blade)
Screwdriver - 1$\frac{1}{2}$ in long x $\frac{1}{4}$ in dia (cross blade)
Screwdriver - 3 in long x $\frac{1}{8}$ in dia (electricians)
Pliers - electricians side cutters
Pliers - needle nosed
Pliers - circlip (internal and external)
Cold chisel - $\frac{1}{2}$ inch
Scriber (this can be made by grinding the end of a broken hacksaw blade)
Scraper (this can be made by flattening and sharpening one end of a piece of copper pipe)
Centre punch
Pin punch
Hacksaw
Valve grinding tool
Steel rule/straight edge
Allen keys
Selection of files
Wire brush (large)
Axle-stands
Jack (strong scissor or hydraulic type)

Special tools

The tools in this list are those which are not used regularly, are expensive to buy, or which need to be used in accordance with their manufacturers' instructions. Unless relatively difficult mechanical jobs are undertaken frequently, it will not be economic to buy many of these tools. Where this is the case, you could consider clubbing together with friends (or a motorists' club) to make a joint purchase, or borrowing the tools against a deposit from a local garage or tool hire specialist.

The following list contains only those tools and instruments freely available to the public, and not those special tools produced by the vehicle manufacturer specifically for its dealer network. You will find occasional references to these manufacturers' special tools in the text of this manual. Generally, an alternative method of doing the job without the vehicle manufacturer's special tool is given. However, sometimes, there is no alternative to using them. Where this is the case and the relevant tool cannot be bought or borrowed you will have to entrust the work to a franchised garage.

> *Valve spring compressor*
> *Piston ring compressor*
> *Balljoint separator*
> *Universal hub/bearing puller*
> *Impact screwdriver*
> *Micrometer and/or vernier gauge*
> *Dial gauge*
> *Universal electrical multi-meter*
> *Cylinder compression gauge*
> *Lifting tackle*
> *Trolley jack*
> *Light with extension lead*

Buying tools

For practically all tools, a tool factor is the best source since he will have a very comprehensive range compared with the average garage or accessory shop. Having said that, accessory shops often offer excellent quality tools at discount prices, so it pays to shop around.

There are plenty of good tools around at reasonable prices, but always aim to purchase items which meet the relevant national safety standards. If in doubt, ask the proprietor or manager of the shop for advice before making a purchase.

Care and maintenance of tools

Having purchased a reasonable tool kit, it is necessary to keep the tools in a clean serviceable condition. After use, always wipe off any dirt, grease and metal particles using a clean, dry cloth, before putting the tools away. Never leave them lying around after they have been used. A simple tool rack on the garage or workshop wall, for items such as screwdrivers and pliers is a good idea. Store all normal spanners and sockets in a metal box. Any measuring instruments, gauges, meters, etc, must be carefully stored where they cannot be damaged or become rusty.

Take a little care when tools are used. Hammer heads inevitably become marked and screwdrivers lose the keen edge on their blades from time to time. A little timely attention with emery cloth or a file will soon restore items like this to a good serviceable finish.

Working facilities

Not to be forgotten when discussing tools, is the workshop itself. If anything more than routine maintenance is to be carried out, some form of suitable working area becomes essential.

It is appreciated that many an owner mechanic is forced by circumstances to remove an engine or similar item, without the benefit of a garage or workshop. Having done this, any repairs should always be done under the cover of a roof.

Wherever possible, any dismantling should be done on a clean flat workbench or table at a suitable working height.

Any workbench needs a vice: one with a jaw opening of 100 mm (4 in) is suitable for most jobs. As mentioned previously, some clean dry storage space is also required for tools, as well as the lubricants, cleaning fluids, touch-up paints and so on which become necessary.

Another item which may be required, and which has a much more general usage, is an electric drill with a chuck capacity of at least (8 mm) $\frac{5}{16}$ in. This, together with a good range of twist drills, is virtually essential for fitting accessories such as wing mirrors and reversing lights.

Last, but not least, always keep a supply of old newspapers and clean, lint-free rags available, and try to keep any working area as clean as possible.

Spanner jaw gap comparison table

Jaw gap (in)	Spanner size
0.250	$\frac{1}{4}$ in AF
0.277	7 mm
0.313	$\frac{5}{16}$ in AF
0.315	8 mm
0.344	$\frac{11}{32}$ in AF; $\frac{1}{8}$ in Whitworth
0.354	9 mm
0.375	$\frac{3}{8}$ in AF
0.394	10 mm
0.433	11 mm
0.438	$\frac{7}{16}$ in AF
0.445	$\frac{3}{16}$ in Whitworth; $\frac{1}{4}$ in BSF
0.472	12 mm
0.500	$\frac{1}{2}$ in AF
0.512	13 mm
0.525	$\frac{1}{4}$ in Whitworth; $\frac{5}{16}$ in BSF
0.551	14 mm
0.563	$\frac{9}{16}$ in AF
0.591	15 mm
0.600	$\frac{5}{16}$ in Whitworth; $\frac{3}{8}$ in BSF
0.625	$\frac{5}{8}$ in AF
0.630	16 mm
0.669	17 mm
0.686	$\frac{11}{16}$ in AF
0.709	18 mm
0.710	$\frac{3}{8}$ in Whitworth; $\frac{7}{16}$ in BSF
0.748	19 mm
0.750	$\frac{3}{4}$ in AF
0.813	$\frac{13}{16}$ in AF
0.820	$\frac{7}{16}$ in Whitworth; $\frac{1}{2}$ in BSF
0.866	22 mm
0.875	$\frac{7}{8}$ in AF
0.920	$\frac{1}{2}$ in Whitworth; $\frac{9}{16}$ in BSF
0.938	$\frac{15}{16}$ in AF
0.945	24 mm
1.000	1 in AF
1.010	$\frac{9}{16}$ in Whitworth; $\frac{5}{8}$ in BSF
1.024	26 mm
1.063	$1\frac{1}{16}$ in AF; 27 mm
1.100	$\frac{5}{8}$ in Whitworth; $\frac{11}{16}$ in BSF
1.125	$1\frac{1}{8}$ in AF
1.181	30 mm
1.200	$\frac{11}{16}$ in Whitworth; $\frac{3}{4}$ in BSF
1.250	$1\frac{1}{4}$ in AF
1.260	32 mm
1.300	$\frac{3}{4}$ in Whitworth; $\frac{7}{8}$ in BSF
1.313	$1\frac{5}{16}$ in AF
1.390	$\frac{13}{16}$ in Whitworth; $\frac{15}{16}$ in BSF
1.417	36 mm
1.438	$1\frac{7}{16}$ in AF
1.480	$\frac{7}{8}$ in Whitworth; 1 in BSF
1.500	$1\frac{1}{2}$ in AF
1.575	40 mm; $\frac{15}{16}$ in Whitworth
1.614	41 mm
1.625	$1\frac{5}{8}$ in AF
1.670	1 in Whitworth; $1\frac{1}{8}$ in BSF
1.688	$1\frac{11}{16}$ in AF
1.811	46 mm
1.813	$1\frac{13}{16}$ in AF
1.860	$1\frac{1}{8}$ in Whitworth; $1\frac{1}{4}$ in BSF
1.875	$1\frac{7}{8}$ in AF
1.969	50 mm
2.000	2 in AF
2.050	$1\frac{1}{4}$ in Whitworth; $1\frac{3}{8}$ in BSF
2.165	55 mm
2.362	60 mm

Jacking and towing

Before jacking-up the car, ensure that it is on level ground and apply the handbrake firmly. There are two jacking points on each side of the car adjacent to each wheel and marked with an embossed triangle. The jack lifting hook must engage with the ridge on the body underframe (photos).

If the car is being jacked-up for maintenance purposes, axle stands or wooden blocks must be used; never work beneath the car with only the tool kit jack supporting it.

Emergency towing points are provided at the front and rear of the car but should only be used for short distances (photos). When being towed, remember that extra effort will be required on the footbrake pedal, as the vacuum servo pump will not be working with the engine stationary.

Spare wheel location

Jacking-up the car

Front towing eye

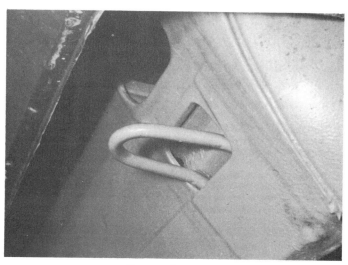

Rear towing eye

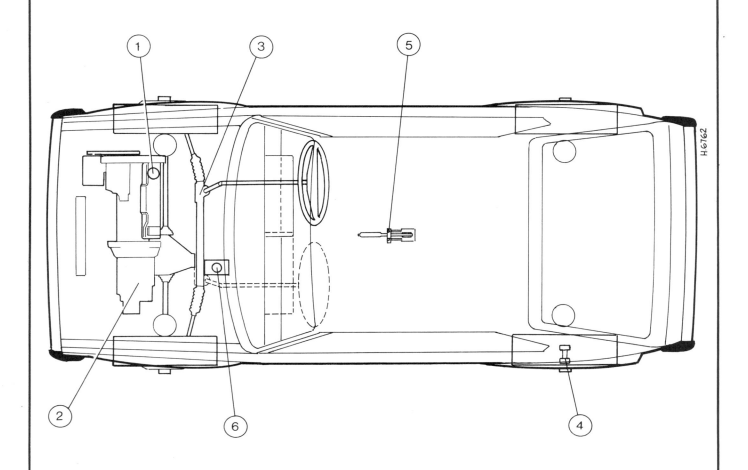

Recommended lubricants and fluids

Component or system	Lubricant type or specification
Engine (1)	Multigrade oil: SAE 20W/50
Gearbox (2)	Hypoid gear oil: GL4, SAE 80 or 80W/90
Rack and pinion unit (3)	Special VW lubricant
Rear wheel bearings (4)	Lithium based grease
Handbrake compensator (5)	Lithium based grease
Clutch cable	Lithium based grease
Braking system (6)	Hydraulic fluid to SAE J1703 or DOT 3

Note: The above are general recommendations only. Lubrication requirements may vary with operating conditions and from territory to territory. If in doubt consult the operator's handbook or your VW dealer.

Routine maintenance

Maintenance is essential for ensuring safety and desirable for the purpose of getting the best in terms of performance and economy from the car. Over the years the need for periodic lubrication – oiling, greasing and so on – has been drastically reduced, if not totally eliminated. This has unfortunately tended to lead some owners to think that because no such action is required the items either no longer exist or will last for ever. This is a serious delusion. It follows, therefore, that the largest initial element of maintenance is visual examination which may lead to repairs or renewals.

Every 250 miles (400 km) or weekly – whichever comes first

Engine
    Check oil level and top-up if necessary (photos)
    Check coolant level and top-up if necessary

Electrical system
    Check operation of all lights
    Check wipers and horn
    Check windscreen washer fluid level (photos)
    Check battery electrolyte level and top-up with distilled water if necessary

Steering
    Check tyre pressures, including spare (photo)
    Examine tyres for wear or damage
    Check steering for smooth and accurate operation

Brakes
    Check reservoir fluid level
    Check brake efficiency

Removing the oil level dipstick

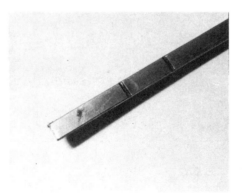

Oil level dipstick minimum and maximum marks. Difference between marks is 1 litre (1.75 Imp pints, 2 US pints)

Topping-up the engine oil

Windscreen washer reservoir

Tailgate washer reservoir

Using a tyre pressure gauge

First 5000 miles (7500 km) or 6 months – whichever comes first

Engine
Tighten the cylinder head bolts
Check and, if necessary, adjust the valve clearances
Change the engine oil (photo)
Examine the engine for oil and water leaks

Fuel system
Drain the water in the fuel filter
Check and, if necessary, adjust the idling speed

Clutch
Check the clutch play and adjust, if necessary

Gearbox
Examine the gearbox and final drive for oil leaks

General
Road test and check the function of all controls

First 10 000 miles (15 000 km) or 12 months – whichever comes first

Repeat this service every 10 000 miles (15 000 km)/12 months, but alternate this and the following service at 5000 mile (7500 km)/6 month intervals

Engine
Check and, if necessary, adjust the valve clearances
Change the engine oil
Renew the engine oil filter
Examine the engine for oil and water leaks
Examine all drivebelts for wear and damage, renew if necessary and/or adjust their tension

Cooling system
Check the antifreeze strength
Check the coolant level and top-up, if necessary
Check the condition and security of all hoses and clips

Fuel and exhaust systems
Drain the water in the fuel filter
Reset the air cleaner intake (where applicable)
Check and, if necessary, adjust the idling speed
Check the condition and security of the exhaust system

Clutch
Check the clutch play and adjust, if necessary

Gearbox
Examine the gearbox and final drive for damage or oil leaks
Check the gearbox and final drive oil level and top-up, if necessary (photos)

Braking system, wheels and tyres
Examine the brake pipes and hoses for leakage or damage
Check the front and rear brake linings for wear
Adjust the rear brakes (where applicable)
Check the operation of the handbrake and adjust, if necessary (where applicable)
Check the fluid level in the master cylinder and top-up, if necessary
Check the tyres for condition and tread depth
Check the tyre pressures

Electrical system
Check the operation of all lights, direction indicators and horn
Check the operation of the wipers and washers and, if necessary, top-up the washer reservoir
Check the battery electrolyte level and top-up with distilled water, if necessary
Check the headlight aim and adjust if necessary
Check the function of all electrical accessories and instruments

Suspension, steering and drivebelts
Check for play or damage in all suspension and steering balljoints and linkages
Check the steering gear bellows and balljoint rubber boots for damage or deterioration
Check for play or damage to the driveshafts and inspect the CV joint boots for leakage or deterioration

Bodywork and fittings
Lubricate all locks and hinges (not steering lock)
Examine the underbody sealant for damage
Check the door locks and window regulators for adjustment and/or operation

General
Road test and check the function of all controls

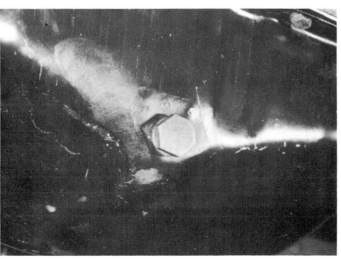

Engine sump drain plug

Transmission filler plug

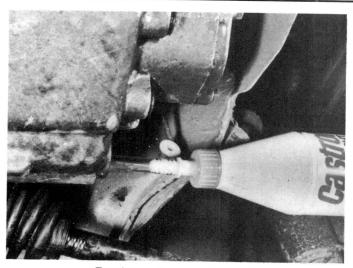

Topping-up the transmission oil

First 15 000 miles (22 500 km) or 18 months – whichever comes first

---

Repeat this service every 10 000 miles (15 000 km)/12 months, but alternate this and the preceding service at 5000 mile (7500 km)/6 month intervals

Engine
Change the engine oil

Cooling system
Check the coolant level and top-up, if necessary

Fuel system
Drain the water in the fuel filter (1983 models onward)

Braking system
Check the front brake linings for wear
Check the fluid level in the master cylinder and top-up, if necessary

Electrical system
Check the battery electrolyte level and top-up with distilled water, if necessary

Bodywork and fittings
Lubricate the bonnet lock and door check straps

Every 20 000 miles (30 000 km) or 2 years – whichever comes first

---

Engine
Check and, if necessary, adjust the valve clearances
Check the condition and tension of the toothed drivebelt; renew, if necessary

Fuel system
Renew the fuel filter
Renew the air filter element

Every 2 years

Cooling system
Renew the coolant

Braking sysem
Renew the brake fluid and check the brakes for operation

Chapter 1 Engine

For modifications, and information applicable to later models, see Supplement at end of manual

Contents

Specifications

Engine – general

Type	Four-cylinder in-line diesel, water cooled with overhead camshaft
Bore	76·5 mm (3·012 in)
Stroke	80·0 mm (3·150 in)
Capacity	1471 cc (89·8 cu in)
Compression ratio	23·5 : 1
Maximum output (DIN)	37 kW (50 bhp) @ 5000 rpm
Maximum torque (DIN)	82·0 Nm (56·5 lbf ft) @ 3000 rpm

Cylinder block and pistons

Material	Cast iron
Number of main bearings	5
Cylinder out of round – maximum	0·04 mm (0·0016 in)
Piston to cylinder clearance:	
New part	0·03 mm (0·011 in)
Wear limit	0·07 mm (0·027 in)

Piston sizes	Piston dia (mm)	Cylinder bore (mm)
Standard – 1	76·48	76·51
Standard – 2	76·49	76·52
Standard – 3	76·50	76·53

Three oversizes are available in steps of 0·25 mm

Piston rings

Side clearance:

Upper compression ring	0·06 – 0·09 mm (0·002 – 0·0035 in)
Lower compression ring	0·05 – 0·08 mm (0·0019 – 0·0031 in)
Oil scraper ring	0·03 – 0·06 mm (0·0011 – 0·002 in)

Wear limit:
    Compression rings . . . .   0·02 mm (0·0007 in)
    Oil scraper ring . . . .   0·15 mm (0·0059 in)
Ring gap:
    Compression rings . . . .   0·3 – 0·5 mm (0·012 – 0·020 in)
    Oil scraper ring . . . .   0·25 – 0·40 mm (0·010 – 0·016 in)
    Wear limit . . . .   1·0 mm (0·039 in)

Crankshaft

Main bearing journals:
    Standard . . . .   54·00 mm (2·126 in)
    1st undersize . . . .   53·75 mm (2·116 in)
    2nd undersize . . . .   53·50 mm (2·106 in)
    3rd undersize . . . .   53·25 mm (2·097 in)
    Maximum out-of-round . . . .   0·03 mm (0·0012 in)
Connecting rod journals:
    Standard . . . .   46·00 mm (1·811 in)
    1st undersize . . . .   45·75 mm (1·801 in)
    2nd undersize . . . .   45·50 mm (1·791 in)
    3rd undersize . . . .   45·25 mm (1·781 in)
    Maximum out-of-round . . . .   0·03 mm (0·0012 in)

Main bearings

Bearing radial clearance . . . .   0·03 – 0·08 mm (0·0012 – 0·0031 in)
Wear limit . . . .   0·17 mm (0·0066 in)
Crankshaft endplay (measured at No 3 bearing) . . . .   0·07 – 0·17 mm (0·003 – 0·0066 in)
Wear limit . . . .   0·37 mm (0·015 in)

Connecting rod bearings

Bearing radial clearance . . . .   0·028 – 0·088 mm (0·0011 – 0·0034 in)
Wear limit . . . .   0·12 mm (0·004 in)
Maximum side clearance . . . .   0·37 mm (0·014 in)

Camshaft

Maximum endplay . . . .   0·15 mm (0·006 in)

Valves

Inlet:
    Length . . . .   104·8 mm (4·125 in)
    Head diameter . . . .   34·0 mm (1·338 in)
    Stem diameter . . . .   7·97 mm (0·314 in)
    Seat width . . . .   2·0 mm (0·078 in)
    Seat angle . . . .   45°
Exhaust:
    Length . . . .   104·6 mm (4·117 in)
    Head diameter . . . .   31·00 mm (1·220 in)
    Stem diameter . . . .   7·95 mm (0·313 in)
    Seat width . . . .   2·4 mm (0·44 in)
    Seat angle . . . .   45°
Valve clearance – cold:
    Inlet . . . .   0·15 – 0·25 mm (0·006 – 0·010 in)
    Exhaust . . . .   0·35 – 0·45 mm (0·014 – 0·018 in)
Valve clearance – hot:
    Inlet . . . .   0·20 – 0·30 mm (0·008 – 0·012 in)
    Exhaust . . . .   0·40 – 0·50 mm (0·016 – 0·020 in)

Lubrication system

Oil pump . . . .   Gear type
Backlash between gears . . . .   0·20 mm (0·008 in) max.
Endplay . . . .   0·15 mm (0·006 in) max.
Oil pressure . . . .   1·96 kgf/cm² (28 lbf/in²) minimum at 2000 rpm with oil temperature
    of 80°C (176°F)
Oil capacity . . . .   3·5 litres (6 Imp pints, 7·4 US pints)

Torque wrench settings

	kgf m	lbf ft
Camshaft bearing caps	2·0	14
Camshaft sprocket	4·5	33
Connecting rod caps	4·5	33
Crankshaft sprocket	8·0	56
Crankshaft pulley	2·0	14
Crankshaft bearing caps	6·5	47
Cylinder head bolts (engine cold):		
Stage 1	7·5	55
Stage 2	Additional $\frac{1}{4}$ turn to each bolt	
Engine to transmission	5·5	40
Engine mounting to body	4·0	29

Torque wrench settings

	kgf m	lbf ft
Driveshaft flange bolts	4·5	33
Fuel pump mounting plate	2·5	18
Fuel pump to mounting plate	2·5	18
Fuel injection pipes	2·5	18
Intermediate shaft flange	2·5	18
Intermediate shaft pulley	4·5	32
Oil drain plug	3·0	21
Oil pump to engine	2·0	14
Oil pump cover bolts	1·0	7
Oil sump bolts	2·0	14
Oil pressure switch	1·2	8·5
Oil filter adapter to block	2·0	18
Drivebelt tensioner locknut	4·5	32
Fuel injection pump sprocket	4·5	32
Fuel injectors	7·0	51
Manifolds to cylinder head	2·5	18
Exhaust pipe to manifold	2·5	18
Clutch pressure plate to crankshaft	7·5	54
Flywheel to clutch assembly	2·0	14
Vacuum pump clamp bolt	1·4	10
Valve cover bolts	0·6	4

1 General description

The four-cylinder, in-line, water-cooled engine has a cast iron cylinder block and an aluminium cylinder head. The crankshaft is supported in five main bearings.

The overhead camshaft is driven by a toothed drivebelt from a sprocket on the crankshaft. The belt also drives the intermediate shaft which in turn drives the oil pump and vacuum pump. The fuel injection pump, also driven by the toothed drivebelt, is mounted on the left-hand side of the engine.

The camshaft lobes press on the bucket type tappets which bear directly on the end of the valve stems. A steel disc, available in different thicknesses, is fitted on each tappet to provide for adjustment of the valve clearances.

The spark plugs as used on petrol engines are replaced by fuel injectors which inject atomised fuel into the pre-combustion chambers in the cylinder head when the piston is at the top of the compression stroke. The compression ratio is 23·5:1 (about three times that of petrol engines) and the heat generated by the high compression of the intake air ignites the vapourised fuel. Electrically heated glow plugs are fitted to each pre-combustion chamber to assist cold starting.

The engine is supported on flexible mountings. These are attached to a bracket at the front of the engine (drivebelt end) and one at the rear of the transmission, a side support to the frame behind the engine and torque reaction damper from the left-hand side of the engine to the frame below the radiator.

2 Major operations possible with the engine in the car

1 The following operations can be carried out with the engine in the car. Removal and refitting of the following:

(a) Cylinder head assembly*
(b) Toothed drivebelt†
(c) Fuel injection pump
(d) Crankshaft front oil seal†
(e) Intermediate shaft oil seal†
(f) Oil sump and oil pump‡
(g) Pistons and connecting rods‡
(h) Engine mountings

* Requires preliminary draining of coolant
† Requires preliminary draining of coolant and removal of radiator
‡ Requires draining of coolant and oil

3 Major operations requiring engine removal

1 It is necessary to remove the engine from the car when removing and refitting the following:

(a) Crankshaft rear oil seal
(b) Crankshaft and main bearings
(c) Intermediate shaft

4 Engine removal – general

1 The engine and transmission can be removed as an assembly. Alternatively, the transmission can be removed first, as described in Chapter 5, and then the engine removed as a separate unit.

2 If the engine and transmission are being removed as a single assembly, it must be lowered out of the engine compartment and removed from under the car. If the transmission is removed first then the engine can be hoisted out of the engine compartment.

3 For removal of the engine/transmission assembly a 330 lbs (150 kg) capacity hoist will be required. The car must be raised and supported on axle stands, or other suitable supports, placed under the bodyframe. Make sure it is high enough to allow the engine/transmission assembly to be withdrawn from underneath the car.

4 When disconnecting wiring, control cables and hoses, label them so that they can be identified to their correct locations and thus avoid any confusion when the engine is being refitted.

5 Have suitable containers available to hold small items so that they will not get lost.

5 Engine/transmission assembly – removal

1 Disconnect the cables from the battery.

2 Mark the position of the bonnet hinges, then remove the four hinge to bonnet bolts and lift away the bonnet with the help of an assistant. Place the bonnet safely out of the way where it will not get scratched or damaged.

3 Unscrew the battery hold-down clamp securing bolt and remove the clamp. Lift the battery out of the engine compartment, taking care not to spill any of the electrolyte.

4 Drain the cooling system as described in Chapter 2. Remove the sump drain plug and drain the oil into a suitable container. Refit the drain plug.

5 Slacken the securing clips and remove the radiator top and bottom hoses. Disconnect the hose to the coolant expansion tank.

6 Disconnect the wiring from the fan motor at the connector and the wiring from the thermoswitch on the radiator.

7 Remove the radiator lower securing nuts. Release the radiator from the upper securing clip, then tilt the radiator towards the engine and lift it up off the bottom mounting supports. Remove it from the engine compartment complete with fan.

8 Remove the alternator as described in Chapter 7, and the air conditioning compressor (if fitted) as described in Chapter 2.

9 Disconnect the fuel supply and return lines from the fuel injection pump. Disconnect the servo vacuum hose from the vacuum pump.

10 Disconnect the accelerator and cold start cables from the levers on the fuel pump. Lift away the accelerator cable complete with support bracket.

11 Disconnect the wiring from the stop solenoid on the fuel pump and from the glow plugs on the cylinder head.

12 Disconnect the wiring from the oil pressure switch, at the rear of

Fig. 1.1 Disconnect the fuel lines and accelerator cable from the fuel injection pump (Sec 5)

6	Fuel supply line	8	Accelerator cable
7	Fuel return line	9	Cable support bracket

5.19 Tying the driveshafts to one side when removing the engine

Fig. 1.2 Remove the exhaust pipe support and disconnect the exhaust pipe from the exhaust manifold (Sec 5)

16	Support bracket	18	Flange securing nuts
17	Support rod	19	Gearbox mounting

Fig. 1.3 Disconnect the gear selector linkage (Sec 5)

13	Relay lever	15	Selector rod
14	Connecting rod		

the cylinder head, and from the coolant temperature switch located on the thermostat housing.

13 Disconnect the wiring from the starter motor and the reversing light switch.

14 Slacken the securing clips and remove the heater hoses.

15 Remove the fuel filter mounting bolts and place the filter assembly on the wheel housing. It is not necessary to disconnect the fuel lines from the filter assembly.

16 Raise the front of the car and support it securely on axle stands.

17 Slacken the clutch cable adjuster, refer to Chapter 4, and remove the cable from the operating lever. Tie the cable out of the way.

18 Undo the clamp bolt and remove the speedometer cable drive from the transmission. Plug the hole in the casing to prevent dust or moisture entering the gearbox.

19 Disconnect the driveshafts from the transmission by removing the bolts from the driveshaft flanges with an Allen key. Support the shafts so that the rubber boots will not get damaged (photo).

20 Remove the exhaust pipe support and the exhaust pipe to exhaust manifold bolts, then lower the exhaust pipe.

21 Remove the gear shift relay lever and disconnect the shift linkage connecting rod from the transmission. Disconnect the selector rod at the rear.

22 Undo the securing bolts and remove the front transmission mounting complete by taking the bracket off the frame and the bracket from

the engine/transmission. Remove the earth strap from the transmission (photos).

23 From underneath the car remove the mounting bracket which holds the unit to the body. The mounting is secured to the body by three nuts and to the transmission by two nuts (photos).

24 Position the lifting gear, fit the sling and take the weight of the engine. The engine is now supported at both ends. Undo the nuts securing the mountings at the front of the engine and at the rear of the transmission. Remove the nuts securing the bracket to the transmission. Lift slightly on the hoist, then remove the mounting bolts and pull the engine/transmission assembly away from the mounting brackets.

25 Turn the roadwheels fully to the right and position the left-hand driveshaft along the wishbone and the right-hand driveshaft pointing towards the front of the car. Make a final check that all wiring and control cables have been disconnected and tucked out of the way, then carefully lower the assembly to the ground and remove it from under the car (photos).

6 Separating the transmission from the engine

1 The engine must be supported so that the transmission can be withdrawn. Either support the engine so that the transmission overhangs the bench or remove the transmission from the engine while the

5.22A Removing the front transmission mounting bolt

5.22B Earth strap location on front transmission mounting

5.23A Rear transmission mounting location

5.23B Locating peg on rear transmission mounting

5.23C Removing the transmission rear mounting (engine out of car for clarity)

5.25A Lowering the engine to the ground with a hoist

5.25B Lifting the body over the engine with a hoist

5.25C Hook location when lifting body

6.3A TDC hole plug

assembly is suspended on the hoist.

2   Undo the securing bolts and remove the starter motor.

3   Remove the plug from the TDC marker hole in the bellhousing. Rotate the crankshaft, using a spanner on the crankshaft sprocket bolt, until the cut-out on the flywheel (76° BTDC) is aligned with the pointer on the clutch housing (photos). This is necessary to prevent the flywheel fouling the housing as the transmission is withdrawn from the engine.

4   Remove the securing bolts and lift away the cover plate (arrowed in Fig. 1.4) over the driveshaft flange.

5   Remove the transmission-to-engine securing bolts and lift away the cover plate. Withdraw the transmission from the engine. **Do not** insert wedges to separate the units or you will damage the mating faces; rock the transmission carefully to free it from the two locating dowels. Withdraw the transmission carefully, taking care not to put any stress on the transmission mainshaft or the clutch pushrod which may damage them (photo).

7   Engine ancillary components – removal

1   Before basic engine dismantling begins remove the following components;

    (a) Air cleaner
    (b) Vacuum pump
    (c) Intake and exhaust manifolds
    (d) Water pump assembly
    (e) Fuel injectors
    (f) Oil filter
    (g) Oil pressure switch
    (h) Clutch pressure plate assembly and friction disc

2   Information on the removal and refitting of these components can be found in the relevant Chapters throughout this manual.

6.3B Flywheel alignment marks when separating engine and transmission

Fig. 1.4 Removing the cover plate (arrowed) (Sec 6)

8 Engine dismantling – general

1   It is best to mount the engine on a dismantling stand but if one is not available, then place the engine on a strong bench so as to be at a comfortable working height. Failing this the engine can be stripped down on the floor, but take care to avoid grit coming in contact with the internal parts of the engine.

2   During the dismantling process the greatest care should be taken to keep the exposed parts free from dirt. As an aid to achieving this, it is a sound scheme to clean the outside of the engine thoroughly (away from the working area), removing all traces of oil and congealed dirt, before dismantling begins.

3   Use paraffin or a good grease solvent. The latter compound will make the job much easier, as, after the solvent has been applied and allowed to stand for some time, a vigorous jet of water will wash off all the solvent and the grease and dirt. If the dirt is very thick, work the solvent into it with a stiff brush.

4   As the engine is dismantled, clean each part in a bath of paraffin. Never immerse parts with oilways in paraffin, eg the crankshaft, but to clean, wipe down with a paraffin dampened rag. Oilways can be cleaned out with wire. If an air line is available all the parts can be blown dry and the oilways blown through as an added precaution.

5   Re-use of old engine gaskets and oil seals is a false economy and can give rise to oil and water leaks, if nothing worse. To avoid the possibility of trouble with leaks after the engine has been reassembled always use new gaskets and oil seals.

6   Do not throw the old gaskets away as it sometimes happens that an immediate replacement cannot be obtained and the old gasket is then very useful as a template. As the gaskets are removed hang them up on suitable hooks or nails.

7   When dismantling the engine it is best to work from the top down, with the engine supported in an upright position. Ensure that it is well supported so that it will not fall over when tight nuts and bolts are being slackened. When the stage where the oil sump has to be removed is reached, the engine can be turned on its side and all the other work carried out with it in this position.

8   Wherever possible, refit nuts, bolts and washers finger tight from where they were removed. This helps avoid possible loss, or doubt as to where they belong. If they cannot be refitted then lay them out in such a fashion that it is clear where they belong.

9 Toothed drivebelt – removal and refitting (engine in car)

1   Release the four securing clips and remove the air cleaner cover and filter. Remove the CAV type fuel filter where fitted (Chapter 3).

2   Undo the eight bolts or nuts securing the valve cover and remove them, the two strengthening strips and the valve cover (photo).

6.5 Separating the transmission from the engine

9.2 Valve cover and retaining nuts

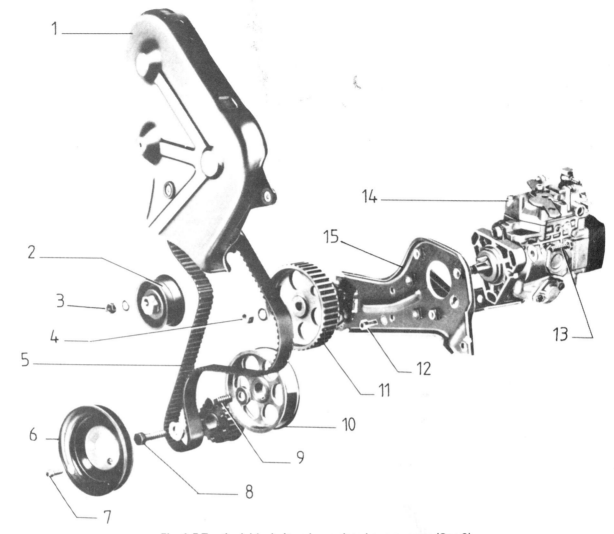

Fig. 1.5 Toothed drivebelt and associated components (Sec 6)

1	Belt cover	6	Crankshaft pulley
2	Belt tensioner	7	Pulley securing bolt
3	Tensioner locknut	8	Crankshaft sprocket securing
4	Pump sprocket securing nut		bolt
5	Drivebelt		

9	Intermediate shaft pulley bolt
10	Intermediate shaft pulley
11	Fuel injection pump sprocket
12	Injection pump mounting

	plate securing bolt
13	Injection pump securing bolt
14	Fuel injection pump
15	Mounting plate

9.4A The crankshaft pulley

9.4B Removing the crankshaft pulley

9.5 Removing the engine drivebelt cover

Remove the valve cover gasket.

3   Slacken the alternator mounting bolts, then push the alternator towards the engine and remove the alternator drivebelt.

4   Undo the crankshaft pulley securing bolts with an Allen key and remove the pulley (photos).

5   Remove the securing bolts and lift away the drivebelt cover (photo). Later models have two covers.

6   Remove the plug from the TDC marker hole on the clutch bellhousing. Rotate the crankshaft, using a spanner on the crankshaft sprocket retaining bolt, until No 1 piston is at TDC on the compression stroke, (both valves closed, cam lobes pointing upwards) and the notch on the flywheel is aligned with the pointer on the bellhousing (Fig. 1.6).

7   Lock the camshaft in position to prevent it from turning while the belt is removed. VW Tool No 2065 is specified for this operation, but a metal bar of suitable dimensions is just as good (photo). Lock the fuel injection pump sprocket in the set position with a locking pin of suitable diameter. Again a special VW tool (No. 2064) is available, but a bolt will serve just as well (photo).

8   Slacken the drivebelt tensioner locknut and unscrew the tensioner adjuster to release the tension from the belt.

9   Undo the drivebelt shield securing bolts. Remove the belt shield and the drivebelt.

10   When fitting a new belt check that the TDC mark on the flywheel is aligned with the pointer on the bellhousing, then slacken the camshaft sprocket securing bolt half a turn and free the sprocket from the camshaft by tapping it with a plastic hammer.

11   Fit the new drivebelt on the sprockets and remove the locking pin from the injection pump sprocket.

12   Turn the belt tensioner clockwise to tension the belt and check the tension between the camshaft sprocket and injection pump sprocket with tool VW210. If this tool is not available, refer to paragraph 14. Adjust the tension so that the scale on tool VW210 reads 12–13, then tighten the camshaft sprocket bolt and the tensioner locknut to the specified torque.

13   Remove the locking fixture from the camshaft.

14   Turn the engine through two revolutions in the normal direction of rotation, then strike the belt with a plastic hammer between the camshaft sprocket and the injection pump sprocket. Now re-check the belt tension and, if necessary, re-adjust. If the tool VW210 is not available a reasonably accurate tension of the belt (as a temporary measure) can be achieved by adjusting the belt tensioner until the belt will twist only 90° when held between the finger and thumb midway between the camshaft sprocket and the fuel injection pump sprocket.

15   Check the fuel injection pump timing, refer to Chapter 3.

16   The remainder of the refitting procedure is the reverse of removal. When refitting the alternator drivebelt adjust the belt tension as described in Chapter 7. Always use a new gasket when refitting the valve cover.

Fig. 1.6 TDC notch on flywheel aligned with pointer (Sec 9)

9.7A Method of locking the camshaft with a metal bar

9.7B Using a bolt to lock the fuel injection pump sprocket

Fig. 1.7 Checking the drivebelt tension with VW tool 210 (Sec 9)

10 Crankshaft pulley, drivebelt and tensioner, fuel injection pump and crankshaft sprocket – removal

1   Undo the four socket headed bolts securing the crankshaft pulley to the crankshaft sprocket and remove the pulley. Remove the belt cover securing bolts and the cover.
2   Before removing the toothed drivebelt, check the belt tension. If the belt is held between the finger and thumb, midway between the camshaft sprocket and the fuel injection pump sprocket, it should be just possible to twist it through ·90°. If it is too slack, adjust it by slackening the locknut and turning the tensioner clockwise. If the belt cannot be tensioned correctly, this means that it has stretched and a new belt must be obtained.
3   Remove the two bolts securing the drivebelt shield and lift away the shield.
4   Release the drivebelt tension and remove the drivebelt.
5   Remove the drivebelt tensioner (photos).
6   Remove the crankshaft sprocket by unscrewing the securing bolt and then pulling off the sprocket, using a suitable puller. Prevent the

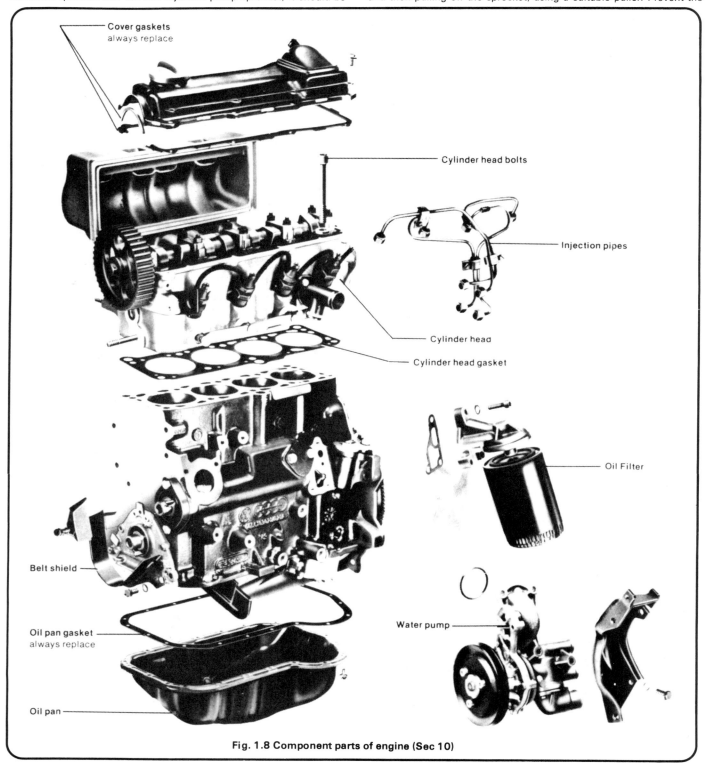

Fig. 1.8 Component parts of engine (Sec 10)

10.5A Drivebelt tensioner location

10.5B Removing the drivebelt tensioner

10.5C Removing the drivebelt tensioner pivot stud

crankshaft from rotating by jamming the flywheel starter ring gear.

7   Slacken the injection pump sprocket securing nut, but do not take it off. Using a suitable two-legged puller, with the centre screw locating on the sprocket securing nut, pull the sprocket to free it on the pump shaft, then remove the puller, nut and sprocket. Fig. 1.9 shows the sprocket being removed using tool VW203b.

8   Remove the bolts securing the injection pump to the pump mounting plate and lift away the fuel injection pump.

9   Remove the bolts attaching the alternator mounting bracket, the engine mounting and injection pump mounting plate to the engine block and lift away the bracket and plate (photos).

11 Camshaft and cylinder head – removal

Note: *Although removal of the camshaft is described in this Section with the cylinder head fitted on the engine, the cylinder head can be removed as an assembly complete with the camshaft. Always remove the fuel injectors and glow plugs before working on the cylinder head.*

1   Undo the valve cover securing bolts, lift off the strengthening strips and remove the valve cover and valve cover gasket.

2   Remove the camshaft bearing caps. These have to be refitted in their original positions. They are numbered 1 to 5 (Fig. 1.11), the cap marked No 1 being the one at the sprocket end of the camshaft. The numbers on the caps are not always on the same side, but note that the bearing position is offset and the caps can only be fitted one way round. Undo the nuts securing bearing caps 5, 1 and 3 in that order and lift off the caps. Now undo the nuts securing 2 and 4 caps, in an alternate and diagonal sequence, and the camshaft will lift them up under pressure of the valve springs. Remove the caps and lift out the camshaft complete with sprocket and oil seal (photos).

3   The bucket-type tappets are now exposed and can be lifted out. Take out each one in turn, prise the steel disc out of the tappet by inserting s small screwdriver blade each side and lift the disc away. On the underside of the disc a number is engraved (eg 3.65), this is the thickness of the disc in millimetres. Note the number, then clean the

Fig. 1.9 Removing the injection pump sprocket with puller VW 203b (Sec 10)

disc and refit it on the tappet with the number side down (not visible). The eight tappets must be refitted in their original positions in the cylinder head so label them to identify their correct locations. Also record the thickness of the tappet discs for use at reassembly (photos).

4   The next job is to remove the cylinder head bolts. These are located in the well of the head and have polygon socket heads which require a special socket spanner. Undo and remove the bolts in the reverse order of the tightening sequence shown in Fig. 1.12.

5   When all ten bolts have been removed lift the cylinder head from the cylinder block. It may need tapping with a plastic hammer to loosen it, but **do not** try to prise it loose by using wedges between the head and the block as this will result in damage to the mating faces of the head and block.

10.9A Alternator mounting bracket

10.9B Injection pump mounting plate (front view)

10.9C Injection pump mounting plate (side view)

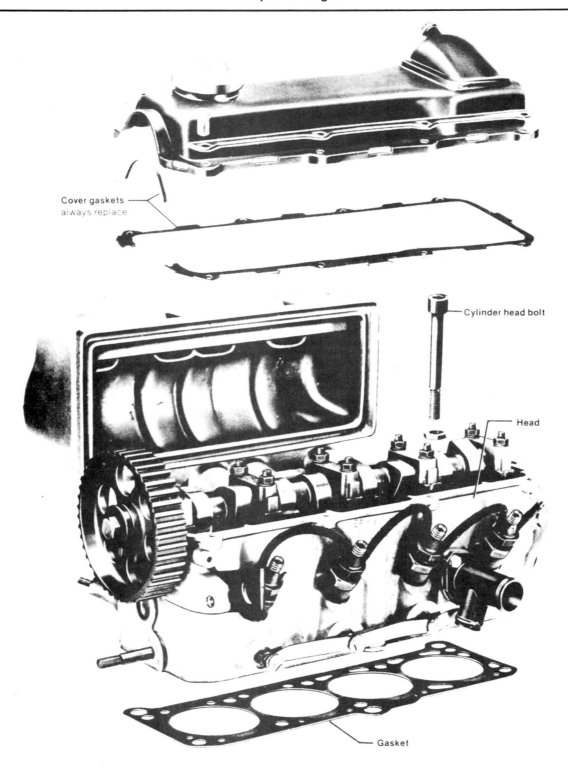

Cover gaskets — always replace

Cylinder head bolt

Head

Gasket

Fig. 1.10 Cylinder head assembly (Sec 11)

6   Remove the cylinder head gasket. **Note:** There are four different thicknesses of cylinder head gasket used, according to the amount the piston projects above the top face of the cylinder block. They are identified by notches and numbers on the gasket, arrowed in Fig. 1.13. Always fit a gasket of the same thickness as the one removed if the same pistons and block are being refitted. If the block or pistons are being renewed then the amount the piston projects (at TDC) above the top face of the block must be measured to determine the thickness of the cylinder head gasket required. See Section 42.

12 Oil sump and oil pump – removal

1   Turn the engine on its side. Undo the securing bolts, which may be hexagon or socket type heads, and remove the sump (photo).
2   The oil pump complete with strainer can now be removed after undoing the two socket headed bolts which secure it to the crankcase (photos).

11.2A Removing a camshaft bearing cap retaining nut

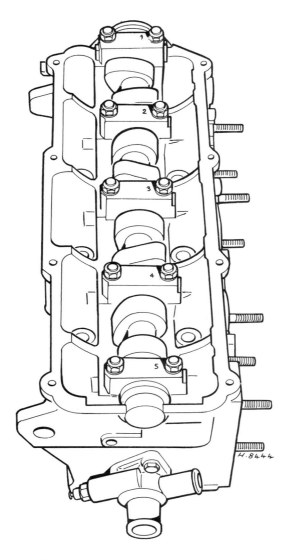
Fig. 1.11 The camshaft bearing caps are numbered 1-5 (Sec 11)

11.2B Removing a camshaft bearing cap

11.3A Removing a tappet assembly

11.3B Removing a tappet disc

11.3C Tappet disc thickness identification

Fig. 1.12 Tightening sequence for cylinder head bolts (Sec 11 and 42)

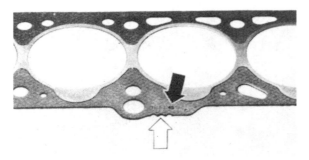

Fig. 1.13 The cylinder head gasket thickness is identified by notches (white arrow) and numbers (black arrow) (Sec 11 and 42)

13 Intermediate shaft, piston and connecting rod assemblies and crankshaft – removal

1   The intermediate plate will have been lifted off the transmission locating dowels when the clutch assembly was removed. Now remove the six bolts securing the crankshaft rear oil seal flange to the engine block. Remove the flange, with oil seal, and the gasket.

2   Remove the intermediate shaft pulley securing bolt and washer and pull off the pulley. Undo the two bolts securing the intermediate shaft oil seal flange to the block. Remove the flange and O-ring, then withdraw the intermediate shaft taking care not to lose the Woodruff key or damage the bearings in the cylinder block (photos).

3   Undo the five bolts securing the crankshaft front oil seal flange to the front of the block, then remove the flange, with oil seal, and the gasket.

4   It is important that all bearing caps are refitted in exactly the same

12.1 Removing the sump

12.2A Oil pump retaining bolts

12.2B Removing the oil pump

13.2A Removing the intermediate shaft pulley

13.2B Removing the intermediate shaft oil seal flange

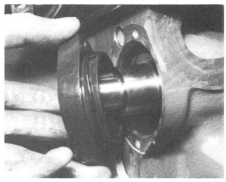

13.2C Intermediate shaft flange O-ring ...

13.2D ... and Woodruff key

13.2E Removing the intermediate shaft

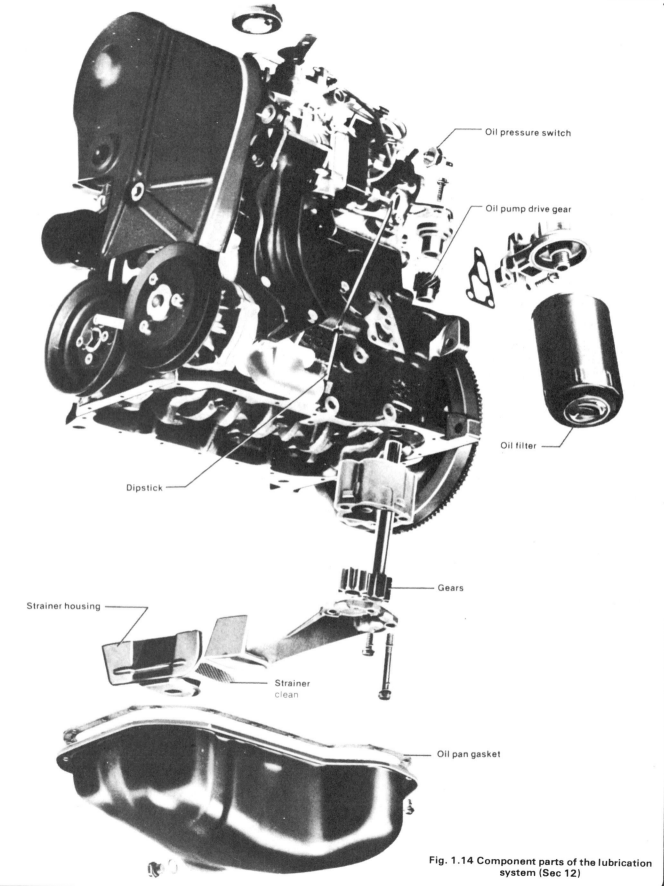

Oil pressure switch

Oil pump drive gear

Oil filter

Dipstick

Gears

Strainer housing

Strainer clean

Oil pan gasket

Fig. 1.14 Component parts of the lubrication system (Sec 12)

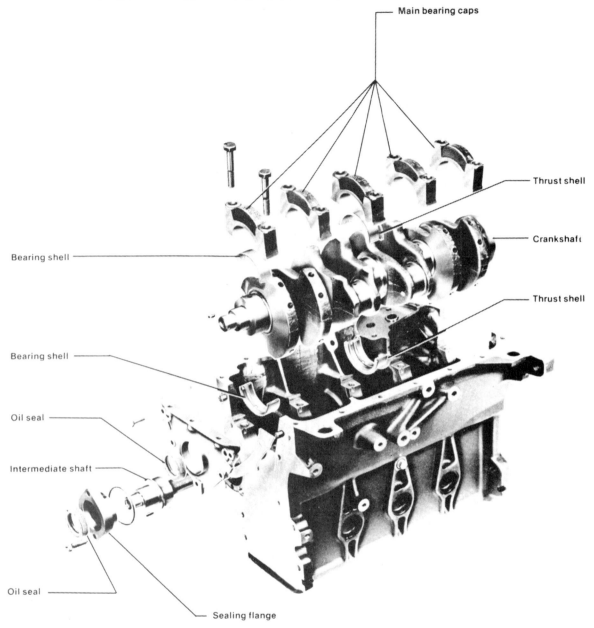

Main bearing caps

Thrust shell

Crankshaft

Thrust shell

Bearing shell

Bearing shell

Oil seal

Intermediate shaft

Oil seal

Sealing flange

Fig. 1.15 Exploded view of cylinder block, crankshaft and intermediate shaft (Sec 13)

position. This also applies to the shell bearings and pistons if they are not being renewed. Using a centre punch mark the connecting rod bearing caps and rods No 1 to No 4, No 1 being the one at the front of the engine (drivebelt end). Note that the forged marks on the connecting rods are toward the intermediate shaft. Mark the tops of the pistons to identify them to their respective cylinder bores. Note that the arrow stamped on the top of the pistons points towards the front of the engine.

5   Undo the nuts securing the No 1 connecting rod cap and remove the cap complete with bearing shell (photos). Push the piston and connecting rod assembly out of the cylinder block through the top. Do not force it, if there is difficulty draw the assembly back and you will probably find a ridge of carbon at the top of the cylinder bore. Remove this with a scraper. If there is a metal ridge reduce the sharp edge of this as well but take care not to score the cylinder bore. The piston and connecting rod should now slide out of the bore.

6   Refit the cap on the connecting rod the right way round and then proceed to remove the other piston and connecting rod assemblies (photos).

7   Note that the main bearing caps are numbered 1 to 5 and that the number is on the opposite side of the engine to the oil pump location, with No 1 bearing at the drivebelt end.

8   Before removing the caps, push the crankshaft to the rear and measure the endplay at No 3 main bearing with a feeler gauge. The endplay should not exceed the specified wear limit. If it exceeds this figure the main bearings must be renewed irrespective of their condition.

9   Remove the main bearing cap securing bolts and lift off the caps and shell bearings.

10 The crankshaft can now be lifted out of the crankcase. Remove the bearing shells from the crankcase. If the bearing shells are not being renewed, make sure they are identified so that they can be refitted in their original positions.

14 Gudgeon pins – removal and refitting

1   Remove a circlip from one end and then push the gudgeon pin out.

Fig. 1.16 Make identifying marks on the top of the pistons (Sec 13)

13.5A Removing a connecting rod cap retaining nut ...

13.5B ... and a connecting rod cap

13.6A Connecting rod and cap identification punch marks

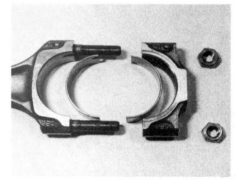

13.6B Connecting rod big-end components

14.1A Removing a gudgeon pin retaining circlip

14.1B Removing a gudgeon pin

14.2 A connecting rod small-end bush

If it is tight, raise the temperature of the piston to 60° C (140° F) with hot water and the pin will slide out easily (photos).

2 Check the play in the connecting rod bush. If the pin seems loose and can be rocked at all then either the pin or the bush (or both) is worn. New bushes can be pressed into the connecting rod, if necessary, but they must then be reamed out to size to fit the gudgeon pin. This job should be left to your local VW garage as the bush must be reamed square to the connecting rod and without a suitable reaming fixture this is unlikely to be achieved (photo).

3 When assembling the piston to the connecting rod, make sure the arrow on the piston crown points to the front (drivebelt end) then push in the gudgeon pin and fit the retaining circlip.

15 Piston rings – removal

1 To remove the piston rings, slide them carefully over the top of the piston, taking care not to scratch the aluminium alloy. Do not slide them off the bottom of the piston skirt. It is very easy to break the cast iron piston rings if they are pulled off roughly, so this operation should be carried out with extreme care. It is helpful to make use of an old feeler gauge by sliding it behind the ring and removing the ring using a

twisting action.

2   Lift one end of the piston ring out of its groove and insert under it the end of the feeler gauge.

3   Run the feeler gauge slowly round the piston. As the ring comes out of its groove, apply a slight upward pressure so that it rests on the land above. It can then be eased off the piston with the feeler gauge stopping it from slipping into an empty groove if it is any but the top ring that is being removed.

16 Valves – removal

1   If the camshaft and tappets were not removed when the cylinder head was removed, refer to Section 11, paragraphs 2 and 3 and remove them now.

2   Using a valve spring compressor tool, compress the valve springs

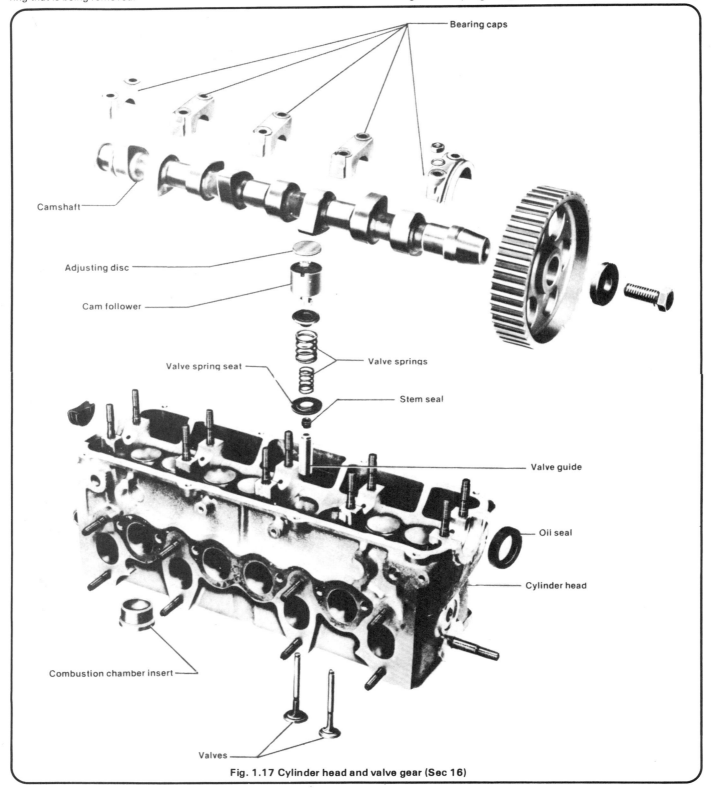

Fig. 1.17 Cylinder head and valve gear (Sec 16)

enough to free the collets, then lift out the collets (photo). When compressing the springs ensure that the valve spring retainer does not damage the valve stem.

3   Release the spring compressor and lift out the valve spring retainer, the springs and the valve spring seat (photos).

4   Remove the valve stem oil seal using needle nosed pliers and withdraw the valve from the underside of the cylinder head (photo). Repeat for the other seven valves.

5   Keep the valves, springs, retainer, valve spring seat and collets in the right order by using a piece of cardboard with holes numbered 1 to 8 (No 1 being the valve nearest the drivebelt end). Alternatively use an internally divided box.

6   Refer to Section 39 for the refitting of the valves.

17 Lubrication system – description

1   The pressed steel oil sump, attached to the underside of the crankcase, acts as a reservoir for the engine oil. The gear type oil pump drains oil through a strainer located under the oil level in the sump, and delivers it under pressure along a short passage and into the full flow oil filter. The oil pressure is regulated by means of a pressure relief valve located within the oil pump. The valve is staked in position and cannot be serviced.

2   From the filter the oil flows to the oil pressure switch, screwed into the rear of the cylinder head, and then to the main oil gallery. From the

16.2 Compressing a valve spring to expose the split collets

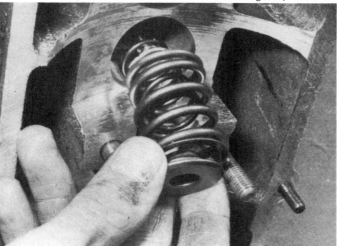
16.3A Removing a retainer and valve springs

16.3B Valve spring seat location

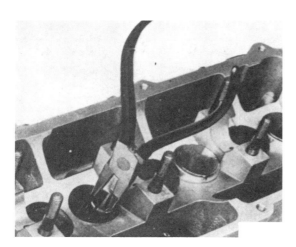
Fig. 1.18 Removing the valve stem seals (Sec 16)

16.4 Removing an inlet valve

main oil gallery, oil is fed to each of the five main bearings and through drillings in the engine block and cylinder head to the camshaft bearings.

3   Drillings in the crankshaft enable oil from the main bearings to be fed to the connecting rod bearings. From there, oil is splashed on to the piston pins and cylinder walls.

18 Positive crankcase ventilation (PCV) system

1   The closed crankcase ventilation system eliminates emission of fumes and vapour from the crankcase to atmosphere by directing the fumes back through the intake system.

2   Blow-by gases pass through the hose from the valve cover to the air cleaner air intake and are then drawn into the combustion chamber.

19 Oil pump – overhaul

1   Refer to Fig. 1.14. The strainer gauge may be removed when the cap is levered off with a screwdriver. Clean the gauge, replace it and refit the cap (photos).

2   Remove the two small bolts and take the cover away from the body.

3   Remove the gears and wash the body and gears in clean paraffin. Dry them and reassemble the gears, lubricating them with clean engine oil. Measure the backlash between the gears with a feeler gauge (Fig. 1.19). This should be 0.05 to 0.20 mm (0.002 to 0.008 in).

4   Now place a straight-edge over the pump body along the line joining the centre of the two gears and measure with a feeler gauge the axial clearance between the gears and the straight-edge (Fig. 1.20). This must not be more than 0.15 mm (0.006 in).

5   If all is well, check that the shaft is not slack in its bearings, and reassemble the pump for fitting to the engine.

6   If there is any doubt about the pump it is recommended strongly that a replacement be obtained. Once wear starts in a pump it progresses rapidly. In view of the damage that may follow a loss of oil pressure, skimping the oil pump repair is a false economy.

20 Engine components – examination for wear

When the engine has been stripped down and all parts properly cleaned, decisions have to be made as to what needs renewal and the following sections tell the examiner what to look for. In any borderline case it is always best to decide in favour of a new part. Even if a part may still be serviceable its life will have been reduced by wear and the

19.1A The oil pump strainer

19.1B Removing the oil pump strainer cap

Fig. 1.19 Checking the backlash between the pump gears (Sec 19)

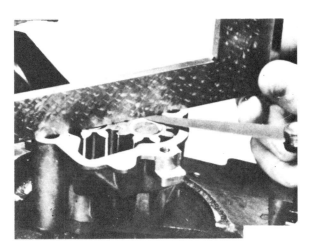

Fig. 1.20 Using a straight-edge and feeler gauge to measure the axial clearance (Sec 19)

degree of trouble needed to replace it in the future must be taken into consideration. However, these things are relative and it depends on whether a quick 'survival' job is being done or whether the car as a whole is being regarded as having many thousands of miles of useful and economical life remaining.

21 Crankshaft – examination and renovation

1 Look at the main bearing journals and the crankpins and if there are any scratches or score marks then the shaft will need regrinding. Such conditions will nearly always be accompanied by similar deterioration in the matching bearing shells.

2 Each bearing journal should also be round and can be checked with a micrometer or caliper gauge around the periphery at several points. If there is more than 0.0254 mm (0.001 in) of ovality regrinding is necessary.

3 A main VW agent or motor engineering specialist will be able to decide to what extent regrinding is necessary and also supply the special undersize shell bearing to match whatever may need grinding off.

4 Before taking the crankshaft for regrinding check also the cylinder bore and pistons as it may be advantageous to have the whole engine done at the same time.

22 Main and big-end bearings – examination and renovation

1 With careful servicing and regular oil filter changes bearings will last for a very long time but they can still fail for unforeseen reasons. With big-end bearings an indication is a regular rhythmic loud knocking from the crankcase. The frequency depends on engine speed and is particularly noticeable when the engine is under load. This symptom is accompanied by a fall in oil pressure although this is not normally noticeable unless an oil pressure gauge is fitted. Main bearing failure is usually indicated by serious vibration, particularly at higher engine revolutions, accompanied by a more significant drop in oil pressure and a 'rumbling' noise.

2 Big-end bearings can be removed with the engine still in the car. If the failure is sudden and the engine has a low mileage since new or overhaul this is possibly worth doing. Bearing shells in good condition have bearing surfaces with a smooth, even matt silver/grey colour all over. Worn bearings will show patches of a different colour when the bearing metal has worn away and exposed the underlay. Damaged bearings will be pitted or scored. It is always worthwhile fitting new shells as their cost is relatively low. If the crankshaft is in good condition, it is merely a question of obtaining another set of standard size shells. A reground crankshaft will need new bearing shells as a matter of course.

23 Cylinder bores – examination and renovation

1 A new cylinder is perfectly round and the walls parallel throughout its length. The action of the piston tends to wear the walls at right angles to the gudgeon pin due to side thrust. This wear takes place principally on that section of the cylinder swept by the piston rings.

2 It is possible to get an indication of bore wear by removing the cylinder head with the engine still in the car. With the piston down in the bore first signs of wear can be seen and felt just below the top of the bore where the top piston ring reaches and there will be a noticeable lip. If there is no lip it is fairly reasonable to expect that bore wear is not severe and any lack of compression or excessive oil consumption is due to worn or broken piston rings.

3 If it is possible to obtain a bore measuring micrometer, measure the bore diameter. Refer to Fig. 1.21 and measure at points 1, 2 and 3, first in direction A and then in direction B. If the out-of-round exceeds the maximum specified then a rebore is required.

4 Any bore which is significantly scratched or scored will need reboring. This symptom usually indicates that the piston or rings are damaged also. In the event of only one cylinder being in need of reboring it will still be necessary for all four to be bored and fitted with new oversize pistons and rings. Your VW agent or local motor engineering specialist will be able to rebore and obtain the necessary matched pistons. If the crankshaft is undergoing regrinding also, it is a good idea to let the same firm renovate and reassemble the crankshaft and

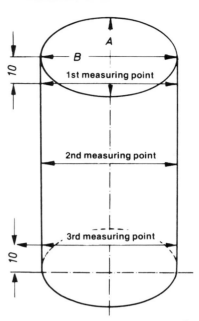

Fig. 1.21 Checking the cylinder bore for wear (Sec 23)

pistons to the block. A reputable firm normally gives a guarantee for such work.

24 Pistons and piston rings – inspection

1 Worn pistons and rings can usually be diagnosed when the symptoms of excessive oil consumption and lower compression occur and are sometimes, though not always, associated with worn cylinder bores. Compression testers that fit into the fuel injector hole are available and these can indicate where low compression is occurring. Wear usually accelerates the more it is left so when the symptoms occur, early action can possibly save the expense of a rebore.

2 Another symptom of piston wear is piston slap – a knocking noise from the crankcase not to be confused with big-end bearing failure. It can be heard clearly at low engine speed when there is no load (idling for example) and much less audible when the engine speed increases. Piston wear usually occurs in the skirt or lower end of the piston and is indicated by vertical streaks in the worn area which is always on the thrust side. It can also be seen where the skirt thickness is different.

3 Piston ring wear can be checked by first removing the rings from the pistons as described in Section 15. Then place the rings in the cylinder bores from the top, pushing them down about 40 mm (1½ inches) with the head of a piston (from which the rings have been removed) so that they rest square in the cylinder. Then measure the gap at the ends of the ring with a feeler gauge (Fig. 1.22). If it exceeds that given in the Specifications at the beginning of this Chapter then new rings are required.

4 The grooves in which the rings locate in the piston can also become enlarged through wear. The clearance between the ring and the piston, in the groove, should not exceed that given in the Specifications (Fig. 1.23).

5 It is seldom that a piston is only worn in the ring grooves and the need to renew them for this fault alone is hardly ever encountered.

25 Connecting rods – examination

1 Connecting rods are not subject to wear but in extreme circumstances such as engine seizure they could be distorted. Such conditions may be visually apparent but where doubt exists they should be changed. The bearing caps should also be examined for indications of filing down which may have been attempted in the mistaken idea that bearing slackness could be remedied in this way. If there are such signs then the connecting rods should be renewed.

2 The connecting rods are supplied in sets of four: therefore if one rod is defective they must all be renewed.

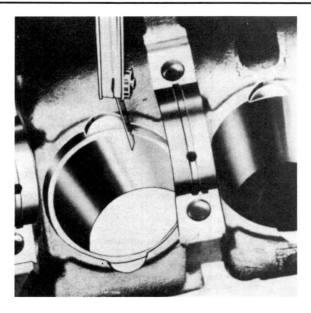

Fig. 1.22 Checking the piston ring gap (Sec 24)

Fig. 1.23 Checking the piston ring clearance in the piston ring grooves (Sec 24)

Fig. 1.24 Checking the camshaft endplay with tool VW387 (Sec 26)

3   If the gudgeon pin bush (small-end bearing) is worn it can be renewed, refer to Section 14.

26 Camshaft and bearings – examination

1   Examine the camshaft bearing journals and cam lobes for wear or scoring. The main decision to take is what degree of wear justifies replacement, which is costly. Scoring or damage to the bearing journals cannot be removed by grinding. Renewal of the camshaft is the only solution.
2   The cam lobes may show signs of ridging or pitting on the high points. If ridging is light then it may be possible to smooth it out with a fine oilstone. The lobes, however, are surface hardened and once this is penetrated wear will take place very rapidly.
3   The camshaft bearings form part of the cylinder head and in the event of wear occurring on these, the complete cylinder head will have to be renewed.
4   Fit the camshaft in the cylinder head without the valves and check that the endplay does not exceed that given in the Specifications. Fig. 1.24 shows the camshaft endplay being checked using a dial gauge.

27 Intermediate shaft – examination and renovation

1   Check the fit of the intermediate shaft in its bearings. If there is excessive play the shaft must be compared with a new one. If the shaft is in good order and the bearings in the block are worn this job is beyond your scope, you may even need a new block so seek expert advice.
2   Check the teeth of the brake booster vacuum pump drivegear for scuffing or chipping. Check the condition of the drivebelt sprocket.
3   There is an oil seal in the intermediate shaft retaining flange. This should be renewed if there are any signs of leakage. To do this, remove the drivebelt pulley and withdraw the flange from the shaft. The oil seal can now be prised out and a new one pressed in. Note that the intermediate shaft rotates anti-clockwise, and the seal must be fitted in accordance with the arrow marked on it (photo).
4   Always fit a new O-ring on the retaining flange before assembling it to the cylinder block.

28 Flywheel – examination

Inspect the friction surface of the flywheel for cracks and scoring. Inspect the ring gear for worn or chipped teeth. If defective the complete flywheel assembly should be renewed. Reconditioning of the flywheel is not recommended due to the balancing which is carried out during manufacture. If a new flywheel is fitted, the TDC mark will be put on it during manufacture.

27.3 Intermediate shaft retaining flange. Arrow below left-hand paint spot indicates direction of shaft rotation

29 Crankshaft oil seals – removal and refitting

1   The rear (flywheel end) oil seal is located in an aluminium housing. Remove the old seal, clean the housing and press in the new seal (photo). Ease it in carefully and press it fully home using either a flat plate in a large vice or a mandrel press. If the seal housing is fitted to the crankcase, make a suitable disc and using two clutch pressure plate to crankshaft bolts, press the seal into position. Fig. 1.25 shows VW tool 2003/1 being used to fit the seal. **Do not** hammer the seal into position: if the lip of the seal is damaged, oil will seep through and find its way on to the clutch friction disc.

2   The front oil seal (sprocket end) is also located in an aluminium housing. Prise out the old seal and press in a new one (photo). Press it in to a depth of $\frac{3}{32}$ in (2 mm) below the face of the housing. This seal can be renewed with the engine in the car provided you have the special tools required: tool No 10–219 to extract the old seal and tool No 10–203 to fit the new one. Those tools are also required if the intermediate shaft oil seal is to be renewed with the engine in the car.

30 Cylinder head and piston crowns – decarbonisation

Note: *When the pistons are at TDC they project above the surface of the cylinder block. Take care when cleaning the top of the block not to damage the pistons.*

1   Always remove the injectors and glow plugs before working on the cylinder head. When decarbonising the cylinder head, insert a drift through the fuel injector holes and drive out the pre-combustion chamber inserts as shown in Fig. 1.26.

2   When the cylinder head is removed, either in the course of an overhaul or for inspection of bores or valve condition when the engine is in the car, it is normal to remove all carbon deposits from the piston crowns and heads.

3   This is best done with a cup shaped wire brush and an electric drill and is fairly straightforward when the engine is dismantled and the pistons removed. Sometimes hard spots of carbon are not easily removed except by a scraper. When cleaning the pistons with a scraper, take care not to damage the surface of the piston in any way.

4   When the engine is in the car certain precautions must be taken when decarbonising the piston crowns in order to prevent dislodged pieces of carbon falling into the interior of the engine which could cause damage to cylinder bores, piston and rings – or if allowed into the water passages – damage to the water pump. Turn the engine so that the piston being worked on is at the top of its stroke and then mask off the adjacent cylinder bores and all surrounding water jacket orifices with paper and adhesive tape. Press grease into the gap all round the piston to keep carbon particles out and then scrape all carbon away by hand carefully. Do not use a power drill and wire brush when the engine is in the car as it will be virtually impossible to keep

29.1 Engine rear oil seal and housing

Fig. 1.25 Fitting a new rear seal in its housing (Sec 29)

29.2 Engine front oil seal and housing

Fig. 1.26 Using a drift to drive out the pre-combustion chamber inserts (Sec 30)

all the carbon dust clear of the engine. When completed, carefully clear out the grease around the rim of the piston with a matchstick or something similar – bringing any carbon particles with it. Repeat the process on the other piston crown. It is not recommended that a ring of carbon is left around the edge of the piston on the theory that it will aid oil consumption. This was valid in the earlier days of long stroke low revving engines but modern engines, fuels and lubricants cause less carbon deposits anyway and any left behind tends merely to cause hot spots.

31 Valves and valve seats – examination and renovation

1   Examine the heads of the valves for pitting and burning, especially the heads of the exhaust valves. The valve seats should be examined at the same time. If the valve seats are so badly worn or burned that they cannot be refaced then the cylinder head will have to be renewed.
2   If the pitting on the valve and valve seat is very slight this can be corrected by grinding the valves and seats together with coarse, and then fine, grinding paste. Where bad pitting of the seats has occurred it will be necessary to recut the seats and fit new valves. Recutting of the valve seats should be left to your local VW garage or local engineering works. Normally it is the valves that are too badly worn for refacing, and the owner can purchase a new set of valves and match them to the seats by hand grinding. Inlet valves can be refaced on a valve grinding machine. Exhaust valves **must not** be machine ground. Grind by hand only against the valve seat.
3   Valve grinding is carried out as follows: Smear a trace of coarse carborundum paste on the seat face and apply a suction grinder tool to the valve head. With a semi-rotary motion, grind the valve head to its seat, lifting the valve occasionally to redistribute the grinding paste. When a dull matt even surface finish is produced on both the valve seat and the valve, wipe off the paste and repeat the process with fine carborundum paste, lifting and turning the valve to redistribute the paste as before. A light spring placed under the valve head will greatly ease this operation. When a smooth unbroken ring of light grey matt finish is produced, on both valve and valve seat faces, the grinding operation is completed.
4   Scrape away all carbon from the valve head and the valve stem. Carefully clean away every trace of grinding compound, taking great care to leave none in the ports or in the valve guides. Clean the valves and valve seats with a paraffin soaked rag then with a clean rag, and finally, if an air line is available, blow the valves, valve guides and valve ports clean.

32 Valve guides and springs – examination and renovation

1   Wear in the valve guides may be checked by fitting a new valve in the guide and observing the amount that the head of the valve will move sideways when the end of the valve stem is flush with the top of the valve guide. The maximum permitted movement for intake and exhaust valves is 1.30 mm (0.051 in) when a new valve is used. Fig. 1.28 shows a dial gauge being used to measure the side movement of the valve.
2   If the side movement exceeds the permitted maximum, new valve guides will be required. This is a job for your VW garage or local engineering works, as the guides have to be fitted using a press and then reamed to the specified dimension.
3   Examine the valve springs for distortion and damage. If possible compare the free length against a new spring. If it is shorter it must be renewed.

33 Cylinder head – examination

1   Examine the cylinder head for cracks or other damage. The machined face of the head should be smooth and free of pitting and burrs.
2   Check the surface of the head for distortion. Place a straight-edge along the centre of the machined face of the head. Make sure there are no ridges at the extreme ends and using a feeler gauge check for distortion. If the straight-edge is held firmly on the head and feelers in excess of 0.1 mm (0.004 in) can be inserted between the straight-edge and the head, a new cylinder head is required.

Fig. 1.27 Grind in the valves with a semi-rotary motion (Sec 31)

Fig. 1.28 Checking a valve guide for wear with tool VW387 (Sec 32)

Fig. 1.29 Using a straight-edge and feeler gauge to check the cylinder head for distortion (Sec 33)

34 Engine reassembly – general

1   To ensure maximum life with minimum trouble from a rebuilt engine, not only must everything be correctly assembled, but everything must be spotlessly clean; all the oilways must be clear, locking washers and spring washers must always be fitted where

indicated and all bearing and other working surfaces must be thoroughly lubricated during assembly.

2   Before assembly begins renew any bolts or studs, the threads of which are in any way damaged, and whenever possible use new spring washers.

3   Apart from your normal tools, a supply of clean rag, an oil can filled with engine oil (an empty plastic detergent bottle thoroughly washed out and cleaned, will do just as well), a new supply of assorted spring washers, a set of new gaskets, and a torque spanner should be collected together.

4   Sit down with a pencil and paper and list all those items which you intend to renew and acquire all of them before reassembly. If you have had experience of shopping around for parts you will appreciate that they cannot be obtained quickly. Do not underestimate the cost either. Spare parts are relatively much more expensive now.

35 Crankshaft, oil seal housings and intermediate shaft – refitting

1   Place the cylinder block upside down on the bench.

2   Thoroughly clean the main bearing seatings and fit the main bearing upper shells. Note that the upper shells have lubrication grooves, whereas the shells in the bearing caps are without lubrication grooves. No 3 main bearing shell has small flanges (photo). If the old bearings are being refitted it is essential that they go back in their original locations.

3   Lubricate the bearings and crankshaft journals with engine oil and then lower the crankshaft onto the bearings (photos).

4   Fit the lower half of the bearing shells in the main bearing caps. Fit the caps in their correct locations (No 1 at the sprocket end and No 5 at the flywheel end), then insert the securing bolts and tighten them to the specified torque (photos). NOTE: The caps are fitted with the

35.2 Fitting No 3 main bearing upper shell

35.3A Lubricating the main bearing shells

35.3B Refitting the crankshaft

35.4A No 3 main bearing cap and bearing shell

35.4B Refitting No 3 main bearing cap

35.4C Main bearing caps are numbered for correct location

35.4D Tighten the retaining bolts to the specified torque

35.4E Sprocket end main bearing cap fitted position

35.5 Checking crankshaft endfloat with a feeler gauge

35.6A Fitting the rear oil seal housing gasket ...

35.6B ... and the rear oil seal and housing

35.6C Tightening the rear oil seal housing retaining bolts

35.7 Fitting the front (sprocket end) oil seal and housing

37.2 Ring compressor fitted to a piston

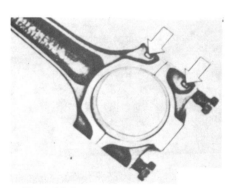

Fig. 1.30 Connecting rod casting mark locations (arrowed) (Sec 37)

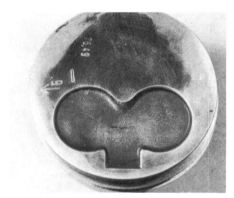

37.3 Piston crown, showing front facing arrow

37.4 Fitting a piston into a cylinder bore

37.5 Connecting rod and cap markings

37.6 Tightening a big-end bearing cap retaining nut

37.8 Checking the connecting rod side clearance with a feeler gauge

numbers on the side opposite to the oil pump location.

5   Tap the crankshaft to the rear as far as it will go and check the clearance between the flange of No 3 bearing and the crankshaft with a feeler gauge to measure the endplay (photo). The endplay should not exceed that specified; if it does then the bearings must be renewed. Check that the crankshaft is free to rotate, if it is not, then the bearings and journals must be rechecked.

6   Lubricate the rear end of the crankshaft. Using a new gasket, fit the rear oil seal housing complete with oil seal. Fit the six securing bolts (photos).

7   Lubricate the front end of the crankshaft and position a new gasket on the engine block. Fit the front oil seal housing, complete with oil seal, and securing bolts (photo).

8   Fit the intermediate shaft in the cylinder block. When inserting the shaft take care not to damage the bearings.

9   Fit the intermediate shaft retaining flange complete with oil seal. Use a new O-ring between the flange and the block. Fit the two securing bolts and tighten them to the specified torque.

36 Piston rings – refitting

1   Ensure that the piston ring grooves are clean.

2   Fit the rings on the pistons by reversing the removal procedure, refer to Section 15.

3   All three rings are marked TOP and must be fitted with the TOP mark towards the piston crown. Start with the oil scraper ring first and then the compression rings.

4   When fitted in their grooves, generously lubricate the rings and piston with engine oil and position the gaps at 120° intervals.

37 Piston and connecting rod assemblies – refitting

1   Position the engine block on its side.

2   Fit a piston ring compressor on the first piston (photo). Lubricate the crankshaft connecting rod journal with engine oil.

3   Insert the piston and connecting rod assembly in to the cylinder bore. Ensure that it is the correct assembly for that particular bore and that the arrow on the piston crown is pointing towards the drivebelt end with the casting marks on the connecting rod (see Fig. 1.30) facing towards the intermediate shaft (photo).

4   Using the shaft of a hammer, tap the piston into the cylinder bore, collecting the ring compressor as the rings go into the bore (photo).

5   Pull the connecting rod onto the crankshaft journal and fit the cap, making sure it is the right way round (photo).

6   Fit the connecting rod cap securing nuts and tighten them to the specified torque (photo). Check that the crankshaft is free to rotate and that there are no high spots causing binding.

7   Repeat this procedure for the other three piston assemblies, checking that the crankshaft is free to rotate after the fitting of each assembly.

8   After all the assemblies are fitted, check the connecting rod side clearance. Push the connecting rod against the crankshaft web and measure the gap at the other side with a feeler gauge (photo). The clearance should not exceed the specified value. If it does then the

bearings must be renewed.

9   Turn the crankshaft and position No 1 piston at TDC (top dead centre).

38 Oil pump, sump and crankshaft sprocket – refitting

1   Clean the mating faces of the engine block and oil pump. Position the oil pump, complete with strainer, on the block and fit the two securing bolts. Tighten the securing bolts to the specified torque (photo).

2   Ensure that the mating faces of the engine block and the oil sump are clean and free of burrs, then position a new sump gasket on the engine block using a sealant compound to keep it in place.

3   Apply sealant to the joint face of the sump, then assemble the sump to the block and fit the securing bolts. Tighten the bolts in a progressive and even manner (photo).

4   Fit the drivebelt sprocket on the front end of the crankshaft. Ensure that it is driven on squarely so that it does not displace or damage the Woodruff key on the crankshaft. Make sure that it is driven fully home, using a piece of suitable diameter steel tubing.

39 Valves, pre-combustion chamber inserts, fuel injectors and glow plugs – refitting

1   With the valves having been ground in (Section 31) and kept in their correct order, assemble the valves and springs in the cylinder head.

2   Fit the valve stem oil seal on the valve guide. With a packet of new oil seals is a small plastic sleeve. This is fitted over the valve stem and lubricated and then the seal should be pushed on over the plastic sleeve until it seats on the guide. This must be done with a special tool VW 10–204 which fits snugly round the outside of the seal and pushes it on squarely. If the seal is assembled without the plastic sleeve the seal will be damaged and oil consumption will become excessive. If you cannot put them on properly then ask the agent to do it for you.

3   Insert the valve in the head and fit the valve spring seat followed by the two valve springs and the valve spring retainer.

4   Using a valve spring compressor, compress the valve springs until the split collets can be slid into position. When the collets are located in the groove in the valve stem (photo), release the compressor. Using a plastic hammer tap the valve stem to check that the collets are properly seated.

5   Fit the other seven valves using the same procedure.

6   Fit the pre-combustion chamber inserts in the cylinder head.

7   Fit the fuel injectors and the glow plugs.

40 Tappets and camshaft – refitting

1   Insert the tappets in their original positions in the cylinder head. Ensure that the engraved (numbered) side of the tappet discs are facing downwards (invisible) (photo).

2   Lubricate the camshaft bearings with engine oil.

38.1 Refitting the oil pump

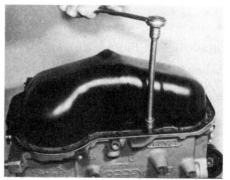
38.3 Tightening the sump retaining bolts

39.4 Fitted position of the valve split collets

40.1 Disc recess on the valve tappet

40.3A Fitting the camshaft front oil seal

40.3B Refitting the camshaft

3   Slide a new camshaft oil seal into position on the front (drivebelt end) of the camshaft and fit the camshaft on the cylinder head (photos).

4   Fit the bearing caps and tighten them down evenly and progressively to the specified torque (photo). Before tightening the securing nuts ensure that the caps are the right way round as the bearings are off centre. Note that the numbers stamped on the caps are not always on the same side.

5   Fit the drivebelt sprocket on the camshaft and tighten the securing bolt (photos).

6   The cylinder head is now ready for fitting on the engine block, except that the valve clearances have not been adjusted. Valve clearance adjustment is described in the next Section.

41 Valve clearances – adjustment

1   Valve clearance adjustment consists of measuring the clearance between the heel of the cam and the steel disc in the top of each tappet, calculating any error and replacing the disc if necessary with one of the thickness required to obtain the specified clearance.

2   The 26 different thicknesses of tappet disc available range from 3.00 mm to 4.25 mm in steps of 0.05 mm, which means that the purchase of a set of feeler gauges graduated in millimetres would be an advantage. Otherwise a lot of calculation will be necessary and a set of conversion tables to transpose 0.05 mm steps into thousandths of an inch. Referring to the table in paragraph 7, the thinnest disc is 3.00 mm (0.1181 in). The thickness progresses at the rate of 0.05 mm (0.001969 in) and since feeler gauges measure only to the nearest thousandth, 0.001969 in may be taken for practical purposes as 0.002 in. By calculating 25 size increases at this rate the thickest disc, 4.25 mm, becomes 0.1681 in whereas its true value is 0.1673 in. The error over the total range is thus 0.0008 in which is acceptable.

3   If routine checking and adjustment of the valve clearances is to be done with the engine in the car, first remove the air cleaner and duct and the valve cover. The engine can be turned over by using a spanner on the crankshaft sprocket bolt or by engaging top gear and pushing the car as required. The procedure for checking the clearance after overhaul is the same, except that during an engine overhaul the adjustment discs will already have been removed and cleaned and the thickness etched on the back of the disc will be known.

4   If the cylinder head is on the bench the camshaft can be turned by the sprocket.

5   Using a feeler gauge measure the clearance between the tappet adjusting disc and the heel of the cam (photo). Make a note of the clearance. Counting from the timing belt end of the engine, the valves are numbered:

Inlet   2 – 4 – 5 – 7
Exhaust   1 – 3 – 6 – 8

6   Repeat this procedure for all the valves in turn, rotating the camshaft as necessary, and then compare the measurements with the clearances given in the Specifications at the beginning of this Chapter. Clearances that are set cold must be rechecked with the engine coolant temperature at approximately 35° C (95° F) and, if necessary, re-adjusted.

7   Make a table of the actual clearances and then calculate the error from the specified clearance as shown in the following example:

	Inlet valve	Exhaust valve
Specified clearance	0.20–0.30 mm (0.008–0.012 in)	0.40–0.50 mm (0.016–0.020 in)
Measured clearance	0.15 mm (0.006 in)	0.55 mm (0.022 in)
Insert disc that is	0.10 mm (0.004 in) thinner	0.10 mm (0.004 in) thicker

Discs are available in the following thicknesses:

Thickness (mm)	Part Number	Thickness (mm)	Part Number
3.00	056 109 555	3.65	056 109 568
3.05	056 109 556	3.70	056 109 569
3.10	056 109 557	3.75	056 109 570
3.15	056 109 558	3.80	056 109 571
3.20	056 109 559	3.85	056 109 572
3.25	056 109 560	3.90	056 109 573
3.30	056 109 561	3.95	056 109 574
3.35	056 109 562	4.00	056 109 575
3.40	056 109 563	4.05	056 109 576
3.45	056 109 564	4.10	056 109 577
3.50	056 109 565	4.15	056 109 578
3.55	056 109 566	4.20	056 109 579
3.60	056 109 567	4.25	056 109 580

8   As the discs are in steps of 0.05 mm, the required disc can be obtained once the thickness of the disc at present fitted is known. If you have dismantled the cylinder head you will know the thickness etched on the back of the disc (provided you remembered to record it), but if you do not then the disc will have to be removed to find out. If you have VW tools 10–209 and 10–208, the job of removing the adjusting disc from the top of the tappet is very straightforward, but we managed using the tool shown in the photograph, a small screwdriver and thin long-nosed pliers. With the camshaft positioned to give the maximum clearance (cam lobe pointing upwards) the tappet is pushed down with tool 10–209, or its counterpart, against the valve spring while the disc is removed with tool 10–208, or prised up with a small screwdriver and lifted out with the pliers. When fitting the disc always ensure that the side with the thickness marked on it is towards the tappet (photos).

9   If the adjustment is made with a cold engine it must be checked again when the engine is hot, and if the cylinder head has been overhauled it must be checked again after 1000 miles (1600 km).

10 If the adjustment was carried out with the engine in the car refit the valve cover and air cleaner.

11 It is suggested that you keep a record of the disc sizes fitted as this can save time at the next check by allowing you to calculate the thickness of disc required without having to remove the old disc.

42 Cylinder head, drivebelt tensioner, intermediate shaft pulley, fuel injection pump and drivebelt – refitting

1   Support the engine on the sump with wooden blocks. Clean the top face of the block.

40.4 Camshaft front bearing cap refitted

40.5A The camshaft drivebelt sprocket

40.5B Fitting the camshaft drivebelt sprocket

41.5 Checking the valve clearances with a feeler gauge

41.8A Tappet compressing tool

41.8B Using the tappet compressing tool

41.8C Compress the tappet ...

41.8D ... prise out the disc ...

41.8E ... and remove the disc with long nosed pliers

2   Four thicknesses of cylinder head gasket are used according to how much the pistons protrude (at TDC) above the top face of the cylinder block. They are as follows:

Piston projection in mm (in)	Gasket thickness in mm (in)	Identification (no of notches)	Part No
0.43–0.63 (0.017–0.025)	1.3 (0.051)	2	068 103 383
0.63–0.82 (0.025–0.032)	1.4 (0.055)	3	068 103 383C
0.82–0.92 (0.032–0.036)	1.5 (0.059)	4	068 103 383G
0.92–1.02 (0.036–0.040)	1.6 (0.063)	5	068 103 383H

3   If the same cylinder block and pistons are being refitted ensure that the new gasket is the same thickness as the one that was removed. The identification marks on the gasket are shown arrowed in Fig. 1.13. If either the pistons or the cylinder block is being renewed then the amount that the pistons protrude above the face of the block must be measured to determine the thickness of gasket required. VW tools 382/7 and 385/17 are specified for measuring piston projection; alternatively, use a straight-edge and feeler blades as shown (photo).

4   Position the new cylinder head gasket on the cylinder block with the side marked OBEN facing upwards (photos).

5   Lift the cylinder head on to the block and insert bolts 8 and 10 (see Fig. 1.12) first to centre the head. We used two $\frac{7}{16}$ in drills in the bolt holes to act as guides when lowering the head onto the cylinder block (photos).

6   Fit the other cylinder head bolts and tighten them in the sequence shown in Fig. 1.12 to the specified Stage 1 torque (photo). Then tighten the bolts further, in the same sequence, to the specified Stage 2 torque. **Note:** *Do not re-tighten the bolts after 1000 miles (1600 km).*

7   Fit the fuel injection pump mounting plate on the front of the engine block.

8   Fit the drivebelt tensioner on its mounting stud. Do not tighten the

42.3 Checking the piston protrusion with a feeler gauge and straight-edge

42.4A Fitting the cylinder head gasket

42.4B Cylinder head gasket upper facing and identifying marks

42.5A Using two drills for cylinder head location

42.5B Refitting the cylinder head

42.6 Tightening the cylinder head bolts

locknut at this stage.

9   Fit the pulley on the intermediate shaft and tighten the securing bolt to the specified torque (photo).

10 Turn the camshaft so that both cams for No 1 cylinder are in the valves-closed position (both cam lobes pointing upwards) and lock the camshaft in this position, refer to Section 9.

11 Check that No 1 piston is still at TDC (see Section 37). If there is any doubt, use setting tool No 2068 after refitting the clutch (Section 45). It is not possible to judge the piston position through the swirl chambers.

12 Assemble the fuel injection pump to the mounting plate, align the marks on the pump and the mounting plate (Fig. 1.31) and fit the securing bolts.

13 Fit the sprocket on the injection pump shaft and tighten the securing nut to the specified torque.

14 Turn the pump sprocket to line up the mark on the sprocket with the mark on the mounting plate, then lock the injection pump sprockets with a suitable locking pin, refer to Section 9.

15 Slacken the camshaft sprocket securing bolt approximately half a turn and then using a plastic hammer tap the sprocket free of the taper

42.9 Tightening the intermediate shaft pulley retaining bolt

Fig. 1.31 Injection pump alignment marks (Sec 42)

on the camshaft.

16 Check that the engine is still at TDC (compression stroke) on No 1 cylinder and fit the drivebelt and the drivebelt shield (photos).

17 Remove the locking pin from the fuel injection pump sprocket and tension the drivebelt by turning the belt tension adjuster as required.

18 VW tool 210 is required to measure the belt tension. If the tool is not available, refer to Section 9, paragraph 14. Measure the tension at the point midway between the camshaft sprocket and the fuel injection pump sprocket. When the belt is correctly tensioned the scale on tool VW 210 will read 12–13. Tighten the drivebelt tensioner locknut.

19 Tighten the camshaft sprocket securing bolt to the specified torque and remove the camshaft locking tool (photo).

20 Turn the crankshaft through two complete revolutions in the normal direction of rotation, then remove the play in the drive by striking the belt once with a plastic hammer between the pump and camshaft sprockets. Recheck the belt tension and re-adjust if necessary.

21 Check the fuel injection pump timing as described in Chapter 3.

43 Water pump, crankshaft pulley, valve cover and vacuum pump – refitting

1 Fit the water pump and thermostat housing assembly, complete with alternator adjusting strap. Ensure that the mating faces of the housing and the engine block are clean and use a new O-ring seal between the pump housing and the block.

2 Bolt the crankshaft pulley to the crankshaft sprocket. Tighten the four securing bolts to the specified torque.

3 Fit the alternator mounting bracket. Don't forget the earth strap which is connected to one of the bolts.

4 Fit a new valve cover gasket on the cylinder head. Ensure that the rubber seal at the rear end and the seal on the front camshaft bearing cap are properly seated, then fit the valve cover, the strengthening strips and securing bolts.

5 Fit the drivebelt cover (photo).

6 Fit the hose between the water pump housing and the cylinder head.

7 Using a new O-ring, fit the brake servo vacuum pump. Ensure that the drive on the end of the pump shaft engages with the oil pump driveshaft and fit the clamp plate and securing bolt (photos).

8 Using a new gasket fit the heater hose connection, complete with coolant temperature switch, on the rear end of the cylinder head.

44 Oil filter adapter, fuel pipes and oil pressure switch – refitting

1 Using a new gasket, fit the oil filter adapter and tighten the securing bolts to the specified torque (photo). The oil filter cartridge screws into the adapter, and is hand tightened only, but do not fit the filter at this stage as it may get damaged when fitting the engine in the car.

2 Screw the oil pressure sender switch into the rear end of the cylinder head and tighten it to the specified torque.

3 Fit the injection pump-to-fuel injector pipes.

45 Intermediate plate and clutch and flywheel assembly – refitting

1 Fit the intermediate plate on the engine block, it locates on the two transmission locating dowels (photo).

2 The flywheel is bolted to the clutch pressure plate. For information on the fitting of the clutch assembly and the flywheel refer to Chapter 4, Section 4.

46 Inlet and exhaust manifolds and air cleaner – refitting

1 Clean the joint faces of the cylinder head and the intake and exhaust manifolds. Fit a new gasket over the exhaust manifold studs.

2 Fit the intake and exhaust manifolds and tighten the socket headed securing bolts and nuts in an even and progressive manner.

42.16A Refitting the drivebelt shield

42.16B Drivebelt location over camshaft and injection pump sprockets

42.16C Drivebelt location over tensioner and intermediate pulley

42.19 Tightening the camshaft sprocket securing bolt

43.5 Refitting the drivebelt cover (engine in car)

43.7A Brake servo vacuum pump (exhauster) drive blade on the oil pump driveshaft (early type oil pump)

43.7B Brake servo vacuum pump drivegear, showing slot for oil pump shaft (early models)

44.1 Refitting the oil filter adaptor

45.1 Cylinder block to transmission intermediate plate retaining bolt locations

3   Fit a new filter element on the air cleaner and fit the air cleaner on the intake manifold. Secure it in position with the four spring retaining clips.

47   Engine – refitting in the car

1   Assemble the transmission to the engine in the reverse order to that described in Section 6 for separating it from the engine. If the clutch has been disturbed, centralise it as described in Chapter 4.

2   Refitting the engine/transmission assembly in the car is the reverse of the removal procedure described in Section 5.

3   When fitting the engine mounting bolts, insert all the bolts loosely and then align the power unit so that there is no twisting or undue stress on the rubber parts of the mountings, refer to Figs. 1.32, 1.33 and 1.34. Tighten the bolts to the specified torque (photo).

4   Reconnect the driveshafts and tighten the flange bolts to the specified torque, refer to Chapter 8.

5   Connect the transmission shift linkage, refer to Chapter 5 for linkage adjustment procedure.

6   Connect the clutch cable and adjust the clutch pedal free movement, refer to Chapter 4.

7   Fit the speedometer cable drive in the transmission. Connect the exhaust pipe tro the exhaust manifold flange.

8   Fit the alternator (don't forget the earth strap), refer to Chapter 7.

9   Smear a new oil filter seal with engine oil and screw the filter cartridge into the oil filter adapter. Tighten the filter by hand, do not use a strap wrench (photo).

10   Connect the accelerator cable and the cold start cable to the fuel injection pump. Adjust the cables as described in Chapter 3.

11   Refit the fuel filter and connect the fuel supply and return pipes to the fuel injection pump.

12   Refit the radiator and fan assembly, refer to Chapter 2, and the air cleaner intake duct. Fit the heater hoses.

13   Reconnect the electrical wiring to the alternator, starter motor, fan motor and fan thermoswitch, oil pressure switch, coolant temperature switch, stop solenoid on the injection pump, glow plugs and the reversing light switch.

14   Fit the vacuum pump-to-brake servo hose.

15   Refill the cooling system with coolant, refer to Chapter 2.

Fig. 1.33 Correct alignment of centre engine mounting (Sec 47)

Fig. 1.32 Correct alignment of rear transmission mounting (Sec 47)

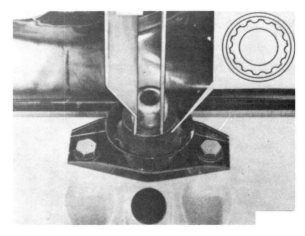

Fig. 1.34 Correct alignment of front engine mounting (Sec 47)

47.3 Engine front mounting

47.9 Oil filter cartridge

16 Refill the sump with engine oil to the correct level. If the transmission was drained, don't forget to refill it with the specified grade of lubricant.
17 Fit the engine compartment bonnet and the battery. Reconnect the battery leads.
18 Finally, check that all electrical wiring and control cables have been connected, all hose clips tightened, and all tools, rags and any other loose items removed from the engine compartment.

48 Engine – initial start-up after overhaul or major repair

1 Make sure that the battery is fully charged and that all lubricants and coolants have been replenished.
2 Bleed the fuel system as described in Chapter 3, then using the glow plugs start the engine and run it to bring it up to normal operating temperature.
3 As the engine warms up there will be odd smells and some smoke from the parts getting warm, particularly the exhaust manifold, and burning off oil deposits. Check for leaks of coolant, oil and fuel which, if serious, will be very obvious. Check also the exhaust pipe and manifold connections as these do not always find their gastight position until the heat and vibration have acted on them and it is almost certain that they will need further tightening. This should be done, of course, with the engine stopped.
4 When normal operating temperature is reached, adjust the idle speed and the maximum rpm as described in Chapter 3.
5 Stop the engine and wait a few minutes, then check to see if any coolant, oil or fuel is leaking while the engine is stopped.
6 Road test the car to check that the engine is giving the necessary power and smoothness. Do not race the engine: if new bearings and/or pistons have been fitted it should be treated as a new engine and run in at a reduced speed, not more than 62 mph (100 km/h) for the first 300 miles (500 km) and not more than 75 mph (120 km/h) for the next 300 miles (500 km). It is not necessary to regulate the speed in the different gears as the engine is automatically governed to approximately 5400 rpm. After 600 miles the speed can be gradually increased to the maximum.

See overleaf for 'Fault diagnosis – engine'

49 Fault diagnosis – engine

Symptom	Reason/s
Engine will not turn over when starter switch is operated	Flat battery Bad battery connections Bad connections at solenoid switch and/or starter motor Starter motor jammed Starter motor defective
Engine turns over but fails to start	Glow plugs or associated wiring defective Injection pump solenoid defective, or mountings or connections loose No fuel reaching the injectors, air in system Injection pump timing incorrect Defective injectors Fuel injection pump defective
Engine starts but runs unevenly and misfires	Air in the fuel system Restricted fuel supply due to blocked filter or fuel lines Defective injectors Idle speed incorrectly adjusted Injection pump timing incorrect Injection pump defective
Excessive exhaust smoke – black or white	Injectors defective Injection pump timing incorrect Maximum rpm adjustment incorrect Injection pump defective
Lack of power	Maximum rpm adjustment incorrect Air in the fuel system Injectors defective Injection pump timing incorrect Injection pump defective Blocked air cleaner filter element Valve clearances incorrect Burnt out valves Worn piston rings and/or cylinder bores
Excessive oil consumption	Oil leaks from gaskets and seals Worn piston rings and/or cylinder bores resulting in oil being burnt in the engine, indicated by excessive blue exhaust smoke Worn valve guides and/or defective valve stem seals
Excessive mechanical noise from the engine	Valve clearances incorrect Worn main and/or big-end bearings Worn cylinders (piston slap)

Chapter 2
Cooling, air conditioning and heating systems

For modifications, and information applicable to later models, see Supplement at end of manual

Contents

Specifications

System type	Thermo-syphon, assisted by belt-driven pump, pressurised
Cooling fan	Electrically driven, thermostatically controlled
Pressure cap release pressure	1·2 to 1·35 kg/cm^2 (17 to 19 lbf/in^2)

Thermostat

Starts to open	80°C (176°F) approx
Fully extended	94°C (200°F) approx
Minimum stroke	7·0 mm (0·27 in)

System capacity (including heater)	6·5 litres (11·4 Imp pints, 13·6 US pints)

Torque wrench settings

	kgf m	lbf ft
Temperature gauge sender	0·7	5
Top hose outlet to cylinder head	2·0	14
Heater hose outlet to cylinder head	1·0	7
Water pump to block	2·0	14
Water pump housings	1·0	7
Water pump pulley to flange	2·0	14

1 General description

1 The engine coolant is circulated by the thermo-syphon method, assisted by a water pump. The radiator cap seals the cooling system which pressurises the system. This has the effect of considerably increasing the boiling point of the coolant.

2 The impeller type water pump is mounted on the side of the engine block and is driven by a V-belt from the crankshaft pulley. This belt also drives the alternator.

3 The electrically operated cooling fan is mounted on the radiator and is controlled by a thermo-switch screwed into the left-hand side of the radiator. As soon as the coolant temperature rises to 90°–95° C (194°–203° F), the fan motor comes into operation, *even if the ignition is switched off*. It is therefore important whenever working near the fan to ensure that the battery is disconnected.

4 The system functions in the following fashion. Cold coolant in the bottom of the radiator circulates up the lower radiator hose to the water pump where it is pushed round the water passages in the cylinder block, cooling the cylinder bores. The coolant then travels up into the cylinder head and circulates round the combustion chambers and valve seats, absorbing more heat, and then, when the engine is at its correct operating temperature, travels out of the cylinder head through the top radiator hose and into the radiator (photo).

5 The coolant passes through the radiator where it is rapidly cooled by the flow of cold air through the radiator core, which is created both

1.4 Cylinder head coolant hose connector.
A – Radiator top hose
B – Water pump hose

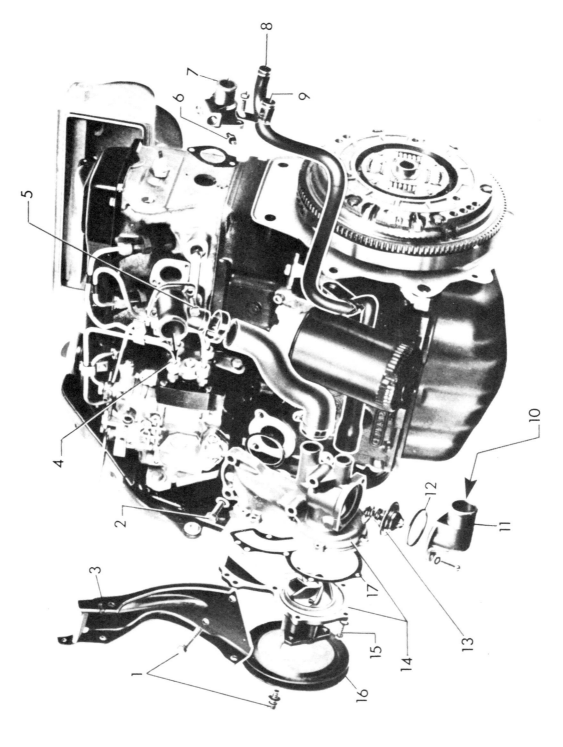

Fig. 2.1 Cooling system components (Sec 1)

1　Bolts
2　Water pump retaining bolts
3　Alternator bracket
4　To radiator top hose

5　Bolt
6　Temperature gauge sender
7　To heater
8　From heater

9　To expansion chamber
10　From radiator bottom hose
11　Water pump inlet elbow

12　O-ring
13　Thermostat
14　Water pump

15　Bolt
16　Pulley
17　Gasket

by the fan and by the motion of the car. The coolant, now much cooler, reaches the bottom of the radiator, when the cycle is repeated.

6   When the engine is cold the thermostat, which is a valve located in the water pump housing that opens and closes according to the temperature of the coolant, restricts the circulation of the coolant in the engine. Only when the correct minimum operating temperature has been reached, as given in the Specifications, does the thermostat begin to open, allowing the coolant to return to the radiator.

7   Engine coolant flows from an outlet connection on the rear end of the cylinder head (which also houses the temperature sender switch) through a hose to the heater radiator inside the car, and then returns through a hose to the water pump housing. The heater radiator is contained within the heater assembly which also houses a blower fan.

2   Cooling system – draining

1   It is best to drain the cooling system with the engine cold, but if this is not possible, the pressure must be released prior to draining the water. To do this, place a cloth over the expansion chamber cap and turn it slowly in an anti-clockwise direction until pressure is heard to escape, then stop turning.

2   Allow all the pressure to escape, then continue turning the cap anti-clockwise and remove it (photo). Be sure to keep your hand away from the escaping steam as otherwise you may be scalded.

3   If the coolant is to be retained for further use, place a suitable container beneath the water pump.

4   Move the heater controls inside the car to the hot position.

5   Disconnect the bottom hose from the water pump inlet elbow, and the heater hose return pipe from the water pump body (photo). Alternatively, remove the thermostat as described in Section 9.

3   Cooling system – flushing

1   After some time the radiator and engine waterways may become restricted or even blocked with scale or sediment, causing the engine to overheat. The coolant will appear rusty or dark in colour and when this occurs, the system should be flushed.

2   With the bottom hose and heater hose disconnected from the water pump and the thermostat removed, disconnect the top hose from the radiator and insert a water hose into the top of the radiator. Allow water to run through the radiator until it flows clear from the bottom hose.

3   Insert the water hose into the radiator top hose and allow water to run through the engine until it emerges clean from the water pump. Squeeze the by-pass hose occasionally to ensure that water circulates through all the engine waterways.

4   In severe cases of contamination the system should be reverse flushed. To do this, remove the radiator and insert the water hose in the bottom outlet with the radiator inverted. Continue flushing until clear water flows from the top of the radiator.

4   Cooling system – filling

1   Refit the thermostat if removed, and reconnect the radiator and heater hoses.

2   Make sure that the heater controls are set at the hot position.

3   Pour coolant of the specified mixture (see next Section) into the expansion chamber to the 'MIN' or cold water level mark (photo).

4   Fit the pressure cap to the expansion chamber and run the engine at a fast tick-over for 15 seconds.

5   Top-up the coolant level in the expansion chamber to the 'MIN' mark or slightly above and refit the pressure cap. When the engine is at normal operating temperature the coolant level will be nearer the 'MAX' level mark.

6   Never fill a hot engine with cold water, otherwise damage may occur to the cylinder head and block.

5   Antifreeze mixture

1   The coolant should be renewed every two years, not only to maintain the antifreeze properties but also to prevent corrosion in the system which would otherwise occur as the strength of the inhibitors

2.2 Removing the pressure cap

2.5 Pit view of the bottom hose and water pump inlet elbow

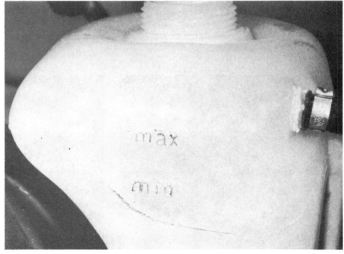
4.3 Expansion chamber level marks

in the coolant become progressively less effective.

2   Before adding antifreeze to the system, check all hoses and clips for deterioration and renew them as necessary. Flush the system as described in Section 3.

3   Mix the solution of antifreeze and water in a clean container; the total capacity of the system is given in the Specifications. The strength of the mixture can be determined from the following table:

Protection to outside temperature of	Quantity of Antifreeze	Water
-25°C (-13°F)	40%	60%
-35°C (-31°F)	50%	50%

4   When topping-up the cooling system always use a solution of the same strength as that already circulating in order to avoid dilution.

6 Radiator – removal, inspection, cleaning and refitting

1   Drain the cooling system as described in Section 2.

2   Disconnect the battery negative terminal.

3   Disconnect the thermo-switch wires from the left-hand side of the radiator (photo).

4   Disconnect the wiring plug from the radiator fan motor (photo).

5   Loosen the clips and disconnect the top and bottom hoses from the radiator (photo).

6   Disconnect the expansion chamber hose from the radiator. If the clamp type of clip is fitted, it will be necessary to obtain a screw type clip before refitting the hose.

7   Unscrew and remove the mounting nuts, slide the radiator sideways to disengage the upper mounting clip, and withdraw the radiator from the engine compartment (photos).

8   Unscrew the retaining bolts and remove the cowl complete with fan motor.

9   Radiator repair is best left to a specialist but minor leaks can be cured using a proprietary product, in many cases without removing the radiator.

10 Clear the radiator of flies and small leaves with a soft brush or by

hosing, and flush it if necessary as described in Section 3.

11 Refitting is a reversal of removal.

7 Pressure cap – testing

If leakage can be heard from the pressure cap or if the cooling system requires constant topping-up, the cap should be tested. Most garages have test equipment and, if the cap does not open within the specified limits, it should be renewed.

8 Fan and thermo-switch – testing and renewal

1   To test the fan motor, disconnect the plug and connect a 12 volt supply to the terminals. If the motor does not operate the brushes may be worn or sticking. To dismantle the motor, remove the fan blades and through bolts; the end brackets can now be removed but note the location of the shims which determine the armature endfloat. Clean the commutator and renew the brushes if necessary, then reassemble the motor in the reverse order.

2   If the thermo-switch is thought to be faulty, it should be removed, after draining the cooling system, and tested in a container of heated water. With a 12 volt test lamp and lead connected to the terminals, or alternatively an ohmmeter, the switch contacts should close when the temperature of the water reaches 90° C (194° F) If the switch is proved faulty, it must be renewed.

3   Should the switch contacts fail to close at any time resulting in overheating due to the fan not operating, the two terminals can be connected together as an emergency measure in order to reach the nearest repair garage.

9 Thermostat – removal, testing and refitting

1   A faulty thermostat will prevent the engine from running at the

6.3 Radiator fan thermo-switch location

6.4 Fan motor and wiring plug

6.5 Radiator top hose connection

6.7A Radiator lower mounting

6.7B Radiator upper mounting clip

6.7C Removing the radiator assembly

most efficient operating temperature. If overheating occurs, considerable damage to the engine may result. If the thermostat is suspect it should be removed and tested.

2   Drain the cooling system as described in Section 2.

3   Unscrew the two retaining bolts and remove the inlet elbow from the bottom of the water pump (photo).

4   Prise out the rubber O-ring and withdraw the thermostat (photos).

5   To test whether the unit is serviceable, suspend it by a piece of string in a pan of water being heated. The thermostat should commence to open at the specified temperature and should extend by the specified stroke when fully open. After cooling, the thermostat should return to its fully closed position.

6   Refitting is a reversal of removal, but fit a new O-ring if necessary.

10 Water pump – removal and refitting

1   Drain the cooling system as described in Section 2.

2   Remove the alternator as described in Chapter 7.

3   Remove the air conditioner compressor where fitted (Section 15).

4   Unbolt the alternator bracket from the cylinder block and water pump and remove the earth lead.

5   Disconnect the by-pass hose from the water pump, also the heater hose if not already removed (photo).

6   Unscrew the bolts securing the water pump to the cylinder block.

7   Remove the water pump complete with pulley, then prise out the rubber O-ring.

8   Unbolt the pulley from the water pump flange.

9   Unscrew the retaining bolts and separate the two halves; if they are tight, use a wooden mallet to tap them free.

10   The removal sequence above is the best one to follow with the engine in the car. If the engine is out of the car, you may prefer to follow the sequence shown in the photographs and separate the two halves of the water pump before removing the rear half from the block (photos).

11   Remove the gasket and clean the two surfaces. Remove the thermostat as described in Section 9.

12   The impeller and housing are serviced as one unit; if the driveshaft is faulty or a leak is present, the whole assembly must be renewed.

13   Refitting is a reversal of removal, but always use a new gasket and O-rings, and tighten all bolts to the specified torque wrench settings. Adjust the drivebelt as described in Chapter 7 and refill the cooling system as described in Section 4.

11 Temperature gauge sender unit – renewal and testing

1   The unit is screwed into the coolant flange at the flywheel end of the cylinder head (photo).

2   Before removing it drain the coolant from the radiator.

3   The resistance varies as the temperature increases. To check the sender disconnect the lead and using an ohmmeter, check the resistance cold and again with the engine hot. The cold resistance should be 270 ohms ± 5% and the normal working temperature resistance 150 ohms ± 5%. If it is not within these limits it should be renewed. It will be noted that the resistance decreases with rise in temperature.

12 Heating system – description

1   The heating system consists of a heat exchanger, blower motor and fan, a control box behind the dashboard, a control valve in the engine compartment (photo) and an extensive ducting system. Refer to Figs. 2.2 and 2.3.

2   The coolant is fed to the heat exchanger from the connection on the rear end of the cylinder head. The coolant is drawn through the heat exchanger and back to the water pump housing. The temperature of the coolant is in excess of 90°C (194°F) when it leaves the cylinder head. The quantity of coolant circulating depends upon how much the valve is opened, so that the heat available to the car interior is controlled in this way.

3   The heater cover is located in the engine compartment next to the windscreen wiper motor. Under the cover, operated by a control cable

9.3 Removing the water pump inlet elbow

9.4A Removing the thermostat

9.4.B Thermostat location aperture in the water pump

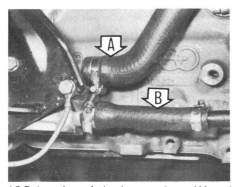
10.5 Location of the by-pass hose (A) and heater hose (B) on the water pump

10.10A If the engine is out of the car, first remove the water pump pulley ...

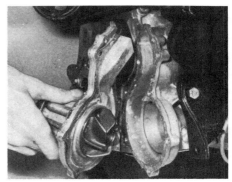
10.10B ... separate the two halves ...

10.10C ... and remove the rear half from the block

11.1 Temperature gauge sender units
A – Engine coolant
B – Heater control

12.1 Heater control valve in the engine compartment

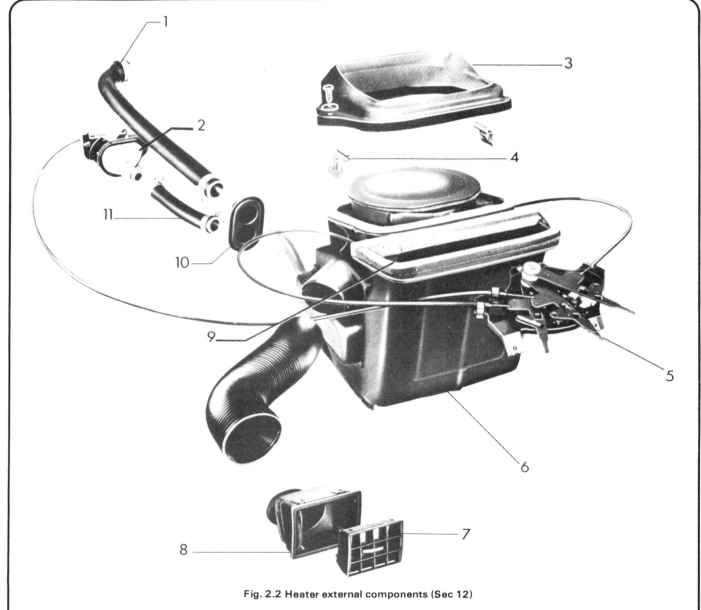

Fig. 2.2 Heater external components (Sec 12)

1	Heater hose to cylinder head	4	Clips	7	Air outlet
2	Control valve	5	Heater controls	8	Fresh air vent
3	Heater cover	6	Housing	9	Air outlet

10 Grommet
11 Heater hose to control valve

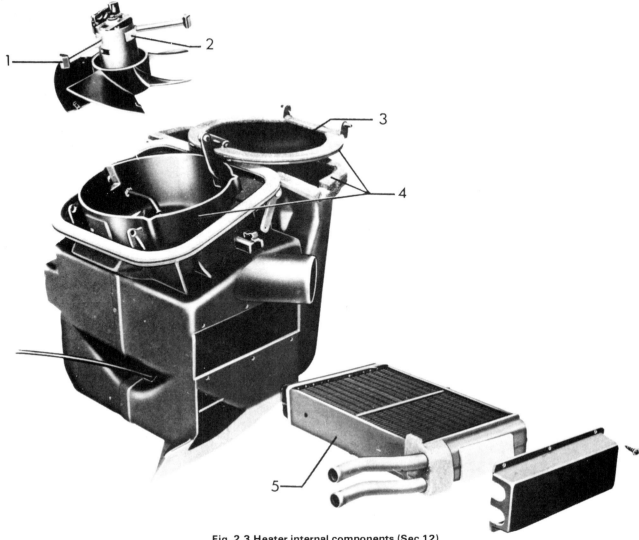

Fig. 2.3 Heater internal components (Sec 12)

1 Clip	4 Gaskets
2 Fan motor	5 Heat exchanger
3 Cut-off flap	

from the control box, is a circular dished flap. This controls the amount of air admitted to the system, and can close the system completely if so wished. Directly under the flap is the fan motor and fan. The fan motor has three speeds.

4   The air is forced into the fresh air housing where it is directed to the footwell air vents by the left-hand lever A on the control panel (see Fig. 2.4) or to the mixed vents for the windscreen and side windows by the right-hand control lever A.

5   Heated air is available through all the ventilation vents except the ones at each end of the dashboard which are for fresh unheated air only. Fig. 2.5 shows a later type of heater which operates in a similar manner (photo).

13 Heating system components – removal and refitting

1   Refer to Figs. 2.2 and 2.3. The heater cover can be removed from the back of the engine compartment by extracting the two plastic retaining pegs. This gives access to the cut-off flap and its actuating lever. Disconnect the cable and unhook one pivot of the cut-off flap. The flap may now be removed.

2   The fan motor is located in the throat of the inlet to the fresh air housing and may be lifted out. Disconnect the fan cable by pulling off the clip.

3   The housing is held to the body of the heater by two metal clips

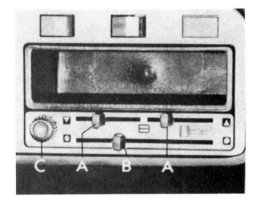

Fig. 2.4 Heater control panel (Sec 12)

A   Air distribution levers
B   Temperature control
C   Fan speed control knob

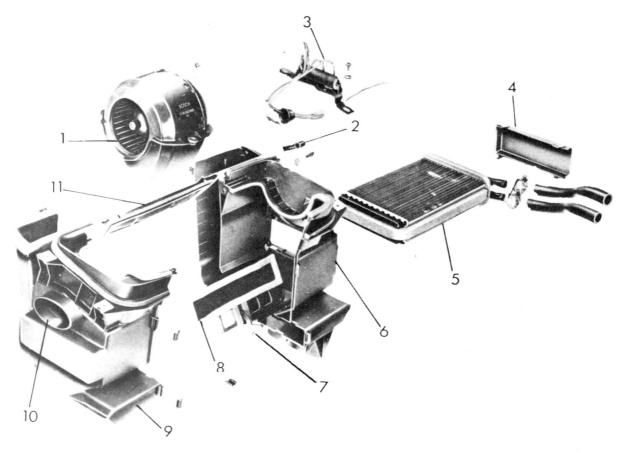

Fig. 2.5 Exploded view of the later type heater (Sec 12)

1	Rotary fan unit	4	Cover	7	Control flap clamp	10	Hose connection
2	Lever	5	Heat exchanger	8	Control flap	11	Cut-off flap
3	Series resistance	6	Housing half	9	Housing half		

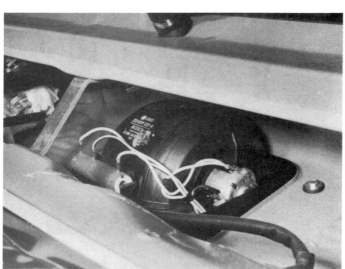

12.5 Later type heater motor location

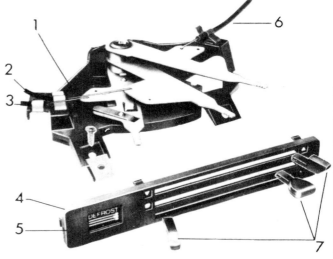

Fig. 2.6 Heater controls on early models (Sec 14)

1	Fresh air controls	5	Trim plate
2	Heater valve cable	6	Footwell flap cable
3	Cut-off flap cable	7	Control knobs
4	Bulb holder		

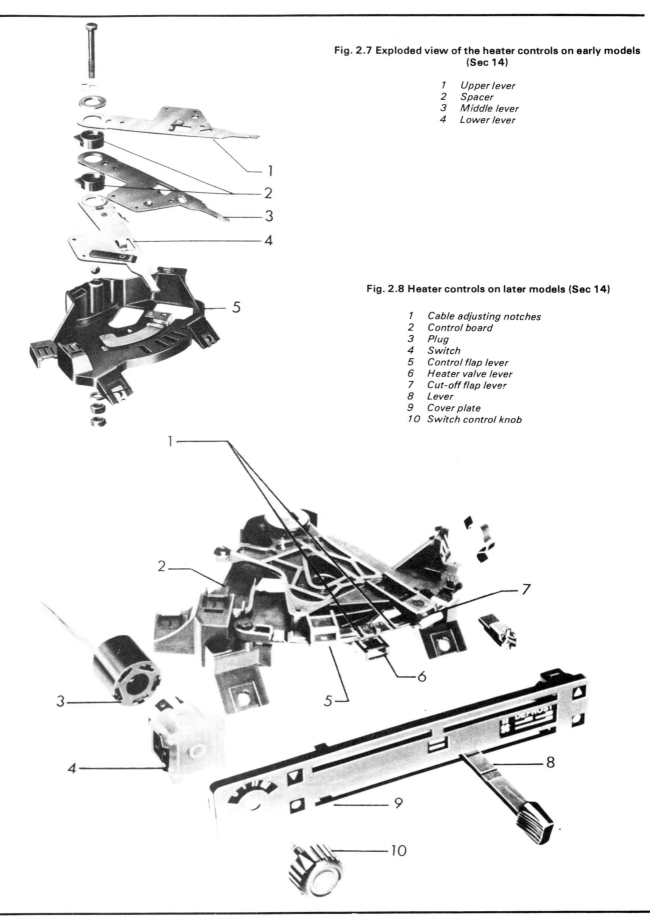

Fig. 2.7 Exploded view of the heater controls on early models (Sec 14)

1　Upper lever
2　Spacer
3　Middle lever
4　Lower lever

Fig. 2.8 Heater controls on later models (Sec 14)

1　Cable adjusting notches
2　Control board
3　Plug
4　Switch
5　Control flap lever
6　Heater valve lever
7　Cut-off flap lever
8　Lever
9　Cover plate
10　Switch control knob

which are difficult to locate and even more difficult to release. In the centre of the clip is a tongue or retaining spring, this must be pressed in and the clip will come undone. There is a clip on each side of the housing and once these are free the housing can be drawn off the heat exchanger. The large air ducts to the dashboard outlets pull out of the housing.

4   The heat exchanger must be removed after the fresh air housing. Two pipes go through the double grommet and are connected to the coolant hoses. It will be necessary to drain the cooling system before these hoses are disconnected.

5   Refitting is the reverse of the removal procedure. Fitting the clips is a bit tricky, the tab of the clip should be pushed into the retainer on the fresh air housing and the housing lifted squarely until the spring clicks into position.

6   Unless the heat exchanger leaks, the control cables break or the fan motor fails to work, it is best to leave well alone. The dismantling and reassembly is not a long job but you can get into difficulties when trying to get the housing clips off, and on, and unless the job is done carefully the housing may crack or split.

14 Heater controls – removal and refitting

1   The control unit is located in the centre of the dashboard. It is accessible after the radio has been removed, or on cars without a radio, the glovebox. Once the radio is extracted the control unit may be seen. Disconnect the battery earth strap and undo the two crosshead screws holding the control unit and it may be eased forward.

2   The middle lever controls the heater valve. It is reasonably easy to unhook the bowden cable and extract it through the bulkhead.

3   The upper and lower cables control the airflow. Although the cable for the upper lever is visible at its far end, right at the bottom of the fresh air housing it is necessary to dismantle the housing to renew it. The outer end of the lever cable operates the flap under the heater cover. This may be got at by removing the heater cover but you will probably break the plastic dowels when extracting them, so get some new ones before tackling the job.

4   It is best to renew the heater cables completely if the inner cable snaps. In this way the exact length required is obtained. We found it a

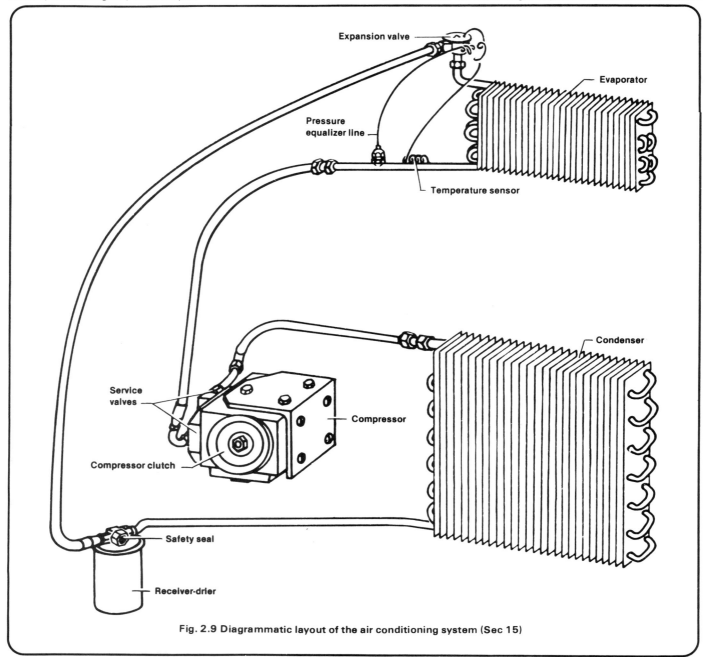

Fig. 2.9 Diagrammatic layout of the air conditioning system (Sec 15)

good thing to fit new cable clamps too, as the old ones seem to distort when removed.

5 Fig. 2.8. shows the later type of control. The removal and refitting procedure is almost identical for both types.

15 Air conditioning system – general

1 The unit works on exactly the same principle as a domestic refrigerator, having a compressor, a condenser and an evaporator. The condenser is attached to the car radiator system. The compressor, belt-driven from the crankshaft pulley, is installed on a bracket on the engine. The evaporator is installed in a housing under the dashboard which takes the place of the normal fresh air housing. This housing also contains a normal heat exchanger unit for warming the intake air. The evaporator has a blower motor to circulate cold air as required.

2 The system is controlled by a unit on the dashboard similar to the normal heater control in appearance.

3 The refrigerant used is difluorodichloromethane (CF_2CL_2) more commonly known as Frigen F12 or Freon F12. It is a dangerous substance in unskilled hands. As a liquid it is very cold and if it touches the skin there will be cold burns and frostbite. As a gas it is colourless and has no odour. Heavier than air it displaces oxygen and can cause asphyxiation if pockets of it collect in pits or similar workplaces. It does not burn, but even a lighted cigarette, causes it to breakdown into constituent gases, some of which are poisonous to the extent of being fatal. So if you have an air-conditioner and your car catches fire, you have an additional problem.

4 We strongly recommend that even trained refrigeration mechanics do not adjust the system unless they have had instruction by VW. The notes for VW personnel cover 25 pages. For the remainder we suggest that the system is left entirely alone, except for the adjustment of the compressor drivebelt, which should have 10 to 15 mm (0.4 to 0.6 inch) deflection in the centre when depressed by the thumb.

5 Removal and refitting of the air conditioner compressor is straightforward as can be seen from Fig. 2.10, but the refrigerant circuit **must**

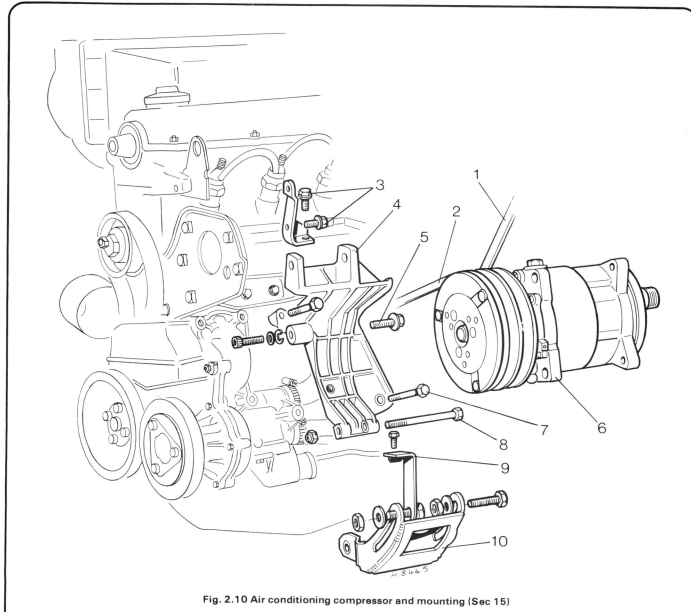

Fig. 2.10 Air conditioning compressor and mounting (Sec 15)

1	Alternator drivebelt	3	Bolts	6	Compressor – bolt must	8	Bolt
2	Water pump and compressor drivebelt	4	Bracket		be at top	9	Hose bracket
		5	Bolt	7	Bolt	10	Tensioner

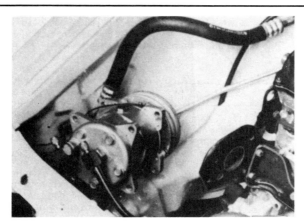

Fig. 2.11 Place the air conditioning compressor on the side of the engine compartment when removing the engine (Sec 15)

not be opened. The compressor must be placed on the side of the engine compartment when removing the engine, but only move it to the point where the flexible refrigerant hoses are in no danger of being stretched.

6   When a situation arises which calls for the removal of one of the air conditioning system components, have the system discharged by your VW agent or a qualified refrigeration engineer. Similarly have the system recharged by him on completion.

7   During the winter period operate the air conditioner for a few minutes each week to keep the system in good order.

8   Periodically, clean the condenser of dirt and insects, either by washing with a cold water hose or by air pressure. Use a soft bristly brush to assist removal of dirt jammed in the condenser fins.

16 Fault diagnosis – cooling, air conditioning and heating systems

Symptom	Reason/s
Overheating	Low coolant level
	Faulty pressure cap
	Thermostat sticking shut
	Drivebelt incorrectly adjusted
	Clogged radiator matrix
	Incorrect engine timing
	Corroded system
	Faulty cooling fan motor or thermo switch
	Blown head gasket
Cool running	Incorrect thermostat
	Faulty cooling fan motor or thermo switch
Slow warm-up	Thermostat sticking open
Coolant loss	Faulty pressure cap
	Split hose
	Leaking water pump
	Loose hose clip
	Blown head gasket
Air conditioning not working	Drivebelt incorrectly adjusted
	Faulty compressor

Chapter 3 Fuel and exhaust systems

For modifications, and information applicable to later models, see Supplement at end of manual

Contents

Specifications

Fuel injection pump

Type	Distributor
Make	Bosch or CAV

Air cleaner element .... Paper

Preheating .... Glow plug in each cylinder

Fuel grade .... CN 45 min (UK), Number 2 (USA)

Fuel tank capacity .... 45 litres (9·9 Imp gal, 11·8 US gal)

Torque wrench settings

	kgf m	lbf ft
Injection pump mounting bolt	2·5	18
Fuel pipes	2·5	18
Fuel pump unions (Bosch)	4·5	32
Injection pump sprocket	4·5	33
Injectors	7·0	51
Injector upper to lower section (Bosch)	7·0	51
Injector upper to lower section (CAV)	7.0	51
Fuel tank strap	2·5	18
Manifolds to cylinder head	2·5	18

1 General description

The fuel system comprises a rear mounted fuel tank located below the rear of the car, a mechanical fuel injection pump driven by the engine timing drivebelt, and injectors screwed into the cylinder head which inject fuel oil into pre-combustion or ante chambers.

A fuel filter is incorporated in the fuel line between the tank and injection pump. It is important to renew the filter at the specified intervals, since the fuel oil is used to lubricate the precision made injection pump. Both the injection pump and the injectors are connected to a fuel return pipe which allows excess fuel to return to the fuel tank.

Two types of injection pump may be fitted, one made by Bosch or one by CAV. Both are of the distributor type incorporating a distribution rotor.

The cold start system comprises preheater glow plugs located in the pre-combustion chambers, and a linked device on the injection pump for advancing the injection timing and increasing the idle speed. In addition, an internal automatic device provides extra fuel at engine cranking speed. A relay linked with the starter motor continues to operate the glow plugs during starting.

A shut-off solenoid is incorporated into the fuel supply circuit in the injection pump. The solenoid valve is shut when de-energised and open when energised, thus when the ignition key is switched on the circuit is open and when it is switched off the supply is stopped.

The servicing of fuel injection components is a complex subject and also requires the use of specialised equipment in dust-free surroundings. The home mechanic is therefore advised to attempt only the procedures described in this Chapter. Even so, the work **must** be carried out under conditions of the utmost cleanliness. Remember also that fuel oil is detrimental to rubber components such as water hoses and toothed drivebelts.

Emission control

Unlike its petrol (gasoline) engined counterpart, the design of the Golf diesel engine is such that satisfactory emission control is achieved without the addition of special equipment or devices, only a crankcase ventilation system (see Chapter 1) being fitted. In order to maintain this desirable condition however, the state of the engine and fuel system must be faultless and regular servicing and adjustment must not be neglected.

2   Air cleaner element – renewal

1   The air cleaner element should be renewed at the specified intervals (see Routine Maintenance). Earlier renewal may be required if the car is operated in very dusty conditions.
2   To remove the element, prise the spring clips up and withdraw the housing from the inlet manifold casting (photo).
3   Remove the element and, if it is to be re-used, shake it to displace all the accumulated dust and dirt (photo).
4   Clean the interior of the housing and manifold casting with a paraffin moistened cloth and wipe dry (photo).
5   Refitting is a reversal of removal, but make sure that the retaining clips are fully engaged with the recesses on the top and bottom of the inlet manifold casting. At the same time, the crankcase ventilation hose from the casting to the valve cover can be removed and cleaned out with paraffin (photo).

3   Fuel filter – renewal and maintenance

1   The fuel filter is located on the right-hand side of the engine compartment by the suspension strut upper bearing (photos). It must be renewed every 20 000 miles (30 000 km) in order to prevent excessive wear occurring in the injection pump.
2   *On cars fitted with the Bosch system,* unscrew the filter canister with a filter wrench, or a spanner if a hexagon is provided on the bottom of the canister. Hold the canister in a cloth and do not tilt it otherwise fuel will spill from it.
3   Discard the old filter canister.
4   Smear a film of diesel fuel onto the sealing ring of the new canister, then tighten it onto the housing using hand pressure only (photo).
5   Early models were provided with a primer pump to fill the system with fuel prior to starting but this has now been discontinued. The system does not need bleeding even though a primer is provided; the engine should be turned with the starter until it starts, then accelerated several times.
6   With the engine running, check the filter canister for fuel leaks, then stop the engine.
7   A water drain tap is provided at the bottom of the filter in order to drain off any accumulated moisture from the fuel (photo). Periodically the tap should be loosened to allow the water to drain out, then tightened when clear fuel flows. Loosen the vent screw on top of the filter housing and have an assistant operate the starter without operating the glow plugs. Tighten the vent screw as soon as clear fuel flows from it.
8   *On cars fitted with the CAV system,* first loosen the filter retaining bolt located in the centre of the upper housing. Do not fully unscrew it at this stage.
9   Wipe the filter upper and lower housings clean with a paraffin moistened cloth.
10   Unscrew the filter mounting nuts and lift the filter from the mounting bracket.
11   Remove the centre bolt, separate the housings, and remove the filter element.
12   Discard the old element and clean any accumulated sediment from the lower housing.
13   When fitting the new element, make sure that the sealing rings are correctly located as shown in Fig. 3.3 and smear their contact faces with a little fuel oil. Tighten the centre bolt, then bleed the fuel system as described in Section 4.
14   The CAV filter also incorporates a water drain tap (refer to paragraph 7). To drain the water, loosen the breather screw on the upper housing, then loosen the drain plug. Tighten both screws when clear fuel emerges

4   Bleeding the fuel system

1   *On cars fitted with the Bosch system,* bleeding is unnecessary, even if the fuel tank has run dry. However, the battery will be required to turn the engine during the time it takes to fill the system, and

2.2 Removing the air cleaner housing

2.3 The air cleaner element

2.4 Intake manifold and air cleaner base casting

2.5 Crankcase ventilation hose connection to the valve cover

3.1A Fuel filter location

3.1B Fuel filter mounting bracket

3.4 The fuel filter canister seal and housing

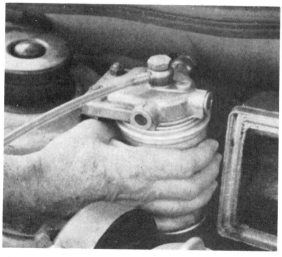

Fig. 3.1 Tightening the fuel filter canister on the Bosch system
(Sec 3)

3.7 Fuel filter canister water drain tap

Fig. 3.2 Fuel filter element retaining bolt (1) and mounting nuts (2)
on the CAV system (Sec 3)

battery discharge can be avoided where the primary facility is fitted as described in the next paragraph.

2   To fill the Bosch system, first loosen the vent screw on the filter housing. Operate the primer pump until the fuel emerging from the screw is free of air bubbles, then tighten the screw (Fig. 3.4). If the engine refuses to start after this, loosen two injector unions and turn the engine with the starter until fuel emerges, then tighten the unions.

3   *On cars fitted with the CAV system,* bleeding is recommended after removing any component or after running out of fuel. First operate the hand lift pump until fuel is visible in the inlet pipe free of air bubbles.

4   Loosen the vent screw on the injection pump next to the throttle lever 1 or 2 turns, and turn the engine with the starter for 15 seconds. If the engine starts before the end of this period, switch it off and tighten the vent screw. With the screw tightened, the engine may be started in the normal manner (Figs. 3.5 and 3.6).

5   Fuel tank – removal, servicing and refitting

1   Disconnect the battery negative terminal.

2   Unscrew the drain plug and drain the fuel into a suitable container.

3   Remove the brake fluid reservoir filler cap and tighten it down onto a piece of polythene sheeting; this will reduce the loss of brake fluid in subsequent operations.

4   Chock the front wheels. Jack-up the rear of the car and support it

on axle stands.

5   Disconnect the brake line hoses on each side of the car, just forward of the rear axle mountings (Fig. 3.8). Plug the ends to prevent the entry of dirt.

6   Unscrew and remove the axle mounting nuts from each side of the car, and lower the rear axle beam as far as the handbrake cable guides will allow.

7   Remove the exhaust silencer mounting rubbers and lower the silencer.

8   Loosen the securing clip and disconnect the fuel supply hose from the tank.

9   Note the location of the engine supply and return pipes, then disconnect them from the tank.

10 Remove the retaining straps and lower the tank sufficiently to disconnect the fuel gauge sender unit wires, breather pipe and drain pipe.

11 Withdraw the fuel tank from under the car.

12 A leak in the fuel tank should be repaired by specialists or alternatively a new tank fitted. Never be tempted to solder or weld a fuel tank.

13 If the tank is contaminated with sediment or water, it can be swilled out using several changes of fuel, but if any vigorous shaking is required to dislodge accumulations of sediment, the fuel gauge sender unit should first be removed as described in Section 6.

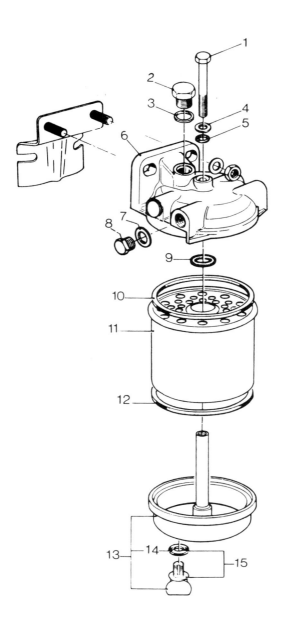

Fig. 3.4 Bosch fuel filter element (1), vent screw (2), primer (3), and drain tap (4) (Sec 4)

Fig. 3.5 CAV fuel filter primer pump (A) and outlet pipe (B) (Sec 4)

Fig. 3.3 Exploded view of the CAV fuel filter (Sec 3)

1   Retaining bolt
2   Vent plug
3   Washer
4   Washer
5   Sealing ring
6   Filter head
7   Washer
8   Plug
9   Sealing ring
10 Sealing ring
11 Element
12 Sealing ring
13 Filter base
14 Sealing ring
15 Drain tap

Fig. 3.6 CAV injection pump vent (1) (Sec 4)

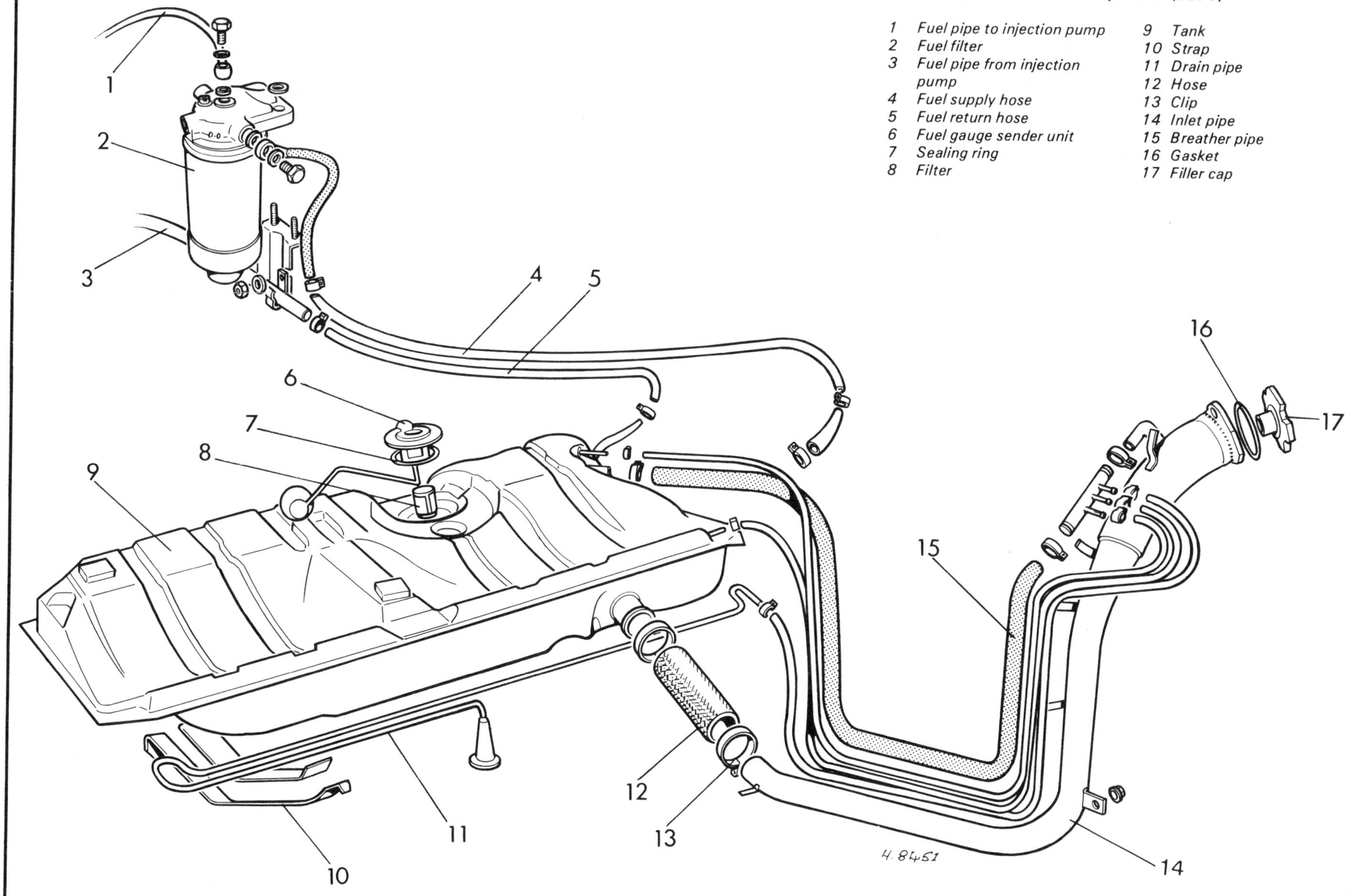

65

Fig. 3.7 Fuel tank components (Sec 5)

1 Fuel pipe to injection pump
2 Fuel filter
3 Fuel pipe from injection
   pump
4 Fuel supply hose
5 Fuel return hose
6 Fuel gauge sender unit
7 Sealing ring
8 Filter
9 Tank
10 Strap
11 Drain pipe
12 Hose
13 Clip
14 Inlet pipe
15 Breather pipe
16 Gasket
17 Filler cap

H.8451

Fig. 3.8 Axle mounting nuts (white arrows) and brake line hose
(black arrow) (Sec 5)

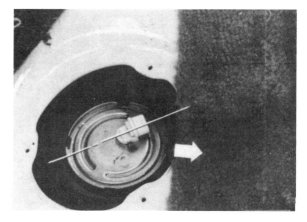

Fig. 3.9 Fuel gauge sender unit installed position. Arrow indicates front
of car (Sec 6)

14 Refitting is a reversal of removal, but the following additional
points should be noted:

  (a) *Renew the hose clips if they are unserviceable*
  (b) *Make sure that the breather and drain pipes are not trapped*
  (c) *Adjust the handbrake cable as described in Chapter 6*
  (d) *Bleed the brake hydraulic system as described in Chapter 6;*
       make sure that the polythene sheeting is removed from the
       reservoir filler cap
  (e) *Bleed the fuel system (if applicable) as described in Section 4*

Fig. 3.10 Removing the injection pump sprocket (Sec 7)

---

6 Fuel gauge sender unit – removal and refitting

1 Disconnect the battery negative terminal.
2 Remove the rear seat, unscrew the retaining screws and lift the
sender cover away.
3 Pull the wiring connector from the sender unit, then wipe away
any dirt from the surrounding area with a paraffin moistened cloth.
4 Twist the sender unit to disengage the bayonet type fitting and
withdraw it from the fuel tank.
5 Remove the sealing ring. Where fitted, clean the filter located on
the bottom of the unit.
6 Refitting is a reversal of removal, but the sealing ring should be
rubbed with graphite powder prior to refitting, and the sender terminal
must face the direction shown in Fig. 3.9 when fully installed.

---

7 Fuel injection pump – removal and refitting

It is not possible to test and repair the injection pump without
special test equipment. If the pump is suspect it should be removed
and taken to a garage housing the necessary facilities or to a diesel
service centre for testing and any repairs that may be necessary.
Fortunately fuel injection pumps are very reliable and seldom give any
trouble.
1 Disconnect the earth cable from the battery negative terminal.
2 Remove the toothed drivebelt as described in Chapter 1, Section
9.
3 Slacken the pump sprocket retaining nut a few threads, but do not
take it off. Using a suitable two-legged puller, free the sprocket from
the pump shaft (Fig. 3.10 shows VW tool 203b being used), then
remove the puller, retaining nut and sprocket (photo).

7.3 Fuel injection pump sprocket mounting taper and key

7.4 Fuel distribution pipe connections on the injection pump

7.5 Fuel stop solenoid terminal (arrowed) on the Bosch injection pump

7.6 Accelerator cable connection to the throttle lever (Bosch system)

7.7 Cold start cable connection on the injection pump (Bosch system)

7.8A Injection pump front mounting plate and accelerator cable bracket (Bosch system)

7.8B Injection pump rear mounting bolt and plate (Bosch system)

4   Disconnect the fuel lines from the injection pump and cover the union with a clean cloth to prevent the entry of dirt or moisture (photo).

5   Disconnect the electrical lead from the stop solenoid on the pump (photo).

6   Disconnect the accelerator cable from the pump lever, undo the accelerator cable bracket securing nuts and lift away the cable complete with bracket (photo).

7   Disconnect the cold start cable from the pump lever (photo).

8   Remove the injection pump mounting bolts and lift away the pump (photos). Do not unscrew the bolts securing the rear mounting plate to the injection pump.

9   To refit the pump, insert the securing bolts and tighten them

finger-tight. Position the injection pump so that the mark on the pump body is aligned with the mark on the mounting plate, as shown in Fig. 3.11, and tighten the bolts to the specified torque.

10   Reconnect the fuel pipes and hoses (photo). Tighten the fuel pipes to the specified torque. Do not overtighten as this can result in fuel leakage.

11   Fit the injection pump sprocket. Tighten the securing nut to the specified torque.

12   Check that the flywheel TDC mark is still aligned with the pointer on the bellhousing, then turn the pump sprocket to align the mark on the sprocket with the mark on the pump mounting plate, see Fig. 3.12

Fig. 3.11 Injection pump and mounting plate alignment marks

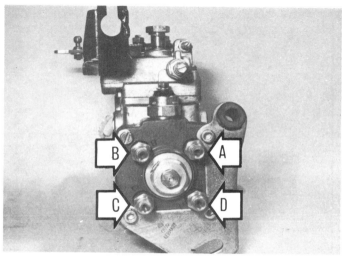

7.10 The fuel distribution pipe unions on the injection pump (Bosch system). A – No 1 injector B – No 3 injector C – No 4 injector D – No 2 injector

Fig. 3.12 Bosch injection pump alignment marks (black arrow), and locking pin (white arrow) (Sec 7)

7.12A Flywheel TDC notch and bellhousing pointer

7.12B Injection pump timing marks (arrowed)

Fig. 3.13 TDC setting fixture for use when engine removed (Sec 8)

Fig. 3.14 Bosch injection pump timing plug (arrowed) (Sec 8)

Fig. 3.15 Checking the Bosch injection pump timing with a dial gauge (Sec 8)

(photos). Now lock the sprocket in position with a stepped pin of suitable diameter, as described in Chapter 1, Section 9.

13 Refit and tension the drivebelt as described in Chapter 1, Section 9.

14 Refer to Section 8 and adjust the injection pump timing.

15 Reconnect the electrical lead to the stop solenoid and refit the accelerator cable and bracket, and the cold start cable, to the pump. Adjust the cables, if necessary, as described in Sections 10 and 11.

16 For the remainder of the refitting procedure, refer to Chapter 1, Section 9, then bleed the fuel system if necessary as described in Section 4.

8 Injection pump timing (Bosch system) – checking and adjusting

1 Turn the engine until No 1 piston is at TDC on compression stroke (both valves closed, cam lobes pointing upwards) and the TDC notch on the flywheel is in alignment with the pointer on the bellhousing. If the transmission is removed, a setting fixture is required to determine the TDC point. Fig. 3.13 shows VW tool No 2068 being used.

2 Remove the plug from the pump cover (Fig. 3.14) and screw in an adapter and dial gauge in place of the plug as shown in Fig. 3.15. The dial gauge should have a range of 0 to 3 mm.

3 Screw the adapter in until the gauge shows a reading of 2.5 mm, then slowly turn the crankshaft anti-clockwise until the needle on the gauge stops moving. Now zero the dial gauge with a 1 mm preload.

4 Rotate the crankshaft in a clockwise direction to align the TDC notch on the flywheel with the pointer and check that the gauge reads 0.83 mm.

5 Adjust, if necessary, by slackening the pump mounting bolts and turning the pump to adjust the lift to 0.83 mm, then retighten the mounting bolts to the specified torque.

6 If the correct lift cannot be achieved the valve timing must be checked.

7 Refer to Chapter 1, Section 9 and remove the valve cover and drivebelt cover.

8 Ensure that the engine is set with No 1 piston at TDC on the compression stroke and then lock the camshaft in position with tool 2065, or a suitable substitute.

9 Check that the lockpin fits in the holes in the pump sprocket and injection pump mounting plate. If the pin cannot be located in both holes the valve timing will have to be adjusted.

10 To adjust the valve timing, slacken the drivebelt tensioner locknut, then slacken the camshaft sprocket retaining nut half a turn and free the sprocket from the taper on the camshaft by tapping it with a plastic hammer. This will allow the sprocket to be rotated independently of the camshaft.

11 Now rotate the injection pump sprocket to align the mark on the sprocket with the mark on the pump mounting plate, see Fig. 3.12, and fit the locking pin to lock the pump sprocket in position.

12 Adjust the tension of the drivebelt as described in Chapter 1, Section 9, then tighten the camshaft sprocket retaining bolt to the specified torque.

13 Remove the camshaft locking tool and the pump sprocket lockpin.

14 Recheck the injection pump timing.

15 Refit the drivebelt cover and valve cover, refer to Chapter 1, Section 9.

9 Injection pump timing (CAV system) – checking and adjusting

1 Follow the instructions given in Section 8, paragraph 1.

2 Clean the area surrounding the inspection cover on the injection pump, then remove the retaining screws and withdraw the cover. Check that the cold start control is fully released.

3 With No 1 piston at TDC as set in paragraph 1, the fixed pointer must be in alignment with the mark which passes through the hole on the rotor driveplate (see Fig. 3.16). If necessary, loosen the pump flange retaining bolts and the mounting bracket bolt at the rear, and turn the injection pump as required.

4 When the adjustment is correct, tighten the bolts and check the timing by turning the engine through two complete revolutions until No 1 piston is at TDC again.

5 Refit the inspection cover and tighten the retaining screws.

Fig. 3.16 CAV injection pump timing pointer (A) and drilled mark (B) (Sec 9)

10 Accelerator cable – adjustment

Note: *The following paragraphs refer to the Bosch system, but the same principles apply to the CAV system.*

1 Ensure that the ball-pin on the pump lever is pointing upwards and is opposite the line marked on the lever (Fig. 3.17 and photo).

2 Check that the accelerator cable is located in the upper hole of the cable support bracket, indicated by the black arrow in Fig. 3.17 (photo).

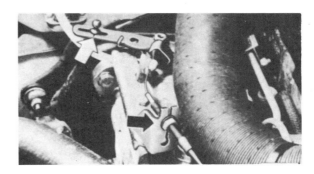

Fig. 3.17 Throttle lever ball-pin mark (white arrow) and accelerator cable location (black arrow) (Sec 10)

10.1 Bosch injection pump, showing the throttle lever

10.2 Injection pump end of the accelerator cable

10.3 Accelerator cable adjustment locknuts (arrowed) (Bosch system)

Fig. 3.18 Cold start cable components (Bosch system) (Sec 11)

1 Washer   2 Lockwasher   3 Pin

11.3 Bosch injection pump, showing the cold start lever

Fig. 3.19 Idle speed adjusting screw (arrowed) on the Bosch
injection pump (Sec 12)

Fig. 3.20 Maximum speed adjusting screw (arrowed) on the Bosch
injection pump (Sec 12)

3   Have an assistant depress the accelerator fully, then adjust the cable by turning the locknuts as necessary until the pump lever just contacts the maximum rpm adjusting screw without putting any strain on the cable (photo).

4   With the cable correctly adjusted, ensure that the adjusting nuts are locked against the cable support bracket, and then check the operation of the cable while your assistant operates the accelerator pedal.

11   Cold starting cable – adjustment

Refer to the note at the beginning of Section 10.

1   When the cold starting cable knob on the dashboard is pulled out, this advances the fuel injection pump timing by 2.5° and thus improves starting.

2   When fitting the cable to the pump insert the washer (1 in Fig. 3.18) onto the cable, then fit the outer cable in the bracket wih the rubber bush.

3   Connect the inner cable to the cold start lever by inserting the cable in pin (3) and then fit the lockwasher (2) (photo).

4   Move the lever as far as possible in the direction of the arrow (Fig. 3.18), then while holding the lever in this position, pull the inner cable tight and lock it in the pivot pin by tightening the clamp screw.

12   Idle speed and maximum speed – checking and adjusting

Checking and adjustment of the idle speed and maximum speed requires the use of special equipment, adaptor VW 1324 and tester VW 1267, so this is a job for your local VW garage. For owners who have access to this equipment the checking and adjustment procedure is described below.

1   Connect the test equipment to the engine in accordance with the instructions printed on the equipment.

2   Start the engine and warm it up to normal operating temperature, engine oil temperature at 50°–70°C (122°–158°F).

Idle speed (Bosch system)

3   Check that the idle speed is between 770 and 870 rpm, if not, slacken the idle adjusting screw locknut and screw the adjusting screw in or out as necessary to obtain the correct idle speed.

4   Hold the adjusting screw to prevent it turning and tighten the locknut.

Maximum speed without load (Bosch system)

5   Move the pump lever to the full throttle position and check that the engine speed is between 5400 and 5450 rpm. If necessary adjust by slackening the adjusting screw locknut, arrowed in Fig. 3.20, and

turning the adjusting screw to obtain the specified setting.

6   Tighten the adjusting screw locknut.

7   Remove the test equipment.

Idle speed (CAV system)

8   Check that the cold start control is fully released.

9   Increase the engine speed to 2000 rpm several times, then allow it to idle. The idle speed should be between 760 and 860 rpm.

10   If adjustment is necessary, first loosen the locknut on the idle speed stabilising screw (see Fig. 3.21) and back off the screw from the throttle shaft. The screw may be locked with locking wire and a lead seal, and the owner is warned that warranty conditions may be infringed if the seal is disturbed.

11   Loosen the idle speed adjustment locknut and adjust the screw until the engine speed is between 820 and 840 rpm. Tighten the locknut.

12   Turn the idling speed stabilising screw clockwise until the engine speed just starts to rise, then back it off $\frac{1}{2}$ to 1 turn and tighten the locknut.

13   Increase the engine speed to 2000 rpm several times and recheck the idling speed.

Maximum speed without load (CAV system)

14   Start the engine and fully open the throttle; the maximum engine speed should be between 5450 and 5650 rpm. **Note**: *If the setting is too high, do not exceed 5850 rpm.*

15   If adjustment is necessary, loosen the locknut and adjust the stop screw (arrowed in Fig. 3.22) as required. Tighten the locknut.

13   Fuel injectors – removal and refitting

1   Injector failure is usually indicated by knocking in one or more cylinders, engine overheating, loss of power, smoky black exhaust and increased fuel consumption. To locate a faulty injector run the engine at a fast idle (engine at normal operating temperature) and slacken the pipe union on each injector in turn. If there is no drop in engine speed when a pipe is slackened then that injector is faulty.

2   Stop the engine, then disconnect the fuel pipe and leak off pipes from the injector (photo).

3   Unscrew the injector from the cylinder head with a 27 mm ring spanner (photos).

4   Remove the heat shield from the bottom of the injector hole in the cylinder head (photo). Discard the heat shield.

5   Fit a new heat shield and then screw the injector into the cylinder head and tighten it to the specified torque.

6   Reconnect the fuel pipes to the injector and tighten the union nut to the specified torque. Do not overtighten as this may result in fuel leakage if the union nut is distorted.

Fig. 3.21 Idle speed stabilising screw (1) and adjusting screw (2) on the CAV injection pump. Arrow indicates locknut (Sec 12)

Fig. 3.22 Maximum speed adjusting screw (arrowed) on the CAV injection pump (Sec 12)

13.2 Injector and fuel pipe union

13.3A Removing an injector

13.3B A Bosch injector, showing leak-off outlets

13.3C An injector nozzle

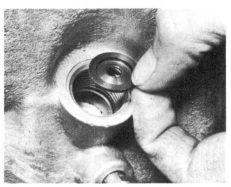

13.4 Removing an injector heat shield

14 Fuel injectors – testing

1   A pressure pump is required for testing the fuel injectors. Fig. 3.23 shows an injector being tested with pressure pump VW 1322. For those owners having access to a fuel injector test pump the testing procedure is described in the following paragraphs.
WARNING: *Never expose your hands to injector spray as working pressure can cause the fuel oil to penetrate the skin.*
2   Connect the injector to the test pump as shown in Fig. 3.23.

Spray testing
3   Close the valve on the pump to isolate the gauge.
4   With rapid short strokes of the test pump lever, 4 to 6 strokes per second, the spray should be even and stop cleanly after each stroke. The injectors must not drip.

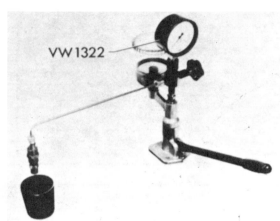

VW 1322

Fig. 3.23 Testing an injector with a pressure pump (Sec 14)

Breaking pressure test
5   Open the valve on the test pump so that the gauge will register.
6   Press the pump lever down very slowly and note the pressure at which the injector works. The specified pressure is 120–130 atm (Bosch) or 120–128 atm (CAV). Adjust, if necessary, by altering the shims as described in Section 15. A thicker shim will increase the breaking pressure – a thinner shim will lower the breaking pressure. Shims are supplied in various thicknesses according to the type of system installed. Increasing the shim thickness by 0.05 mm increases the breaking pressure by approximately 5 atmospheres (5.0 kgf/cm^2) and pro rata.

Leakage test
7   With the pump gauge working, very slowly press down on the pump lever until the gauge is registering approximately 110 atmospheres (110 kgf/cm^2), then hold the pressure for 10 seconds and check that there is no fuel leakage from the tip of the nozzle during this period.
8   Repair or renew a faulty injector.

15 Fuel injectors – servicing

1   The injectors can be dismantled for cleaning, renewal of defective ports and adjustment.
2   Clamp the upper part of the injector in a vice and slacken the lower part, then remove it from the vice, turn it over and clamp the lower part in the vice. This will prevent the internal parts falling out as the upper part is unscrewed.
3   Remove all the parts and clean them in diesel fuel. Keep all the parts belonging to the injector together and do not interchange them with parts from another injector. The needle and nozzle are supplied as a matched set. Always renew the heat shield.
4   Assemble the parts in the order shown in Fig. 3.24 and tighten the upper and lower parts to the specified torque.
5   Test and, if necessary, adjust the breaking pressure, refer to Section 14.

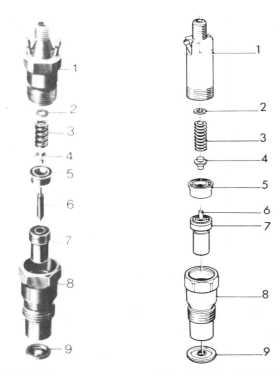

Fig. 3.24 Injector components — Bosch (left) and CAV (right) (Sec 15)

1 *Body*	4 *Seat*	7 *Nozzle*
2 *Shim*	5 *Nozzle holder*	8 *Nut*
3 *Spring*	6 *Needle*	9 *Heat shield*

16 Glow plugs – removal and refitting

1   Provided the glow plugs are working correctly and the engine starts satisfactorily, there is no need to remove the glow plugs except to clean them when the injectors are serviced, normally at 60 000 mile (96 000 km) intervals or every 4 years, whichever occurs first.

2   To remove the glow plugs, first disconnect the battery negative terminal.

3   Unscrew the terminal nuts and remove the bus bar noting that the supply wire is connected to No 4 cylinder (photos).

4   Unscrew the glow plugs and remove them from the cylinder head (photos).

5   Clean any accumulations of carbon from the glow plug tips and apply a little graphite grease to the threads.

6   Refitting is a reversal of removal.

17 Fuel pipes and unions

1   To ensure correct sealing, all fuel pipe unions should only be tightened to the specified torque (photo). Bending of fuel pipes must also be avoided and it is preferable to remove a pipe completely, rather than leave one end attached and bend the other.

2   When fitting fuel distribution pipes to the Bosch injection pump, first tighten the unions into the pump head to the specified torque, then tighten the pipe nuts to the specified torque (photo). The unions and seals should be renewed if a leak occurs after installing them in this manner.

3   Refer to Fig. 3.25 and note that on the Bosch injection pump the inlet union bolt (A) differs from the return union bolt (B). The latter incorporates a restrictor and if fitted in the inlet union will result in unsatisfactory performance, 'hunting', smoky exhaust and incorrect engine maximum speed (photos).

16.3A Glow plug supply wire location

16.3B Glow plug bus bar location

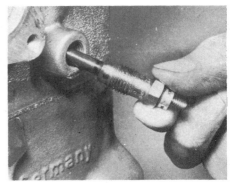

16.4A Removing a glow plug

16.4B Glow plug, showing element tip

17.1 Injection pump leak-off outlet union (Bosch system)

17.2 Fuel distribution pipe locations (Bosch system)

Fig. 3.25 Inlet union (A) and outlet union (B) location on the Bosch injection pump (Sec 17)

17.3A Injection pump inlet union (Bosch system)

17.3B Injection pump inlet union bolt (Bosch system)

18.1A Cylinder head ports, showing manifold gaskets

18.1B Intake manifold mounting on the exhaust manifold

18.2A Exhaust manifold location

18 Manifolds and exhaust system

1   The intake manifold is bolted to the cylinder head and incorporates four separate induction passages, each communicating with a single cylinder. Always use a new gasket when installing, and tighten the bolts evenly to the specified torque (photos).

2   The exhaust manifold is located just below the intake manifold and is attached to the cylinder head by eight studs. The four gaskets must be renewed whenever the exhaust manifold is removed, and the retaining nuts should always be tightened to the specified torque. The

lower end of the exhaust manifold is supported by two brackets (photos).

3   The exhaust system comprises three sections: (a) front pipe and expansion unit which is corrugated and attached to the manifold flange, (b) intermediate pipe and (c) rear section incorporating the silencer. The system is mounted to the body underframe by rubber O-rings (photos).

4   At six monthly intervals, the exhaust system should be examined for leaks and deterioration. Very often a small leak can be repaired by welding, but if the deterioration is extensive the particular section must be renewed. Never ignore a leak, as poisonous gases may seep into

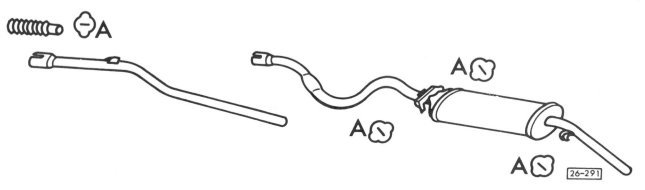

Fig. 3.26 Exhaust system components (Sec 18)

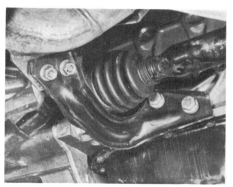

18.2B Right-hand exhaust manifold support bracket

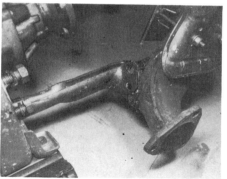

18.2C Left-hand exhaust manifold support bracket

18.3A Centre exhaust mounting and joint

18.3B Rear exhaust mounting

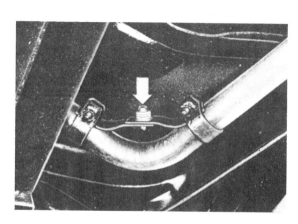

Fig. 3.27 Damping bracket fitted to the rear exhaust section (Sec 18)

18.6A Fitting the expansion unit to the exhaust manifold ...

18.6B ... showing the gasket and flange bolts

the car interior and cause drowsiness.

5   Removal of the exhaust system is best achieved by disconnecting and removing the rear section first, then removing the front section.

6   Refitting is a reversal of removal, but before tightening the intermediate clamps and the triangular flange, the system should be positioned to give uniform loading of the mounting rubbers. It is important to note that a damping bracket is fitted to the bend in the rear section (Fig. 3.27) and when fitting a new section, the bracket must be transferred from the old section. If it is unserviceable, the bracket must be renewed. Always fit a new gasket between the expansion unit and the exhaust manifold (photos).

19 Fault diagnosis – fuel and exhaust systems

Symptom	Reason/s
Engine does not start	Lack of fuel
	Battery discharged
	Stop solenoid faulty or fuse blown
	Glow plug relay faulty
	Fuel filter blocked
	Fuel supply hose trapped
	Injection timing incorrect
	Injection pump or injectors faulty
Uneven idling	Incorrect idle speed adjustments
	Loose fuel pipe or union
	Rear injection pump bracket broken
	Air in fuel system
	Faulty injectors
	Injection timing incorrect
	Injection pump faulty
Smoky exhaust	Choked air cleaner element
	Injection pump adjustments incorrect
	Faulty injectors
	Injection timing incorrect
	Injection pump faulty
High fuel consumption	Choked air cleaner element
	Leaking fuel pipe or union
	Return pipes blocked
	Injection pump adjustments incorrect
	Faulty injectors
	Injection timing incorrect
	Injection pump faulty

Chapter 4 Clutch

For modifications, and information applicable to later models, see Supplement at end of manual

Contents

Specifications

Type . . . . Single dry plate, diaphragm spring, cable operated

Clutch pedal free travel . . . . 15 mm ($\frac{5}{8}$ inch)

Driven plate (friction disc)
Maximum out of true (at 179 mm dia) . . . . 0·4 mm (0·015 in)
Minimum depth of lining above rivets . . . . 0·6 mm (0·023 in)

Pressure plate
Maximum inward taper . . . . 0·3 mm (0·012 in)

Torque wrench settings

	kgf m	lbf ft
Pressure plate to crankshaft	7·5	54
Flywheel to pressure plate	2	14
End cover plate	1·5	11

1 General description

Unlike the clutch on most engines, the clutch pressure plate is bolted to the crankshaft flange and the flywheel, which is dish shaped, is bolted to the pressure plate with the friction disc being held between them. This is in effect the reverse of the more conventional arrangement where the flywheel is bolted to the crankshaft flange and the clutch pressure plate bolted to the flywheel (Fig. 4.1).

The release mechanism consists of a metal disc, called the release plate, which is clamped in the centre of the pressure plate by a retaining ring. In the centre of the release plate is a boss into which the clutch pushrod is fitted. The pushrod passes through the centre of the main driveshaft of the gearbox, which is tubular, and is housed in a release bearing situated at the back of the gearbox. A single finger lever presses on this bearing when the shaft to which it is splined is turned by operation of the cable from the clutch pedal. In effect the clutch lever pushes the clutch pushrod, which in turn pushes the centre of the release plate inwards towards the crankshaft. The outer edge of the release plate presses on the pressure plate fingers forcing them back towards the engine and removing the pressure plate friction face from the friction disc, thus disconnecting the drive. When the clutch pedal is released the pressure plate reasserts itself clamping the friction disc firmly against the flywheel and restoring the drive.

It is not possible to dismantle the clutch pressure plate, if it is defective it must be renewed as an assembly.

2 Clutch pedal free travel – adjustment

1 There should be 15 mm ($\frac{5}{8}$ inch) of free travel downwards on the clutch pedal before the lever on the gearbox begins to turn the withdrawal mechanism shaft. At this point the additional load can be felt at the pedal. This ensures that the withdrawal mechanism is not in contact with the clutch and is not wearing out during normal operation. It also makes certain that the clutch is fully engaged.

2 The easiest way to measure the free play is to use a short wooden strip. Hold it against the pedal with the end on the floor of the car. Mark the position of the top of the clutch pedal. Next make a mark 15 mm ($\frac{5}{8}$ inch) from the first mark, and replace the strip alongside the pedal as before. Press down the pedal until the end of the free play is felt and make another mark. This mark should coincide with your second mark. If it does not then the cable must be adjusted until it does. 3 mm ($\frac{1}{8}$ in) either way does not matter. Keep the piece of wood in your tool box for subsequent checks.

3 The cable is adjusted at the gearbox end. At the bracket on the gearbox where the outer cable (cable sheath) ends there are two locknuts. Slacken these, and turn the adjuster. Undo it to shorten the free play, screw it in to increase free play (Fig. 4.2). Two people make the job easier, one to check the measurement, one to do the adjustment.

3 Clutch cable – removal and refitting

1 Slacken off the cable adjuster until it is possible to disconnect the cable from the operating lever on the transmission. Remove the inner and outer cable from the operating lever on the transmission. Remove the inner and outer cable from the bracket on the transmission casing (photos).

2 Working under the facia unhook the cable from the clutch pedal, and then withdraw the cable through the grommet in the bulkhead.

3 Refitting is the reverse of the removal procedure. Adjust the clutch pedal free travel as described in Section 2.

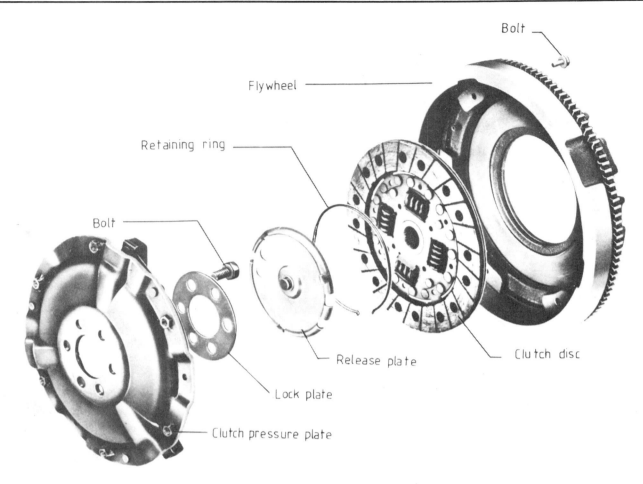

Fig. 4.1 Exploded view of clutch assembly (Sec 1 and 4)

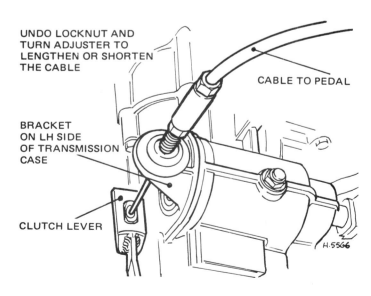

Fig. 4.2 Clutch cable adjustment (Sec 2)

UNDO LOCKNUT AND
TURN ADJUSTER TO
LENGTHEN OR SHORTEN
THE CABLE

CABLE TO PEDAL

BRACKET
ON LH SIDE
OF TRANSMISSION
CASE

CLUTCH LEVER

4 Clutch – removal and refitting

1 Support the engine and remove the transmission as described in Chapter 5. Clamp the flywheel to prevent it turning and remove the bolts holding the flywheel to the pressure plate in diagonal fashion. Release each one two or three threads at a time until they are all slack and then take them out. The flywheel and the friction disc may now be removed. Note which way the disc is fitted (Fig. 4.1).

2 Examine the pressure plate surface. If it is clean and free from scoring there is no reason to remove it unless the friction disc shows signs of oil contamination.

3 If the plate surface is defective then it must be removed. Note exactly where the ends of the retaining ring are located (it must be refitted in this way later), and prise the ring out with a screwdriver. The release plate may now be removed. The pressure plate is held to the crankshaft flange by six bolts fitted using a thread locking compound (photos). These will be difficult to remove as they were tightened to a high torque before the locking fluid set, so the plate must be held with a clamp.

4 Refitting of the clutch is the reversal of removal. Use thread locking compound on the bolts securing the plate to the crankshaft flange if they have been removed and tighten them to the specified torque. Make sure that the retaining ring is correctly seated (Fig. 4.3 and photos). Take care that no oil or grease is allowed to get onto the pressure plate or friction surfaces.

5 When refitting the clutch disc make sure the greater projecting boss which incorporates the torsion springs is furthest from the engine, then fit the flywheel over the pressure plate. Fit the securing bolts and tighten them finger-tight only.

3.1A Clutch operating lever and cable

3.1B Clutch inner cable connection to operating lever

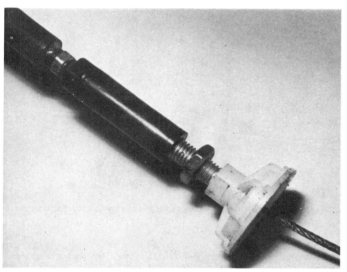

3.1C Clutch adjustment and locknut

4.3A Removing the clutch release plate (retaining ring already extracted)

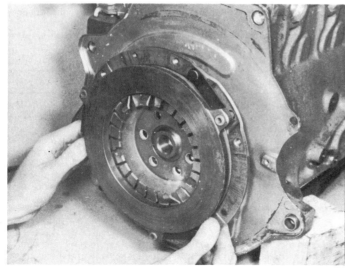

4.3B Removing the clutch pressure plate

Fig. 4.3 The ends of the retaining ring must rest between the two cut-outs of the release plate as shown – arrowed (Sec 4)

4.4A Refitting the clutch pressure plate

4.4B Flywheel expanding peg for locating pressure plate

**Fig. 4.4 Using VW tool 547 to centre the clutch friction disc
(Sec 4)**

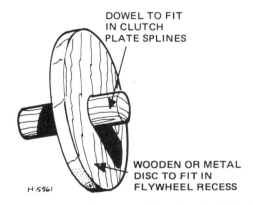

DOWEL TO FIT
IN CLUTCH
PLATE SPLINES

WOODEN OR METAL
DISC TO FIT IN
FLYWHEEL RECESS

H.5561

**Fig. 4.5 Home-made tool for centralising the clutch friction disc
(Sec 4)**

6   The next operation is to centre the clutch disc. If this is not done
accurately the gearbox mainshaft will not be able to locate in the
splines of the clutch disc hub, and it will be impossible to fit the
gearbox. The best centralising tool is VW 547 which fits in the
flywheel and has a spigot which fits exactly in the centre of the clutch
disc hub (Fig. 4.4). If you cannot borrow or hire tool VW 547 then we
suggest you make up a tool as shown in Fig. 4.5. Once the clutch disc
is centred correctly, tighten the securing bolts in a diagonal sequence
to the specified torque and check the centralisation again (photo).
7   When refitting the transmission, put a smear of multi-purpose
grease on the end of the clutch pushrod at the release plate end.

5   Clutch assembly – inspection

1   The most probable part of the clutch to require attention is the friction disc. Normal wear will eventually reduce its thickness. The lining
must stand proud of the rivets by not less than 0.6 mm (0.025 inch).
At this measurement the lining is at the end of its life and a new friction plate is needed.
2   The friction disc should be checked for run-out if possible. Mount
the disc between the centres of a lathe and measure the run-out at
175 mm diameter. The quoted limit is given in the Specifications.
However, this requires a dial gauge and a mandrel. If the clutch has
not shown signs of dragging then this test may be passed over, but if it
has we suggest that expert help be sought to test the run-out (Fig.
4.6).
3   Examine the pressure plate. There are three important things to
check. Put a straight-edge across the friction surface and measure any
bow or taper with feeler gauges. This must not exceed the specified
value. The fingers of the diaphragm will be rough. Scoring of up to 0.3
mm (0.012 ins) is acceptable. If the surface is rough enough to

4.6 Using a vernier caliper to double check the clutch disc
centralisation

Fig. 4.6 Checking the friction disc for run-out (Sec 6)

damage the release bearing remove the burrs with a stone. If in doubt consult the VW agent.

4   The rivets which hold the spring fingers in position must be tight. If any of them are loose the pressure plate must be scrapped. Finally, the condition of the friction surface. Ridges or scoring indicate undue wear and unless they can be removed by light application of emery paper it would be better to renew the plate.

5   The flywheel friction surface must be similarly checked.

6   So far the inspection has been for normal wear. Two other types of damage may be encountered. The first is overheating due to clutch slip. In extreme cases the pressure plate and flywheel may have radial cracks. Such faults mean that they require renewal. The second problem is contamination by oil or grease. This will cause clutch slip but probably without the cracks. There will be shiny black patches on the friction disc which will have a glazed surface. There is no cure for this, a new friction disc is required. In addition it is **imperative** that the source of contamination be located and rectified. It will be either the engine rear oil seal, or the gearbox front oil seal, or both. Examine them and renew the faulty ones before fitting a new disc. Failure to do this will mean dismantling the transmission again very shortly. The fitting of new seals is discussed in Chapters 1 and 5.

6   Clutch release mechanism – removal and refitting

1   The clutch release mechanism is accessible after removal of the gearbox end cover plate. Undo the four securing screws and remove the cover plate (photo). The clutch torque shaft with its finger is now visible (Fig. 4.8).

2   The finger is held in place by two circlips and a spring. The two circlips can now be removed and the shaft, finger and return spring removed from the casing (photos).

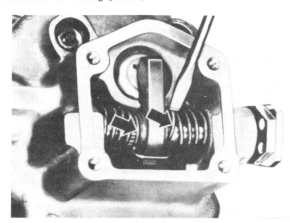

Fig. 4.8 View of clutch release mechanism with gearbox end cover removed. Arrows indicate location of the two circlips (Sec 6)

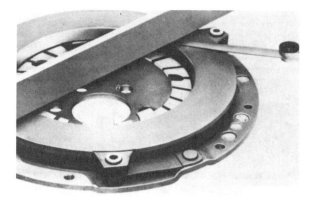

Fig. 4.7 Checking the inward taper of the pressure plate friction surface (Sec 4)

3   Lift out the clutch release bearing and guide sleeve (photo). The pushrod cannot be withdrawn until the transmission is in the car.

4   Rotate the clutch release bearing: if it is noisy or feels rough it must be renewed. Inspect the shaft oil seal for wear or deterioration

6.1 Removing the gearbox end cover plate

6.2A Removing the clutch release finger retaining circlips

6.2B Removing the clutch release torque shaft

6.3 Removing the clutch release bearing

6.5 Fitted position of the clutch release finger return spring

and renew it, if necessary.

5   Refitting is the reverse of the removal procedure. When fitting the return spring ensure that the bent ends bear against the gearbox casing and the centre part hooks into the clutch finger (photo). Always use a new gasket when fitting the end cover.

7   Fault diagnosis – clutch

There are four main faults to which the clutch and release mechanism are prone. They may occur by themselves or in conjunction with any of the other faults. They are clutch squeal, slip, spin and judder.

Clutch squeal

1   If on taking up the drive or when changing gear, the clutch squeals, this is a good indication of a badly worn clutch release bearing.

2   As well as regular wear due to normal use, wear of the clutch release bearing is much accentuated if the clutch is ridden, or held down for long periods in gear, with the engine running. To minimise wear of this component the car should always be taken out of gear at traffic lights and for similar holdups.

Clutch slip

3   Clutch slip is a self-evident condition which occurs when the clutch pedal free travel is insufficient, the clutch friction plate is badly worn, when oil or grease have got onto the flywheel or pressure plate faces, or when the pressure plate itself is faulty.

4   The reason for clutch slip is that, due to one of the faults listed above, there is either insufficient pressure from the pressure plate, or insufficient friction from the friction plate to ensure solid drive.

5   If small amounts of oil get onto the clutch, they will be burnt off under the heat of clutch engagement, and in the process, gradually darken the linings. Excessive oil on the clutch will burn off leaving a carbon deposit which can cause quite bad slip, or fierceness, spin and judder.

6   If clutch slip is suspected, and confirmation of this condition is required, there are several tests which can be made.

7   With the engine in second or third gear and pulling lightly up a

moderate incline sudden depression of the accelerator may cause the engine to increase in speed without any increase in road speed. Easing off on the accelerator will then give a definite drop in engine speed without the car slowing.

8   In extreme cases of clutch slip the engine will race under normal acceleration conditions.

9   If slip is due to oil or grease on the linings a temporary cure can sometimes be effected by squirting carbon tetrachloride into the clutch. The permanent cure is, of course, to renew the clutch friction disc and trace and rectify the oil leak.

Clutch spin

10   Clutch spin is a condition which occurs when the release arm travel is excessive, there is an obstruction in the clutch either on the mainshaft splines or in the operating lever itself, or oil may have partially burnt off the clutch linings and have left a resinous deposit which is causing the clutch disc to stick to the pressure plate or flywheel.

11   The reason for clutch spin is that due to any, or a combination of the faults just listed, the clutch pressure plate is not completely freeing from the centre plate even with the clutch pedal fully depressed.

12   If clutch spin is suspected, the condition can be confirmed by extreme difficulty in engaging first gear from rest, difficulty in changing gear, and very sudden take up of the clutch drive at the fully depressed end of the clutch pedal travel as the clutch is released.

13   Check that the clutch cable is correctly adjusted and, if in order, the fault lies internally in the clutch. It will then be necessary to remove the clutch for examination and to check the gearbox mainshaft.

Clutch judder

14   Clutch judder is a self evident condition which occurs when the gearbox or engine mountings are loose or too flexible, when there is oil on the faces of the clutch friction plate, or when the clutch pressure plate has been incorrectly adjusted during assembly.

15   The reason for clutch judder is that due to one of the faults just listed, the clutch pressure plate is not freeing smoothly from the friction disc, and is snatching.

16   Clutch judder normally occurs when the clutch pedal is released in first gear or reverse gear, and the whole car shudders as it moves backwards or forwards.

Chapter 5 Transmission

For modifications, and information applicable to later models, see Supplement at end of manual

Contents

Specifications

Type
.... Four forward speeds (all synchromesh), one reverse. Final drive integral with main gearbox. Transfer to front wheels by double CV jointed driveshafts

Gear ratios
1st	3·45 : 1
2nd	1·94 : 1
3rd	1·37 : 1
4th	0·969 : 1
Reverse	3·17 : 1
Final drive	3·89 : 1

Oil capacity
.... 1·25 litres (2·2 Imp pints, 2·65 US pints)

Oil type
.... Hypoid oil marked GL4. SAE 80 or 80W/90

Torque wrench settings

	kgf m	lbf ft
Transmission to engine bolts	5·5	40
Driveshaft flange bolts	4·5	32
Engine mounting bolts	5·5	40
Pinion shaft bearing retainer bolts	4·0	29
Housing flange joint bolts	2·0	14
End cover plate bolts	1·5	11
Selector shaft cover	4·5	32
Selector shaft detent plunger	2·0	14
Reverse gear shaft lock bolt	2·0	14
Mainshaft bearing retaining nuts	1·5	11

1 General description

The transmission assembly is bolted to the rear of the engine. The larger section of the casing, the gearbox housing, is withdrawn from the bearing housing leaving the gear trains and the differential unit in the bearing housing.

The mainshaft can be removed complete, but the pinion shaft must be completely dismantled, while held in the bearing housing, before it can be removed. Only after the removal of the pinion shaft can the differential unit be lifted out. The drive for the speedometer is provided by the helical teeth on the pinion shaft.

The clutch release mechanism is housed in the rear of the gear casing and is accessible after removal of the end cover plate. The release shaft bearing and sleeve can be removed while the gearbox is in the car (see Chapter 4).

The inner selector shaft operates one of the three shift rods. These are controlled by gear detents and interlocks located in the gearbox housing. The 1st/2nd gear shift rod operates a fork which engages with the synchromesh hub for 1st/2nd gear on the pinion shaft. A similar arrangement operates the 3rd/4th gearchange, moving gears on the mainshaft. A third shift rod operates the reverse gearchange by means of a relay lever. The reverse gear is located in the end of the gearbox housing on a short shaft which is pressed into the casing. The shaft does not rotate. Reverse gear has a plain metal bush and no roller or ball bearings.

Power is transferred to the differential unit by a helical gear on the pinion shaft which meshes with the ring gear on the differential unit. The drive flanges can be removed without removing the transmission assembly from the car, see Chapter 8, and the oil seals renewed. For all other repairs to the transmission the assembly must be removed from the car.

2 Transmission removal – general

1   The transmission is removed downwards so the car must be raised from the ground to provide sufficient height for the withdrawal of the gearbox from underneath. The ideal arrangement is to work over a pit, but axlestands or similar suitable supports under the body can be used. Note however that you must be able to rotate the wheels when disconnecting the driveshafts from the transmission drive flanges. Approximately 60 cm (24 inches) clearance is required to withdraw the transmission assembly from under the car.

2   Since the engine will be left unsupported at the rear it is necessary to make provision to take its weight. If a suitable hoist is available this will be a simple matter, but if not, a support similar to that shown in Fig. 5.1 can be made and placed in position with the end supports resting in the channels which house the bonnet sides on top of the wings. Alternatively the engine can be supported from underneath with blocks placed under the sump but this method means that the car cannot be moved while the transmission is out of the car.

3 Transmission – removal and refitting

1   Support the engine as described in Section 2.
2   Remove the ground strap from the battery negative terminal.
3   Remove the drain plug and drain the transmission oil into a suitable container.
4   For purposes of this Section, the front of the transmission is regarded as the end nearest the engine. Left and right are as if you are standing at the left-hand side of the car behind the transmission looking towards the engine.
5   Remove the plastic plug from the timing access hole in the bellhousing. Rotate the crankshaft until the cut-out on the flywheel is opposite the pointer on the clutch housing (Fig. 5.2). This lines up the recess in the flywheel with the driveshaft flange and unless this is done the transmission will not come away from the engine.
6   Remove the clamp bolt and lift out the speedometer drive cable and pinion assembly (photos). Plug the hole to prevent any dirt or small items getting into the gearbox.
7   Pull the wiring plug from the reversing light switch. Disconnect the clutch cable, refer to Chapter 4.
8   Undo the three left-hand gearbox mounting bolts and lift away the mounting and the earth strap.
9   Undo the upper gearbox-to-engine bolts and remove them.
10   Remove the retaining clips and disconnect the shift linkage from the selector shaft lever and the relay lever.
11   Disconnect the leads from the starter motor, then remove the securing bolts and lift away the starter.
12   Remove the engine mounting support from the body and the engine.

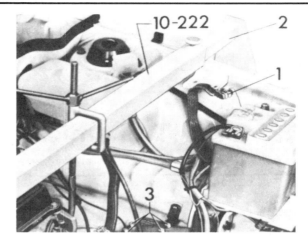

Fig. 5.1 Engine support bar necessary when removing the transmission only (Sec 2)

1   Battery earth strap
2   Engine support bar
3   Left-hand transmission mounting bolts

Fig. 5.2 Removal cut-out location on the flywheel (Sec 3)

3.6A Removing the speedometer drive cable

3.6B Speedometer drive cable and driven gear

13 Remove the mounting which attaches the transmission to the car body. It is best to remove it completely from the rubber mounting on the transmission.

14 Undo the socket bolts securing the left-hand driveshaft to the transmission drive flange with an Allen key and remove the CV joint from the flange. Cover the CV joint with a plastic bag and tie the shaft out of the way. Rotate the roadwheel as necessary to get at each bolt in sequence. Repeat this procedure to disconnect the right-hand driveshaft.

15 Just below the driveshaft flange is a nut, (18 in Fig. 5.3), remove this and then the bolts securing the flywheel cover plate and the smaller cover plate on the sump. Remove the small cover plate, the large plate remains on the engine.

16 With the help of an assistant pull the transmission off the locating dowels and lower it to the ground (photo). When removing the transmission keep it level with the engine until the clutch pushrod and gearbox mainshaft are withdrawn from the boss of the clutch friction disc. This will prevent any stress being put on the mainshaft which could damage the shaft.

17 Refitting is the reverse of the removal procedure. When positioning the transmission check that the flywheel recess is in the correct position, see paragraph 5, before trying to slide the assembly into position. As the gearbox mainshaft splines have to enter the clutch friction disc boss it may be necessary to rotate the crankshaft slightly to align the splines. Use a spanner on the crankshaft sprocket centre bolt to turn the crankshaft.

18 Tighten the driveshaft flange bolts, the transmission-to-engine bolts and the mounting bolts to the specified torques. Refill the transmission with the correct grade of oil.

19 Check the gear selector operation and adjust the clutch pedal free travel if necessary, refer to Chapter 4.

4 Transmission overhaul – general

1 The overhaul of the transmission assembly requires a number of special tools, and adjustments are critical if the job is to be done successfully. For this reason we do not recommend that the home mechanic should attempt a complete overhaul. However, the transmission can be dismantled and the following Sections describe the dismantling and overhaul procedures.

2 The dismantling of the final drive is described only as far as removing the differential unit from the casing. It is considered that the overhaul of the differential unit is not within the capacity of the owner who does not have the necessary jigs and fixtures required for this work and therefore, this aspect of the overhaul procedure has not been included.

3 Before dismantling the transmission, decide first if it is worthwhile from an economic point of view. If it has done a high mileage and is in generally poor condition then the cost of new parts could be more than the cost of an exchange unit.

5 Transmission – separating the housings

1 Remove the clutch pushrod. Undo the four bolts securing the gearbox end cover plate and remove the cover plate. This will give access to the clutch release mechanism. Lift out the clutch release bearing and sleeve.

2 There are two circlips one on each side of the clutch release lever (Fig. 5.5). Later models may only have one circlip. Remove these and slide the operating shaft out of the housing, collecting the return spring and release lever as the shaft is withdrawn. Note that there is a master spline on the shaft and that the release lever will fit on the shaft in one way only.

3 Prise out the plastic cap from the centre of the drive flange and remove the circlip and spring washer. Withdraw the flange using a suitable puller. Fig. 5.4 shows VW tool 391 being used to pull off the flange (photos). There is no need to remove the opposite driveshaft flange.

4 Remove the selector shaft detent plunger and the lockbolt for the reverse gear shaft. Remove the reversing light switch (photos).

5 On the side of the housing below the clutch withdrawal shaft is the cover for the selector shaft. Using a plug spanner, remove this cover and lift off the spring seat, then remove the two detent springs. Later transmissions have only one spring (photo).

6 Withdraw the selector shaft from the housing (photos).

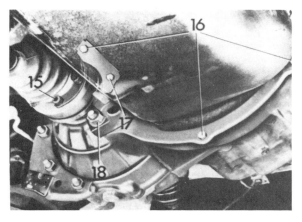

Fig. 5.3 Flywheel cover plate (Sec 3)

15 Driveshaft retaining bolt
16 Large cover plate bolts
17 Small cover plate bolt
18 Nut

3.16 Removing the transmission from the engine

Fig. 5.4 Tool for removing the drive flanges (Sec 5)

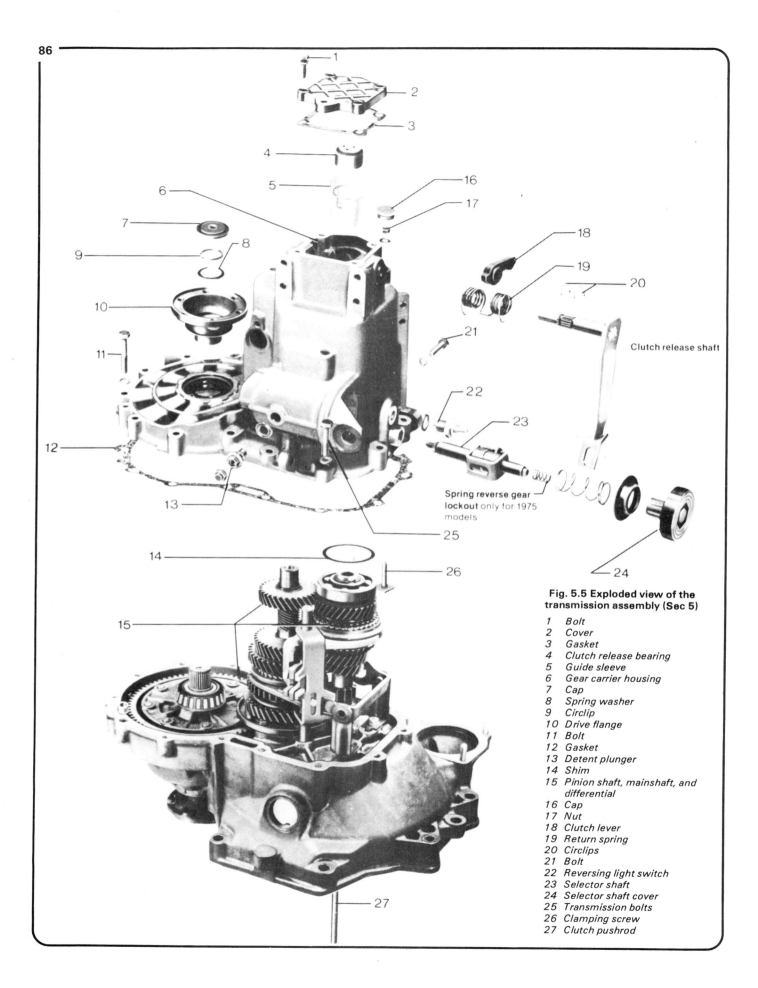

Clutch release shaft

Spring reverse gear lockout only for 1975 models

Fig. 5.5 Exploded view of the transmission assembly (Sec 5)

1 Bolt
2 Cover
3 Gasket
4 Clutch release bearing
5 Guide sleeve
6 Gear carrier housing
7 Cap
8 Spring washer
9 Circlip
10 Drive flange
11 Bolt
12 Gasket
13 Detent plunger
14 Shim
15 Pinion shaft, mainshaft, and differential
16 Cap
17 Nut
18 Clutch lever
19 Return spring
20 Circlips
21 Bolt
22 Reversing light switch
23 Selector shaft
24 Selector shaft cover
25 Transmission bolts
26 Clamping screw
27 Clutch pushrod

5.3A Removing a drive flange plastic cap

5.3B Drive flange showing circlip and spring washer

5.3C Withdrawing a drive flange with a puller

5.4A Selector shaft detent plunger

5.4B Removing the selector shaft detent plunger

5.4C Removing the reverse gear shaft lockbolt

5.4D Removing the reversing light switch

5.5 Removing the selector shaft cover and spring

5.6A Removing the selector shaft

5.6B The gear selector shaft

5.7A Removing the plastic caps to expose the mainshaft bearing clamp retaining nuts

5.7B Showing the three mainshaft bearing clamp retaining nuts

Fig. 5.6 Mainshaft bearing clamp nut locations, showing the plastic caps (arrowed) (Sec 5)

5.9 Removing the gear carrier housing

Fig. 5.7 Separating the transmission casings using the special tool VW 391 (Sec 5)

A   7 mm bolt

7   On the end of the gear carrier housing (where the clutch withdrawal mechanism is located) are two plastic caps. Prise these out and undo the nuts underneath them. There is a third nut inside the housing from which the clutch withdrawal mechanism was removed, this must also be removed (photos). If these nuts are not removed, the mainshaft bearing cannot be pulled out of the casing and the casing will fracture if pressure is applied to draw it off the bearing housing. The three nuts which must be removed are shown in Fig. 5.6, with the plastic caps (arrowed) already removed.
8   Undo and remove the 14 bolts securing the two casings together. Twelve of these bolts are M8 x 50 and two are M8 x 36, note where the shorter bolts are fitted.
9   The casings are now ready for separation. Fig. 5.7 shows VW tool 391 being used. Secure the tool in the holes for the cover plate with

two 7 mm bolts and then screw the centre screw down on the top of the mainshaft until is just touches. Fasten a bar or piece of angle iron across the bellhousing in such a manner as to support the end of the mainshaft and then continue to screw in the centre screw of the tool until the casing is pulled away, leaving the mainshaft bearing complete on the mainshaft. Lift away the gear carrier housing (photo). On top of the bearing there may be one or more shims, collect them and label them to ensure that they can be identified at reassembly. The needle bearing for the pinion shaft will remain in the gear carrier housing; it can be removed, if necessary, using a suitable extractor.

6   Mainshaft, pinion shaft and differential – removal

1   Refer to Fig. 5.8. The mainshaft assembly can be removed quite easily, but the pinion shaft assembly must be partially dismantled before the pinion shaft and the differential unit can be removed.
2   Remove the two shift fork shaft circlips and withdraw the shaft from the bearing housing, then lift away the shift fork set (photos).
3   Remove the circlip retaining the 4th speed gear on the pinion shaft, then lift the mainshaft out of its bearing in the bearing housing and at the same time remove the 4th speed gear from the pinion shaft (photos). The mainshaft needle bearing and oil seal will remain in the bearing housing.
4   Remove the circlip retaining the 3rd speed gear on the pinion shaft. This circlip is used to adjust the axial play of the 3rd speed gear and must be refitted in the same position, so label it for identification at reassembly. Remove the 3rd speed gear (photos).
5   Remove the 2nd speed gear and then the needle bearing from over its inner sleeve (photos).
6   To remove the rest of the gears a long hooked puller will be required. Fig. 5.9 shows VW tool 447h being used with a suitable puller (A). Before pulling off the synchro hub/sleeve and 1st speed gear remove the reverse gear by tapping the reverse gear shaft out of its seating, then lift the shaft and gear away (photo).
7   Remove the plastic stop button from the end of the pinion shaft and fit the puller under the 1st speed gear. Note that the pinion shaft bearing retainer has two notches to accommodate the puller legs. Pull the gear and synchro hub off the shaft. Tape the synchro unit together to prevent it coming apart.
8   Remove the needle bearing and thrust washer. Note that the flat side of the washer is towards the 1st speed gear (photos).
9   Remove the four nuts or bolts securing the pinion bearing retainer and lift off the retainer. The pinion shaft is seated in a taper roller bearing, and can now be removed from the bearing housing (photos).
10 Remove the second drive flange as described in Section 5, paragraph 3, and then lift the differential unit out of the bearing housing (photo). We do not recommend trying to overhaul the differential unit, if it is in any way suspect seek advice from your VW agent.

Fig. 5.8 Exploded view of transmission gears (Sec 6)

1 Nut
2 Main shaft bearing
3 Shift fork set
4 Circlips
5 Reverse gear shift fork stop sleeve
6 Pinion shaft gears
7 Bearing retainer
8 Reinforcement plate (when fitted)
9 Pinion shaft
10 Differential
11 Reverse gear and shaft
12 Drive flange
13 Circlip
14 Cap

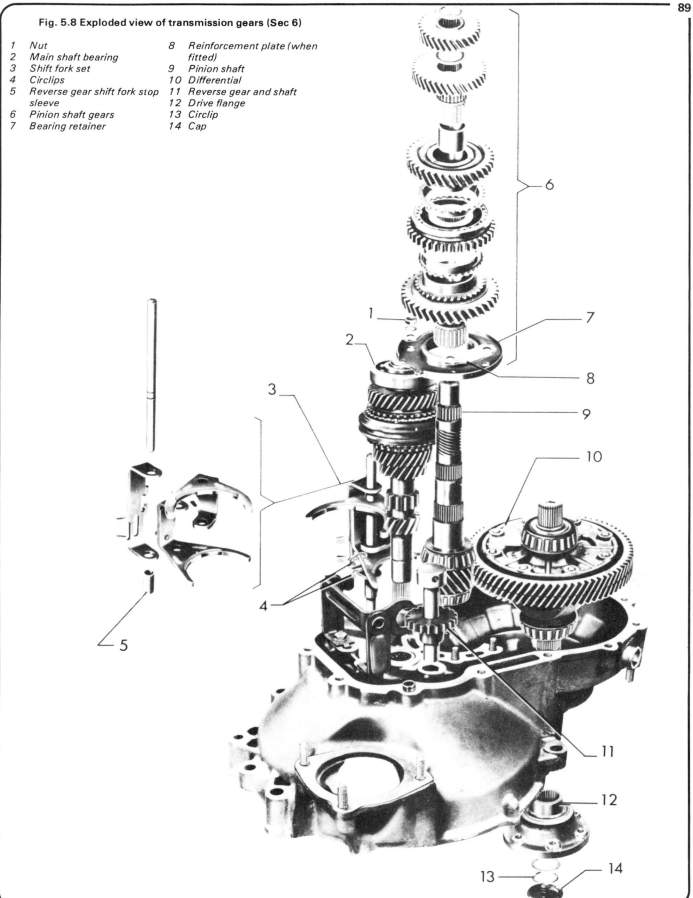

6.2A Removing a shift fork shaft circlip (arrowed)

6.2B Removing the shift fork shaft

6.2C Removing the shift fork set

6.3A Removing the 4th speed gear retaining circlip (pinion shaft)

6.3B Removing the mainshaft assembly

6.4A Removing the 3rd speed gear retaining circlip (pinion shaft)

6.4B Removing the 3rd speed gear from the pinion shaft

6.5A Removing the 2nd speed gear from the pinion shaft

Fig. 5.9 Removing the 1st gear from the pinion shaft (Sec 6)

A   VW puller US 1078

6.5B 2nd speed gear needle roller location on the pinion shaft

6.6 Reverse gear and shaft

6.8A 1st speed gear needle roller bearing

6.8B Removing the 1st speed gear thrust washer

6.9A Removing the pinion bearing retainer bolts

6.9B Removing the pinion bearing retainer

6.9C The pinion or output shaft

6.10 The differential unit on the bearing housing

7 Bearing housing – overhaul

1   Clean the housing using a grease solvent, remove all oil and sludge. Renew both the oil seals (photo). Fill the space between the lips of the seals with multi-purpose grease before fitting. The drive flange oil seal must be driven in as far as it will go. Fig. 5.10 shows VW tool 194 being used, but a piece of suitable diameter steel tubing can also be used.

2   The mainshaft needle bearing may be removed, if necessary, with a suitable extractor. Do not remove the bearing unless it is defective as it is likely to be damaged during removal (photo).

3   If the outer races of the differential bearings are defective then it will be necessary for the casings and the differential unit to be taken to the VW agent for servicing.

4   The starter motor shaft should be tried in the starter bush. If undue wear is apparent, remove the bush with a puller and fit a new one.

7.1 Mainshaft oil seal in the bearing housing

Fig. 5.10 Fitting the drive flange oil seal with the special tool (Sec 7)

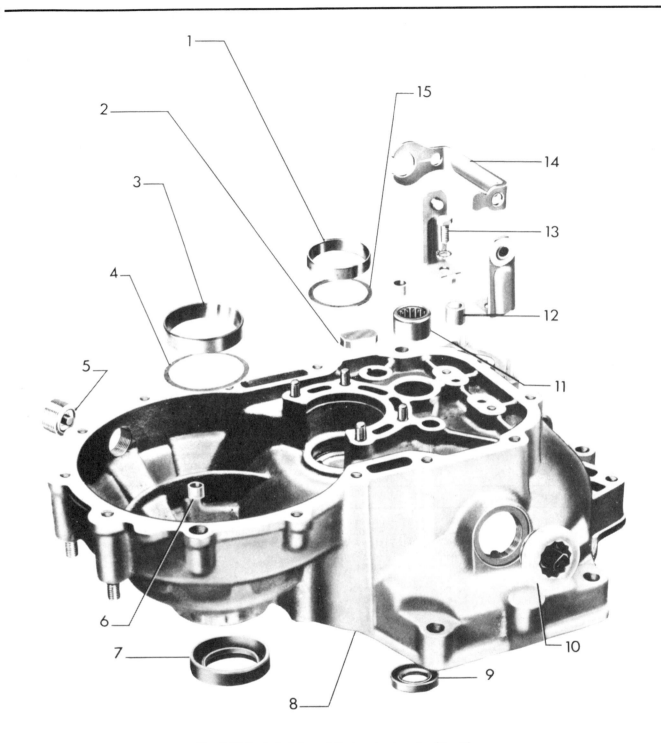

Fig. 5.11 Exploded view of the bearing housing (Sec 7)

1	Pinion bearing outer race	8	Bearing housing
2	Magnet	9	Mainshaft oil seal
3	Differential bearing outer race	10	TDC sender unit (early models)
		11	Mainshaft needle bearing
4	Shim	12	Starter bush
5	Drain plug	13	Bolt
6	Dowel sleeve	14	Reverse shift fork
7	Drive flange oil seal	15	Shim

7.2 Mainshaft needle bearing in the bearing housing

8 Gear carrier housing – overhaul

1   There are three oil seals to renew: one for the clutch operating lever, one for the selector shaft, and a large one for the drive flange. In each case prise out the old seal, noting which way round it is fitted. Fill the seal lips with multi-purpose grease and drive the seals squarely into the housing using a suitable mandrel or piece of tubing (photos).

2   The needle bearing for the pinion shaft is difficult to extract unless the correct extractor is available, see Fig. 5.13. The shaft may be tried in the bearing without having to remove the bearing (photo).

3   If the outer race of the final drive is renewed, the complete unit must be taken to the VW agent for setting up with the correct shims (photo).

9 Pinion shaft taper bearings

1   The large and small bearings accurately locate the pinion shaft gear with the crownwheel of the differential. If either bearing is defective then both must be renewed. In the removal process the bearings are destroyed. New ones have to be shrunk on and the shim under the smaller bearing changed for one of the correct size.

2   This operation is quite complicated and requires special equipment for preloading of the shaft and measurement of the torque required to rotate the new bearings. In addition the shim at the top of

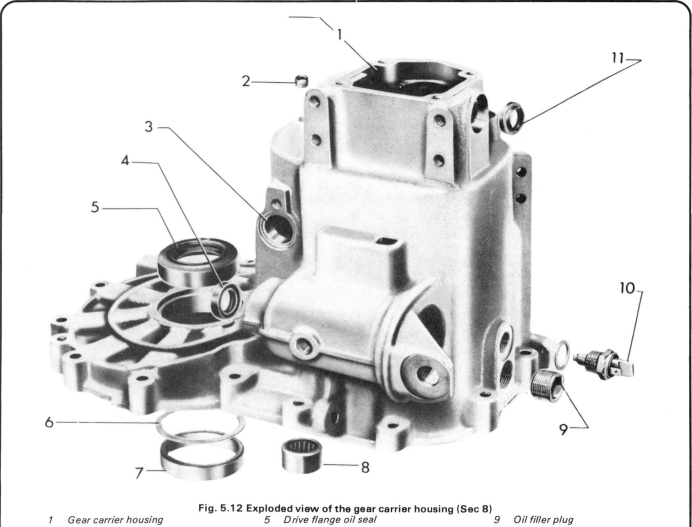

Fig. 5.12 Exploded view of the gear carrier housing (Sec 8)

1 Gear carrier housing	5 Drive flange oil seal	9 Oil filler plug
2 Oil level plug	6 Shim	10 Reversing light switch
3 Speedometer drive aperture	7 Differential bearing outer race	11 Clutch operating lever oil
4 Selector shaft oil seal	8 Mainshaft needle bearing	seal

8.1A Clutch operating lever oil seal

8.1B Selector shaft oil seal

8.1C Drive flange oil seal location in the gear carrier housing

Fig. 5.13 Using an extractor (A) to remove the pinion shaft needle bearing from the gear carrier housing (Sec 8)

8.2 Pinion shaft needle bearing location in the gear carrier housing

8.3 Differential bearing outer race location in the gear carrier housing

10.2A Removing the 4th speed gear from the mainshaft

10.2B Removing the 4th speed gear needle roller bearing

10.4A 3rd speed gear needle roller bearing location on the mainshaft

the mainshaft and the axial play at the circlip of the 3rd speed gear on the pinion shaft will be affected. This will mean selection of a new shim and circlip. There are six different thicknesses of circlip. Therefore it is recommended that if these bearings require renewal, the work should be left to your VW agent.

10 Mainshaft – dismantling and reassembly

1 Refer to Fig. 5.14. Remove the ball bearing retaining circlip and then, supporting the bearing under the inner race, press the shaft out of the inner race. VW tool 402 can be used to remove the bearing but a suitable tool can be made from a piece of steel. At assembly the bearing is pressed into the gear carrier housing and the shaft pressed into the race.

2 Remove the thrust washer, 4th speed gear, and the needle bearing together with the synchro ring from the mainshaft (photos).

3 Remove the circlip, then support the 3rd speed gear and press the mainshaft through the 3rd/4th synchro hub. Tape the synchro unit together to prevent it from coming apart.

4 Remove the needle bearing to complete the dismantling of the shaft (photos).

5 Should the clutch pushrod be loose in the mainshaft the bush may be driven out of the end of the shaft and a new bush and oil seal fitted. If the shaft is to be renewed then the tolerances will be affected and this means going back to the agent with his special tools and gauges. The problem is the play between the 2nd speed gear on the pinion shaft and 3rd speed gear on the mainshaft when both shafts are fitted. This must be 1.0 mm (0.040 in). Adjusting this also requires a new shim on the top of the ball bearing between the bearing and the gear carrier housing.

6 If gears on either shaft are to be renewed then the mating gear on the other shaft must be renewed as well. They are supplied in pairs only.

7 The inspection of the synchro units is dealt with in Section 11.

8 When reassembling the mainshaft, lightly oil all the parts.

9 Fit the 3rd speed gear needle bearing and the 3rd speed gear. Press on the 3rd/4th gear synchro hub and fit the retaining circlip. When pressing on the synchro hub and sleeve, turn the rings so that the keys and grooves line up. The chamfer on the inner splines of the hub must face 3rd gear (photos).

10 On transmission up to N. 18065, fit the thrust washer and 4th speed gear. Later transmissions have a ball bearing with a wider inner race and the thrust washer is not fitted. If the old type bearing is being replaced with a new type, the 4th gear thrust washer must be left out.

11 The mainshaft ball bearing should now be pressed into the gear carrier housing. Ensure that the same shim/s removed at dismantling are refitted between the bearing and the casing. The bearing is fitted in the housing with the closed side of the ball bearing cage towards the 4th speed gear. Insert the clamping screws and tighten the clamping

10.4B The mainshaft completely dismantled

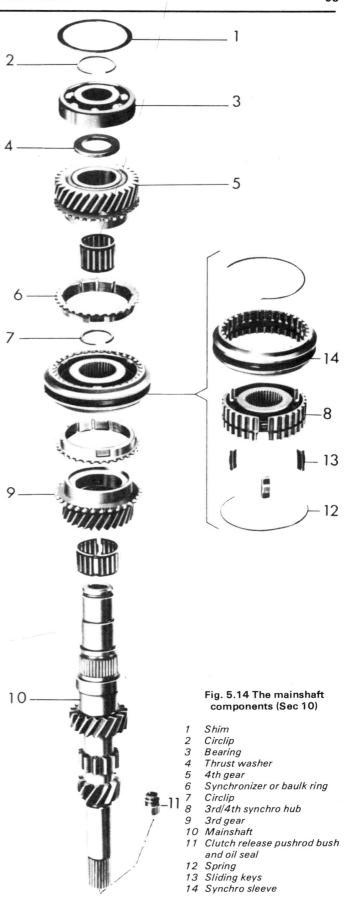

Fig. 5.14 The mainshaft components (Sec 10)

1 Shim
2 Circlip
3 Bearing
4 Thrust washer
5 4th gear
6 Synchronizer or baulk ring
7 Circlip
8 3rd/4th synchro hub
9 3rd gear
10 Mainshaft
11 Clutch release pushrod bush and oil seal
12 Spring
13 Sliding keys
14 Synchro sleeve

10.9A Fitting the 3rd speed gear to the mainshaft

10.9B 3rd speed gear baulk ring location

10.9C Fitting the 3rd/4th synchro assembly to the mainshaft

10.9D 3rd/4th synchro hub retaining circlip fitted on the mainshaft

10.11A Fitting the mainshaft ball bearing into the gear carrier housing

10.11B Correct location of mainshaft ball bearing outer race clamps

screw nuts to the specified torque (photos).

Note: The endplay will have to be adjusted if either of the bearings, the thrust washer or mainshaft have been renewed, so the help of a VW agent with the necessary special tools and gauges will be required.

11 Synchroniser units – inspection

1   Synchroniser units are supplied as an assembly, parts should not be interchanged.
2   When synchro baulk rings are being renewed, it is advisable to fit

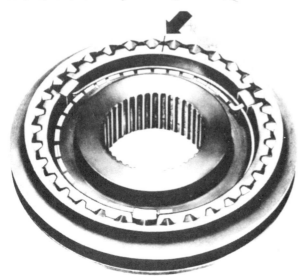

Fig. 5.15 Synchro hub and sleeve mating marks (Sec 11)

new blocker bars (sliding keys) and retaining springs in the hub. This will ensure that full advantage is taken of the new, unworn cut-outs in the rings.

3   The splines on the inner hub and outer sleeve are matched, either by selection on assembly or by wear patterns during use. Those matched on assembly have etched lines on the inner hub and outer sleeve so that they can be easily realigned. For those with no marks, scribe a line on the hub and sleeve before dismantling (see Fig. 5.15) to ensure correct alignment at reassembly.

4   When examining for wear there are two important features to check:

(a)   *The fit of the splines. With the keys removed, the inner and outer sections of the hub should slide easily with minimum backlash or axial rock. The degree of permissible wear is difficult to specify, no movement at all is exceptional, yet excessive movement will affect operation and result in jumping out of gear. If in doubt consult your VW agent*

(b)   *Selector fork grooves and selector forks should not exceed the maximum permissible clearance of 0.012 in (0.3 mm). The wear can be either on the fork or in the groove, so try a new fork in the existing sleeve groove first to see if the clearance is reduced considerably. If not then a new synchro assembly is needed.*

5   The fit of the synchro ring on the gear is also important. Press the ring onto the gear and check the gap with feeler gauges. Refer to Fig. 5.16, the dimension (a) must not be less than 0.5 mm (0.020 in).

12 Differential unit – inspection

1   A faulty differential will cause a lot of noise while the car is in motion. However, it may go a long way making a noise without getting any worse. If you decide it needs renewing then renew it as a unit.
2   There are several problems. If a new differential is fitted then a new crownwheel to an old shaft is inviting noise. It may be possible for

Fig. 5.16 Synchro ring wear limit dimension (a) (Sec 11)

the agent to build the old differential if only the taper bearings are at fault, and he may be able to fit a new crownwheel to your differential if only the crownwheel is damaged. It is worth asking, but most likely you will need a replacement differential.

13 Differential, pinion shaft and mainshaft – reassembly in bearing housing

1   Refit the differential unit in the casing. Using tool VW 391, fit the drive flange to the bearing housing and fit the spring washer, retaining circlip and cap.
2   Check that the mainshaft ball bearing is correctly fitted in the gear carrier housing, plastic cage towards the casing, and that the bearing clamp bolt nuts are tight.
3   Fit the pinion shaft complete with its taper bearings into the bearing housing, so that the pinion gear meshes with the crownwheel (photo).
4   Fit the bearing retaining plate and the four securing bolts (photo). Fit the 1st speed gear thrust washer with its flat side up (towards the 1st gear). Fit the needle roller cage.

13.3 Fitting the pinion shaft into the bearing housing

5   Slide the 1st speed gear over the needle bearing. Warm the synchro hub a little and press it into position. The hub will slide on if heated to 120°C (250°F) and it can then be tapped into position. Make sure that the grooves are in line with the shift keys in the 1st/2nd synchro to avoid damage to the baulk ring on assembly. The shift fork groove in the operating sleeve should be nearer 2nd gear and the groove on the hub nearer 1st gear (photos).
6   The inner race for the 2nd speed gear needle bearing must be fitted next and pressed down as far as it will go.
7   Fit the reverse idler gear and shaft with the shaft aligned as shown

13.4 Tightening the pinion shaft bearing retaining plate bolts

13.5A Assembling the 1st speed gear to the pinion shaft

13.5B 1st speed gear baulk ring location

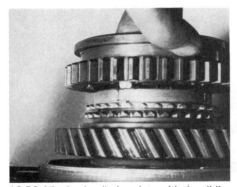

13.5C Aligning baulk ring slots with the sliding keys in the 1st/2nd synchro assembly

13.5D Fitting the 1st/2nd synchro assembly to the pinion shaft

13.5E Using a metal tube to drive the 1st/2nd synchro assembly onto the pinion shaft

in Fig. 5.17. Use a plastic hammer to drive the shaft into the casing.

8   Fit the 2nd speed gear needle bearing on the pinion shaft and the 2nd gear with the shoulder downwards.

9   Warm the 3rd speed gear and press it down over the splines with the collar thrust face towards the 2nd gear.

10   Fit the 3rd gear retaining circlip and using feeler gauges measure the play between the gear and the circlip. It must be less than 0.008 in (0.20 mm). If it is more, a thicker circlip must be fitted. The following table gives the sizes available:

Part no	Thickness (mm)	Thickness (in)	Colour
020 311 381	2.5	0.098	brown
020 311 381 A	2.6	0.102	black
020 311 381 B	2.7	0.106	bright
020 311 381 C	2.8	0.110	copper
020 311 381 D	2.9	0.114	yellow
020 311 381 E	3.0	0.118	blue

11   At this stage the mainshaft must be fitted in position on the bearing housing. Slide it into the needle bearing in the casing and fit the shift forks in the operating sleeves. Insert the retaining circlips. Fit the reverse gear shift fork (photos).

12   Fit the 4th speed gear and its retaining circlip on the pinion shaft. Finally insert the stop button for the pinion shaft needle bearing in the end of the pinion shaft.

13   The bearing housing and shafts are now assembled ready for the assembly of the gear carrier housing to the bearing housing, which is described in the next Section (photo).

Fig. 5.17 Reverse idler gear shaft alignment (Sec 13)

14 Transmission – reassembling the housings

1   Check that the reverse gear shaft is in the correct position, see Fig. 5.17, and set the gear train in neutral. Fit a new gasket on the bearing housing flange.

13.11A Fitting the shift forks

13.11B Fitting the reverse shift fork pivot posts

13.11C Reverse shift fork assembly

13.11D Reverse shift fork to gear assembly

13.13 Bearing housing assembly ready for fitting of the gear carrier housing

2   Lower the gear carrier housing over the shafts onto the bearing housing flange, checking that the pinion shaft is aligned with the pinion shaft needle bearing in the casing, and drive the mainshaft into its bearing, using a suitable mandrel on the inner race. A piece of suitable diameter steel tube can be used. Ensure that the mainshaft is supported on a block of wood when driving the mainshaft into the bearing.

3   Insert the 14 bolts which secure the two housings together and tighten them to the specified torque.

4   Fit the circlip over the end of the mainshaft, working through the release bearing hole. Insert the clutch pushrod into the mainshaft. Ensure that the circlip is properly seated, then fit the clutch release bearing and sleeve assembly (photos).

5   Fit the clutch release shaft and lever. Ensure that the spring is hooked over the lever in the centre and that the angled ends rest against the casing. The shaft can be inserted in the lever in one position only. Fit the two circlips, one each side of the lever.

6   Position a new gasket on the end of the housing and fit the end cover plate and four securing screws. Tighten the screws to the specified torque.

7   Lubricate the selector shaft and insert it into the casing. When it is in position, fit the spring and screw in the shaft cover with a plug spanner, tightening it to the specified torque.

8   Fit the selector shaft detent plunger. This has a plastic cap. Only if the housing, selector shaft or plunger are faulty and new ones are

required should the plunger need adjusting. If necessary, adjust as follows:

(a) Refer to Fig. 5.18. Slacken the locknut and screw in the adjusting sleeve until the lockring lifts off the adjusting sleeve

(b) Screw the adjusting sleeve out until the lockring just contacts the sleeve

(c) Check that the lockring lifts as soon as the shaft is turned. Tighten the locknut and fit the plastic cap

9   Fit the reverse gear shaft lockbolt and the reversing light switch.

15 Gearshift linkage – adjustment

1   Align the holes in the lever housing cover plate with the holes in the bearing plate, A in Fig. 5.19, and check that the threaded holes B are in the middle of the slots. If they are not, turn the bearing plate through 180°. Tighten the lever bearing.

2   Slacken the shift rod clamp bolt (Fig. 5.20) to permit the selector lever to move on the shift rod. Pull the boot off the lever housing and push it back out of the way (photo).

3   Refer to Fig. 5.21. Ensure that the shift finger is in the centre of

14.4A Fitting the circlip over the end of the mainshaft

14.4B Inserting the clutch pushrod into the mainshaft

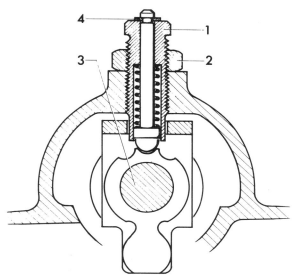

Fig. 5.18 Cross-sectional view of the selector shaft detent plunger (Sec 14)

1 Adjusting sleeve	3 Selector shaft
2 Locknut	4 Spring clip

Fig. 5.19 Gear lever housing cover. Arrows show alignment holes (Sec 15)

Fig. 5.20 Gear shift rod clamp bolt (arrowed) (Sec 15)

15.2 Shift rod clamp bolt and rubber boot

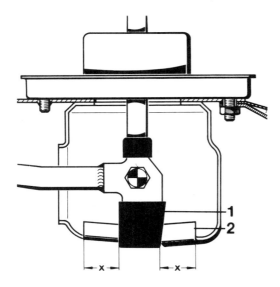

Fig. 5.21 Gear shift finger (1) and stop plate (2) (Sec 15)

Fig. 5.22 Gear shift rod adjusting dimension (a) (Sec 15)

the stop plate and that dimension X is the same on both sides.

4   Now adjust the shift rod so that dimension a in Fig. 5.22 is 0.75 in (20 mm), then tighten the clamp bolt.

5   Check the operation of the gearshift linkage by selecting each gear in turn. If the linkage is spongy or binding check the adjustment of the selector shaft detent plunger, refer to Section 14, paragraph 8.

---

16 Gearchange lever and linkage – removal and refitting

1   Unscrew the gearchange lever knob. Release the rubber gaiter from the gear lever housing and pull it off the lever.

2   Release the boot from under the lever housing, slide it forward on the shift rod and remove the clevis pin securing the shift rod to the gearchange lever (photo).

3   Undo the two lever bearing assembly securing bolts then lift out the bearing and lever together.

4   To remove the linkage, first refer to Fig. 5.23. When disconnecting the front and rear selector rods, prise back the ends of the plastic clips before pulling the rods off the selector and relay levers (photos).

5   Refitting is the reverse of the removal procedure. When fitting the gearshift linkage rod note that the ends are bent at different angles, 90° and 95°. The 95° end, arrowed in Fig. 5.23, is connected to the selector shaft lever. Lubricate all the pivot points and friction surfaces with grease. Adjust the gearshift linkage as described in Section 15 (photos).

16.2 Gear lever boot location

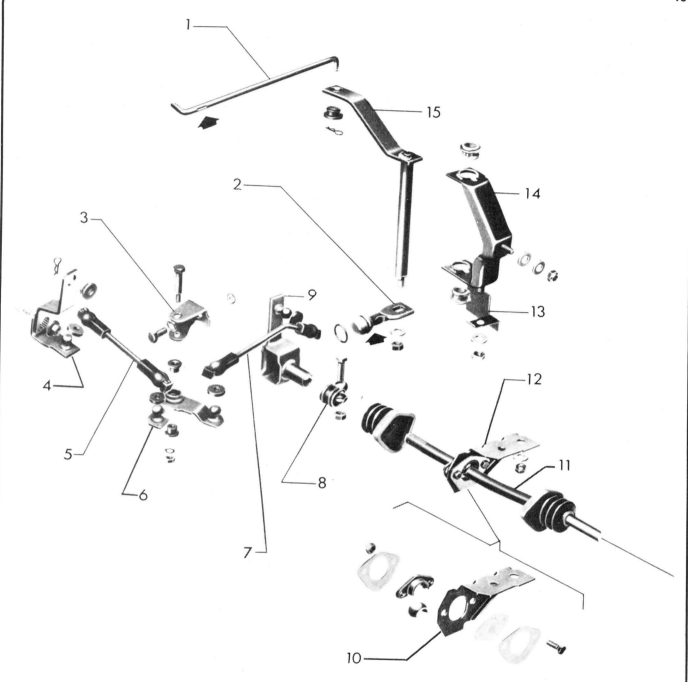

Fig. 5.23 Exploded view of the gearchange linkage (Sec 16)

1	Linkage rod with 95° angled end (arrowed)	4	Selector shaft lever
2	Lever	5	Front selector rod
3	Relay lever bracket	6	Relay lever
		7	Rear selector rod

8	Shift rod clamp	12	Shift rod bearing assembly
9	Selector lever	13	Protective plate
10	Bearing plate	14	Relay shaft bracket
11	Shift rod	15	Relay shaft

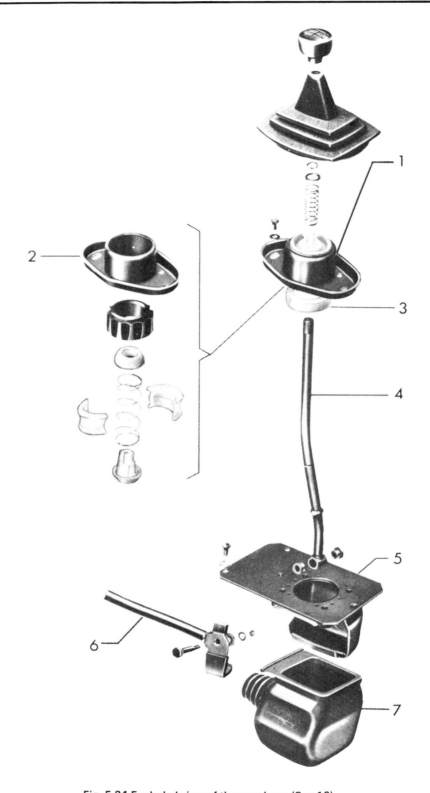

Fig. 5.24 Exploded view of the gear lever (Sec 16)

1	Gear lever bearing assembly	3	Spacer	5	Gear lever housing	7	Gear lever boot
2	Gear lever bearing plate	4	Gearshift lever	6	Shift rod		

16.4A Removing the gearchange linkage crank pivot bolt

16.4B Removing the gearchange linkage crank and bushes

16.4C Removing the gearchange linkage crank bracket

16.5A The gearchange relay shaft location

16.5B The gearchange relay shaft and connecting link

16.5C Selector shaft lever location

17 Fault diagnosis – transmission

It is sometimes difficult to decide whether all the effort and expense of dismantling the transmission is worthwhile to cure a minor irritant such as a whine or where the synchromesh can be beaten by a rapid gearchange. If the noise gets no worse consideration should be given to the time and money available, for the elimination of noise completely is almost impossible, unless a complete new set of gears and bearings is fitted. New gears and bearings will still make a noise if fitted in mesh with old ones.

Symptom	Reason/s
Synchromesh not giving smooth change	Worn baulk rings or synchro hubs
Jumps out of gear on drive or over-run	Weak detent spring Worn selector forks Worn synchro hubs
Noisy rough whining and vibration	Worn bearings, chipped or worn gears
Gear difficult to engage	Clutch fault Gearshift mechanism out of adjustment

Chapter 6 Braking system, wheels and tyres

For modifications, and information applicable to later models, see Supplement at end of manual

Contents

Specifications

Type .... Hydraulic, servo-assisted. Dual circuit diagonally connected. Front – disc brakes. Rear – drum brakes

Handbrake .... Cable operated, acting on rear brakes

Front brakes (disc)
Caliper piston diameter	44 mm (1·73 in)
Disc diameter	239 mm (9·4 in)
Disc thickness (new)	12 mm (0·47 in)
Disc thickness (min) after refinishing	10·5 mm (0·41 in)
Pad thickness (new)	14 mm (0·55 in)

Rear brakes (drum)
Drum internal diameter	180 mm (7·08 in)
Drum internal diameter (max) after refinishing	181 mm (7·13 in)
Wheel cyinder bore diameter	14·29 mm (0·56 in)
Lining thickness:	
Riveted	5 mm (0·20 in)
Wear limit	2·5 mm (0·097 in)
Bonded	4 mm (0·16 mm)
Wear limit	1·5 mm (0·060 in)
Lining width	30 mm (1·2 in)

Master cylinder bore diameter .... 20·64 mm (0·81 in)

Brake servo diameter .... 177·8 mm (7·0 in)

Wheels and tyres

Wheels	4½J x 13 or 5J x 13 with 45 mm offset	
Tyres	Radial ply 145SR or 155SR	
Tyre pressures	**Front**	**Rear**
Half load	1·7 bar (24 lbf/in²)	1·7bar (24 lbf/in²)
Full load	1·8 bar (26 lbf/in²)	2·2 bar (31 lbf/in²)

Torque wrench settings

	kgf m	lbf ft
Front hub nut	24·0	174
Caliper to wheel bearing housing	6·0	43
Disc to hub	0·7	5
Splash plate to hub	0·8	6
Backplate to stub axle	3·0	22
Wheel nuts	9·0	65
Servo to adapter	1·0	14
Master cylinder to servo	1·5	11
Brake hoses to caliper/wheel cylinder	1·0	7
Brake pipes to master cylinder	1·0	7

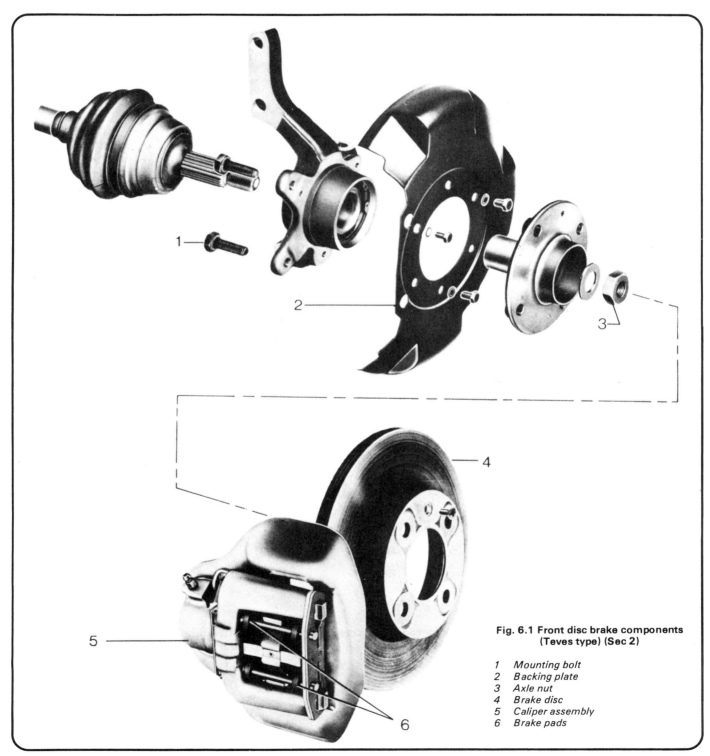

**Fig. 6.1 Front disc brake components
(Teves type) (Sec 2)**

1 Mounting bolt
2 Backing plate
3 Axle nut
4 Brake disc
5 Caliper assembly
6 Brake pads

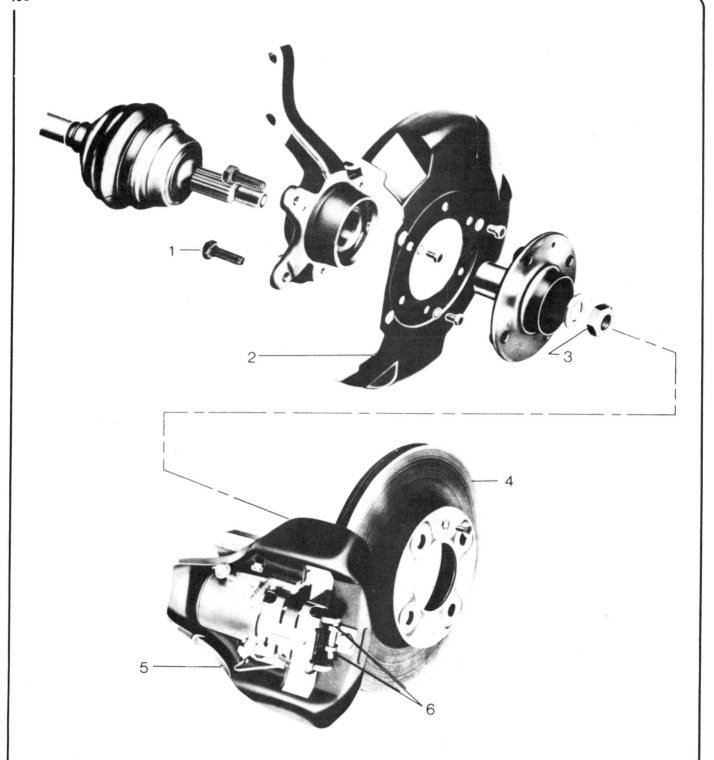

Fig. 6.2 Front disc brake components (Girling type) (Sec 2)

1	Mounting bolt	3	Axle nut	5	Caliper assembly
2	Backing plate	4	Brake disc	6	Brake pads

1 General description

The main braking system is operated hydraulically. The vacuum powered servo is fitted between the brake pedal and the master cylinder to reduce the pressure required at the brake pedal to operate the brakes. A pressure regulator is fitted to the rear brakes.

The system is fail-safe, with dual hydraulic circuits connecting the brakes diagonally: the right front wheel and the left rear wheel are supplied by one circuit and the left front wheel and the right rear wheel by the other circuit. If one circuit fails there will still be one front and one rear brake working. If the pressure in either of the circuits is too low a warning light on the instrument panel will light up to warn the driver.

The front wheels are fitted with floating caliper disc brakes. Two makes of caliper may be found, those made by Girling and those made by Teves. The latter are stamped 'Ate'. The rear wheels are fitted with drum brakes. The handbrake is cable operated, and applies the rear brakes only. The equalizer bar is located at the bottom of the handbrake lever.

A vacuum pump, gear driven from the intermediate shaft, is mounted on the front side of the engine in the position normally occupied by the distributor on petrol (gasoline) engines and supplies vacuum for the operation of the servo. This is necessary because of the low inlet manifold vacuum of diesel engines.

2 Front brakes – general description

1 One of two types of floating caliper is used on the cars covered by this manual: one type is made by Teves (Ate) and the other by Girling. Refer to Figs. 6.1 and 6.2 to see the differences.
2 The Teves caliper has a fixed mounting frame bolted to the stub axle and a floating frame held in position on the mounting frame and able to slide on the mounting frame in a direction 90° to the face of the disc. Fixed to the floating frame is a hydraulic cylinder with piston and seals. The friction pads are held in the mounting frame by pins and a spreader spring.
3 When the brake pedal is pressed the piston is forced against the inner (direct) brake pad pushing it against the disc. The reaction causes the floating frame to move away until the floating frame presses against the outer (indirect) pad, pushing that one against the disc. Further pressure holds the disc between the two pads.
4 The Girling, commonly known as the Girling A type single cylinder caliper, works on a different principle. The cylinder is fixed to the stub axle and contains two pistons. The caliper body which carries the pads is free to slide along grooves in the cylinder body. One piston pushes the direct pad against the disc and the other piston pushes the floating caliper so that the indirect pad is forced against the disc.
5 Despite the obvious structural differences the two calipers are interchangeable but must be changed as pairs (ie, two Teves or two Girlings but not one of each).
6 The brake pads on both types of caliper are identical.

3 Disc pads (Teves caliper) – inspection and renewal

1 Brake pads wear more quickly than drum brake shoes. They should be checked for wear at the intervals specified in Routine Maintenance. The thickness of the pad (including the backing plate) must not be less than the dimension given in the Specifications. If the pads wear below this thickness then damage to the brake disc may result. Measure the pad thickness through the holes in the roadwheels, see Figs. 6.3 and 6.4.
2 To remove the pads, jack-up the front of the car and remove the wheels. Using a suitable drift tap out the pins securing the disc pads (photos). On some cars there may be a wire securing clip fitted round these pins. This should be pulled off. If there is no clip the pins will have sleeves.
3 Remove the spreader and pull out the inner, direct pad. If you are going to put the pads back then they must be marked so that they go back in the same place. Use a piece of wire with a hook on the end to pull the pad out. Now lever the caliper over so that there is space between the disc and the outer pad, ease the pad away from the caliper onto the disc and lift it out (photo).
4 Clean out the pad holder and check that the rubber dust cover is

Fig. 6.3 Brake disc pad thickness dimension (a) including backplate not to be less than 6 mm ($\frac{1}{4}$ in) (Sec 3)

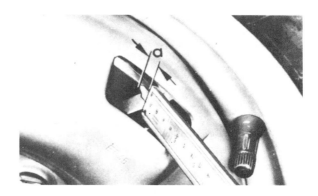

Fig. 6.4 Using vernier calipers to check the brake disc pad thickness (a) (Sec 3)

3.2A Disc pad pin retaining clip location (Teves type)

not damaged. Insert the outer pad and fit it over the projection on the caliper (photo). It will be necessary to push the piston in to insert the inner pad. This will cause the master cylinder reservoir to overflow unless action is taken to prevent it. Either draw some fluid out of the reservoir or slacken the bleeder screw (photo).
5 Push the piston in and check that the edges of the raised face of the piston are at 20° to the face of the caliper (photo). Make a gauge

3.2B Removing the disc pad retaining pins (Teves type)

3.3 Removing an outer disc pad (Teves type)

3.4A Caliper projection engaged in outer disc pad recess (Teves type)

3.4B Caliper bleeder screw location (Teves type)

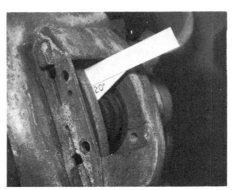

3.5 Check the angle of the piston projections

3.6 Disc pad spreader and retaining pins assembled to the caliper (Teves type)

out of cardboard if necessary. If the angle is more or less, turn the piston until the angle is correct.

6   Insert the inner pad, fit the spreader and the pins (photo). Fit a new locking wire if the type of pin requires it.

7   Do not forget to shut the bleed screw if it was opened as soon as the piston has been forced back. We do not like this method because there is a chance of air entering the cylinder and we do not like spare brake fluid about on the caliper while working on the friction pads.

8   Work the footbrake a few times to settle the pistons. Now repeat the job for the other wheel.

9   Replace the roadwheels, lower to the ground and take the car for a test run.

4   Disc pads (Girling caliper) – inspection and renewal

1   In general, the method is the same as for the Teves caliper (Section 3) with the following differences.

2   Lever off the pad spreader spring with a screwdriver, and pull out the pins with pliers after removing the screw which locks them in position.

3   Remove and refit the pads as with the Teves caliper. Fit the pins and the locking screw. A repair kit for brake pads will include new pins and retainer so use them.

4   The pad spreader spring is pressed on. The arrow must point in the direction of rotation of the disc when the car is travelling forward.

5   Calipers, pistons and seals (Teves) – removal, inspection and refitting

1   Support the front of the car on stands and remove the wheels.

2   If it is intended to dismantle the caliper then the brake hoses must be removed, plugged and tied out of the way.

3   Mark the position of the brake pads and remove them if the caliper is to be dismantled.

4   Remove the two bolts holding the caliper to the stub axle (photo).

This should not be done while the caliper is hot.

5   Withdraw the caliper from the car and take it to a bench.

6   Refer to Fig. 6.5. A repair kit should be purchased for the overhaul of the caliper.

7   Ease the floating frame away from the mounting frame. Press the brake cylinder and guide spring off the floating frame. The cylinder may now be dismantled.

8   Remove the retaining ring and the rubber boot. The next problem is to remove the piston which is probably stuck in the piston seal. The obvious way is to blow it out using air pressure in the hole which normally accommodates the hydraulic pressure hose. However, be

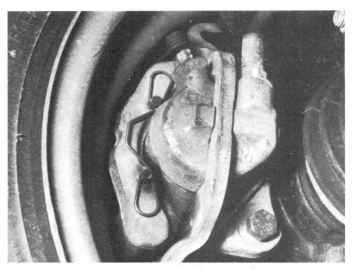

5.4 Caliper lower retaining bolt location (Teves type)

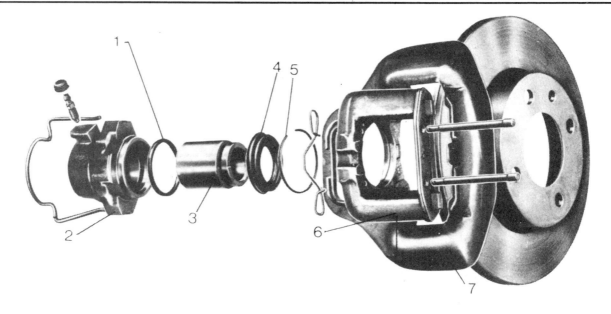

Fig. 6.5 Exploded view of the brake caliper (Teves type) (Sec 5)

1	O-ring seal	5	Circlip
2	Cylinder	6	Mounting frame
3	Piston	7	Floating frame
4	Dust cap		

careful. The piston may be stuck in the seal but when it does come out it will come quickly. Fit the cylinder in a vice with a piece of wood arranged to act as a stop for the piston. If you do not, as most people do not, have a ready supply of compressed air use a foot pump. Low air pressure is all that is normally required.

9   When the piston is out of the cylinder clean carefully the bore of the cylinder and the piston with brake fluid or methylated spirit.

10 It is difficult to define wear on the piston. When it has been cleaned it should have a mirror finish. Scratches or dull sections indicate wear. The inside of the bore must be clean with no scratches or distortion. If there is any doubt renew the whole unit. In any case renew the seal and dust excluder. Dip the cylinder in clean brake fluid. Coat the piston and seal with brake rubber grease (Ate) and press the piston and seal into the cylinder. Install new dust excluder and its retaining ring. Fit a new locating spring and knock the cylinder onto the floating frame with a brass drift.

11 Refit the floating frame to the mounting frame and set the piston recess at an inclination of 20° to the lower guide surface of the caliper (where the pad rests), as described in Section 3.

12 Bolt the mounting frame onto the stub axle and fit the pads. Refit the wheel and lower to the ground.

13 Top-up the brake fluid reservoir and bleed the brakes as described in Section 23.

14 Road test the car to check the operation of the brakes.

6   Calipers, pistons and seals (Girling) – removal, inspection and refitting

1   Refer to Fig. 6.6. The general rules for overhaul are the same as for the Teves (Section 5) but with the complication of the extra piston.

2   Remove the cylinder and floating mounting from the stub axle and press them apart. Again use air pressure to dislodge the pistons and be careful that they do not come out suddenly. Clean the pistons and bore carefully. Use a Girling kit of seals and parts. Wash the cylinder and pistons with clean brake fluid and reassemble.

3   In this case the pistons and cylinder are bolted to the front suspension. The caliper sliding frame must move easily over the cylinder casting. Tighten the holding bolts to the specified torque.

7   Disc pad wear indicators – general

1   A built-in method of indicating to the driver that the brake pads require renewing is fitted on cars for the USA and certain other territories. Refer to Fig. 6.7. The chamfer (arrow B in the illustration) on both sides of the brake disc has a lug about 25 mm (1 in) long flush with the face of the disc. The pads have a thin extension piece (A) on the bottom which is coated with wear resistant material. When the pads are worn to the permissible limit the extension on the pad makes contact with the lug on the disc. This causes a vibrating or pulsating effect at the foot pedal, thus indicating to the driver that pad renewal is a matter of urgency.

2   Discs and brake pads of this type may be fitted to cars not so originally fitted.

8   Front brakes – squeaking pads

If the pads squeal or squeak excessively, relief from this problem may be obtained by removing and cleaning the pads and holders and then applying sparingly a substance known as 'Plastilube'. This substance **must not** be applied to friction surfaces but to the ends, sides and back of the pad. It should also be applied to the pins and spreader and the sliding surfaces of the floating caliper.

9   Rear brakes – general description

1   One of two types of drum brake is found on the Golf/Rabbit models. The early models are equipped with manually adjusted brakes; from 1979 self-adjusting brakes are fitted.

2   With the manually adjusted type, the shoes are held against the connecting link by a U-spring. The shoes are adjusted through a hole in the backplate, using a screwdriver to rotate the brake shoe adjuster.

3   The construction of the self-adjusting brakes is similar to the type found on earlier models except that the U-spring is replaced by two coil springs and the adjusting mechanism consists of a pushrod, wedge and springs. Refer to Fig. 6.9. A single operation of the brake

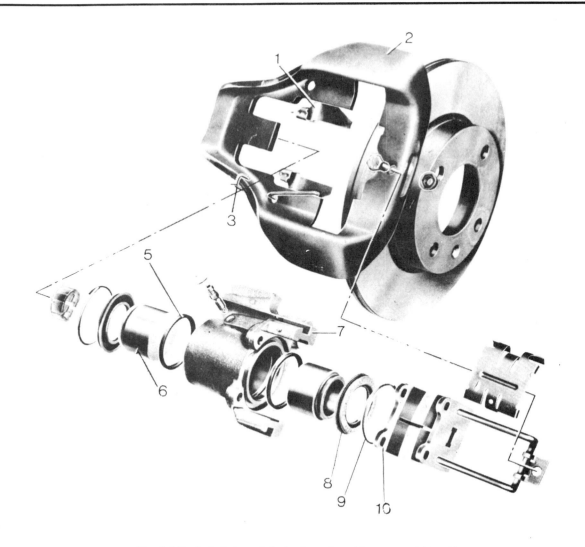

Fig. 6.6 Exploded view of the brake caliper (Girling type) (Sec 6)

1	Clip	5	Sealing ring	8	Dust cap
2	Frame	6	Piston	9	Circlip
3	Retaining spring	7	Cylinder housing	10	Brake pads
4	Support				

Fig. 6.7 Brake pad wear indicator system (Sec 7)

For A and B see text

pedal sets a fixed clearance between the brake drum and the brake shoes. As the linings wear and shoe travel becomes greater than the fixed clearance, the wedge is moved downwards by the arrangement of the pushrod and the springs. This movement of the wedge alters the effective length of the pushrod and thus automatically adjusts the position of the brake shoes in relation to the brake drum.

10 Rear brakes (manually adjusted type) – adjustment of shoes and handbrake

Note: Adjustment of the handbrake on models with self-adjusting rear brakes is only necessary if the handbrake lever or cables have been removed and refitted, or the cables have stretched after a high mileage, refer to Section 12.

Brake shoe adjustment

1   Chock the front wheels, then jack-up the rear of the car and support it on axle stands or other suitable supports.
2   Find the adjuster access hole on the backplate. It is just below the wheel cylinder bleed screw. Remove the rubber plug from the hole.
3   Move the handbrake lever to the fully off position. Depress the lever on the brake pressure regulator valve (Section 21) towards the valve body. This will release any pressure in the right-hand pipeline.
4   Through the access hole in the left-hand rear brake backplate a toothed wheel is visible. Using a screwdriver, lever the adjuster wheel teeth upwards (handle of the screwdriver down) until the brake linings bind on the drum. Now back-off (work the screwdriver the other way) the adjuster until the roadwheel will rotate without the drum dragging on the brake shoes. Refit the rubber plug in the adjuster access hole.
5   Repeat this procedure to adjust the other rear brake, but note that this time the adjuster works in the reverse direction, (lever the teeth of the adjuster downwards to bring the shoes in contact with the brake drum).

Handbrake adjustment

6   After the footbrake is correctly adjusted the handbrake may be adjusted, if it fails to lock the rear wheels after the control lever is pulled over three or four notches. Remove the handbrake lever boot securing screws and pull up the boot. Pull the handbrake lever up two notches from the fully off position. Tighten each of the adjusting nuts a little at a time, keeping the equalizer bar level, until neither of the rear wheels can be turned by hand. Release the handbrake lever and check that the rear wheels rotate freely. Tighten the locknuts.
7   If the equalizer bar is positioned at an acute angle after the correct adjustment has been achieved then one of the cables has been stretched and must be renewed, refer to Section 25.

11 Rear brakes (manually adjusted type) – removal and refitting

1   Slacken the roadwheel bolts. Chock the front wheels, jack-up the rear of the car and support it on axle stands or other suitable supports. Release the handbrake lever.
2   Take off the hub cap, remove the split-pin and the locking ring. Remove the hub nut and pull the brake drum off the stub axle. The thrust washer and wheel bearing will come off with the drum. Set the drum on one side for inspection (Section 13). **Note:** It may be necessary to back-off the brake shoes to remove the brake drum, refer to Section 10.
3   The brake assembly is now exposed. **Do not** depress the brake pedal from now on. Remove the large U-spring and unhook the two springs at the bottom of the brake shoes. Take off the leaf springs from the steady pins and remove the shoes from the backplate. It will be necessary to unhook the handbrake cable to remove the shoes. The adjuster rod will come away with the shoes. The backplate can be removed, if necessary, by undoing the four securing bolts and lifting away the backplate and stub axle.
4   Overhaul of the brake drum and shoes is dealt with in Section 13

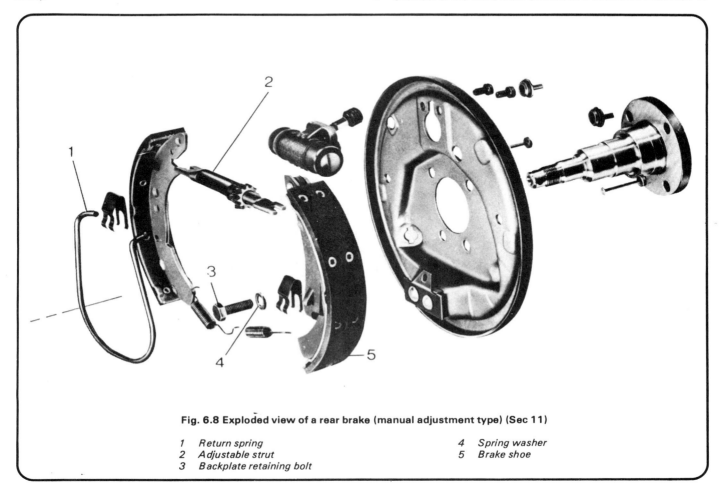

Fig. 6.8 Exploded view of a rear brake (manual adjustment type) (Sec 11)

1 Return spring	*4 Spring washer*
2 Adjustable strut	*5 Brake shoe*
3 Backplate retaining bolt	

and the wheel cylinder in Section 14.

5   Refitting is the reverse of the removal procedure. Fit the hand-brake cable to the trailing shoe lever, locate the shoes on the backplate and fit the steady pins. Fit the bottom springs. Lever the shoes apart and fit the adjuster rod. Finally fit the U-spring.

6   Refit the drum and bearing. Adjust the bearing as described in Chapter 9. Refit the roadwheel and adjust the brakes, refer to Section 10. If the wheel cylinder was removed, bleed the hydraulic system as described in Section 23.

12 Rear brakes (self-adjusting type) – removal and refitting

1   Refer to Fig. 6.9. Repeat the operations described in Section 11, paragraphs 1 and 2, but note that the self-adjusting mechanism will have kept the lining right up to the drum and the adjuster must be backed off before the drum can be removed. To do this insert a screwdriver through a roadwheel bolt hole and push the adjusting wedge right up, then withdraw the brake drum (photo). **Do not** depress the brake pedal from now on.

2   Using a pair of pliers remove the washers retaining the shoe steady springs by depressing them and rotating them through 90° and remove the springs (photo).

3   Pull the bottom ends of the shoes out of the support and unhook the lower return spring (photo).

4   Pull back the spring on the handbrake cable and disconnect the cable from the operating lever.

5   Using pliers, unhook the wedge spring and upper return spring, then lift away the brake shoes (photo).

6   The brake wheel cylinder can be removed, if necessary, as described in Section 14.

7   The backplate can be removed, if necessary, by undoing the four securing bolts and lifting away the backplate and stub axle.

8   To disconnect the pushrod from the brake shoe, clamp the shoe in a vice, unhook the locating spring and lift away the pushrod.

9   Overhaul of the brake drum and shoes is dealt with in Section 13 and the wheel cylinder in Section 14.

10 Refitting is the reverse of the removal procedure. When inserting the wedge, the lug on the wedge must be towards the backplate. After fitting the brake drum adjust the wheel bearing as described in Chapter 9. If the wheel cylinder was removed, bleed the hydraulic system as described in Section 23.

Note: The brakes are automatically adjusted when the footbrake pedal is depressed. Do this several times.

11 Refit the roadwheels and lower the car to the ground. Road test the car to check the operation of the brakes.

13 Brake shoes and drums – inspection and renovation

1   One of two types of shoe is used. One type has the lining riveted to the brake shoe and the other has the lining bonded to the shoe. When the lining thickness is worn to less than the wear limit specified at the beginning of this Chapter the shoes must be renewed.

2   The linings must be free from oil or hydraulic fluid contamination, have smooth surfaces and be free from scoring. If any of these defects are present the shoes must be renewed and the cause of the defect discovered and rectified.

3   The four shoes on the rear axle must be renewed at the same time. It is not recommended that DIY owners should attempt to reline the riveted type of brake shoe. It is much better to obtain new shoes.

4   Drums must be smooth and unscored. Any scoring or grooves on the inside diameter must be removed by machining in a lathe. The diameter after machining must not exceed the maximum specified.

5   The drum must also be inspected for cracks, ovality or other damage.

14 Wheel cylinder – removal, overhaul and refitting

1   The wheel cylinder is fastened to the backplate by two screws. It may be removed only after the brake shoes are lifted away from it. It is not necessary to dismantle the shoes from the backplate.

2   Disconnect the hydraulic hose from the cylinder and plug the hose. The screws holding the cylinder to the plate may be difficult to extract. Brake fluid is a good penetrating oil so moisten the threads with a little fluid.

3   An exploded view of a rear wheel cylinder is shown in Fig. 6.10.

4   To dismantle, remove the dust caps and blow the pistons out with low air pressure. Be careful when doing this that the pistons do not come out too quickly. Muffle the cylinder with a large piece of rag.

5   Wash the bores and pistons with clean brake fluid and examine for mirror finish and scratches. If there is any blemish discard the complete unit and fit a new one. Always fit new seals and dust caps. Coat

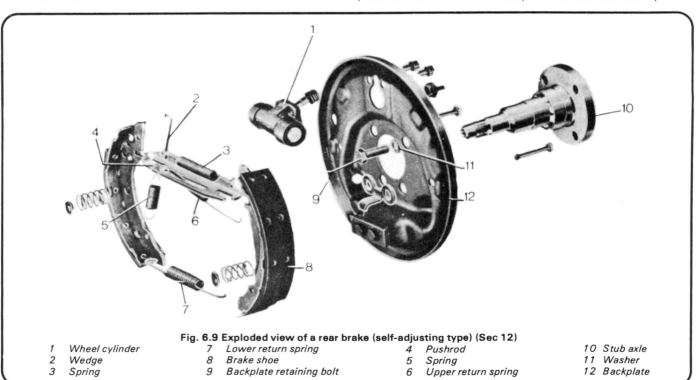

Fig. 6.9 Exploded view of a rear brake (self-adjusting type) (Sec 12)

1	Wheel cylinder	7	Lower return spring	4	Pushrod	10	Stub axle
2	Wedge	8	Brake shoe	5	Spring	11	Washer
3	Spring	9	Backplate retaining bolt	6	Upper return spring	12	Backplate

12.1 Removing the rear brake drum

12.2 Removing the brake shoe steady springs

12.3 Lower return spring location on rear brakes (self-adjusting type) and handbrake cable and operating lever location

12.5 View of the rear brakes showing spring and strut locations (self adjusting type)

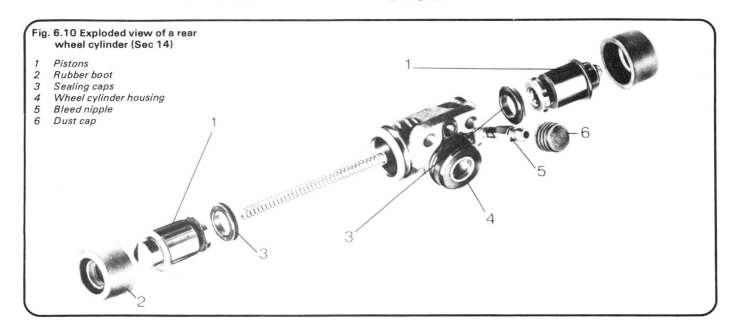

Fig. 6.10 Exploded view of a rear wheel cylinder (Sec 14)

1 Pistons
2 Rubber boot
3 Sealing caps
4 Wheel cylinder housing
5 Bleed nipple
6 Dust cap

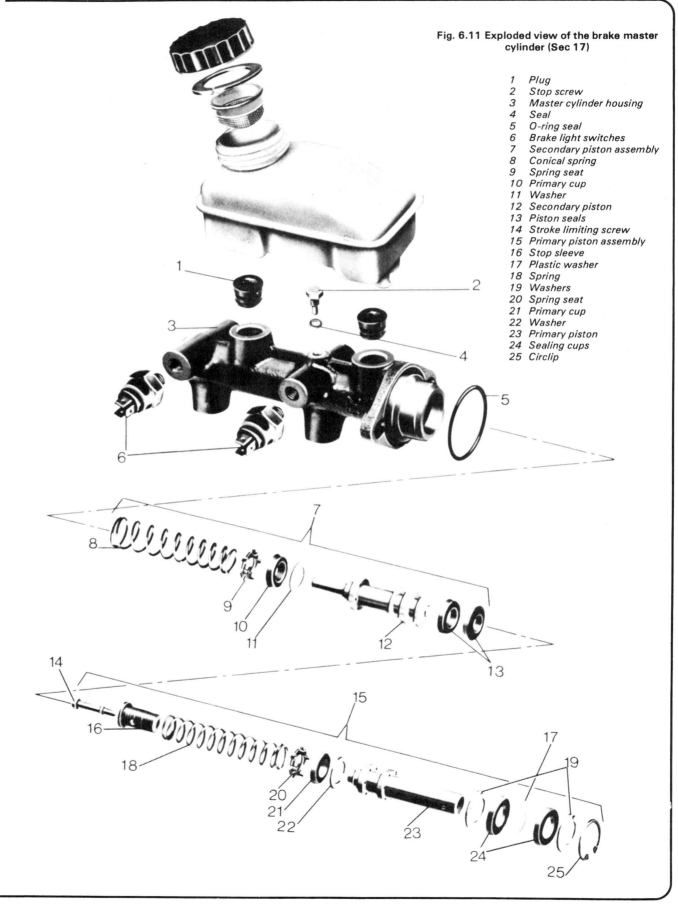

Fig. 6.11 Exploded view of the brake master cylinder (Sec 17)

1 Plug
2 Stop screw
3 Master cylinder housing
4 Seal
5 O-ring seal
6 Brake light switches
7 Secondary piston assembly
8 Conical spring
9 Spring seat
10 Primary cup
11 Washer
12 Secondary piston
13 Piston seals
14 Stroke limiting screw
15 Primary piston assembly
16 Stop sleeve
17 Plastic washer
18 Spring
19 Washers
20 Spring seat
21 Primary cup
22 Washer
23 Primary piston
24 Sealing cups
25 Circlip

them with a little brake rubber grease before fitting and make sure the seals are the right way round.

6   Refitting is the reverse of the removal procedure. Bleed the hydraulic system as described in Section 23 and road test the car to check the operation of the brakes.

15 Brake hydraulic system – description and operation

1   The master cylinder has two pistons, the front or secondary supplying pressure to the left-hand front wheel and the right-hand rear wheel. The rear, or primary, piston supplies pressure to the right-hand front wheel and the left-hand rear wheel. Inspection of the unit will show four pipes leading from the main casting to the wheel cylinders and calipers.

2   Brake fluid is supplied from the fluid reservoir, the white plastic container which feeds both circuits through the master cylinder.

3   When the brake pedal is pressed the pushrod moves the primary piston forward so that it covers the port to the fluid reservoir. Further movement causes pressure to build up between the two pistons exerting pressure on the secondary piston which also moves forward covering the port to the fluid reservoir. The pressure now builds up in the pipe.

4   If the pipes of the secondary piston circuit fracture or the system fails in some way the secondary piston will move forward to the end of the piston compressing the conical spring and sealing the outlet port to the left front and right rear brakes. The primary piston circuit will continue to operate.

5   Failure of the primary piston circuit causes the piston to move forward until the stop sleeve contacts the secondary piston and the primary piston simultaneously when pressure will again be applied to the secondary piston circuit.

6   The various springs and seals are designed to keep the pistons in the right place when the system is not under pressure.

7   Pressure switches are screwed into the cylinder body and operate the stoplights and warning lamps.

16 Master cylinder – removal and refitting

1   The master cylinder is mounted on the front of the brake servo unit in the engine compartment (photo).

2   Disconnect the battery earth strap and then the wiring from the brake light and warning light switches on the master cylinder.

3   Disconnect the pipes from the master cylinder and collect the brake fluid, which will drain out, in a suitable container. Take care to avoid brake fluid spilling on paintwork.

4   Undo the nuts securing the master cylinder to the servo unit and lift the master cylinder off the mounting studs. Discard the O-ring located between the master cylinder and the servo.

5   Refitting is the reverse of the removal procedure. Always fit a new O-ring between the master cylinder and the servo unit. Ensure that the wiring and pipes are reconnected to their original locations. Tighten the master cylinder securing nuts and the brake lines to the specified torque.

6   Fill the brake fluid reservoir with fresh fluid (never re-use fluid removed from the system) and bleed the hydraulic system as described in Section 23.

17 Master cylinder – overhaul

1   Clean the outside of the cylinder thoroughly and then set it on a clean area. Work only with clean hands. Obtain an overhaul kit and a quantity of fresh brake fluid in a clean container. Always use all the parts supplied in the overhaul kit.

2   Refer to Fig. 6.11. Undo and remove the brake stoplight and warning light switches.

3   Remove the fluid reservoir by pulling it upwards out of the rubber grommets. Remove the grommets.

4   Remove the stop screw and seal from the top of the cylinder.

5   Push the piston back slightly and then remove the retaining circlip. The contents of the cylinder should now slide out if the cylinder is tilted. If they do not, apply a low air pressure and blow them out. As the parts are removed place them in the order in which they should be refitted.

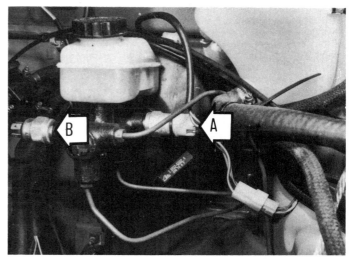

16.1 Brake master cylinder location, showing primary brake circuit stop and warning light switch (A) and secondary brake circuit stop and warning light switch (B)

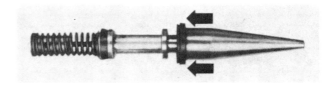

Fig. 6.12 Using a tapered mandrel to fit the master cylinder piston seals (Sec 17)

6   Examine the bore of the cylinder. If it is scored or rusty the cylinder must be renewed. It is possible to hone out slight marks if you have access to the right equipment, but our advice is to fit a new cylinder.

7   Clean the master cylinder with brake fluid or methylated spirit only, never use paraffin or petrol, and ensure that all passageways and holes are clear.

8   The piston seals are not easy to fit. VW make a special taper mandrel, see Fig. 6.12, which just fits on the ends of the piston and then the seal is eased on over the taper. The seals can be fitted without this tool, but take care not to damage them as they slide over the piston lands. Use the fingers only – never a metal tool.

9   Assemble the two pistons with their associated parts. During assembly wet all the parts with fresh brake fluid. Ensure that the primary cups and piston seals are fitted correctly, see Fig. 6.11.

10 Hold the cylinder vertically and insert the complete secondary piston from underneath.

11 Now insert the primary piston and retaining circlip. Fit the stop screw. It may be necessary to move the secondary piston to fit the stop screw fully.

12 Insert the brake fluid reservoir locating grommets in the top of the master cylinder and then fit the fluid reservoir.

18 Servo unit – testing, repair, removal and refitting

1   If the brakes seem to need more pedal pressure than normal a check of the servo is indicated. The brake servo pump should also be checked.

2   First of all check that the hose connecting the vacuum pump to the servo unit is securely attached and in good condition. Then with the engine running disconnect the hose from the servo unit and check that there is suction at the end of the hose. If there is no suction the vacuum pump is defective, refer to Sections 19 and 20.

3   If the vacuum hose and vacuum pump are in order and the servo is still not assisting the brakes the trouble is either a leaking servo diaphragm or a defect in the master cylinder. Check that the sealing ring between the master cylinder and the servo is not leaking.

4   The repairs possible to the servo are very limited. Refer to Fig.
6.13. The O-ring between the servo and the master cylinder should
always be renewed whenever the units are separated. At the rear end
of the servo, the filter and damping washer may be removed from the
sleeve and renewed, note that the slots in the damping washer and
filter should be offset 180° on assembly. Apart from this the servo,
which is a sealed unit, cannot be serviced further.

5   To remove the servo, first remove the master cylinder as described
in Section 16 and plug the hydraulic lines. Disconnect the vacuum
hose from the servo.

6   Remove the clevis pin connecting the servo pushrod to the brake
pedal (LHD models) or to the brake pedal to servo link rod (RHD
models) and unscrew the fork end (photo). Remove the nuts securing
the servo unit to the mounting bracket and lift away the servo.

7   Refitting is the reverse of the removal procedure. Bleed the
hydraulic system as described in Section 23 and adjust the brake pedal
pushrod, refer to Section 26.

19 Brake servo vacuum pump – general description, removal and refitting

1   As the intake manifold vacuum on diesel engines is much less than
that on petrol (gasoline) engines, a vacuum pump is needed to create
enough vacuum for the efficient operation of the brake servo unit.

2   The diaphragm type of pump used is mounted on the location
used by the distributor on spark ignition engines and is driven by a gear
on the intermediate shaft.

3   Slacken the hose clips and disconnect both hoses from the pump.
Disconnect the oil feed at the union on the pump body (photos).

4   Undo the clamp plate securing bolt, remove the clamp plate and
then withdraw the pump from the engine block (photos). Discard the
O-ring.

5   Refitting is the reverse of the removal procedure. Ensure that the
end of the pump drive engages correctly with the oil pump shaft.
Tighten the clamp plate securing bolt to the specified torque.

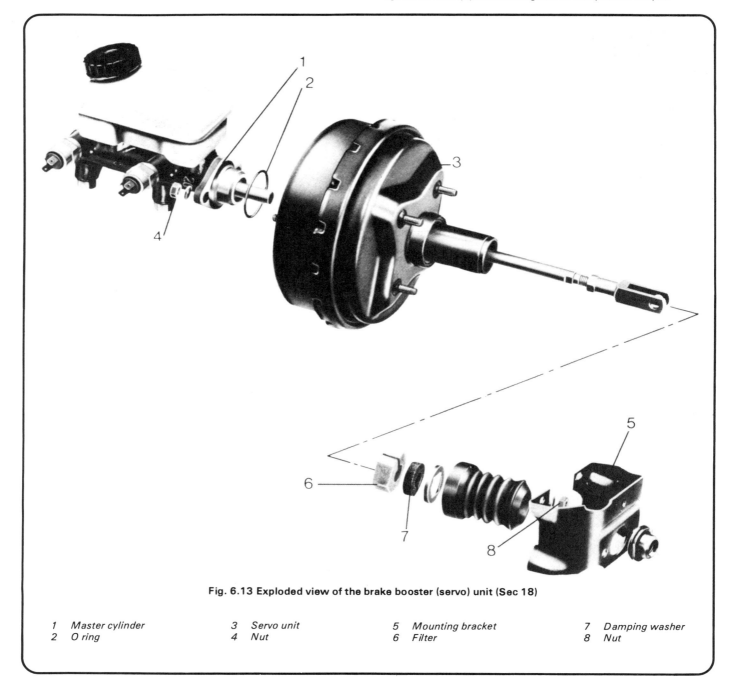

Fig. 6.13 Exploded view of the brake booster (servo) unit (Sec 18)

1	Master cylinder	3	Servo unit	5	Mounting bracket	7	Damping washer
2	O ring	4	Nut	6	Filter	8	Nut

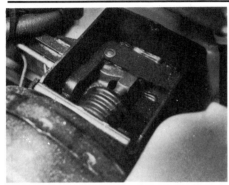

18.6 Brake servo bell crank linkage location (left-hand side)

19.3A Brake servo vacuum pump (exhauster) lower hose connection

19.3B Brake servo vacuum pump (exhauster) upper hose connection and non-return valve

19.3C Brake servo vacuum pump (exhauster) oil feed pipe location

19.4A Brake servo vacuum pump (exhauster) clamp plate

19.4B Removing the brake servo vacuum pump (exhauster)

20 Vacuum pump – overhaul

1   Obtain a vacuum pump repair kit before dismantling the pump. Refer to Fig. 6.15.
2   Make an alignment mark on both parts of the pump body to ensure that they can be reassembled in their original position. Undo the eight securing bolts and separate the top section from the lower part of the body.
3   Undo the diaphragm assembly securing nut and remove the diaphragm and its backing plates. Remove the O-ring.
4   Undo the four securing screws and remove the endplate and gasket.
5   Undo the two securing screws and remove the cover plate, springs, spring seats, valves and washers.
6   Wash all the parts in a cleaning solvent and inspect them for wear and damage. Examine the diaphragm for deterioration or splits. If in doubt, renew it.
7   Fit a new O-ring on the pushrod.
8   Fit the diaphragm and backing plates with the moulded part of the diaphragm towards the top part of the body and the holes in line with the holes in the pump body.
9   Coat the threads of the diaphragm assembly securing nut with a thread locking compound. Fit the nut and tighten it to the specified torque.
10   Assemble the top part loosely to the main body.
11   Working through the endplate opening remove the circlip, arrowed in Fig. 6.14 from the driveshaft, then push the shaft back until the pushrod is free of the driveshaft and the tension is released from the diaphragm.
12   Push the pushrod against the stop in the direction of the arrow in Fig. 6.16 and hold it in this position while tightening the screws securing the top part to the body in a diagonal sequence, a few threads at a time. Push the driveshaft into position and fit the thrust washer and circlip on the end of the shaft.
13   Refit the washers, valves, spring seats and springs. When fitting the valves the spring seats must be towards the housing. Using a new

Fig. 6.14 Brake vacuum pump driveshaft circlip (arrowed) (Sec 20)

gasket, refit the valve cover plate.
14   Using a new gasket, refit the pump body endplate.

21 Brake pressure regulator – description

1   This device is fitted to some models to limit the hydraulic pressure in the rear wheel hydraulic cylinders and so limit the braking force. In effect it should prevent the rear wheels being locked solid by the brakes and so avoid skidding.
2   It is fitted just in front of the rear axle, to which it is attached by a spring. When the brakes are applied sharply the front of the car sinks

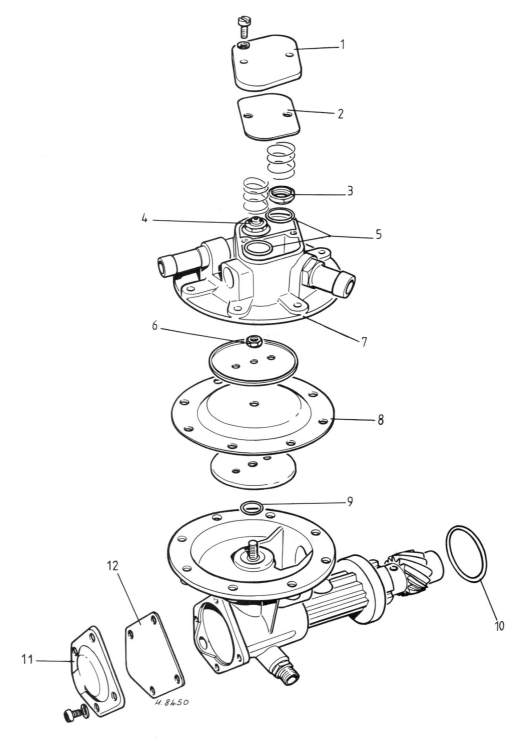

4.8450

Fig. 6.15 Exploded view of the brake vacuum pump (exhauster) (Sec 20)

1	Cover		7	Upper body
2	Gasket		8	Diaphragm
3	Inlet valve		9	O-ring
4	Outlet valve		10	O-ring
5	Sealing washer		11	Cover
6	Nut		12	Gasket

Fig. 6.16 Arrow shows direction to move pushrod of brake vacuum pump to pre-tension the diaphragm (Sec 20)

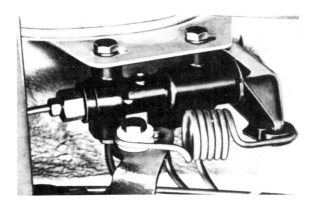

Fig. 6.17 Brake pressure regulator (Sec 21)

and the rear rises a little. This causes the rear axle beam to pivot slightly in its mountings and the pressure on the spring is reduced. This enables a spring inside the valve to restrict the hydraulic pressure available to the rear brakes.

3 When testing and adjusting the pressure regulator it is necessary to position the car body accurately and then to measure the pressures at the front and rear brake bleed nipples when the brakes are applied sharply. The tension of the spring between the regulator and the rear axle beam is then adjusted so that the correct pressures are obtained.

4 This requires special equipment to set the position of the rear suspension springs, and meters to measure up to 100 kgf/cm^2 (1420 lbf/in^2). This job must be left to the VW agent who will have the necessary equipment. Inaccurate setting may result in rear wheel skids or reduced braking efficiency.

5 When bleeding the hydraulic brake system of cars fitted with a pressure regulator, the lever of the regulator should be pressed towards the rear axle.

22 Hydraulic pipes and hoses – inspection and renewal

1 The magnitude of the pressure in the hydraulic lines is not generally realized. The test pressures are 100 kgf/cm^2 (1420 lbf/in^2) for the front brakes. These pressures are with the braking system cold. The temperature rise in the drums and discs for an emergency stop from 60 mph is as much as 80°C (176°F), and during a long descent may reach 400°C (752°F). The pressure must be even further raised

as the temperature of the brake fluid in the cylinder rises. The normal pressure in the hydraulic system when the brakes are not in use is negligible. The pressure builds up quickly when the brakes are applied and remains until the pedal is released. Each driver will know how quick the build up is when equating it to the speed of his own reaction in an emergency brake application.

2 Recent research in the USA has shown that brake line corrosion may be expected to lead to failure after only 90 days exposure to salt spray such as is thrown up when salt is used to melt ice or snow. This in effect makes a four year old vehicle automatically suspect. It is possible to use pipe made of copper alloy used in marine work called 'Kunifer 10' as a replacement. This is much more resistant to salt corrosion, but as yet it is not a standard fitting.

3 All this should by now have indicated that pipes need regular inspection. The obvious times are in the autumn before the winter conditions set in, and in the spring to see what damage has been done.

4 Trace the routes of all the rigid pipes and wash or brush away accumulated dirt. If the pipes are obviously covered with some sort of underseal compound do not disturb the underseal. Examine for signs of kinks or dents which could have been caused by flying stones. Any instances of this means that the pipe section should be renewed, **but before actually taking it out read the rest of this Section.** Any unprotected sections of pipe which show signs of corrosion or pitting on the outer surface must also be considered for renewal.

5 Flexible hoses, running to each of the front wheels and from the underbody to each rear wheel should show no external signs of chafing or cracking. Move them about to see whether surface cracks appear. If they feel stiff and inflexible or are twisted they are nearing the end of their useful life. If in any doubt renew the hoses. Make sure also that they are not rubbing against the bodywork.

6 Before attempting to remove a pipe for renewal it is important to be sure that you have a replacement source of supply within reach if you do not wish to be kept off the road for too long. Pipes are often damaged on removal. If an official agency is near you may be reasonably sure that the correct pipes and unions are available. If not, check first that your local garage has the necessary equipment for making up the pipes and has the correct metric thread pipe unions available. The same goes for flexible hoses.

7 Where the couplings from rigid to flexible pipes are made there are support brackets and the flexible pipe is held in place by a U clip which engages in a groove in the union. The male union screws into it. Before getting the spanners on, soak the unions in penetrating fluid as there is always some rust or corrosion binding the threads. Whilst this is soaking in, place a piece of plastic film under the fluid reservoir cap to minimise loss of fluid from the disconnected pipes. Hold the hexagon on the flexible pipe coupling whilst the union on the rigid pipe is undone. Then pull out the clip to release both pipes from the bracket. For flexible hose removal this procedure will be needed at both ends. For a rigid pipe the other end will only involve unscrewing the union from a cylinder or connector. When you are renewing a flexible hose, take care not to damage the unions of the pipes that connect into it. If a union is particularly stubborn be prepared to renew the rigid pipe as well. This is quite often the case if you are forced to use open ended spanners. It may be worth spending a little money on a special pipe union spanner which is like a ring spanner with a piece cut out to enable it to go round the tube.

8 If you are having the new pipe made up, take the old one along to check that the unions and pipe flaring at the ends are identical.

9 Refitting of the hoses or pipes is a reversal of the removal procedure. Precautions and care are needed to make sure that the unions are correctly lined up to prevent cross threading. This may mean bending the pipe a little where a rigid pipe goes into a fixture. Such bending must not, under any circumstances, be too acute or the pipe will kink and weaken.

10 When fitting flexible hoses take care not to twist them. This can happen when the unions are finally tightened unless a spanner is used to hold the end of the flexible hose and prevent twisting.

11 If a pipe is removed or a union slackened, thereby admitting air into the hydraulic system, then the system must be bled as described in Section 23.

23 Brake hydraulic system – bleeding

1 First locate the bleed nipples on all four brakes. The rear wheel bleed nipples are at the back of the drum at the centre of the hydraulic cylinder. A small dust cap covers the nipple. This will probably be

covered with mud. Clean the mud from the back of the drum, wipe the dust cap and the area around it with a clean rag and the operation may start. The front brake bleed nipples are on the inside surface of the caliper.

2   As fluid is to be pumped out of the system make sure you have plenty of new clean fluid. It must conform to SAE recommendation J1703, J1703R but better still, get the official VW fluid. If other than hydraulic fluid is used the whole system may become useless through failure of piston seals. Top-up the fluid reservoir generously, and keep topping it up at intervals throughout the whole job (photo). On cars fitted with a pressure regulator valve, refer to Section 21, paragraph 5.

3   Start with the rear right-hand wheel. A piece of rubber or plastic hose 4 mm ($\frac{5}{32}$ in) inside diameter and about 600 mm (2 feet) long is required. Fit this over the bleed nipple and immerse the other end in a jar or bottle with some clean brake fluid in it. Fix the hose so that the end of it cannot come out of the brake fluid, and stand the bottle on the ground in a secure place.

4   You will need a helper whose job is to depress the brake pedal when required (but see Section 24, paragraph 6). It is as well to rehearse the operation before opening the bleed nipple valve. Open the valve about one turn and depress the pedal slowly to the floor of the vehicle. As soon as it is on the floor close the bleed valve **before** the pedal is released. Now release the pedal slowly. Brake fluid and air bubbles should have passed down the tube into the bottle. Repeat the operation until no further air bubbles are observed. Make the final tightening at the end of the last down-stroke. Check the fluid reservoir

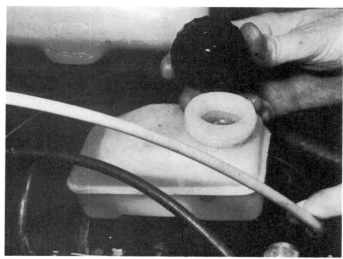

23.2 Removing the brake fluid reservoir filler cap

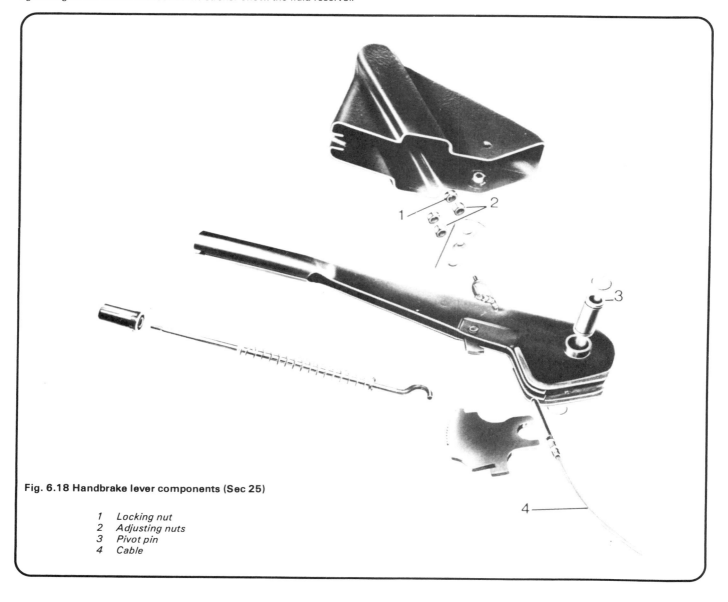

Fig. 6.18 Handbrake lever components (Sec 25)

    1   Locking nut
    2   Adjusting nuts
    3   Pivot pin
    4   Cable

level after every two strokes and top-up if necessary.

5　When you are satisfied that the rear right-hand brake line is clear of air bubbles then wipe down the brake and proceed to the next task; in order left rear, right front caliper, left front caliper.

6　After each session clean down the brakes with care and wash your hands. Brake fluid is poisonous and it is a splendid paint remover. Use a soapy solution and wash any paintwork that has been splashed.

7　Finally, the brake fluid in the jar should be discarded. Never use it for topping-up the brake fluid reservoir, for this always use fresh brake fluid.

24　Brake hydraulic system – changing fluid

1　The brake fluid is hygroscopic, which means that if it is allowed to come into contact with the open air it will absorb moisture. If it does then when the brakes get hot the water will boil and the brakes will not work properly – at the moment when they are needed most.

2　VW recommend that the fluid should be changed every two years—they give a variety of reasons – but the fact that they do recommend it should be reason enough.

3　The change over is simple to do. First of all clean the rear drums, particularly by the bleed nipples, and give the front calipers the same treatment.

4　Connect all four bleed nipples to plastic pipe and suitable containers, then open all four bleed nipples and get a helper to pump the brake pedal until no further fluid comes out.

5　Close the nipples, fill the system with clean brake fluid and then bleed the system as in Section 23.

6　The use of a proprietary pressure brake bleeder will enable the operations described in Section 23 and 24 to be carried out without an assistant.

25　Handbrake lever and cables – removal and refitting

1　To remove the lever, the plastic boot must be removed from the handbrake lever. Refer to Fig. 6.18. Slacken off the locking nut and remove it and the adjusting nut from each cable. Lift off the equalizer bar. Remove the clip from the pivot pin and push the pin out of the housing. The handbrake lever will now lift out leaving the cables in place.

2　The cables run through conduits under the car and then through clips to the rear brake backplate and to the shoe operating lever. It is necessary to remove the brake drum, as described in Sections 11 and 12, to unhook the cable from the operating lever. The cable can then be withdrawn from the conduit.

3　Refitting is the reverse of the removal procedure. Adjust the handbrake as described in Section 10 for manually adjusted rear brakes. The procedure for adjusting the handbrake cable on models with self-adjusting rear brakes (only necessary when the lever and/or cables have been renewed) is the same as for manually adjusted rear brakes.

26　Brake and clutch pedal assembly – removal and refitting

LHD models – refer to Fig. 6.19

1　Both pedals are fitted on the same shaft. Disconnect the clutch cable from the clutch pedal, refer to Chapter 4.

2　Disconnect the brake pedal pushrod clevis from the pedal by removing the clevis pin. Unhook the pedal return spring.

3　Remove the pedal shaft retaining clip, withdraw the shaft and collect the brake and clutch pedals.

4　Refitting of the pedals is the reverse of the removal procedure. After the pedals are fitted check the clutch pedal free play, refer to Chapter 4, and adjust the brake pedal pushrod as follows:

　(a)　*Slacken the clevis locknut and adjust the position of the clevis on the pushrod to obtain a dimension of 206 mm (8.1 in) between the brake servo housing and the clevis hole, indicated by A in Fig. 6.19*

　(b)　*Fit the clevis pin in the second hole in the brake pedal which is 51 mm (2.0 in) from the centre of the pedal bush*

RHD models – refer to Fig. 6.20

5　On RHD models the brake pushrod is connected to the servo unit through left and right-hand bell cranks which are connected by a link rod (photo).

6　The removal and refitting of the pedals is basically the same as for LHD models but note that the pushrod clevis pin and clip are different and that the bell cranks and connecting link are mounted to the brackets attached to the bulkhead.

7　When refitting the assembly, adjust the length of the brake pushrod by positioning the clevis at each end of the pushrod so that dimension B in Fig. 6.20 is 172 mm (6.8 in) and then tighten the locknuts.

8　When fitting the link rod between the bell cranks, adjust the length of the rod so that it is free of play and then tighten the locknuts.

9　Lubricate all friction surfaces inside the car with MOS_2 grease and all the linkage joints in the engine compartment with multi-purpose grease.

27　Tyres – inspection and maintenance

1　These can be an expensive problem if neglected. The most important matter is to keep them inflated at the correct pressure. A table of pressures is given at the start of the Chapter. If the vehicle is driven over rough ground, or over glass in the road, the tread should be inspected to see whether stones or glass fragments are lodged in the tread. These should be removed forthwith.

2　A careful study of the tread once a week will pay dividends. Tyres should wear evenly right across the tread but they rarely do, they are usually replaced because of misuse. A table is given showing some of the main troubles. Study it and watch your tyre treads.

Wear description	Probable cause
Rapid wear of the centre of the tread all round the circumference	*Tyre overinflated*
Rapid wear at both edges of the tread, wear even all round the circumference	*Tyre underinflated*
Wear on one edge of the tyre (a) Front wheels only (b) Rear wheels only	*Steering geometry needs checking Check rear suspension for damage*
Scalloped edges, wear at the edge at regular spacing around the tyre	*Maybe wheel out of balance, or more likely wear on the wheel bearing housing or steering balljoint*
Flat or rough patches on the tread	*Caused by harsh braking Check the brake adjustment*
Cuts and abrasions on the wall of the tyre	*Usually done by running into the kerb*

3　If the tyre wall is damaged the tyre should be removed from the wheel to see whether the inside of the cover is also damaged. If not the dealer may be able to repair the damage.

4　Tyres are best renewed in pairs, putting the new ones on the front and the older ones on the rear. Do not carry a badly worn spare tyre, and remember to keep the spare properly inflated.

5　The Specification to this Chapter gives the recommended grade of tyre to fit the wheels. We suggest you keep to this recommendation. However, if you wish to alter the arrangement there are two golden rules to remember:

　(a)　*Do not fit a radial and a crossply on the same axle. In many countries this is illegal. The braking characteristics are different and you will be inviting an accident*

　(b)　*If you have two radials and two crossplys, the radials MUST be on the rear wheels. This again is bound up with braking characteristics*

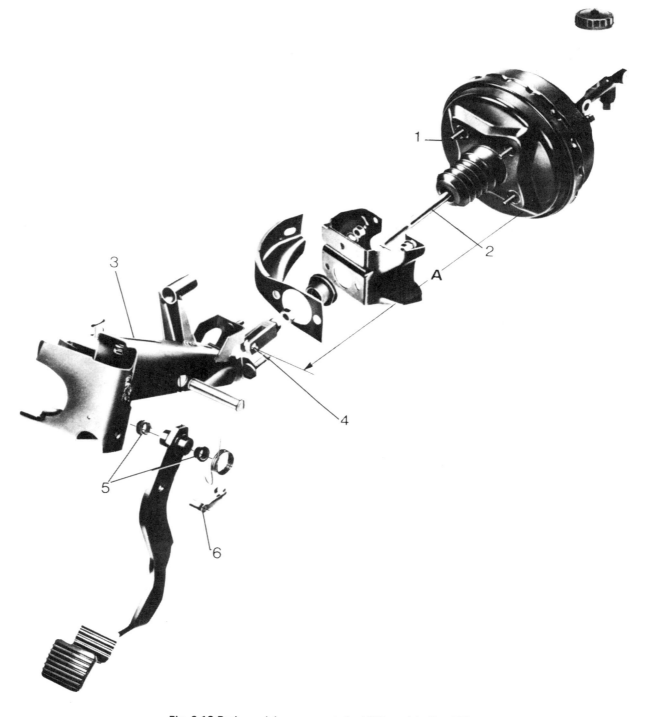

Fig. 6.19 Brake pedal components for LHD models (Sec 26)

| 1 | Servo unit | 3 | Bracket | 5 | Bushes | A = 206 mm (8.1 in) |
| 2 | Pushrod | 4 | Pushrod yoke | 6 | Clevis pin | |

Fig. 6.20 Brake pedal components for RHD models (Sec 26)

1   Steering column and pedal   2   Bushes   4   Right-hand side bell crank   B = 172 mm (6.8 in)
   bracket   3   Adjustable pushrod

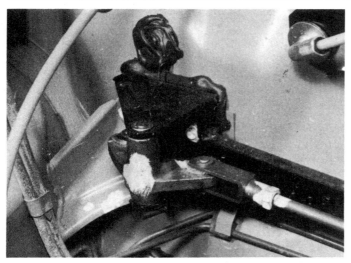

26.5 Brake pedal to servo bell crank linkage (right-hand side) on RHD cars

28 Wheels – inspection and balancing

1   Tyres and wheels should be balanced dynamically when new tyres are fitted. Mark the position of the balance weights and note the size of them. They have been known to fly off. This will affect the steering in the case of the front wheel.

2   If you suspect a wheel is out of balance, jack-up that wheel and spin it gently. Mark the bottom position when it comes to rest. Spin it several times more and note the bottom position each time. If the wheel comes to rest in the same position each time then the wheel and tyre are definitely out of balance and should be taken for balancing. It is best to do this test with the wheel on the rear axle where it may spin more freely.

3   Even though the wheel may be balanced statically (as in paragraph 2) it may still be out of balance dynamically. The only way to check for certain is to have it tested by a specialist.

There are two simple checks to do on the wheel:

(a) *Jack the wheel off the ground and spin the wheel. Place a heavy weight so that it almost touches the rim and watch the clearance between the weight and rim as the wheel spins to see that the rim is not distorted*

(b) *Examine the holes through which the fixing bolts are fitted. If the bolts are allowed to get loose while the car is in service these holes may be elongated. Check the rim for cracks between bolt holes*

29 Fault diagnosis – braking system

Before diagnosing faults in the brake system check that irregularities are not caused by any of the following faults:
       1   *Incorrect mix of radial and crossply tyres*
       2   *Incorrect tyre pressures*
       3   *Wear in the steering mechanism, suspension or shock absorbers*
       4   *Misalignment of the bodyframe*

Symptom	Reason/s
Pedal travels a long way before the brakes operate	Seized adjuster on rear shoes or shoes require adjustment Disc pads worn past limit
Stopping ability poor, pedal pressure firm	Linings, pads, discs or drums worn, contaminated, or wrong type One or more caliper piston or rear wheel hydraulic cylinder seized Loss of vacuum in servo
Car veers to one side when brakes are applied	Brake pads on one side contaminated with oil Hydraulic pistons in calipers seized or sticking Wrong pads fitted
Pedal feels spongy when brakes are applied	Air in the hydraulic system Spring weak in master cylinder
Pedal travels right down with no resistance	Fluid reservoir empty Hydraulic lines fractured Seals in master cylinder head failed
Brakes overheat or bind when car is in motion	Compensating port in master cylinder blocked Reservoir air vent blocked Pushrod requires adjustment Brakes shoes return springs broken or strained Caliper piston seals swollen Unsuitable brake fluid
Brakes judder or chatter and tend to grab	Linings worn Drums out of round Dirt in drums or calipers Discs run-out of true excessive
Brake shoes squeak (rear brake)	Dirt in linings Backplates distorted Brake shoe return springs broken or distorted Brake linings badly worn
Disc pads squeak (front brakes)	Wrong type of pad fitted Pad guide surfaces dirty Spreader spring deficient or broken Pads glazed Lining on pad not secure
Foot pedal must be pressed harder in one position only	Groove in master cylinder pushrod due to wear at sealing cups. Air entering vacuum side of servo
Very high pedal pressure required to operate brakes, linings found to be in good condition and correctly adjusted	No servo assistance Vacuum pump defective

Chapter 7 Electrical system

For modifications, and information applicable to later models, see Supplement at end of manual

Contents

Specifications

System type .... 12 volt, negative earth

Battery rating .... 63 amp-hours

Alternator
Make .... Bosch or Motorola
Maximum output 55 amp/770W
Stator resistance:
    Bosch .... 0·14 to 0·154 ohms
    Motorola .... 0·15 to 0·17 ohms
Rotor resistance:
    Bosch .... 3·4 to 3·7 ohms
    Motorola .... 3·9 to 4·3 ohms
Maximum slip ring ovality .... 0·03 mm (0·001 in)
Brush protrusion:
    New .... 10·0 mm (0·4 in)
    Minimum .... 5·0 mm (0·2 in)
Charging voltage .... 12·5 to 14·5 volts

Starter motor
Type .... Pre-engaged
Output .... 1·1 kW (1·5 hp) or 1·5 kW (2·0 hp)
Brush length – minimum .... 13·0 mm (0·5 in)
Commutator minimum diameter .... 38·5 mm (1·52 in)
Armature endfloat .... 0·1 to 0·15 mm (0·004 to 0·006 in)

Bulbs

	Type No	VW part No (USA)
Sealed beam headlamps	6014	ZVP 118114
Front direction indicator/parking lamps	1034	ZVP 118034
Side marker lamps	1816	ZAP 118816
Rear direction indicator lamps	1073	ZVP 118073
Stop lamps	1073	ZVP 118073
Tail lamps	67	ZVP 118067
Reversing lamps	1073	ZVP 118073

Rear number plate lamp	1816	ZAP 118816
Control illumination	—	N 177512
Instrument illumination	—	N 177512
Indicator and warning lamps	—	N 177512
Interior lamp	211	ZVP 118211

Fuses

For fuse ratings and circuits protected, see Section 33

Torque wrench settings

	kgf m	lbf ft
Starter mounting bracket to transmission	1·6	11
Starter to bracket nuts	0·6	4
Alternator pulley nut	4·0	29
Alternator mounting nuts and bolts	2·0	14
Windscreen wiper arm nut	0·4 to 0·6	3 to 4
Tailgate wiper arm nut	0·4 to 0·6	2·4 to 4·2

1 General description

The major electrical system components comprise a 12 volt battery, of which the negative terminal is earthed, a Bosch or Motorola alternator which is mounted on the left front side of the engine and is driven by a belt from the crankshaft pulley, and a starter motor which is mounted on the right-hand rear of the engine.

The battery supplies current for starting and for the lighting and other electrical circuits. It provides a reserve of electricity when the current consumed by the electrical equipment exceeds that being produced by the alternator. Normally an alternator is able to meet any demand placed upon it.

When fitting electrical accessories to cars with a negative earth system, it is important, if they contain silicone diodes or transistors, that they are connected correctly otherwise serious damage may result to the components concerned. Items such as radios, tape recorders etc, should all be checked for correct polarity.

It is important that both battery leads are disconnected if the battery is to be boost charged. If body repairs are to be carried out using electric arc welding equipment, the alternator must be disconnected otherwise serious damage can be caused to the diodes and regulator. Whenever the battery is disconnected it must always be reconnected with the negative terminal earthed.

2 Battery – removal and refitting

1   The battery is mounted on the left-hand side at the front of the engine compartment. Remove the earth strap (negative) and the positive cable terminal. The battery is held in position by a clamp which fits over a rim at the base. A 13 mm socket spanner preferably with an extension, is needed to undo the clamp nut (photo).

2   Lift the battery out and clean the battery platform. Any sign of corrosion should be neutralized with an alkali solution. Ammonia or ordinary baking powder will do the job. If the corrosion has reached the metal, scrape the paint away to give a bright surface and repaint right away.

3   Refitting is the reverse of removal. Smear the terminals with a little petroleum jelly. **Do not** use grease.

3 Battery – maintenance and inspection

1   Normal weekly battery maintenance consists of checking the electrolyte level of each cell to ensure that the separators are covered by 6 mm ($\frac{1}{4}$ in) of electrolyte. If the level has fallen, top up the battery using distilled water only (photo). Do not overfill. If a battery is over-filled or any electrolyte spilt, immediately wipe away the excess as electrolyte attacks and corrodes any metal it comes into contact with very rapidly.

2   As well as keeping the terminals clean and covered with petroleum jelly, the top of the battery, and especially the top of the cells, should be kept clean and dry. This helps prevent corrosion and ensures that the battery does not become partially discharged by leakage through dampness and dirt.

3   Once every three months remove the battery and inspect the battery securing bolts, the battery clamp plate, tray, and battery leads for corrosion (ie. white fluffy deposits on the metal which are brittle to, touch). If any corrosion is found, clean off the deposits with ammonia and paint over the clean metal with an anti-rust/anti-acid paint.

4   At the same time inspect the battery case for cracks. If a crack is found, clean and plug it with one of the proprietary compounds marketed for this purpose. If leakage through the crack has been

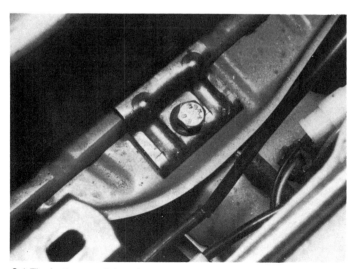

2.1 The battery retaining clamp

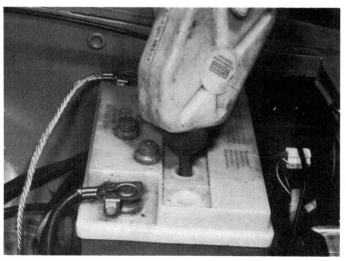

3.1 Topping up the battery with distilled water

excessive then it will be necessary to refill the appropriate cell with fresh electrolyte as detailed later. Cracks are frequently caused to the top of battery cases by pouring in distilled water, in the middle of winter, *after* instead of *before* a run. This gives the water no chance to mix with the electrolyte and so the former freezes and splits the battery case.

5   If topping-up the battery becomes excessive and the case has been inspected for cracks that could cause leakage, but none are found, the battery is being overcharged and the voltage regulator will have to be checked.

6   With the battery on the bench at the three monthly interval check, measure the electrolyte specific gravity with a hydrometer to determine the state of charge and condition of the electrolyte. There should be very little variation between the different cells and if a variation in excess of 0·025 is present it will be due to either:

   (a) *Loss of electrolyte from the battery caused by spillage or a leak, resulting in a drop in the specific gravity of the electrolyte when the deficiency was replenished with distilled water instead of fresh electrolyte*

   (b) *An internal short circuit caused by buckling of the plates or a similar malady pointing to the likelihood of total battery failure in the near future*

7   The specific gravity of the electrolyte for fully charged conditions at the electrolyte temperature indicated, is listed in Table A. The specific gravity of a fully discharged battery at different temperatures of the electrolyte is given in Table B.

8   Specific gravity is measured by drawing up into the body of a hydrometer sufficient electrolyte to allow the indicator to float freely. The level at which the indicator floats indicates the specific gravity.

Table A
Specific gravity – battery fully charged
1·268 at 38°C or 100°F electrolyte temperature
1·272 at 32°C or 90°F electrolyte temperature
1·276 at 27°C or 80°F electrolyte temperature
1·280 at 21°C or 70°F electrolyte temperature
1·284 at 16°C or 60°F electrolyte temperature
1·288 at 10°C or 50°F electrolyte temperature
1.292 at 4°C or 40°F electrolyte temperature
1·296 at −1·5°C or 30°F electrolyte temperature

Table B
Specific gravity – battery fully discharged
1·098 at 38°C or 100°F electrolyte temperature
1·102 at 32°C or 90°F electrolyte temperature
1·106 at 27°C or 80°F electrolyte temperature
1·110 at 21°C or 70°F electrolyte temperature
1·114 at 16°C or 60°F electrolyte temperature
1·118 at 10°C or 50°F electrolyte temperature
1·122 at 4°C or 40°F electrolyte temperature
1·126 at −1·5°C or 30°F electrolyte temperature

4   Battery – charging

1   In winter time when heavy demand is placed upon the battery such as when starting from cold and much electrical equipment is continually in use, it is a good idea occasionally to have the battery fully charged from an external source at the rate of 4 to 6 amps. Always disconnect it from the car electrical circuit when charging.

2   Continue to charge the battery at this rate until no further rise in specific gravity is noted over a four hour period.

3   Alternatively, a trickle charger, charging at the rate of 1·5 amps, can safely be used overnight. Disconnect the battery from the car electrical circuit before charging or you will damage the alternator.

4   Specially rapid 'boost' charges which are claimed to restore the power of the battery in 1 to 2 hours can cause damage to the battery plates through over-heating.

5   While charging the battery note that the temperature of the electrolyte should never exceed 100°F (37.8°C).

6   Make sure that your charging set and battery are set to the same voltage.

5   Battery – electrolyte replenishment

1   If the battery is in a fully charged state and one of the cells maintains a specific gravity reading which is 0·025 or lower than the others, and a check of each cell has been made with a voltage meter to check for short circuits (a four to seven second test should give a steady reading of between 1·2 and 1·8 volts), then it is likely that electrolyte has been lost from the cell with the low reading at some time.

2   Top-up the cell with a solution of 1 part sulphuric acid to 2·5 parts of water, obtainable ready mixed from a service station. If the cell is already fully topped-up draw some electrolyte out of it with a battery hydrometer

3   Continue to top-up the cell with the freshly made electrolyte and to recharge the battery and check the hydrometer readings.

6   Alternator – safety precautions

1   The alternator has a negative earth circuit. Be careful not to connect the battery the wrong way or the alternator will be damaged.

2   **Do not** run the alternator with the output wire disconnected.

3   When welding is being done on the car the battery and the alternator output cable should be disconnected.

4   If the battery is to be charged in the car, both the leads of the battery should be disconnected before the charging leads are connected to the battery.

5   Do not use temporary test connections which may short circuit accidentally. The fuses will not blow, the diodes will burn out.

6   When replacing a burnt out alternator clear the fault which caused the burn out first or a new alternator will be needed a second time.

7   Alternator – drivebelt adjustment

1   The alternator is driven by a belt from the crankshaft pulley. The belt also drives the water pump.

2   The alternator has two lugs on its casing. A bolt threaded through these is mounted in a bracket bolted to the cylinder block (photo). This bolt forms the hinge on which the alternator is mounted. The head of the bolt is a hollow (socket) hexagon which is accessible through a hole in the timing belt cover. This bolt must be slackened before the alternator belt tension may be adjusted.

3   On the bottom of the alternator is yet another lug through which a bolt is fitted to a slotted strap. The strap is hinged on the cylinder block (photo).

4   Thus the alternator may be rotated about the hinge bolt to tighten the drivebelt. The tension in the drivebelt is correct when the belt may be depressed with a thumb as shown in Fig. 7.1 halfway between the crankshaft and alternator pulleys (photo). The bolts should be tightened to hold the alternator in this position.

5   It may be difficult to slacken the socket head bolt. If so, remove the strap, and then remove the bracket with alternator complete. Undo the wiring plug, remove the belt and then take the alternator away. The socket head bolt may then be held in a vice and undone that way.

8   Alternator – testing

1   There is a way of testing the alternator in the car, but it requires a lot of expensive equipment and does not provide much conclusive evidence. Refer to Fig. 7.2. The following are required. A battery cut-out switch, a variable resistance capable of consuming up to 500 watts, an ammeter reading 0–30 amps, a voltmeter reading 0–20v, and a tachometer. A special adaptor is required to enable a tachometer to be used on a Diesel engine. In its absence an estimate of engine speed may suffice.

2   The battery cutout switch is illustrated in Fig. 7.3.

3   Connect up as shown in the diagram in the following manner. Disconnect the battery earth strap and the positive cable. Connect the cut-out switch to the battery positive terminal and then connect the car positive lead to the cut-out switch.

4   So far no interference with the normal circuit. Now arrange an alternative one to take the place of the battery. From the battery cut-out switch connect the variable resistance and ammeter in series to

7.2 The alternator with drivebelt removed, showing the mounting bracket and upper pivot bolt

7.3 Alternator lower mounting and adjusting strap

7.4 The alternator and water pump drivebelt

Fig. 7.1 Checking point for alternator drivebelt tension (Sec 7)

$$a = 10 - 15 \ mm \ (\tfrac{3}{8} - \tfrac{9}{16} \ in)$$

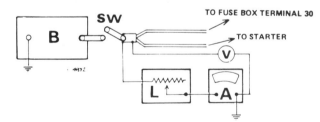

Fig. 7.2 Circuit diagram for testing alternator (Sec 8)

B	Battery	A	Ammeter (0–30 amps)
SW	Battery cut-out switch	V	Voltmeter (0–20 volts)
L	Variable resistance		

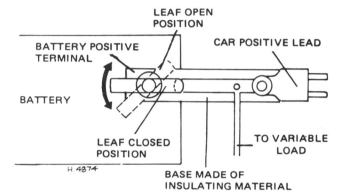

Fig. 7.3 Diagrammatic arrangement of the battery cut-out switch (Sec 8)

the chassis (earth) of the car. Arrange a voltmeter to measure the voltage between the battery cut-out switch and earth. Reconnect the battery earth strap.

5   Start the engine and run it up to 2800 rpm. Set the variable resistance so that the ammeter reading is between 20 and 30 amps. Now open the battery cut-out switch, that is, cut the battery out of the circuit so that the current flows only through the resistance. Alter the resistance to bring the current back to 25 amps. Now read the voltmeter. It should read between 12.5 and 14.5 volts.

6   If the voltmeter reading is outside these limits close the cut-off switch, stop the engine and replace the alternator regulator with a new one (or a borrowed one). Repeat the test. If the desired 12.5 to 14.5 volts is obtained then the old regulator was faulty. If not then the alternator is faulty and must be changed. It seems a lot to do for little reward but the only other way is to take the alternator to an official agent for testing.

9   Alternator (Bosch K1 14V) – overhaul

1   The regulator is fitted into the alternator housing. Remove a small screw and it may be removed. Refer to Fig. 7.4 (photo).

2   Inside it will be seen the two slip ring brushes. These must be free in the guides and protrude at least 5 mm (0·2 in). The new brush protrusion is 10 mm (0·4 in). The brushes may be renewed by unsoldering the leads from the regulator, fitting new brushes and resoldering the leads (Fig. 7.5).

9.1 Alternator wiring plug and regulator locations (Bosch type)

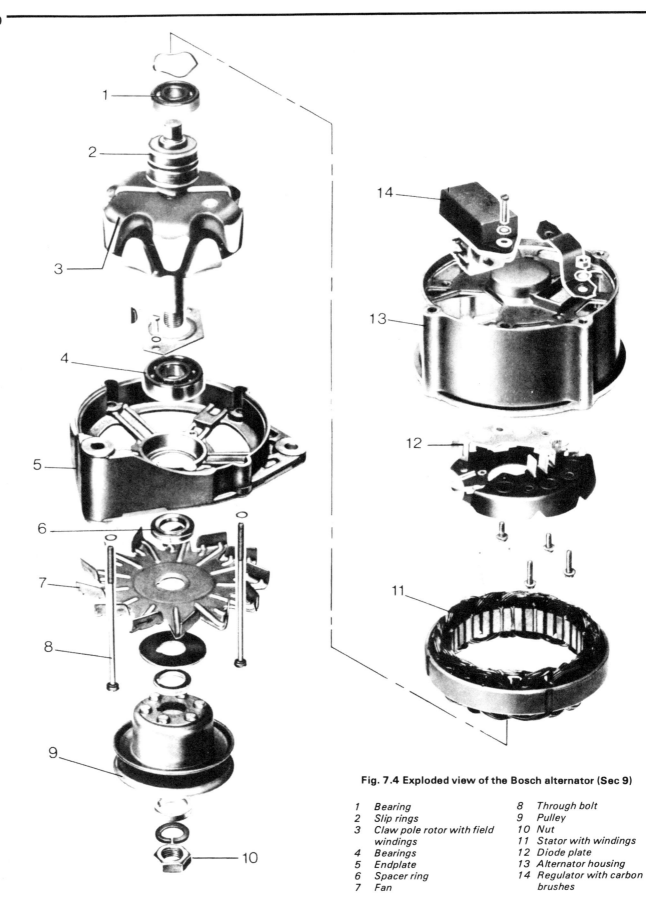

Fig. 7.4 Exploded view of the Bosch alternator (Sec 9)

1	Bearing	8	Through bolt
2	Slip rings	9	Pulley
3	Claw pole rotor with field windings	10	Nut
4	Bearings	11	Stator with windings
5	Endplate	12	Diode plate
6	Spacer ring	13	Alternator housing
7	Fan	14	Regulator with carbon brushes

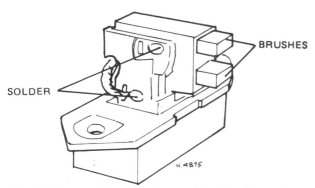

Fig. 7.5 Alternator brush leads are soldered to the regulator (Sec 9)

3   Undo the pulley nut and remove the pulley, the spacer ring, the large washer and the fan. Note which way the fan fits to make assembly easier. There is an arrow showing the direction of rotation.
4   Remove the bracket from the housing which held the wiring plug and if not already removed, take away the regulator.
5   Undo the housing bolts and separate the components. The armature will stay in the endplate and the housing bearing will stay on the shaft. Have a good look at the various components. Clean off all the dust using a soft brush and then wipe clean. Any smell of burnt carbon or signs of overheating must be investigated. Check the slip rings for burning, scoring and ovality. You will have had reason to check the bearings before dismantling, but have a further look now. At this point you must make up your mind whether to do the repair yourself, or whether to take the alternator to a specialist. If you have the tools and the skill, it is possible to renew the bearings, renew the diode carrier complete, clean up the slip rings and to fit a new rotor or stator. It is not possible to repair the winding, renew individual diodes, renew the slip rings or repair the fan.
6   Dealing with the rotor first. The rotor may be removed from the endplate by using a mandrel press. Then take the screws out of the cover over the endplate bearing and press the bearing out of the frame. The slip ring end bearing may be pulled off using an extractor on the inner race. If you pull on the outer race the bearing will be scrapped. Renew the bearings if necessary.
7   The slip rings may be cleaned up with fine glasspaper (not emery paper).
8   Test the rotor electrically. Check the insulation resistance between the slip rings and the shaft. This must be infinity. If it is not there is a short circuit and the armature must be renewed. Get an auto-electrical specialist to confirm your findings first. Check the resistance of the winding. Measure this between slip rings. It should be as specified. If there is an open circuit or high resistance, then again the rotor must be renewed.
9   The stator and the diode carrier are connected by wires. Make a simple circuit diagram so that you know which wire goes to which diode and then unsolder the connections. This is a delicate business as excess heat will destroy the diode and possibly the winding. Grip the

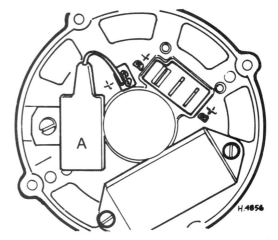

Fig. 7.6 Anti-surge condenser (A) fitted to the alternator (Sec 9)

wire as close as possible to the soldered joint with a pair of long nosed pliers and use as small a soldering iron as possible.
10   The stator winding may now be checked. First check that the insulation is sound. The resistance between the leads and the frame must be infinity. Next measure the resistance of the winding. It should be as specified. A zero reading means a short circuit, and of course a high or infinity reading, an open circuit.
11   The diode carrier may now be checked. Each diode should be checked in turn. Use a test lamp or an ohmmeter. Current must flow only one way; ie, the resistance measured one way must be high and the other way (reverse the leads), low. Keep the current down to 0·8 milliamps and do not allow the diode to heat up. If the resistance both ways is a high one, then the diode is open circuited, a low one, short circuited. If only one diode is defective the whole assembly (diode plate) must be renewed.
12   Reconnect the stator winding to the diode circuit, again be careful not to overheat the diode, and reassemble the stator and diode carrier to the housing.
13   A new diode carrier, or a new stator may be fitted, but be careful to get the correct parts.
14   Assembly is the reverse of dismantling. Be careful to assemble the various washers correctly.
15   It has been found that voltage surge in the electrical system damages the alternator diodes. If this happens when requesting repair of the diode plate ask for and fit a condenser (part no 059 035 271) to prevent this occurring again (Fig. 7.6).

10 Alternator (Motorola type) – overhaul

1   Refer to Fig. 7.7 and 7.8. It will be seen that although the construction is basically the same as the Bosch generator the Motorola differs considerably in detail.

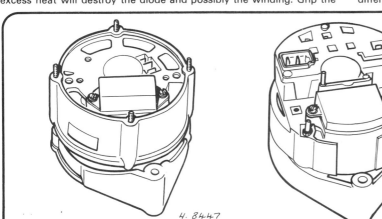

Fig. 7.7 Comparison of Bosch (left) and Motorola (right) alternators (Sec 10)

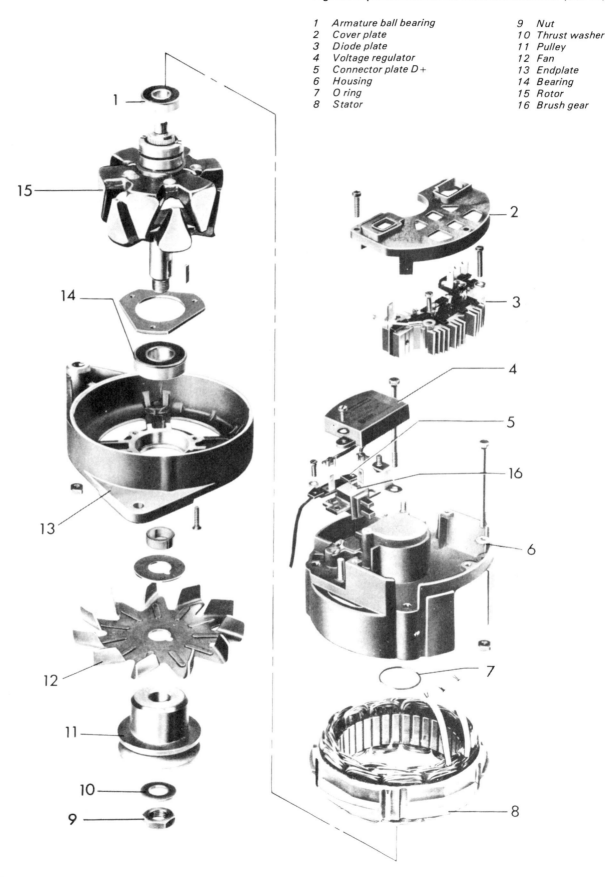

Fig. 7.8 Exploded view of the Motorola alternator (Sec 10)

1 Armature ball bearing
2 Cover plate
3 Diode plate
4 Voltage regulator
5 Connector plate D+
6 Housing
7 O ring
8 Stator

9 Nut
10 Thrust washer
11 Pulley
12 Fan
13 Endplate
14 Bearing
15 Rotor
16 Brush gear

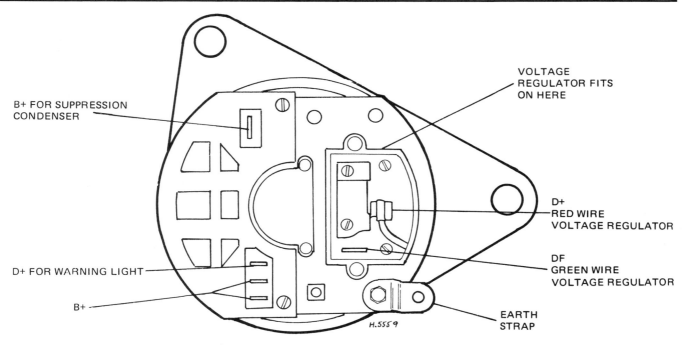

B+ FOR SUPPRESSION CONDENSER

VOLTAGE REGULATOR FITS ON HERE

D+ RED WIRE VOLTAGE REGULATOR

DF GREEN WIRE VOLTAGE REGULATOR

D+ FOR WARNING LIGHT

B+

EARTH STRAP

H.5559

Fig. 7.9 Diagrammatic view of the Motorola alternator endplate with regulator removed (Sec 10)

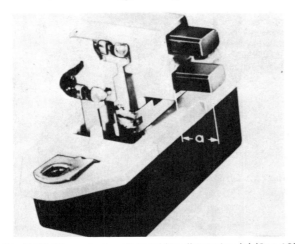

Fig. 7.10 Alternator brush checking dimension (a) (Sec 10)

2   The stator and rotor have the same form as those of the Bosch but the cover, housing and diode plate are of different construction. The earth strap is bolted to the cover, not the hinge as in the case of the Bosch.

3   The same principles apply for overhaul. The rotor should be checked for earth short circuit and continuity. The resistance between slip rings must be as specified, ovality of slip rings must be within limits. Bearings may be drawn off with a puller and renewed if necessary.

4   The stator may be disconnected from the diode plate and the winding tested for open and short circuit. The resistance should be as specified.

5   Once isolated the diode plate may be tested, as in Section 9, and a new one fitted if required. It is not recommended that any attempt be made to renew individual diodes.

6   The routing of the D+ wire inside the cover is important. It must be fitted in the two sets of clips provided or it will interfere with the armature.

7   The voltage regulator connections must be checked. The green wire goes to DF and the red wire to D+ (see Fig. 7.9).

8   The connections on the cover must be checked carefully. A diagram is given for information.

11 Starter motor – testing on engine

1   If the starter motor fails to operate then check the condition of the battery by turning on the headlamps. If they glow brightly for several seconds and then gradually dim, the battery is in an uncharged condition.

2   If the headlamps continue to glow brightly and it is obvious that the battery is in good condition, then check the tightness of the earth lead from the battery terminal to its connection on the body frame particularly, and the other battery wiring. Check the tightness of the connections at the rear of the solenoid. Check the wiring with a voltmeter for breaks or short circuits.

3   If the wiring is in order check the starter motor for continuity using a voltmeter.

4   If the starter motor drive fails to release when the ignition key is released from the start position (indicated by a continuous whirring noise) then the solenoid spring is broken or the drive teeth are jammed in the ring gear. Remove the starter motor for examination.

12 Starter motor – removal and refitting

1   Disconnect the earth strap from the battery negative terminal.

2   Note the routing of the starter motor cables. Disconnect the heavy cable from the battery and pull the leads off the two solenoid terminals (photos).

3   Undo and remove the bolts securing the starter motor to the bellhousing and withdraw the starter motor from the housing.

4   To refit, insert the starter into the transmission bellhousing and locate the armature shaft in the bush in the housing.

5   Fit the starter motor securing bolts and tighten them to the specified torque.

6   Reconnect the wiring to the starter solenoid. Route the battery cable as noted before removal.

13 Starter motor – overhaul

1   Clean the exterior of the starter motor before starting to dismantle it. Refer to Fig. 7.13.

2   Remove the connector strip terminal nut (D) and from the other end remove the two bolts holding the solenoid to the mounting bracket. Now lift the solenoid pull rod so that it is clear of the operating lever and remove the solenoid.

12.2A Battery cable location on the starter solenoid

12.2B Starter motor with leads removed

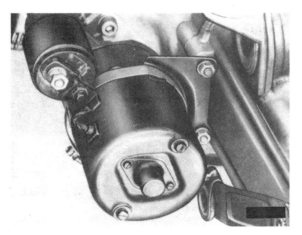

Fig. 7.11 Starter motor mountings (typical) (Sec 12)

Fig. 7.12 Typical starter motor supply cable position
(Sec 12)

3   At the front end of the starter is a cap held by two screws. Remove this and under it there is a shaft with a circlip and bush. Remove the clip.

4   Now remove the through bolts and remove the cover.

5   The brush gear is now visible. Lift the brushes out of the holder and remove the brush holder. The starter body holding the field coils may now be separated from the endplate. This will leave the armature still in the mounting bracket.

6   To remove the mounting bracket from the drive end of the shaft, first push back the stop ring with a suitable tube so that the circlip underneath may be released from its groove. It is not possible to remove the mounting bracket and pinion from the shaft.

7   Finally remove the operating lever pin from the mounting bracket and remove the pinion assembly.

8   Clean and examine the pinion, shaft and lever and inspect for wear. If possible run the armature between centres in a lathe and check that the shaft is not bent. Check the fit of the drive pinion on the shaft. Check that the pinion will revolve in one direction only (one way clutch) and that the teeth are not chipped.

9   Examine the commutator. Clean off the carbon with a rag soaked in petrol. Minor scoring may be removed with fine glass paper. Deep scoring must be removed by machining in a lathe. Commutator copper is harder than the commercial grade, and requires the lathe tool to be ground differently. Unless you have had instruction on machining commutators we suggest that the skimming and under-cutting be left to the expert. The minimum diameter for the commutator is given in the Specifications.

10   Test the armature electrically. Check the insulation between the armature winding and the shaft. To do this connect the negative terminal of the ohmmeter to the shaft and place the positive probe on each commutator segment in turn.

11   Burning on the commutator is usually a sign of an open circuited winding. If you have access to a 'growler' have the armature checked for short circuits.

12   Inspect the field windings for signs of abrasion or stiff and damaged insulation, particularly where the leads leave the coil. Check the field coil for short circuit to the pole piece and for open circuits. Renew if necessary.

13   The brushes must be at least of the specified length and must slide easily in the holder. There are two schools of thought about brush renewal. One says that the entire field coil must be replaced or the brush plate with the armature current brushes. The VW/Audi method is somewhat different.

14   Isolate the brushes, pull them out of the holders and hold them away from the winding. Crush the old brush with a powerful pair of pliers until the lead is free from the brush. Clean the end of the lead and prepare it for soldering. The new brush, obtainable from official agents, is drilled and has a tinned insert. Push the end of the lead into the drilling and splay it out, then using silver solder, solder the brush to the lead.

15   If it is your first attempt at soldering it could be better to get expert help. Use a large soldering iron (250 watts plus), do not let any of the solder creep along the wire and file off any surplus. Do not let the lead get too hot, or damage will occur to the field coils. Use a flat pair of

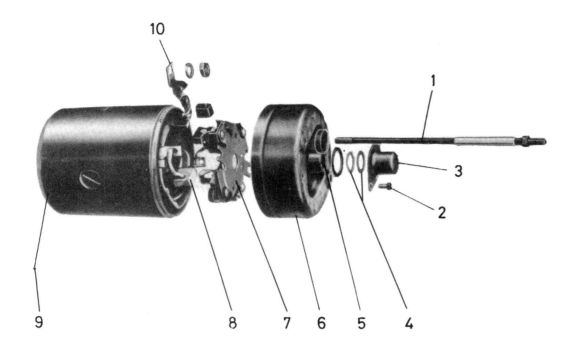

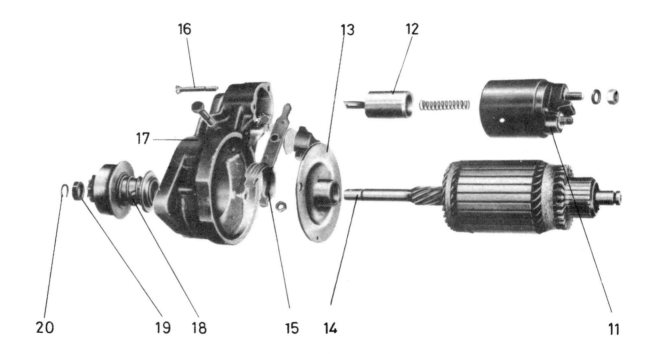

Fig. 7.13 Exploded view of the starter motor (Sec 13)

1 Housing screw (through
   bolt)
2 End cap screw
3 End cap
4 Shims
5 Bush

6 Housing
7 Brush plate
8 Brushes
9 Stator
10 Terminal tag for solenoid

11 Solenoid
12 Solenoid plunger
13 Support bearing
14 Armature
15 Stirrup

16 Solenoid switch screw
17 Mounting bracket
18 Drive pinion
19 Stop ring
20 Circlip

pliers to hold the lead as close to the brush as possible while soldering. These will act as a a heat sink and will also stop the solder getting in the core of the lead.

16 One final word about brushes. Check that you can get new ones before crushing the old ones.

17 Assembly is the reverse of dismantling. Fit the drive pinion and operating lever to the mounting bracket. Fit the drive pinion to the armature shaft. Fit a new lock ring (circlip) and fit the stop ring (groove towards the outside) over the lock ring. Check that the stop ring will revolve freely on the shaft. It fits on the armature shaft outside the pinion.

18 Fit the starter body over the armature to the mounting bracket. See that the tongue on the body fits in the cut-out of the mounting bracket and that the body seats properly on the rubber seating. Smear a little joint compound round the joint before assembly.

19 Fit the two washers onto the armature shaft and install the brush holder over the commutator. In order to get the holder in place with the brushes correctly assembled cut two lengths of wire and bend them to hold up the brush springs while the brushes are fitted over the commutator (photos). Once the four brushes are in place the wires may be withdrawn.

20 Wipe the end of the shaft and oil it, then fit the endcover onto the housing and install the through-bolts. Again seal the joint, and seal the ends of the through-bolts. Now refit the shims and the circlips. If a new armature has been fitted the endplay must be checked. It should be

13.19A Using two clips to hold the brush spring on assembly

13.19B The wire clip (arrowed) fits under the brush spring so that the brush may be lifted easily to enter the plate over the commutator

within the specified limits and is adjusted by fitting appropriate shims.

21 Check that the solenoid lead grommet is in place and refit the solenoid. Use a sealing compound on the joint faces, move the pinion to bring the operation lever to the opening and reconnect pullrod. Seat the solenoid firmly on the mounting bracket in the sealing compound and install the bolts. Reconnect the wire to the starter body (D).

22 The starter may now be refitted to the car.

23 The pinion end of the shaft fits into a bearing in the clutch housing and this can be checked only when the transmission is dismantled. The commutator end of the shaft fits into a bearing bush in the endplate. The old bush may be pressed out if necessary and a new one pressed in. The endplate should be dipped into hot oil for five minutes before the bush is pressed in to give a shrink fit. Grease the bush with multi-purpose grease before fitting the shaft.

14 Headlamps – general

The fixing and beam adjustment for the Golf/Rabbit is generally the same. The main differences are in the type of bulb and method of renewal. The Golf is fitted with renewable bulbs while the Rabbit has sealed beam units.

15 Headlamps and bulbs (Golf) – removal and refitting

1 To remove the bulb, pull off the connector and cover (photo).

2 Press the retaining ring in slightly, turn it anti-clockwise to release it and then lift away the ring.

3 Lift the bulb out of the reflector (photo).

4 Fit a new bulb in the reflector, ensuring that the lug on the bulb plate is located in the recess at the bottom of the reflector.

5 Fit the retaining ring in position, press it in and turn it clockwise to lock in position.

6 Refit the cover and the electrical connector. Ensure that the cover seats correctly on the reflector or water will find its way into the lamp and a new reflector will be required.

7 To remove the reflector it is necessary first to remove the grille by undoing the securing clips and screws. The screws securing the headlamp (not the beam adjusting screws, see Fig. 7.16) can now be removed and the lamp drawn out from the front (photos). The frame and reflector are held together by clamps which must be turned to separate the parts. It is better to renew them as an assembly. If the lamp assembly is renewed adjust the headlamp beam adjustment, refer to Section 23.

16 Headlamp sealed beam unit (Rabbit) – removal and refitting

1 Undo the front grille securing clips and screws and remove the grille.

2 Remove the three securing screws and lift away the sealed beam unit retaining ring (do not alter the setting of the two headlamp beam adjusting screws).

3 Pull the sealed beam unit forward out of the support ring and disconnect the wiring plug from the back of the unit.

4 Connect the plug to a new unit then fit the unit in the support ring ensuring that the three glass lugs are correctly located in the support ring.

5 Fit the retaining ring and securing screws. Refit the front grille.

6 If the headlamp beam adjusting screws are disturbed, the headlamp beam will have to be re-adjusted, refer to Section 23.

17 Front parking light – bulb renewal

1 The parking light on Golf models is inside the headlamp and attached to the headlamp wiring, see Fig. 7.14 (photo). On Rabbit models the parking light bulb is located in the front turn signal lamp.

2 Turn the bulb to the left and pull it out.

3 Fit the new bulb in the holder and turn it to the right.

15.1 Removing the headlamp rear cover

15.3 Removing the headlamp bulb

15.7A Removing the headlamp surround ...

15.7B ... lamp retaining screw ...

15.7C ... and headlamp complete

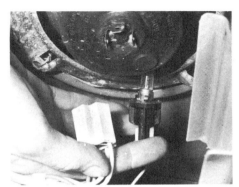
17.1 Removing the parking light bulb

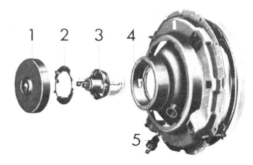

Fig. 7.14 Headlamp and parking light components (Sec 17)

1 Cover
2 Retaining ring
3 Headlamp bulb
4 Reflector
5 Parking light bulb

18 Front turn signal lamp – bulb renewal

1 Remove the two screws securing the lens to the bumper bar (photo). The bulb can now be pressed into the holder, turned to the left and removed.
2 Fit the new bulb. When refitting the lens ensure that the gasket is in good condition and seated correctly. Do not overtighten the lens securing screws or the lens may crack.

19 Light cluster (rear) – bulb renewal

1 Open the tailgate and remove the plastic cover by pressing the lugs outwards (photo).

2 Remove the bulb holder and extract the bulbs as necessary by pressing them in and turning them anti-clockwise.
3 If required, the lens can be removed by unscrewing the retaining nuts (photos).
4 Refitting is a reversal of removal.

20 Interior light – bulb renewal

1 Using a wide bladed screwdriver, prise the lamp from the roof, taking care not to damage the headlining (photo).
2 Remove the festoon type bulb from the spring contacts.
3 Fit the new bulb. Refit the lamp by inserting the switch end first and pressing the remaining end in until the spring clip is fully engaged.

21 Number plate light – bulb renewal

1 Remove the two screws and lift off the lens and cover (photo).
2 Depress the bulb, turn it anti-clockwise, and remove it.
3 Fit the new bulb and refit the lens, taking care not to overtighten the retaining screws.

22 Side markers (USA) – bulb renewal

1 Remove the two retaining screws and pull the unit away from the front wing to expose the rubber cover.
2 Pull off the cover, press the lugs outward, and remove the bulb holder and bulb.
3 Refitting is a reversal of removal.

18.1 Removing the front turn signal lens

19.1 Removing the interior cover from the rear light cluster

19.3A Removing the rear light cluster lens ...

19.3B ... and bulbholder

20.1 The interior lamp and bulb

21.1 Removing the number plate lamp lens and cover

Fig. 7.15 Side marker lens retaining screws (arrowed) (Sec 22)

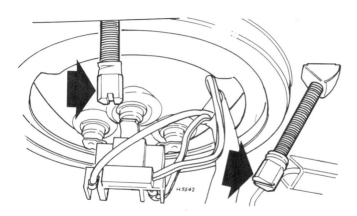

Fig. 7.16 Beam adjustment screws (arrowed) on the Rabbit (Sec 23)

23 Headlamps – beam adjustment

1   Refer to Fig. 7.16 and note the location of the two adjusting screws.
2   It is recommended that the headlamp beams are adjusted by your dealer or service staion. In an emergency use the following procedure.
3   Having ascertained how the beam is to be aimed on dip, whether it must swing to the right or left when dipped, set the car on level ground about 20 feet (6 metres) from a vertical wall or door. The vehicle tyre pressures should be correct and there should be the equivalent of the driver's weight in the driving seat.
4   Mark with relation to the centre-line of the car and the height of the lamps from the ground, the equivalent positions of the lamps on the wall. Using this as a datum, mark the area to which the lights should be directed on dipped beam. Cover one light and switch on. Using the adjusting screws direct the beam to the area required. Cover that light and repeat with the other one. When the beams are correctly focussed on dip the main beams will automatically be correct.

24 Direction indicators and emergency flashers – general

1   The direction indicators are controlled by the left-hand column switch.
2   A switch on the facia board operates all four flashers simultaneously and although the direction indicators will not work when the ignition is switched off the emergency switch over-rides this and the flasher signals continue to operate.
3   All the circuits are routed through the relay on the console and its fuse.
4   If the indicators do not function correctly, a series of tests may be done to find which part of the circuit is at fault.
5   The most common fault is in the flasher lamps, defective bulbs, and dirty or corroded contacts. Check these first, then test the emergency switch. Remove it from the circuit and check its operation. If the switch is in good order refit it and again turn on the emergency

lights. If nothing happens then the relay is not functioning properly and it should be renewed. If the lights function on emergency but not on operation of the column switch then the wiring and column switch are suspect (see Section 25).

25 Steering column switches – removal and refitting

1 There are four switches on the steering column:

(a) *The horn switch pad in the centre of the steering wheel*
(b) *The turn signal/headlight dip and flasher lever on the left of the column*
(c) *The windscreen wiper/washer control lever on the right of the column which, on later models, incorporates the rear window wash/wipe control*
(d) *The steering lock/starter switch on the lower right of the column (see Section 26)*

2 Before commencing dismantling remove the earth strap from the battery.

3 To remove the horn pad simply pull it upwards. It takes a very strong pull, but it does come off that way. Remove the wire connection. Undo the nut and remove the steering wheel.

4 Two crosshead screws hold the two halves of the cover for the column switches together. Remove these and take the lower half of the cover away. The various components of the switches are now visible.

5 From below the switch pull out the three multipin plugs. There is one for each lever switch and one for the starter switch. They will go back only one way so there is no need to mark them. Unscrew the retaining screws which hold the wiper/turn signal switch assemblies in place, and lift the complete switch away.

6 The action of the lever switches may now be tested. If the switch does not move decisively and there is slackness in the linkage, then the switch must be renewed.

7 Assembly is the reverse of removal. When refitting the steering

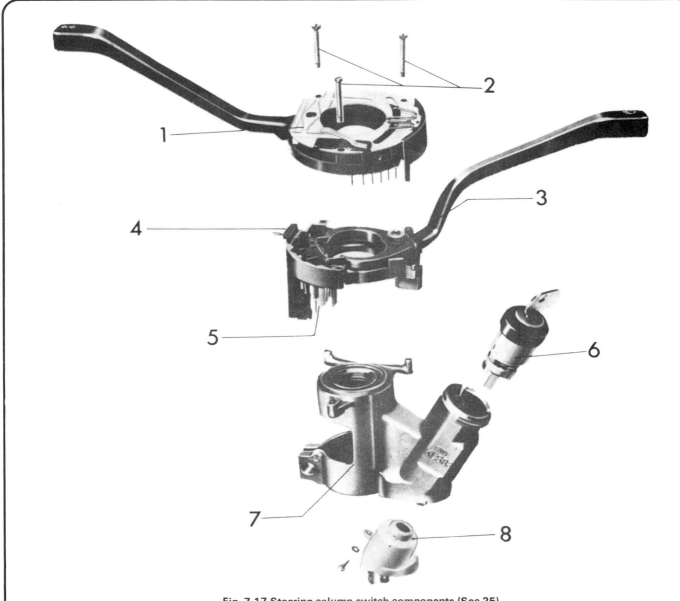

Fig. 7.17 Steering column switch components (Sec 25)

1 Turn signal switch	3 Windscreen wiper switch	5 Headlight dip and flasher switch	6 Lock cylinder	8 Ignition/starter switch
2 Retaining screws	4 Wedge		7 Steering lock housing	

wheel be careful to align the cancelling lug in the right place or the switch levers will be damaged. The roadwheels should be in the straight ahead position, the turn signal switch in the neutral position and the lug to the right.

26 Ignition and steering lock switch – removal and refitting

1   Disconnect the battery negative terminal.
2   Remove the steering wheel and switches as described in Section 25.
3   On early Rabbit models pull out the locking plate with a pair of pliers, insert and turn the ignition key clockwise approximately one thickness of the key, then withdraw the lock and key.
4   On all other models it is necessary to drill a 3·0 mm (0·11 in) diameter hole in the lock housing at the location shown in Fig. 7.18. Do not drill intothe lock cylinder. Insert a length of stout wire through the hole and depress the spring tensioned retaining peg; the cylinder can now be removed with the ignition key.
5   If the lock cylinder is faulty it must be renewed.
6   To remove the switch, first withdraw the switch housing from the top of the steering column. Unscrew the retaining screw and remove the switch.
7   Refitting is a reversal of removal, but with the early type, peen the locking plate into position with a hammer.

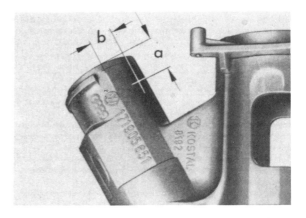

Fig. 7.18 Drilling position when removing the ignition/starter switch (Sec 26)

$a = 12.0$ mm (0.472 in)
$b = 10.0$ mm (0.394 in)

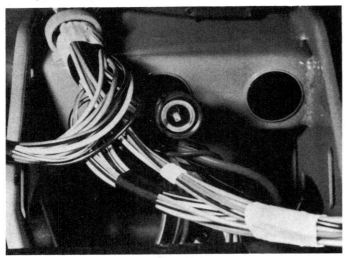

27.5 Speedometer cable location with instrument panel removed

27.7A Instrument panel retaining screw location on RHD cars with glovebox and grille removed

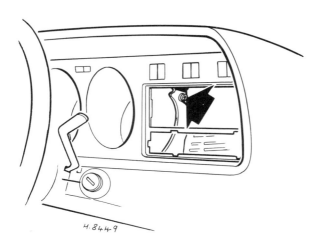

Fig. 7.19 Instrument panel retaining screw (arrowed) on LH drive cars (Sec 27)

27.7B Removing the instrument panel and switches

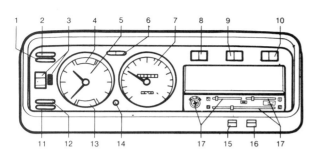

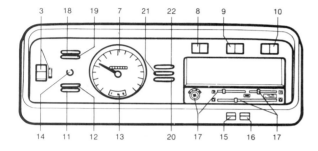

28.1 Rear view of the instrument panel

Fig. 7.20 The two types of instrument panel (Sec 27)

1 Oil pressure warning lamp	13 Fuel gauge
2 Glow plug warning lamp	14 Vacant for accessory
3 Light switch	15 Vacant for accessory
4 Temperature gauge	16 Vacant for accessory
5 Clock	17 Heater and vent levers, fan
6 Main beam, turn signal,	switch
alternator warning lamps	18 Turn signal warning lamp
7 Speedometer	19 Main beam warning lamp
8 Heated rear window switch	20 Glow plug warning lamp
9 Hazard light switch	21 Alternator and coolant
10 Fog light switch	temperature warning lamps
11 Brake warning lamp	22 Oil pressure warning lamp
12 Vacant for accessory	

27 Instrument panel – removal and refitting

1 Disconnect the battery negative terminal.
2 Remove the steering wheel. This is not essential but will facilitate subsequent operations.
3 Pull off the heater control knobs and remove the trim plate.
4 Prise off the radio control knobs, then reach under the radio and depress the two side clips. Ease the radio out from the front of the facia and disconnect the earth and supply wires, speaker plug, and aerial plug.
5 Reach up behind the instrument panel and disconnect the speedometer cable (photo).
6 Remove the glovebox (if fitted).
7 Remove the retaining screw from the rear of the instrument panel (Fig. 7.19) and withdraw the assembly from the facia (photos).
8 Reference to Fig. 7.20 will show that there are two types of instrument panel and therefore the wiring arrangement will depend on the type fitted. The switches can be removed by opening the dovetails and pulling them out; there is no need to disconnect the wires.
9 With the instrument panel removed, the instruments, warning bulbs, and printed circuit can be dismantled from the casing.
10 Refitting is a reversal of removal.

28 Instrument panel – inspection and testing

1 The printed circuit should be examined, preferably using a magnifying glass. Any defects will show up as breaks or short circuits in

Fig. 7.21 Instrument panel 12 point multiplug terminals (Sec 28)

1 Turn signal warning lamp	7 Fuel gauge sender
2 Main beam warning lamp	8 Temperature gauge sender
3 Clock	9 Alternator warning lamp
4 Earth	10 Oil pressure warning lamp
5 Instrument lighting	11 Glow plug lamp
6 Live (+) wire	12 Vacant

which case the printed circuit must be renewed (photo).
2 The various circuits can be tested for continuity using a test lamp and leads or a meter. Figs. 7.21 and 7.23 show the multiplug connection terminals and the applicable circuits.

29 Switches (lighting) – removal, testing and refitting

1 Disconnect the battery negative terminal.
2 Remove the instrument panel as described in Section 27.
3 Move up the dovetail clips and withdraw the switch from the panel (photo).
4 The switches cannot be repaired and if one is proved faulty after testing with a meter or test lamp, it must be renewed.
5 Refitting is a reversal of removal.

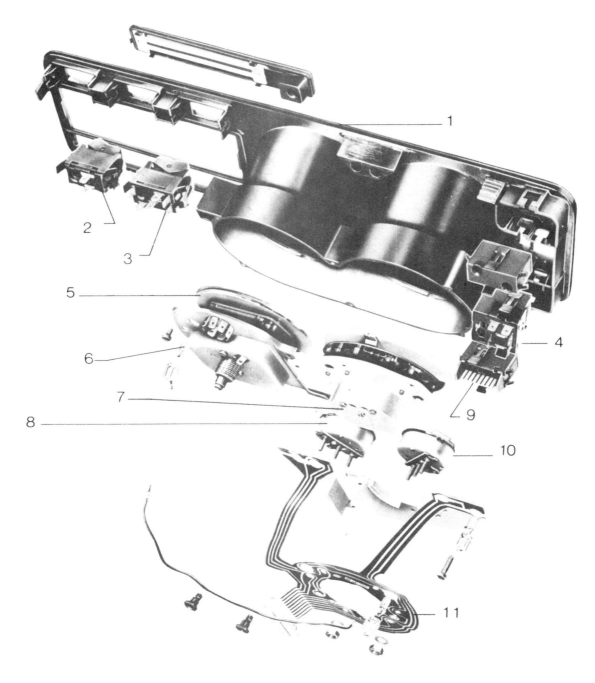

Fig. 7.22 Instrument panel components (Sec 28)

1 Surround
2 Heated rear window switch
3 Hazard flasher switch
4 Light switch
5 Speedometer

6 Bulb
7 Clock (illustration shows tachometer)
8 Fuel gauge

9 Dual brake circuit warning light and seat belt light
10 Coolant temperature gauge
11 Printed circuit

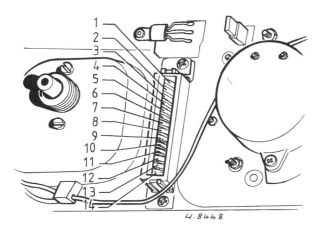

Fig. 7.23 Instrument panel 14 point multiplug terminal (Sec 28)

1	Vacant
2	Turn signal warning lamp
3	Main beam warning lamp
4	Clock
5	Earth
6	Instrument lighting
7	Live (+) wire
8	Fuel gauge sender

9	Coolant temperature or warning switch
10	Alternator warning lamp
11	Oil pressure warning lamp
12	Glow plug warning lamp
13	Vacant
14	Vacant

29.3 Switches, showing the locating lugs

30 Temperature gauge – testing

1　If the gauge is giving innaccurate readings, first test the voltage stabilizer for correct output.

2　If the gauge is receiving the correct voltage from the stabilizer but is still innaccurate, then either the gauge or the sender is faulty, or alternatively the wiring may have a fault.

3　A quick test is to pull the wire off the sender and using a 12v 6 watt bulb as a series resistance and with the ignition switched on touch the bulb centre pin to earth momentarily. Have someone watch the gauge. It should move right across the scale. It is essential to have the bulb in series with the wire or you may damage the gauge. If there is no reading then press a bit harder with your contact. Still no reading, then either the wiring or the gauge are at fault. Check the fuse, if there is one in the circuit for your vehicle. If there is still no reading then the gauge must be extracted for testing separately.

4　If there is a reading then the gauge is not at fault but the sender is suspect. To test the gauge for accuracy disconnect the sender and fit resistances in its place. Ordinary radio resistances will do. A 47 ohm resistance should indicate that the engine is hot. Replace this with a 270 ohm resistor and the needle should register 'cold'. If the gauge does not pass this test then it is not accurate and should be renewed. If the gauge passes the test, but still refuses to indicate that the engine is getting warm, then the sender unit should be renewed.

31 Fuel gauge and sender unit – testing

1　Read paragraph 1 of Section 30 before proceeding.

2　The handbook states that when the needle of the fuel gauge reaches the reserve mark there is about one gallon of fuel in the tank. It is important therefore that the gauge is accurate.

3　There is a very good way of checking the reserve mark. Buy one gallon of fuel, empty the fuel tank, put in the one gallon and check the reading against the reserve mark. If it is possible to arrange to fill the tank from empty to full, one gallon at a time, a piece of thin cardboard fitted to the face of the gauge glass may be marked at each gallon and you will know exactly how much fuel is in the tank at all times.

4　If the gauge is not reading then a simple test is required. A 47 ohm resistor and a 0–12v meter are needed. Underneath the car at the rear on the right-hand side of the fuel tank is the combined fuel hose and fuel gauge wires entry. Switch on the ignition and measure the voltage across the terminals. If there is no voltage pull off the terminal of the wire to the gauge and check the voltage between that terminal and earth. If there is now a reading the sender unit is at fault. Check that the other wire is in fact connected securely to earth. If there is still no reading then either the wiring or the gauge is faulty. Check that all the fuses are in order. To decide whether the gauge or the wiring is at fault the instrument panel must be removed.

5　If the sender unit is faulty then the tank must be drained. Remove the hose clip and pull off the hose. Disconnect the battery earth strap and disconnect the wires from the sender unit. Turn the locking plate until the unit can be withdrawn from the tank, and then remove the fuel pipe and sender unit. There is little that can be done to the sender unit, it is best to take it to an expert, who may be able to repair it or supply a new one.

6　To test the accuracy of the gauge, if it is working, disconnect the gauge wires at the sender unit and insert a 47 ohm resistance between them. Switch on the ignition and the gauge should register full. Substitute a 100 ohm and then a 220 ohm resistor in turn and the needle should be on the second mark and then the reserve mark respectively.

32 Fuse and relay panel – removal and refitting

1　Disconnect the battery negative terminal.

2　Unscrew the crosshead retaining screws and withdraw the panel to expose the multiplug connectors.

3　Note the location of the wiring, then disconnect it and remove the panel.

4　Figs. 7.24 and 7.25 show the various terminals on the panel which will be of assistance when tracing a fault.

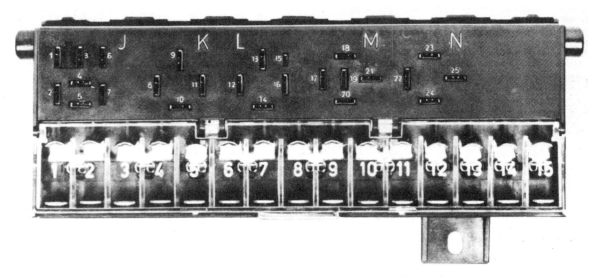

Fig. 7.24 Front view of the fuse and relay panel (Sec 32)

Socket	Contact	Relay terminal	Internal connections	Socket	Contact	Relay terminal	Internal connections
J – dipswitch relay	1	–	J2	M – intermittent wiper washer switch relay	17	15	Bridge for wiper motor on cars without intermittent switch
	2	56	G10, D17				
	3	–	J5, fuses S1 and S2		18	31	
	4	56A	G8, fuses S3 and S4		19	53S	
	5	56B	J3		20	S1	
	6	–	H1 to H7 (terminal 30)		21	53M	
	7	S	E8				
K – heated rear window relay	8	86	D10, L15, M18, N23 (terminal 31)	N – hazard flasher relay	22	49A	D1, E3
	9	30	H1 to H7 (terminal 30)		23	31	D10, L15, K8, M18 (terminal 31)
	10	87	Fuse S5				
	11	85	D7		24	+49	D12
L – Electric fuel pump 1977 on (spark ignition engines only)	12	86	A3		25	C	D6
	13	30	H1 to H7 (terminal 30)				
	14	87	A8				
	15	31	D10, K8, M18, N23 (terminal 31)				
	16	15	Fuses S8 and S9				

33 Fuses and relays – general

1   The fuses are located in the fusebox beneath the left-hand side of the dashpanel. Access to them is gained by lifting the transparent cover (photo).
2   The function of each fuse is given in the following table; the fuse number is as given on the fusebox lid.

Fuse	Amps	Circuit
1	8	Low beam, left
2	8	Low beam, right
3	8	High beam, left and warning light
4	8	High beam, right
5	16	Heated rear window
6	8	Stop lights, hazard flasher system
7	8	Interior light, cigarette lighter, radio
8	8	Turn signals and warning light
9	16	Reversing lights, horn, fuel cut-off valve
10	8	Fresh air fan
11	8	Wipers, washer pump intermittent relay
12	8	Number plate lights
13	8	Right parking light, tail light, and side marker (USA)
14	8	Left parking light, tail light, and side marker (USA)
15	16	Radiator cooling fan

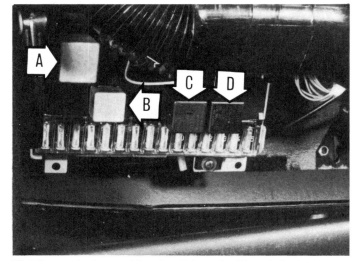

33.1 Fuse and relay panel location. Relays: A – Dip switch relay, B – Heated rear window, C – Intermittent wiper/washer, D – Hazard warning

Fig. 7.25 Rear view of the fuse and relay panel (Sec 32)

A – Front wiring harness socket
B – Test diagnosis socket (early models), vacant (late models)
C – Front wiring harness socket
D – Dashboard wiring harness socket
E – Dashboard wiring harness socket
F – Rear wiring harness socket
G1 – to G6 via fuse S15
G2 – to E7 and M20
G3 – to ignition/starter switch terminal 15

G4 – to fuse S12
G5 – to alternator terminal D+
G6 – to G1 via fuse S15
G7 – to ignition/starter switch terminal X
G8 – to headlight dip relay terminal 56A
G9 – to oil pressure switch
G10 – to light switch terminal 56
H1 to H7 – terminal 30

Additional fuses of 8 amp rating are also located separately above the main fusebox for the rear window wiper/wash system and fog lights (where fitted).

3   To remove a fuse, depress the upper contact spring and lift the fuse out.

4   Always renew a fuse with one of similar rating, and never renew it more than once without finding the source of the trouble.

5   Fit the fuse with the metal strip facing outward. Check that the contacts are free of any corrosion and clean them up with emery tape if necessary.

6   The 50 amp glow plug fuse is contained in a separate fusebox located in the engine compartment on the bulkhead (photo).

7   Relays are plugged into the upper part of the fuse panel and their functions are identified in the photograph 33.1.

33.6 The glow plug fuse

---

34 Horn – testing, removal, and refitting

1   The horn is located on the front crossmember in front of the engine (photo).

2   If the horn fails to operate, first check that the relevant fuse is intact and is firmly fitted between the contacts.

3   Using a test lamp and leads or a voltmeter, check that current is reaching the horn from the supply wire (usually yellow and black) with the ignition switched on. If not, the supply wire is faulty.

4   If current is reaching the supply wire, use the same method to check that current is reaching the horn output terminal. If not, the horn is faulty. If it is, but the horn fails to operate, have an assistant operate the horn push and turn the adjusting screw (if fitted) until the horn operates satisfactorily.

5   If the horn still fails to operate after making the previous tests, connect a wire between the output terminal and earth. If the horn now operates, a fault exists in the horn push or wiring. Use the same method as previously described to trace the fault.

6   To remove the horn, first disconnect the battery negative terminal.

7   Disconnect the horn input and output wires.

8   Unbolt the horn from the mounting bracket.

9   Refitting is a reversal of removal.

34.1 Location of the horn

35.6 Speedometer cable retaining clamp location on the transmission (arrowed)

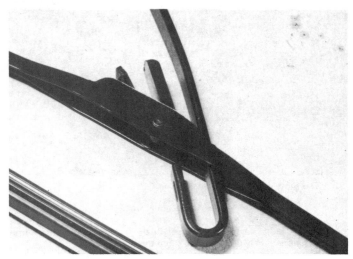

37.1 Removing a wiper blade from the arm

35 Speedometer and speedometer drive – removal and refitting

1   Disconnect the battery negative terminal.
2   Remove the instrument panel as described in Section 27.
3   Remove the voltage stabilizer (where fitted).
4   Unscrew the two retaining screws and remove the speedometer head from the rear of the instrument panel.
5   Refitting is a reversal of removal, but make sure that the cardboard washers are located beneath the retaining screw heads. If these are left out, damage will occur due to earthing; replacements can be made out of ordinary cardboard if necessary.
6   To remove the speedometer cable, remove the retaining screw at the transmission end and withdraw the drivegear (photo).
7   With the cable disconnected from the speedometer head pull it through the grommet hole and remove the cable from the car.
8   Refitting is a reversal of removal, but make sure that the cable is positioned with the minimum amount of curving. The cable must be attached to the plastic retainer near the bulkhead in order to prevent it touching the clutch cable. Do not grease the cable at the head end as this may cause the needle to stick.

36 Radio – fitting guidelines

1   The fitting of a radio to the Golf presents no problems. It may be fitted to the dashboard, or centre console. A centre console with provision for storing small articles may be purchased and the radio installed in that.
2   VW provide a choice of radios to suit the taste and pocket. Pushbutton or manual control is available, and a radio with a built-in cassette tape player, speakers, a lockable aerial and suppression kits is also supplied, with full fitting instructions.
3   There does not seem to be any point in going elsewhere as fitting a set which is not tailored to suit will mean cutting the dashboard about and building separate supports which will get in the way of things in an already crowded space.
4   The console fitting for the radio is particularly attractive as the storage space is somewhat limited, and putting the radio in the dashboard involves pressing out the small glovebox and discarding it.
5   It is important to get advice from the local experts as to the best set for your requirements. VHF gives patchy reception in built-up or hilly areas and if you do a lot of long distance work, a set which functions well at home may be unsuitable in other areas.
6   If 'electrical noise' appears then it is probably due to some unit of the electrical system which is badly worn. Sparking at the alternator slip rings, a defective voltage regulator, fan motor or blower motor may be responsible. The only way to find out is to isolate each item until the noise disappears and then overhaul that item.
7   It is recommended that a small fuse be inserted in the supply cable. A two amp one is sufficient.

37 Wiper blades and arms – renewal

1   To remove a wiper blade, depress the clip with a screwdriver and slide the blade from the arm (photo). On some models it may be possible to renew the wiper rubber separately. Where this type is fitted, use pliers to squeeze the support rail, then withdraw the rubber.
2   To remove a wiper arm, first prise out the cover with a screwdriver then unscrew the retaining nut (photo). Lever the arm off the shaft being careful not to damage the paintwork.
3   When refitting a wiper arm and blade assembly, make sure that the gap between the blade and the windscreen lower edge is as given in Fig. 7.26; the wiper motor must also be in its parked position. The tailgate wiper should be positioned as shown in Fig. 7.28.

38 Windscreen wiper mechanism – removal and refitting

1   Remove the wiper blades and arms as described in Section 37.
2   Disconnect the battery negative terminal, then remove the boot from each spindle and unscrew the retaining nuts.
3   Unplug the connector from the motor terminals.
4   The wiper motor and frame are held in position by a nut on a bracket (photo). Remove this nut and lift the motor and frame away

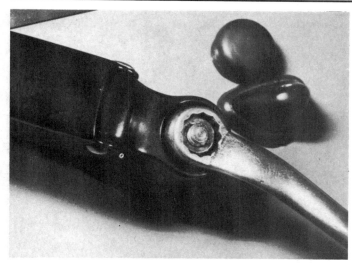

37.2 Unscrewing the wiper arm retaining nut

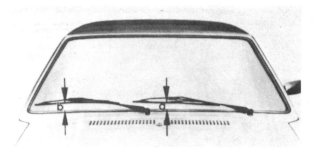

Fig. 7.26 Wiper blade parked position dimensions (Sec 37)

a = 35.0 mm (1.38 in)
b = 65.0 mm (2.56 in)

Note: LHD shown, RHD is mirror image

from the car. The mechanism may now be examined at leisure.

5   The motor may be removed from the frame by undoing two nuts. Alternatively, the motor may be removed from the frame while the frame is still in position but we do not see the point in this as having got so far one might as well have a look at the frame joints as well.

6   Check that all the levers and pins are secure, not worn and are well lubricated.

7   Do not remove the crank from the motor unless the motor is to be replaced with a new one. If this is to be done, connect the multipin plug to the motor before installing the motor, switch on and let the motor run for four minutes. Switch off and the motor will stop in the parking position. Fit the crank in the way shown in Figs. 7.29 and 7.30.

8   Repair is by renewal. Whatever is wrong with the electrical components may only be cured by fitting new ones. The renewal of the column switch is discussed in Section 25. The brush gear is not a

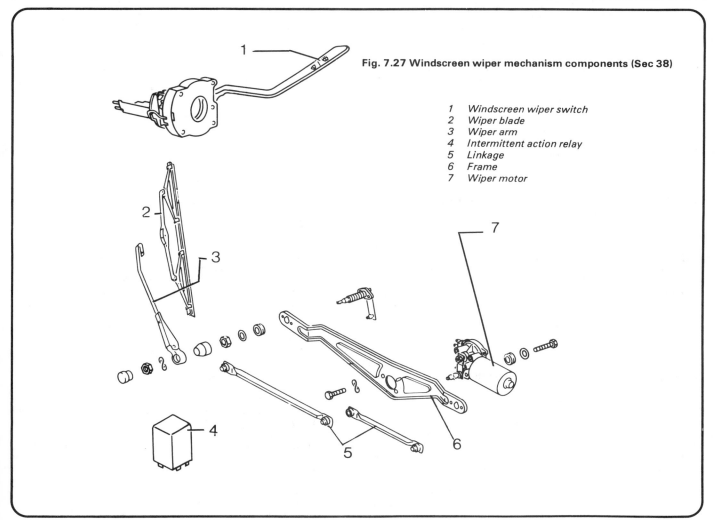

Fig. 7.27 Windscreen wiper mechanism components (Sec 38)

1   Windscreen wiper switch
2   Wiper blade
3   Wiper arm
4   Intermittent action relay
5   Linkage
6   Frame
7   Wiper motor

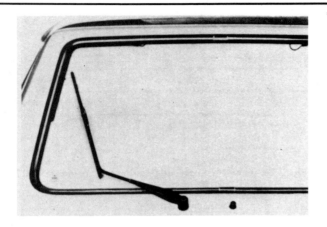

Fig. 7.28 Tailgate wiper blade parked position (Sec 37)

Distance from top of blade to weatherstrip = 30 mm (1.18 in)

38.4 Windscreen wiper motor location

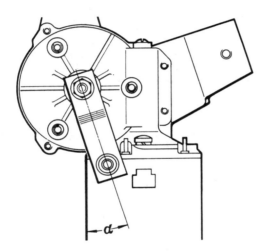

Fig. 7.29 Wiper motor crank parked position on RHD cars (Sec 38)

Angle = 20°

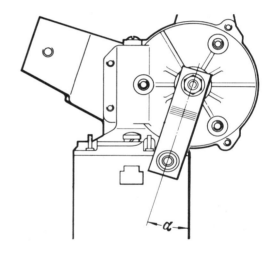

Fig. 7.30 Wiper motor crank parked position on LHD cars (Sec 38)

Angle = 20°

service part so the motor must be renewed if faulty.

9   Inspect the linkage for wear or corrosion. The parts of the linkage are renewable, if required. However, the links are different on left-hand and right-hand drive vehicles.

10   If electrical 'noise' has caused problems with the radio the motor may be replaced by a fully suppressed one.

11   Refitting is a reversal of removal.

39 Tailgate wiper motor – removal and refitting

1   Disconnect the battery negative terminal.

2   Remove the wiper arm and blade as described in Section 37.

3   Remove the boot and unscrew the retaining nut.

4   Extract the inspection panel from the tailgate lower edge and disconnect the wiring from the motor (photo).

5   Unscrew the mounting bolts and withdraw the motor assembly from the inspection aperture, at the same time disengaging it from the mechanism.

6   Unbolt the mechanism from the tailgate and remove it.

7   Refitting is a reversal of removal, but make sure that the motor is in its parked position as shown in Fig. 7.32 before fitting it.

40 Washer jets – adjustment

1   Periodically the washer jets should be adjusted so that the water spray is directed toward the points shown in Fig. 7.33. The tailgate jet should be adjusted to direct spray into the centre of the wiped area.

2   Where headlight washers are fitted, direct the spray into the shaded area shown in Fig. 7.34.

3   The washer pumps are located by the reservoirs (photo).

41 Wiring diagrams – desciption

1   The wiring diagrams included at the end of this Chapter are of the current flow type where each wire is shown in the simplest line form without crossing over other wires.

2   The fuse/relay panel is at the top of the diagram and the combined letter/figure numbers appearing on the panel terminals refer to the multiplug connector in letter form and the terminal in figure form.

3   Internal connections through electrical components are shown by a single line.

4   The encircled numbers along the bottom of the diagram indicate the earthing connecting points as given in the leg end.

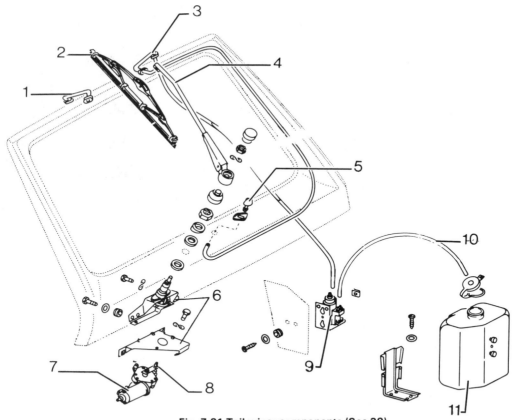

Fig. 7.31 Tail wiper components (Sec 39)

1	Wiring grommet	4	Wiper arm	7	Wiper motor	10	Hose
2	Wiper blade	5	Jet	8	Crank	11	Reservoir
3	Water hose grommet	6	Spindle and frame	9	Washer pump		

39.4 Tailgate wiper motor with inspection cover removed

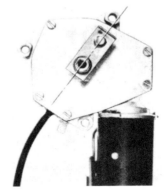

Fig. 7.32 Tailgate wiper motor crank parked position (Sec 39)

Fig. 7.33 Windscreen washer jet adjusting dimensions (Sec 40)

a = 170 to 270 mm (6.7 to 10.6 in)
b = 275 to 325 mm (10.8 to 12.8 in)
c = 305 to 355 mm (12.0 to 14.0 in)
d = 230 to 330 mm (9.0 to 13.0 in)

Note: LHD shown, RHD is mirror image

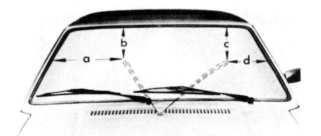

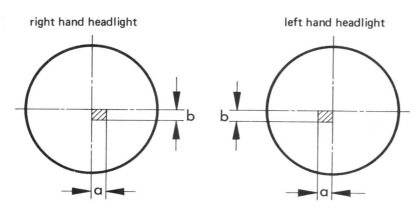

right hand headlight   left hand headlight

Fig. 7.34 Headlight washer adjusting dimensions (Sec 40)

$a = 15$ mm (0.6 mm)
$b = 10$mm (0.4 mm)

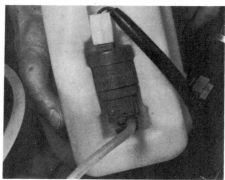

40.3 Windscreen washer reservoir and pump

---

42 Fault diagnosis – electrical system

Symptom	Reason/s
Starter motor fails to turn engine	
No electricity at starter motor	Battery discharged
	Battery defective internally
	Battery terminal leads loose or earth lead not securely attached to body
	Loose or broken connections in starter motor circuit
	Starter motor switch or solenoid faulty
Electricity at starter motor: faulty motor	Starter brushes badly worn, sticking, or brush wires loose
	Commutator dirty, worn, or burnt
	Starter motor armature faulty
	Field coils earthed
Starter motor turns engine very slowly	
Electrical defects	Battery in discharged condition
	Starter brushes badly worn, sticking or, brush wires loose
	Loose wires in starter motor circuit
Starter motor operates without turning engine	
Mechanical damage	Faulty solenoid
	Pinion or flywheel gear teeth broken or worn
Starter motor noisy or excessively rough engagement	
Lack of attention or mechanical damage	Pinion or flywheel gear teeth broken or worn
	Starter motor retaining bolts loose
Battery will not hold charge for more than a few days	
Wear or damage	Battery defective internally
	Electrolyte level too low or electrolyte too weak due to leakage
	Plate separators no longer fully effective
	Battery plates severely sulphated
Insufficient current flow to keep battery charged	Alternator belt slipping
	Battery terminal connections loose or corroded
	Alternator not charging properly
	Short in lighting circuit causing continual battery drain
	Regulator unit not working correctly
Ignition light fails to go out, battery runs flat in a few days	
Alternator not charging	Fan belt loose and slipping, or broken
	Brushes worn, sticking, broken, or dirty
	Brush springs weak or broken
Regulator or cut-out fails to work correctly	Regulator incorrectly set
	Open circuit in wiring of regulator unit

Fuel gauge

Fuel gauge gives no reading

Fuel tank empty!
Electric cable between tank sender unit and gauge broken or loose
Fuel gauge case not earthed
Fuel gauge supply cable interrupted
Fuel gauge unit broken

Fuel gauge registers full all the time

Electric cable between tank unit and gauge earthed

Horn

Horn operates all the time

Horn push either earthed or stuck down
Horn cable to horn push earthed

Horn fails to operate

Blown fuse
Cable or cable connection loose, broken or disconnected
Horn has an internal fault

Horn emits intermittent or unsatisfactory noise

Cable connections loose
Horn incorrectly adjusted

Lights

Lights do not come on

If engine not running, battery discharged
Light bulb filament burnt out or bulbs broken
Wire connections loose, disconnected or broken
Light switch shorting or otherwise faulty

Lights come on but fade out

If engine not running battery discharged

Lights give very poor illumination

Lamp glasses dirty
Reflector tarnished or dirty
Lamps badly out of adjustment
Incorrect bulb with too low wattage fitted
Existing bulbs old and badly discoloured
Electrical wiring too thin not allowing full current to pass

Lights work erratically – flashing on and off, especially over bumps

Battery terminals or earth connection loose
Lights not earthing properly
Contacts in light switch faulty

Wipers

Wiper motor fails to work

Blown fuse
Wire connections loose, disconnected, or broken
Brushes badly worn
Armature worn or faulty
Field coils faulty

Wiper motor works very slowly and takes excessive current

Commutator dirty, greasy, or burnt
Spindle binding or damaged
Armature bearings dry or unaligned

Wiper motor works slowly and takes little current

Brushes badly worn
Commutator dirty, greasy, or burnt
Armature badly worn or faulty

Wiper motor works but wiper blades remain static

Wiper motor gearbox parts badly worn

SYMBOL	EXPLANATION	Sample use
	ALTERNATOR WITH DIODE RECTIFIERS	Golf alternator
	MOTOR	Fan motor, radiator fan
	EXTERNAL WIRING WIRE 10 mm^2 sectional area	Wiring diagram
	WIRE JUNCTION FIXED (SOLDERED)	Relay plate, dash board printed circuit
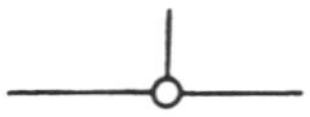	WIRE JUNCTION SEPARABLE	Screw on terminals and eyelets
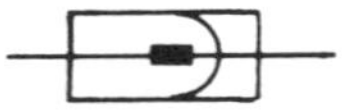	PLUG, SINGLE OR MULTIPIN	T10 written by the side means explanation in the key
	WIRE CROSSING, NOT JOINED	Wiring diagram
	GROUND, OR EARTH	Wiring diagram
	SWITCH CLOSED	Wiring diagram
	SWITCH OPEN	Wiring diagram
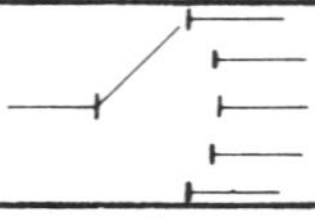	MULTI CONTACT SWITCH	Wiring diagram
	SWITCH, MANUALLY OPERATED	Wiring diagram
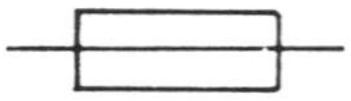	FUSE	
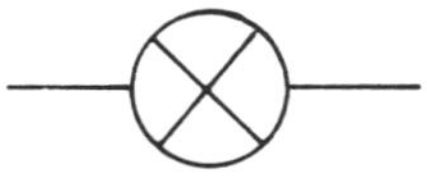	BULB	
	CONDENSER	

H.5550

Fig. 7.35A Current flow diagram symbols

SYMBOL	EXPLANATION	Sample use
	TRANSFORMER, IRON CORE	
	DIODE	Alternator
	TRANSISTOR	Voltage regulator
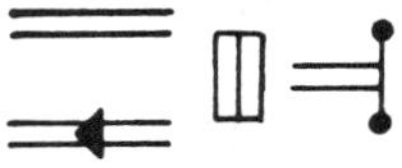	MECHANICAL CONNECTION MECHANICAL CONNECTION SPRING LOADED	Double switch Oil pressure switch
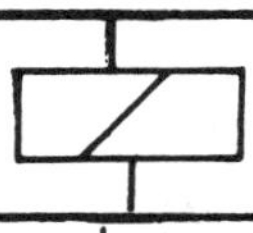	RELAY, COIL	
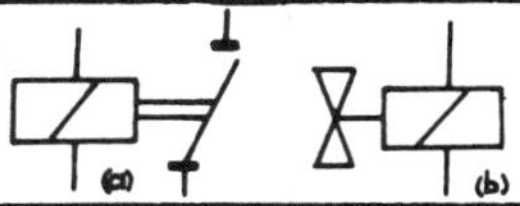	RELAY, ELECTRO MAGNETIC	Headlamp
	HORN	
	RESISTOR	
	POTENTIOMETER	
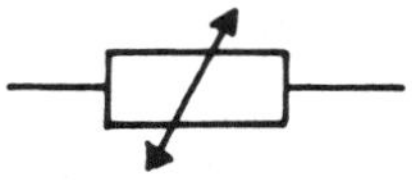	THERMAL RESISTOR AUTOMATIC REGULATING	Temperature sender
	HEATING ELEMENT	Rear window heater
	BATTERY 12 volt	
	MEASURING GAUGE	Fuel gauge Temperature gauge
	SUPPRESSION WIRE	
	CLOCK	
	MECHANICAL PRESSURE SWITCH	Door switch for interior light

Fig. 7.35B Current flow diagram symbols (continued)

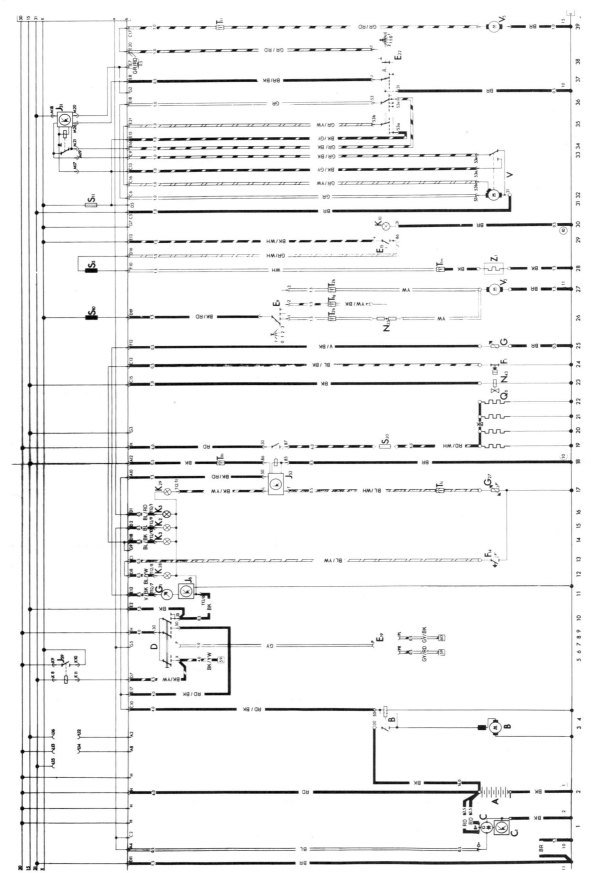

Fig. 7.36A Wiring diagram for 1978 Golf LD (see page 156 for key and page 175 for colour codes)

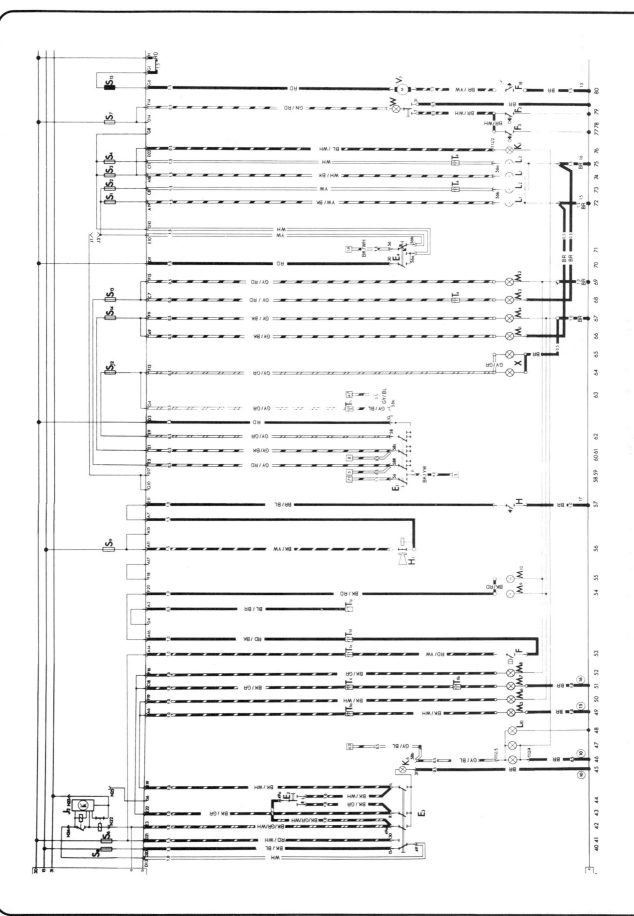

Fig. 7.36B Wiring diagram for 1978 Golf LD (continued) (see page 156 for key and page 175 for colour codes)

Key to wiring diagram Fig. 7.36 for 1978 Golf LD (see page 175 for colour codes)

Designation		in current track
A	Battery	2
B	Starter	3, 4
C	Alternator	1
C 1	Voltage regulator	1
D	Ignition/starter switch	5–10
E 9	Fresh air blower switch	26, 27
E 15	Heated rear window switch	29, 30
E 19	Parking light switch (contact in turn signal switch not fitted – switch not functional)	7, 8, 9
E 22	Wiper switch for intermittent operation	35–38
F 1	Oil pressure switch	24
F 14	Coolant temperature – warning switch*	13
G	Fuel gauge sender	25
G 1	Fuel gauge	11
G 27	Engine temperature sender*	11
J 6	Voltage stabilizer	17
J 31	Wash-wipe intermittent relay	35–36
J 52	Glow plug relay	17–19
J 59	Relief relay for X-contact	5
K 2	Alternator warning lamp	15
K 3	Oil pressure warning lamp	14
K 5	Turn signal warning lamp	16
K 10	Rear window warning lamp	30
K 28	Coolant temperature warning lamp	12
K 29	Glow period warning lamp	17
N 33	Fresh air blower series resistance	37
Q 6	Glow plugs	19–22
S 5, S 10, S 11	Fuses in fuse box	
S 20	Fuse (50 A) for glow plugs (in engine compartment)	19
T 1c	Connector, single, behind dash	
T 1f	Connector, single, in engine compartment	
T 1g	Connector, single, behind dash	
T 1h	Connector, single, behind dash	
T 1m	Connector, single, in luggage compartment, left	
T 2b	Connector, 2 pin, on dash insert	
T 12	Connector, 12 pin, on dash insert	
V	Wiper motor	32–34
V 2	Fresh air blower	27
V 5	Washer pump	39
Z 1	Heated rear window	28
E 1	Lighting switch	58–62
E 2	Turn signal switch	44
E 3	Emergency light switch	40–46
E 4	Headlight dip/flasher switch	70–71
F	Brake light switch	53

Designation		in current track
F 2	Door contact switch, front left	79
F 3	Door contact switch, front right	77
F 18	Thermoswitch for radiator fan	80
H	Horn control	57
H 1	Horn	56
J 2	Emergency light relay	42–44
K 1	Main beam warning lamp	76
K 6	Emergency light warning lamp	45
L 1	Headlight, left	72, 74
L 2	Headlight, right	73, 75
L 10	Instrument panel light	46, 48
M 1	Parking light, left	66
M 2	Tail light, right	69
M 3	Parking light, right	68
M 4	Tail light, left	67
M 5	Turn signal, front left	49
M 6	Turn signal, rear left	50
M 7	Turn signal, front right	51
M 8	Turn signal, rear right	52
S 1 – S 4	}	
S 6 – S 9	} Fuses in fusebox	
S 12 – S 15	}	
T 1a	Connector, single, in engine compartment front left	
T 1b	Connector, single, in engine compartment front right	
T 1d	Connector, single, on brake light switch	
T 1e	Connector, single, behind instrument panel	
T 1i	Connector, single, on brake light switch	
T 1p	Connector, 4 point, behind instrument panel	
T 4	Connector, 12 point, behind instrument panel	
T 12	Connector, 12 point, on instrument panel insert	
V 7	Radiator fan	80
W	Interior light front	79
X	License plate light	64–65
①	Earth wire, battery – body – engine	
②	Earth wire, generator – engine	
⑩	Earthing point, instrument panel	
⑪	Earthing point, steering column support	
⑮	Earthing point, engine compartment, front left	
⑯	Earthing point, engine compartment, front right	
⑰	Earth wire, steering box	

* F 14 and G 27 in one housing. On Golf LD the coolant temperature warning switch F 14 is replaced by a coolant temperature indicator sender.

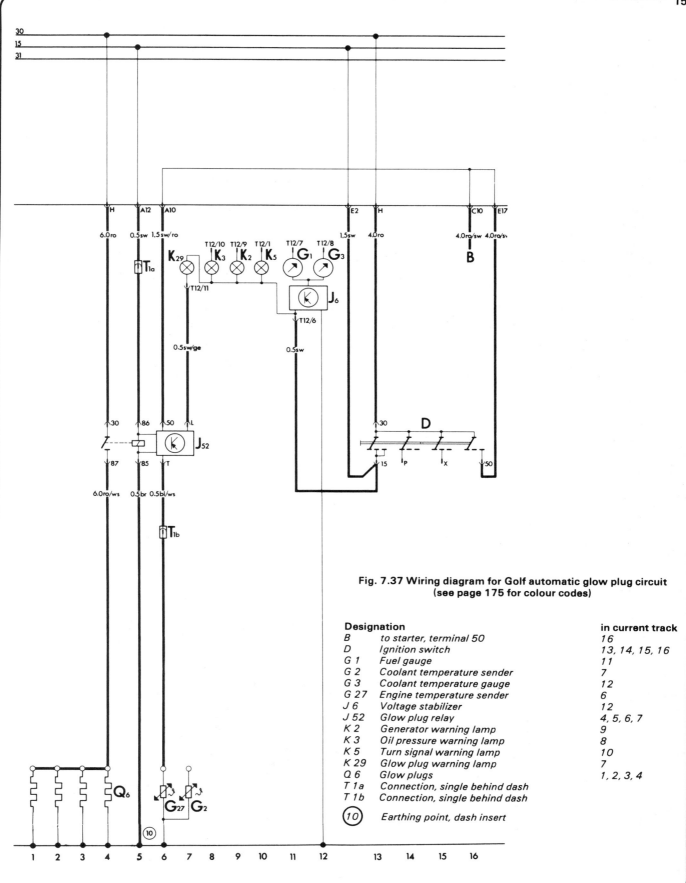

**Fig. 7.37 Wiring diagram for Golf automatic glow plug circuit
(see page 175 for colour codes)**

Designation		in current track
B	to starter, terminal 50	16
D	Ignition switch	13, 14, 15, 16
G 1	Fuel gauge	11
G 2	Coolant temperature sender	7
G 3	Coolant temperature gauge	12
G 27	Engine temperature sender	6
J 6	Voltage stabilizer	12
J 52	Glow plug relay	4, 5, 6, 7
K 2	Generator warning lamp	9
K 3	Oil pressure warning lamp	8
K 5	Turn signal warning lamp	10
K 29	Glow plug warning lamp	7
Q 6	Glow plugs	1, 2, 3, 4
T 1a	Connection, single behind dash	
T 1b	Connection, single behind dash	
⑩	Earthing point, dash insert	

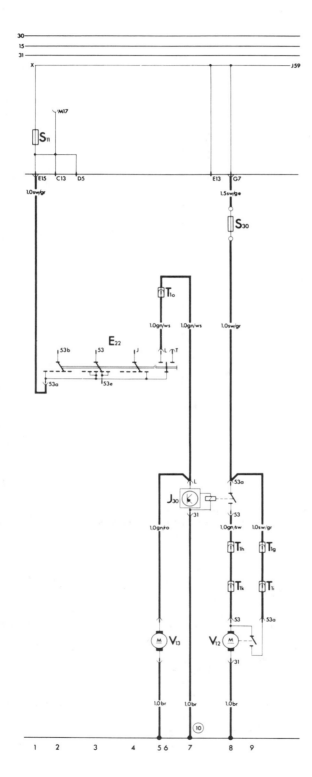

Fig. 7.38 Wiring diagram for Golf rear window wiper and washer circuit (see page 175 for colour codes)

Designation	in current track
E 22 Windscreen wiper switch for intermittent operation	2, 3, 4, 6
J 30 Rear wiper-washer relay	7, 8
J 59 to relief relay for X contact	9
S 11 Fuse 11 in fuse box	1
S 30 Single fuse for rear wiper	8
T 1g Connector, single, in rear left of luggage compartment	
T 1h Connector, single, in rear left of luggage compartment	
T 1i Connector single in tailgate	
T 1k Connector single in tailgate	
T 1o Connector single behind dash	
V 12 Rear wiper motor	8, 9
V 13 Rear washer pump motor	5
⑩ Earth point, dash insert	

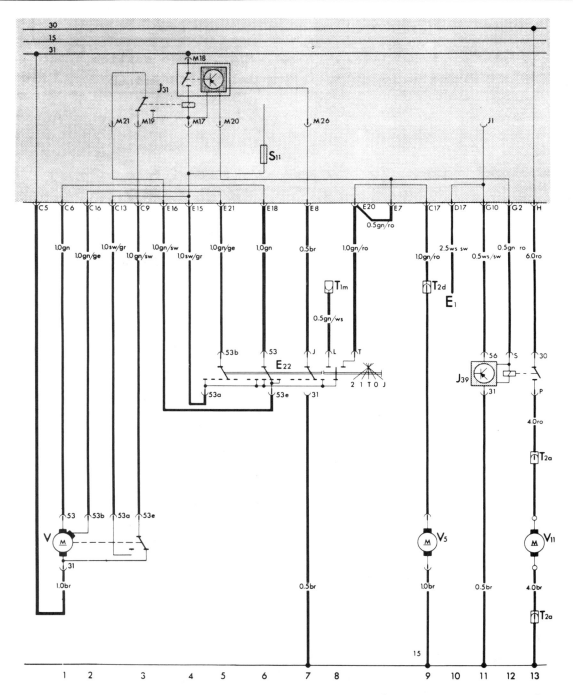

Fig. 7.39 Wiring diagram for Golf headlight washer intermittent facility (see page 175 for colour codes)

Designation		in current track
E 1	to lighting switch	10
E 22	Wiper switch for intermittent operation	5 – 8
J 31	Wash/wipe intermittent relay	3 – 5
J 39	Headlight washer system relay	11 – 15
S 11	Fuse in fuse box	6
T1m	Connector, single, behind instrument panel	
T2a	Connector, two point, near the headlight washer pump	
T2d	Connector, two point, in engine compartment	
V	Windscreen wiper motor	1
V5	Windscreen washer pump motor	9
V11	Headlight washer pump	13
⑮	Earthing point in engine compartment	

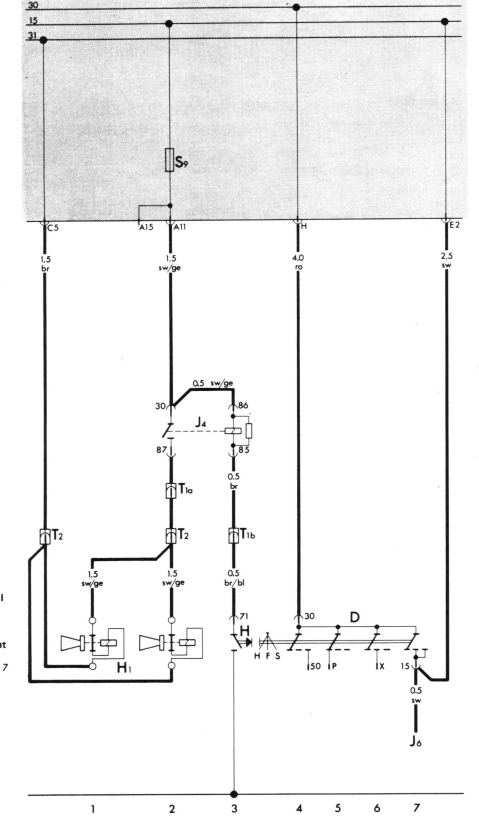

Fig. 7.40 Wiring diagram for Golf dual
   tone horn system (see page 175 for
   colour codes)

Designation		in current track
D	Ignition/starter switch	4, 5, 6, 7
H	Horn plate	3
H 1	Horn	1, 2
J 4	Duel tone horn relay	2, 3
J 6	to voltage stabiliser	7
S 9	Fuse in fuse box	2
T 1a	Connector, single, behind instrument panel	
T 1b	Connector, single, behind instrument panel	
T 2	Connector, two point, near the horns	

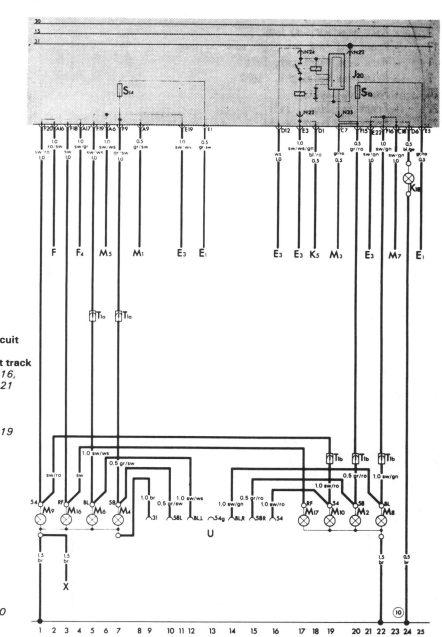

Fig. 7.41 Wiring diagram for Golf trailer circuit
(see page 175 for colour code)

Designation		in current track
E3	to emergency light switch	11, 16, 17, 21
F	to brake light switch	2
F4	to reversing light switch	4
J20	Turn signal/emergency light relay for trailer	17, 19
K 5	to turn signal warning lamp	18
K 18	Warning lamp for trailer	24
M 1	Side light, left	8
M 2	Tail light, right	20
M 3	Side light, right	19
M 4	Tail light, left	7
M 5	Turn signal, front left	8
M 6	Turn signal, rear left	5
M 7	Turn signal, front right	23
M 8	Turn signal, rear right	22
M 9	Brake light, left	1
M 10	Brake light, right	19
M 16	Reversing light, left	3
M 17	Reversing light, right	17
S 13	Fuses in fuse box	7, 20
S 14		
T 1a	Connector, single, in luggage compartment rear left	
T 1b	Connector, single, in luggage compartment rear right	
U	Trailer socket	9, 10
X	to number plate lights	3
⑩	Earthing point, instrument panel	

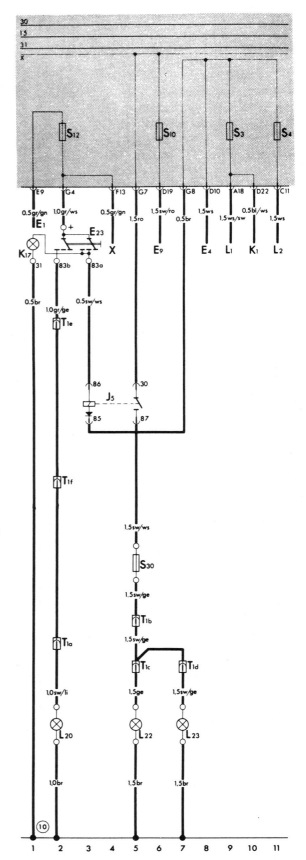

Fig. 7.42 Wiring diagram for Golf fog lights (see page 175 for colour codes)

Designation		in current track
E 1	to lighting switch, terminal 58	1
E 4	to dimmer/flasher switch, terminal 56a	8
E 9	to fresh air blower switch	6
E 23	Front and rear fog light switch	1 - 4
J 5	Fog light relay	4, 5
K 1	Main beam warning lamp	10
K 17	Front and rear fog light warning lamp	1
L 1	Main beam headlight, left	9
L 2	Main beam headlight, right	11
L 20	Rear fog light	2
L 22	Front fog light, left	5
L 23	Front fog light, right	7
S 3, 4	Fuses in fuse box	
S10, 12		5
S 30	Single fuse for fog lights	
T 1a	Connector, single, in luggage compartment	
T 1b	Connector, single, under windscreen washer container	
T 1c	Connector, single, in engine compartment, front left	
T 1d	Connector, single, in engine compartment, right	
T 1e	Connector, single, behind instrument panel	
T 1f	Connector, single, behind instrument panel	
X	to number plate lights	3
(10)	Earthing point, instrument cluster	

Key to wiring diagram Fig. 7.43 for 1977 Rabbit (see page 175 for colour codes)

Note: *Rabbit de Luxe petrol version shown. Use diagram in conjunction with wiring diagram Fig. 7.44 but note the following deletions and additions:*

Deletions	1	Current track 3 to 10 (CIS equipment)
	2	Current track 10 to 16 (Ignition system)
	3	Diagnosis system
	4	EGR components
Additions	1	Glow plug system
	2	Safety belt warning system
	3	Warning light terminal 15 to D20 now via glow plug relay J52 terminal 86

Description		in current track
A	Battery	2
B	Starter	10-12
C	Alternator	1
C 1	Regulator	1
D	Ignition/starter switch	18-21
E 1	Light switch	68-70
E 2	Turn signal switch	51
E 3	Emergency flasher switch	47-50, 52, 53, 55
E 4	Headlamp dimmer/flasher sw.	66, 67
E 9	Fresh air fan switch	83
E 15	Rear window defogger switch	86
E 20	Instrument panel lights sw.	71
E 22	Washer/wiper intermitt. sw.	91-94
E 24	Safety belt switch, left	19
E 25	Safety belt switch, right	19
F	Brake light switch	38, 39
F 1	Oil pressure switch	30
F 2	Door sw./buzzer, front left	45
F 3	Door sw./buzzer, front right	43
F 4	Backup light switch	34
F 9	Park. brake warning light switch	28
F 18	Radiator fan thermo switch	96
F 26	Thermo-time sw. for start. valve	8,9
F 27	Elapsed EGR mileage switch	29
G	Fuel guage sending unit	32
G 1	Fuel gauge	22
G 2	Coolant temperature sending unit	31
G 3	Coolant temperature gauge	23
G 6	Electrical fuel pump	7
G 7	Connections for TDC sensor	24
H	Horn button	37
H 1	Horn	36
J 2	Emergency flasher relay	49,50
J 6	Voltage stabilizer	22
J 9	Rear window defogger relay	85
J 17	Electrical fuel pump relay	6-10
J 31	Washer/wiper intermitt. relay	89,90
J 34	Safety belt warning relay	17-21
K 1	Headlight high beam warning light	65
K 2	Alternator charging warning light	25
K 3	Oil pressure warning light	24
K 5	Turn signal warning light	26
K 6	Emergency flasher warning light	54
K 7	Dual circ. brake/safety belt warn. light	27,28
K 10	Rear window defog. warning light	86
K 22	EGR warning light	29
L 1	Left headlight, high/low beam	61,63
L 2	Right headlight, high/low beam	62,64
L 10	Instrument panel light	71,72
L 15	Ashtray light	52
L 16	Heater lever light	55
L 28	Cigarette lighter light	50
M 1	Parking light, front left	76
M 2	Tail light, right	81
M 3	Parking light, front right	79
M 4	Tail light, left	78

Description		in current track
M 5	Turn signal, front left	57
M 6	Turn signal, rear left	58
M 7	Turn signal, front right	59
M 8	Turn signal, rear right	60
M 9	Brake light, left	40
M 10	Brake light, right	41
M 11	Side marker lights, front	75,80
M 12	Side marker lights, rear	77,82
M 16	Backup light, left	35
M 17	Backup light, right	36
N	Ignition coil	14
N 6	Ballast resistor wire	14
N 9	Control pressure regulator	3
N 17	Cold start valve	8
N 21	Auxiliary air regulator	5
N 23	Speed control resistors for fresh air fan	83
O	Ignition distributor	14,15
P	Spark plug connectors	15,16
Q	Spark plugs	15,16
S	Fuses on fuse/relay panel S1, S2, S3, S4, S5, S6, S7, S8, S10, S11, S12, S13, S14, S15	
S 9	Fuse	33
S 20	Fuse (16A) on fuse/relay panel (on relay J 17)	4

Wire connectors

T	engine compartment	
T 1a	single, behind dashboard	
T 1b	single, behind dashboard	
T 1c	single, behind dashboard	
T 1d	single, behind dashboard	
T 1e	single, trunk rear left	
T 1f	single, behind dashboard	
T 1g	Single, behind dashboard	
T 1h	single, behind dashboard	
T 1i	single, engine compartment, front left	
T 1k	single, engine compartment, front right	
T 1l	single, trunk, rear left	
T 1m	single, trunk, rear right	
T 2a	double, behind dashboard	
T 2b	double, behind dashboard	
T 2c	double, engine comp., front left	
T 2d	double, engine comp., front right	
T 2e	double, behind dashboard	
T 3a	3 point, behind dashboard	
T 4	4 point, behind dashboard	
T 12	12 point, on instrument cluster	
T 20	Diagnosis socket	22
U 1	Cigarette lighter	46
V	Windshield wiper motor	88,89
V 2	Fresh air fan	84
V 5	Windshield washer pump	95
V 7	Radiator cooling fan	96
W	Interior light	42
X	License plate light	73,74
Y	Clock	69
Z 1	Rear window defogger element	85
(1)	Ground strap, batt./body, engine	
(2)	Ground strap alternator to engine	
(10)	Ground connectors, instrument cluster	
(11)	Ground conn., steer. col. support	
(15)	Ground connectors, engine comp. front left	
(16)	Ground connectors, engine comp. front right	

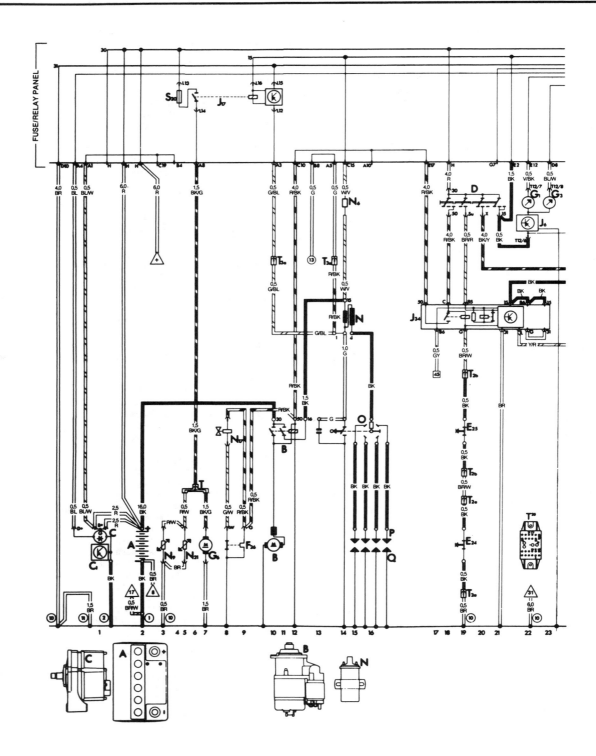

Fig. 7.43A Wiring diagram for 1977 Rabbit (see page 163 for key and page 175 for colour codes)

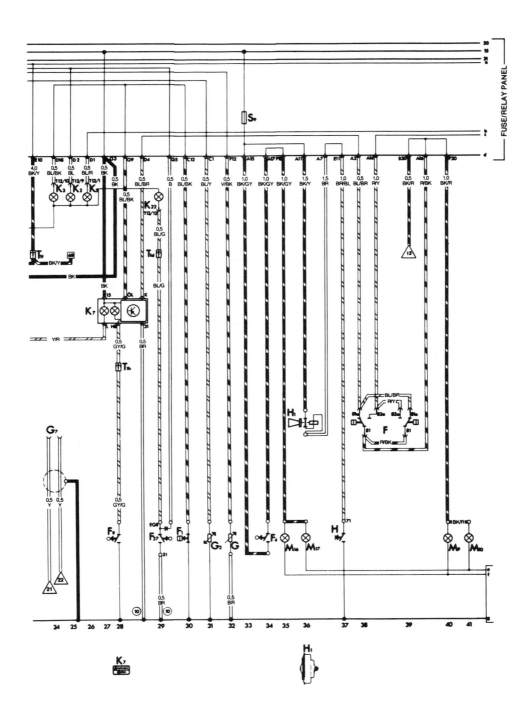

Fig. 7.43B Wiring diagram for 1977 Rabbit (continued) (see page 163 for key and page 175 for colour codes)

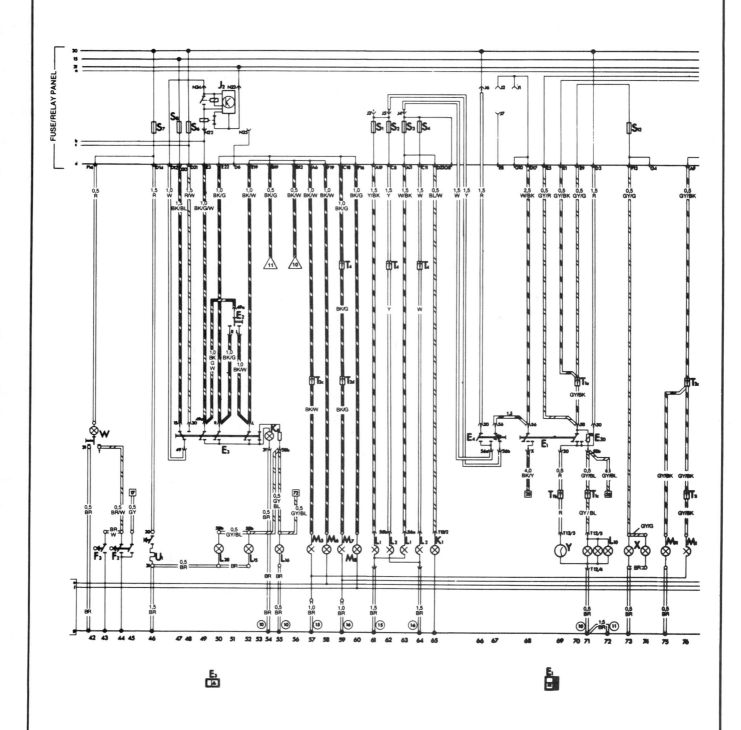

Fig. 7.43C Wiring diagram for 1977 Rabbit (continued) (see page 163 for key and page 175 for colour codes)

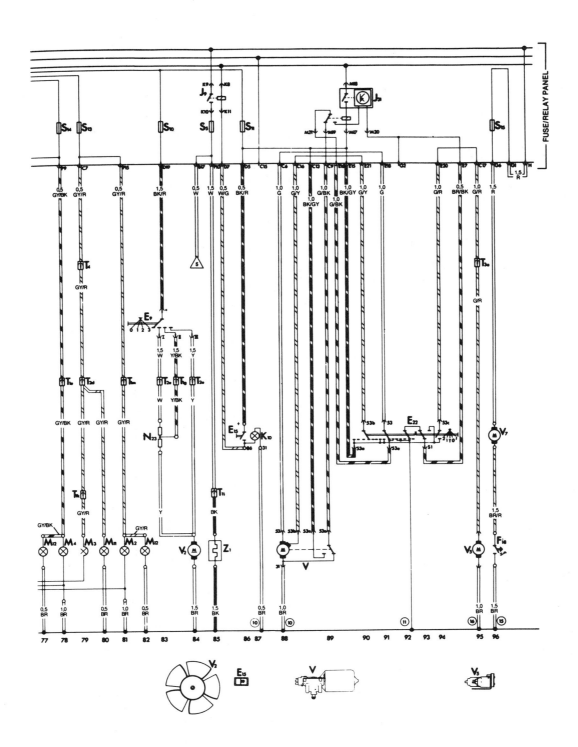

Fig. 7.43D Wiring diagram for 1977 Rabbit (continued) (see page 163 for key and page 175 for colour codes)

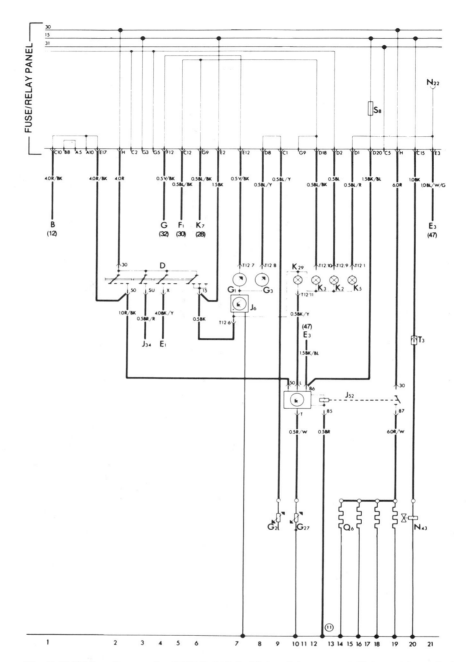

Fig. 7.44 Wiring diagram for 1977 Rabbit (additional) (see page 175 for colour codes)

Note: *Use in conjunction with Fig. 7.43 but note that current track numbers do not correspond*

Description		in current track	Description		in current track
B	to starter, terminal 50	1	J 52	Glow plugs relay (with pre-glow sending unit)	10,12,19
D	ignition/starter switch	2,3,4,5,6	K2	Alternator charging warning light	13
E1	to light switch, terminal X	4	K3	Engine oil pressure warning light	12
E3	to emergency flasher switch	11,21	K5	Turn signal warning light	15
F1	to engine oil pressure switch	5	K7	to dual circuit brake warning light	6
G	to fuel gauge sending unit	4	K29	Pre-glow warning light	10
G1	fuel gauge	7	N43	Fuel cut-off valve	20
G2	Coolant temperature sending unit	9	Q6	glow plugs	14,16,18,19
G3	Coolant temperature gauge	8	S8	Fuse (in fuse box)	17
G27	Engine oil temperature sending unit	10	T3	Wire connector, 3 point; behind dashboard	
J 6	Voltage stabilizer	7	T 12	Wire connector, 12 point; on dashboard cluster	
J 34	to relay for safety belt warning system	3	(11)	Ground connector, steering column support	

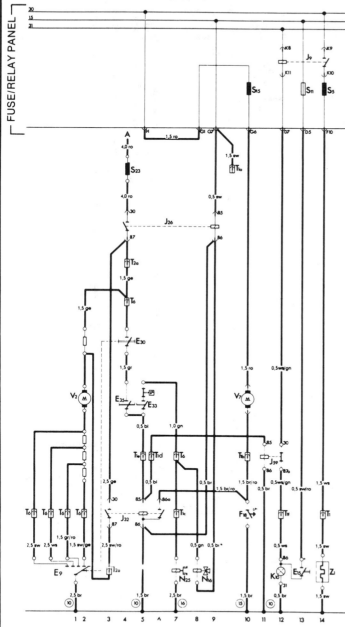

Fig. 7.45 Wiring diagram for air conditioner on 1978 Rabbit (see page 175 for colour codes)

Description		in current track
A	to battery	4
E9	A/C speed control	1,2
E15	defogger switch	12,13
E30	A/C clutch switch (on speed control)	4
E33	temp. control	5
E35	A/C clutch switch (on temp. control)	4
F18	radiator fan thermo sw.	10
J 9	defogger relay	12-14
J 26	A/C on/off relay (on evap. housing)	4-9
J 32	A/C blower motor/rad. fan relay (on evap. housing)	3-6
J 59	defogger cut-out relay	11,12
K10	defogger warn. light	12
N16	two-way valve	8
N25	compressor clutch	7
S5	fuse (16A)	14
S11	fuse (8A)	13
S15	fuse (16A)	10
S23	A/C fuse (25A – on evap. housing)	3

Wire Connectors

T1	single, in trunk
T1 a	single, vacant (on fuse/relay panel)
T1 b	single, in engine comp. (left)
T1 c	single, on compressor
T1 d	single, on evaporator
T1 e	single, behind dash (left)
T1 f	single, behind dash (center)
T 2a	double, behind dash (center)
T 6	6 point, behind dash (center)
V 2	A/C blower motor	2
V 7	radiator cooling fan	10
Z 1	rear window defogger	14

(10) grnd. conn., behind dash

(15) grnd. conn., in engine comp. (left)

(16) grnd. conn., in engine comp. (right)

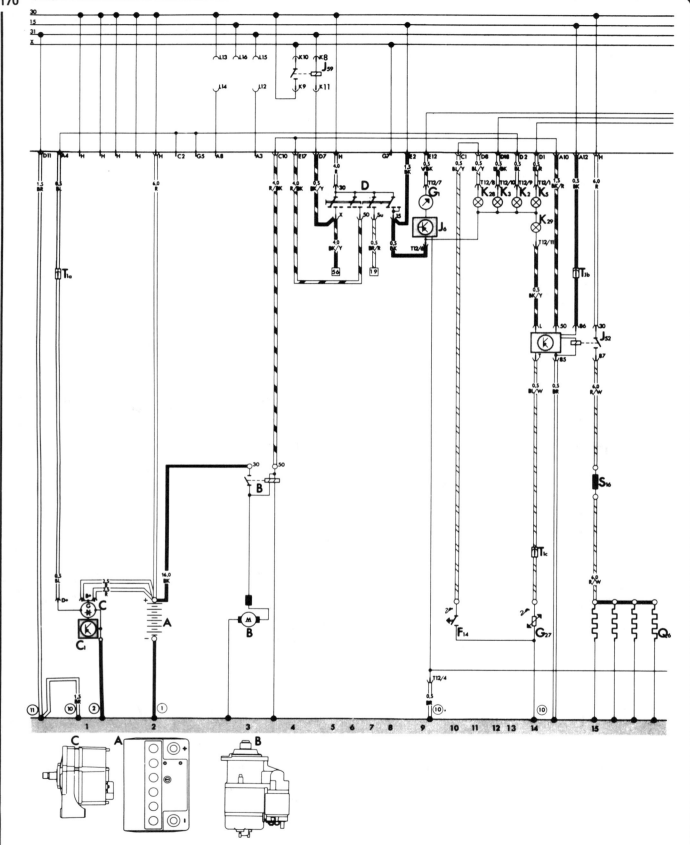

Fig. 7.46A Wiring diagram for 1978 Rabbit Custom (see page 174 for key and page 175 for colour codes)

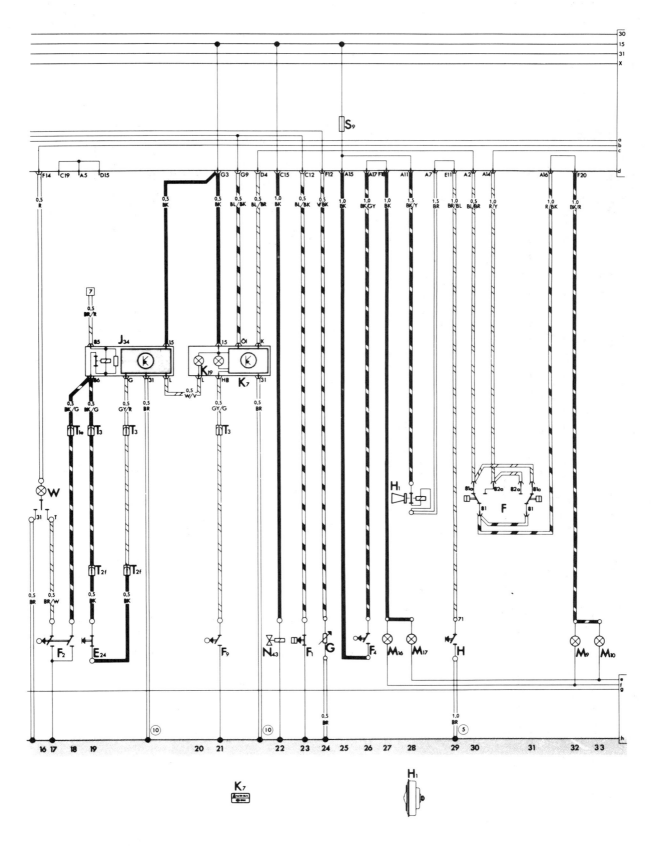

Fig. 7.46B Wiring diagram for 1978 Rabbit Custom (continued) (see page 174 for key and page 175 for colour codes)

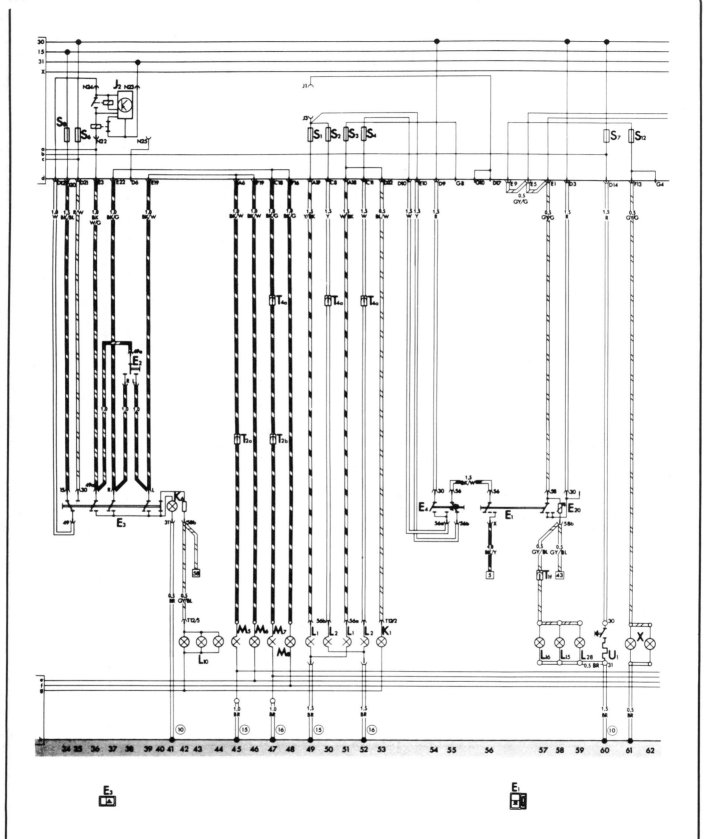

Fig. 7.46C Wiring diagram for 1978 Rabbit Custom (continued) (see page 174 for key and page 175 for colour codes)

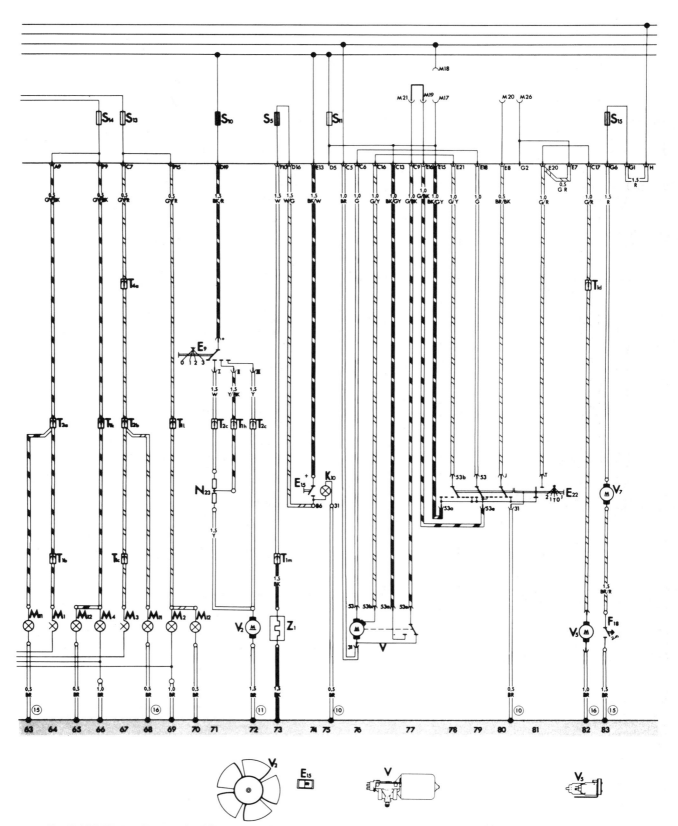

Fig. 7.46D Wiring diagram for 1978 Rabbit Custom (continued) (see page 174 for key and page 175 for colour codes)

Key to wiring diagram Fig. 7.46 for 1978 Rabbit Custom (see next page for colour codes)

Description		in current track
A	Battery	2
B	Starter	3
C	Alternator	1
C1	Regulator	1
D	Glow/starter switch	5-8
E1	Light switch	56-58
E2	Turn signal switch	38
E3	Emergency flasher switch	34-42
E4	Headlight dimmer/flasher switch	54,55
E9	Fresh air fan switch	71,72
E15	Rear window defogger switch	74,75
E20	Instrument panel light switch	58
E22	Windshield washer/wiper intermitt. switch	78-81
E24	Safety belt switch left	19
F	Brake light switch	30,31
F1	Engine oil pressure switch	23
F2	Door/buzzer switch, front left	17,18
F4	Backup light switch	26
F9	Parking brake warning light switch	21
F14	Coolant temperature control switch	10
F18	Radiator cooling fan thermo switch	83
G	Fuel gauge sending unit	24
G1	Fuel gauge	9
G27	Engine temperature sending unit	14
H	Horn button	29
H1	Horn	28
J2	Emergency flasher relay	36-38
J6	Voltage stabilizer	9
J34	Safety belt warning relay	19
J52	Glow plugs relay	14,15
J59	Load reduction relay for X-terminal	4-5
K1	Headlight high beam warning light	53
K2	Alternator charging warning light	13
K3	Engine oil pressure warning light	12
K5	Turn signal warning light	14
K6	Emergency flasher warning light	42
K7	Dual brake system/parking brake warning Light	21
K10	Rear window defogger warning light	75
K19	Safety belt warning light	20
K28	Coolant temperature warning light	11
K29	Pre-glow warning light	14
L1	Head light, left, low/high beam	49,51
L2	Head light, right, low/high beam	50,52
L10	Instrument panel light	42-44
L15	Ashtray light	58
L16	Heater lever light	57
L28	Cigarette lighter light	59
M1	Parking light left	64
M2	Tail light, right	69
M3	Parking light, right	67
M4	Tail light, left	66
M5	Turn signal, front left	45
M6	Turn signal, rear left	46
M7	Turn signal, front right	47
M8	Turn signal, rear right	48
M9	Stop light, left	32
M10	Stop light, right	33
M11	Side markers, front	63,68

Description		in current track
M12	Side markers, rear	65,70
M16	Backup light, left	27
M17	Backup light, right	28
N23	Ballast resistor for fresh air fan	71
N43	Electro-magnetic cut-off switch	22
Q6	Glow plugs	15
S1		
to	Fuses in fuse box	
S15		
S16	Fuse for glow plugs (50 amp)	

Wire connectors

T1a	Single, in engine compartment	
T1b	Single, engine compartment, left	
T1c	Single, engine compartment, right	
T1d	Single, behind dashboard	
T1e	Single, behind dashboard	
T1f	Single, behind dashboard	
T1h	Single, behind dashboard	
T1k	Single, trunk, left	
T1l	Single, trunk, right	
T1m	Single trunk, left	
T2a	Double, engine compartment, front left	
T2b	Double, engine compartment, front right	
T2c	Double, behind dashboard	
T2f	Double, behind dashboard	
T3	3-point, behind dashboard	
T4a	4-point, behind dashboard	
T12	12-point, instrument cluster	
U1	Cigarette lighter	60
V	Windshield wiper motor	76,77
V2	Fresh air fan	72
V5	Windshield washer pump	82
V7	Radiator cooling fan	83
W	Interior light	16
X	Licence plate light	61,62
Z1	Rear window defogger element	73

Ground connectors

(1)	battery/body/engine
(2)	alternator/engine
(5)	steering gear
(10)	instrument cluster
(11)	steering column bracket
(15)	engine compartment, front left
(16)	engine compartment, front right

Black	–	BK
Brown	–	BR
Red	–	R
Orange	–	O
Yellow	–	Y
Green	–	G
Blue	–	BL
Violet	–	V
Grey	–	GY
White	–	W

Wiring diagram colour code for Figs. 7.36, 7.43, 7.44 and 7.46

Where a wire has two or three colours, the main colour is given first, followed by the tracer colour(s)

Blue	–	bl
Brown	–	br
Yellow	–	ge
Green	–	gn
Grey	–	gr
Lilac	–	li
Red	–	ro
Black	–	sw
White	–	ws

Wiring diagram colour code for Figs. 7.37 to 7.42 and 7.45

Where a wire has two or three colours, the main colour is given first, followed by the tracer colour(s)

Chapter 8
Front suspension, steering and driveshafts

For modifications, and information applicable to later models, see Supplement at end of manual

Contents

Specifications

Front suspension

Type	Independent, MacPherson strut, co-axial coil spring and shock absorber with wishbones
Shock absorbers	Hydraulic, telescopic, double acting
Steering knuckle balljoints – max play	2·5 mm (0·10 in)

Steering gear
Type	Rack and pinion with safety column
Overall ratio	17·37 : 1
Steering wheel turns, lock-to-lock	3½
Turning circle, between kerbs	10 metres (33 ft)

Steering alignment
Camber – wheels straight ahead	+ 20′ ± 30′
Max permissible difference between sides	1°
Castor	1° 50′ ± 30′ (not adjustable)
Toe angle (vehicle unladen. Negative angle denotes toe-out)	$-15' \begin{smallmatrix}+ 10'\\- 15'\end{smallmatrix}$

Driveshafts . . . .

	LH – solid	RH – tubular
Length	445 mm (17·5 in)	658 mm (25·9 in)

Torque wrench settings

	kgf m	lbf ft

Suspension
	kgf m	lbf ft
Strut to wing securing nuts	2·0	14
Camber adjusting bolt nut	8·0	58
Strut to steering knuckle bolt	6·0	43
Steering balljoint clamp bolt	3·0	21
Wishbone pivot (front hinge) bolt	6·0	43
Wishbone U-clamp bolt	4·5	32
Driveshaft flange bolt	4·5	32
Hub nut	24·0	173
Shock absorber piston rod nut	8·0	58
Balljoint securing bolts	2·5	18

Steering
	kgf m	lbf ft
UJ clamp bolt to steering column	3·0	21
UK clamp bolt to steering gear	3·0	21
Steering wheel nut	5·0	36
Tie-rod locknut	3·0	21
Tie-rod balljoint nut	3·0	21
Steering gear securing nuts	3·0	21
Steering column switch housing	1·0	7

1 General description

1 The suspension is simple and easily dismantled once the axleshaft nut is undone. This is tightened to a very high torque, and will present a problem for most owner drivers. The ways of overcoming this are discussed in Section 2, paragraph 5.

2 A straightforward MacPherson strut is housed in a bearing in the body and is located at the bottom by a balljoint attached to a wishbone bracket hinged to the frame. The roadwheel and brake are carried on a steering knuckle which is clamped to the bottom of the suspension strut and houses the wheel bearing. The top bolt of the clamp is eccentric and is used to adjust the camber angle. The steering knuckle is referred to throughout as the wheel bearing housing.

3 The drive to the roadwheel from the differential unit is supplied by a shaft with a constant velocity joint (CVJ) at each end. The inner end is flanged and secured by bolts to the final drive flange. The outer end is splined and passes into the splined inner part of the outer CVJ.

4 The CVJ outer race is an integral part of the short wheel axle which is splined into the hub. The hub is carried in a ball bearing in the wheel bearing housing and the whole wheel hub is held in place by the axle nut.

5 An integral part of the wheel bearing housing is a lever extending to the rear of the suspension strut. To this is fastened, by means of a balljoint, the tie-rod which is connected at the inner end to the steering gear. Thus as the tie-rod moves the suspension strut rotates, and with it the wheel is turned in a vertical plane, so steering the car.

6 The coil spring is mounted on a platform attached to the body of the shock absorber. The upper end of the spring is held by a cap and compressed slightly by a nut on the piston rod of the shock absorber. Thus as the spring is compressed the body of the piston moves up over the piston rod, and as the spring expands it pushes the body of the shock absorber down. In this way a controlled damping force is applied to the suspension.

7 The steering column is held in a tube which is fixed to the body. The column runs in a spacer sleeve at the top and a ball bearing at the bottom. A safety feature of the system is the universal joint (UJ) shaft which connects the bottom of the steering column to the steering gear. This is contained in a rubber cover. Besides catering for a change in direction of the drive, it ensures that should the steering gear be driven backwards in an accident such motion would not be transmitted to the steering column.

8 The lower end of the UJ shaft is clamped to the pinion shaft of the rack and pinion mechanism. The casing of this is bolted to the frame with clamps and rubber bushes. As the pinion turns the rack is moved to the right or left. Attached to each end of the rack shaft, by means of balljoints, are the tie-rods which transmit the steering motion to the front wheels. The tie-rods are easily removable. On new vehicles, the right-hand rod only is adjustable for length. Should a replacement for the left-hand rod be required only the adjustable type is available. This is discussed in Section 12.

9 The steering gear may be removed without disturbing the column or front wheels. Adjustment is simply both for wear and correct track.

10 Toe-in and camber angles are easily adjustable but the measurement of these angles requires special equipment and is best left to the VW agent. The castor angle is fixed. If the geometry is incorrect the tyres will wear rapidly. If such wear is apparent the owner is advised to have the geometry checked forthwith.

11 The text is written about LHD vehicles. Obviously the suspension does not differ for RHD but the steering gear differs, if only in the position of the pinion. Repair techniques are the same, and the photographs are of a RHD vehicle.

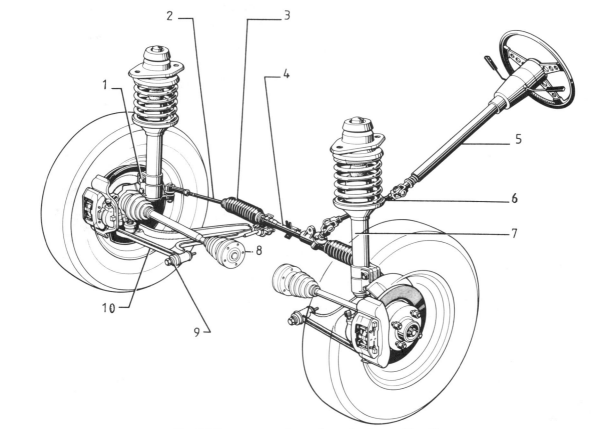

Fig. 8.1 Front suspension and steering layout (Sec 1)

1 Camber adjustment bolt	4 Steering gear	7 Suspension strut	9 Bonded rubber bush (front)
2 Tie-rod	5 Steering column	8 Driveshaft	10 Suspension wishbone
3 Bellows	6 Lower steering shaft		

2   Maintenance

1   Apart from careful periodic inspection, maintenance is not necessary. All bearings and joints are prepacked and have no method of replenishment.
2   Check the state of wear of the tyre treads regularly and if there are signs of uneven wear, action, as described later, is necessary right away.
3   Measure the free-play of the steering wheel as soon as you acquire the vehicle. If this measurement subsequently increases, the reason must be located and corrected.
4   The rubber gaiters and covers must be checked for splits and age hardening. They may be renewed as required.
5   The problem of undoing the axle nut may be solved by using a large lorry type spanner but it should only be done while the car is standing on its wheels. The force required could easily pull the vehicle off an axle stand. It **must** be tightened to the correct torque so this will probably mean going to the agent if the hub has been dismantled. At the same time the steering geometry may be checked.
6   We have deliberately omitted any discussion on the setting of the steering geometry. This operation requires special gauges and extensive experience in using them. For those who have that experience and access to the gauges the necessary angles are given in the Specifications. For the remainder our strong recommendation is to get this job done by the VW agent.
7   With the reservations given in paragraphs 5 and 6 there is no reason why the owner cannot dismantle the steering and suspension and renew worns parts as required. The method of doing these jobs is discussed in the rest of the Chapter.

3   Driveshaft – removal and refitting

1   The driveshafts differ in length and construction. The right-hand shaft is longer than the left-hand shaft and is of tubular construction, while the shorter shaft is solid. In all other respects the shafts are the same.
2   Removal of the shaft does not present many problems. While the vehicle is standing on its wheels, undo the axle nut and slacken the roadwheel studs. Jack-up the front wheels and support the vehicle on axle stands. Remove the roadwheel and turn the steering to full lock, left lock for the left shaft and right for the right shaft.
3   Using an 8 mm Allen key remove the socket head bolts holding the inner CVJ to the final drive flange (photo). Be careful to use a proper key for if the socket head is damaged the result will be time consuming to say the least. These bolts are quite tight for the type of spanner used. Ideally a special hexagon 'screwdriver' bit should be used which will fit a torque wrench, but if one is not available then the bolts should be tightened as hard as possible on reassembly.

3.3 Driveshaft inner joint and final drive flange

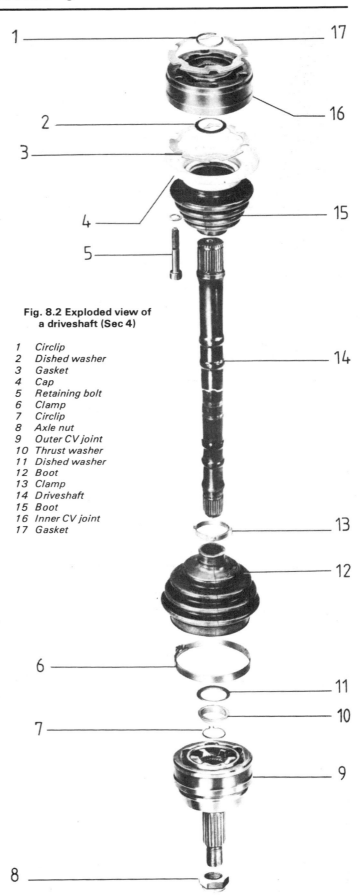

Fig. 8.2 Exploded view of a driveshaft (Sec 4)

1   Circlip
2   Dished washer
3   Gasket
4   Cap
5   Retaining bolt
6   Clamp
7   Circlip
8   Axle nut
9   Outer CV joint
10 Thrust washer
11 Dished washer
12 Boot
13 Clamp
14 Driveshaft
15 Boot
16 Inner CV joint
17 Gasket

3.4 Removing the driveshaft from the final drive flange

4   Once all the bolts are removed the CVJ may be pulled away from the final drive and the shaft removed from the hub (photo).
5   Refitting is the reverse of removal. Clean the splines carefully and smear a little molybdenum based grease on them. The problem of tightening the axle nut is again emphasised, and the nut fitted must be a new one.

4   Driveshaft – dismantling and reassembly

1   Having removed the shaft from the car it may be dismantled for the individual parts to be checked for wear.
2   The rubber boots, clips and thrust washers may be renewed if necessary but the CV joints may only be renewed as complete assemblies. It is not possible to fit new hubs, outer cases, ball cages or balls separately for they are mated to a tolerance on manufacture; it is not possible to buy them either.
3   Start by removing the outer joint (refer to Fig. 8.2). Cut open the 34 mm clip and undo the 88 mm hose clamp. The boot may now be pulled away from the joint. Open the circlip with a pair of circlip pliers and tap the side of the joint. The circlip should spring out of its groove.
4   The outer CV joint may now be removed from the shaft and set aside for examination. The boot, clamp, dished washer and thrust washer may be pulled off the end of the shaft. See Fig. 8.3.
5   If the boot of the inner CV joint is damaged it should be removed and refitted from the outer end and the CV joint on the inner end left in

place. If however, the inner joint is suspected then this too must be removed. Use circlip pliers to remove the circlip from the end of the shaft and press off the CV joint. It will be necessary to ease the plastic cap away from the joint before pressing off the CV joint. The CV joint may now be set aside for inspection.
6   The CV joints should be washed clean and lightly oiled. Press the ball hub and cage out of the joint. Pivot the case through 90° to extract it. Examine the balls and ball tracks for scoring and wear. There should be a bright ring where the ball track runs round the joint but no further scoring. If the joint does not seem satisfactory take it to the VW agent for advice and possible renewal.
7   Assembly is the reverse of dismantling. Fit the inner CV joint first. It should be filled with 90 grams of molydbenum disulphide (MOS$_2$) grease, filling in equal amounts from each side. The grease is obtainable in packets from official agents. Pump the grease in while pressing the CV joint onto the shaft. Pull the joint on until a new circlip may be fitted. The outer diameter of the dished washer should now rest against the CV joint. Refit the plastic cover and the boot.
8   Push a new 34 mm diameter clip onto the shaft, then the boot for the outer CV joint and the boot clamp. Fit the dished washer so that the outer diameter rests against the spacer. Now fit the spacer with the convex side towards the joint.
9   Press a new circlip into the joint and drive the joint onto the shaft using a rubber hammer until the circlip seats in the groove. Pack the joint with 90 grams of MOS$_2$ grease and then refit the boot.
10 Refit the shaft as described in Section 3.

5   Suspension strut – removal and refitting

1   Refer to Fig. 8.4. There are several ways in which the strut may be removed, depending upon the reason for removal and the tools available. If it is possible to remove the components without disturbing the axle nut or the camber, then so much the better.
2   It is quite simple to remove the whole assembly and then remove the damaged parts and renew them. If only the coil spring or shock absorber are to be removed then turn to paragraph 9.
3   Slacken the wheel nuts and support the front of the car on axle stands. Remove the wheel. Remove the socket-head bolts connecting the inner CVJ to the flange and encase the CVJ in a polythene bag. Remove the front brake caliper and hang it up with a piece of wire taking care not to strain the hydraulic hose, refer to Chapter 6.
4   Remove the clamp bolt (photo) from the wheel bearing housing which holds the steering balljoint in place and separate the wishbone from the wheel bearing housing. Undo the tie-rod securing nut and using a puller break the tie-rod balljoint (photo).
5   Remove the two nuts holding the top of the suspension strut to the bodyframe inside the engine compartment (photo). Lower the strut from the frame and take it away complete with driveshaft and disc.
6   The coil spring must be held in compression while the top nut on the rod is removed. There is a special tool VW340 and VW340/5 to do this, see Fig. 8.5, but there are various types of spring compressor

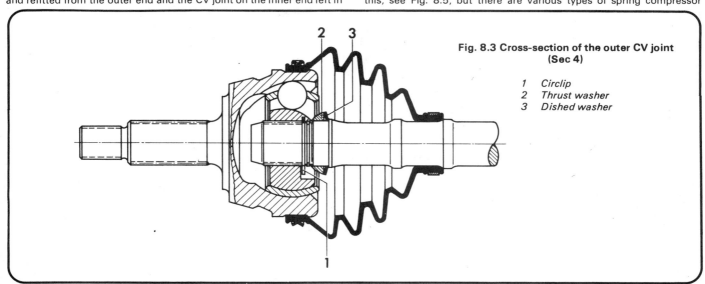

Fig. 8.3 Cross-section of the outer CV joint (Sec 4)

1 Circlip
2 Thrust washer
3 Dished washer

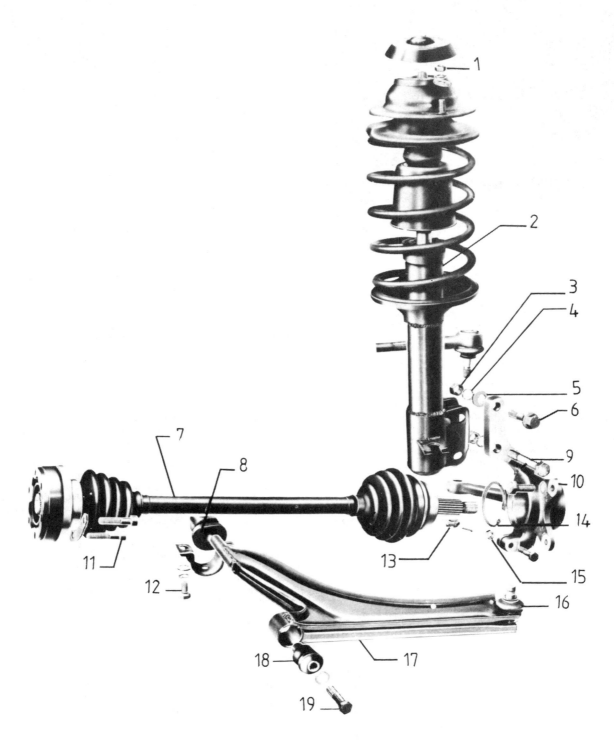

Fig. 8.4 Front suspension components (Sec 5)

1 Nut	6 Camber adjustment bolt	11 Retaining bolt	16 Ball joint
2 Suspension strut	7 Driveshaft	12 Bolt	17 Wishbone
3 Nut	8 Rubber bush	13 Tie-rod nut	18 Rubber bush
4 Washer	9 Bolt	14 Circlip	19 Bolt
5 Eccentric washer	10 Wheel bearing housing	15 Nut	

5.4A Steering balljoint and clamp bolt location

5.4B Tie-rod end and retaining nut location (right-hand side) and driveshaft outer bellows

5.5 Suspension strut upper mounting

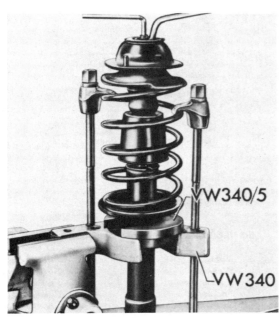

Fig. 8.5 Compressing the front spring with the special tool (Sec 5)

tools which will do the job. The nuts on the compressor tool should be tightened a little at a time on each side until the tension on the piston rod is relieved. The piston rod must be held tight while undoing the nut. There are flats formed on the end of the piston rod which can be held with a spanner. Fig. 8.6 shows details of the suspension strut.

7 Remove the coil spring and test the shock absorbers as in Section 7.

8 If the shock absorber is to be removed then the camber angle setting will be disturbed. To be able to reassemble the strut with the correct camber angle proceed as follows. Locate the top bolt holding the shock absorber clamp to the wheel bearing housing. This is an eccentric bolt (photo). Mark the relative position of the bolt head to the clamp by two centre-punch marks. Undo the camber adjusting bolt and the lower bolt and remove them. Open the clamp with a lever and extract the shock absorber.

9 It is possible to extract the strut without undoing the driveshaft or wishbone. Remove the bolts from the clamp as in paragraph 8, disconnect the top of the strut from the body as in paragraph 5, prise the clamp apart and push the wheel bearing housing off the strut. Lower the strut and remove it.

10 Assembly is the reverse of removal. Refit the shock absorber and coil spring to the wheel bearing housing. The spring must be compressed to start the securing nut. Tighten the nut to the specified torque. Adjust the camber eccentric correctly. Push the top of the

piston rod through the wing into the engine compartment and secure it correctly.

11 Refit the steering balljoint and wishbone to the wheel bearing housing, refit the tie-rod balljoint and then refit the driveshaft to the final drive.

12 Refit the brake caliper, refer to Chapter 6. Refit the roadwheel and lower the car to the ground.

13 If the camber adjusting eccentric bolt has been disturbed, it is advisable to have the camber angle checked at the earliest opportunity to ensure that the bolt has been fitted correctly.

6 Coil springs – inspection and renewal

1 There is not a lot to go wrong but even so the spring may require renewal. If it is broken read Chapter 9, Section 8, paragraphs 2 and 3 and examine the whole suspension very carefully.

2 If a knocking noise is heard from the front suspension when travelling over rough ground then the end coils are bottoming on the next coils. Read Chapter 9, Section 8, paragraph 4 but this time fit the damping sleeve to the top **and** bottom coils.

3 There are six tolerance groups for the coil spring, each group denoted by paint spots. If a spring is faulty make sure the new one is from the same tolerance group. Consult the VW storeman if in doubt about the marking.

4 The method of removal and refitting is given in Section 5.

7 Shock absorbers – inspection and renewal

1 A defective shock absorber will upset the steering and braking so it should be attended to right away. Apart from steering and braking difficulties it usually complains audibly as it operates.

2 A quick and reliable test is done by pushing the car down on the front corner and releasing the pressure suddenly. The car should run to its correct level without oscillation. Any oscillation indicates that the shock absorber is empty.

3 The shock absorber, removed from the suspension strut, should be held by the cylinder body in a vice. Push the piston rod right down and then pull it right out. There should be a firm, even resistance to movement throughout the stroke in both directions. If there is not then the unit is defective. If you are not sure take it to the VW agent and ask for it to be tested against a new one.

4 There is no repair, only renewal. It is not necessary to renew both shock absorbers if only one is faulty but it **must** be replaced by one of the same part number.

5 The method of removal and refitting is given in Section 5.

8 Wishbones – inspection, removal and refitting

1 The balljoint is attached to the wishbone by three 7 mm rivets. Renewal of the balljoint is by drilling out the rivets with a 6 mm drill and attaching the new balljoint with three 7 mm bolts and nuts, tightened to the specified torque.

2 Apart from fitting a new balljoint the pivot bushes may be replaced

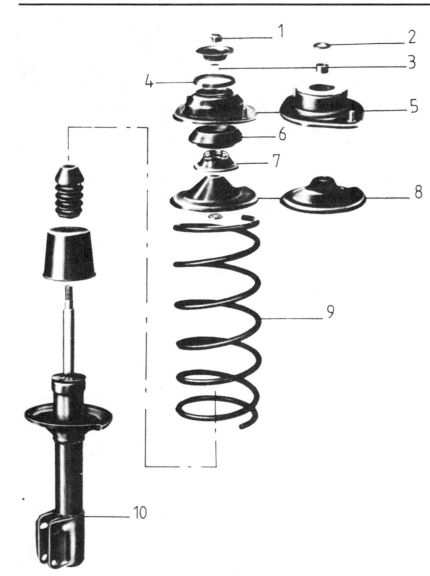

Fig. 8.6 Exploded view of the suspension strut (Sec 5)

1	Nut	6	Rubber damper
2	Washer	7	Strut bearing
3	Spacer sleeve	8	Spring seat
4	End collar	9	Coil spring
5	Bearing	10	Shock absorber

if worn. To do this properly the wishbone must be removed from the vehicle. This is discussed below.

3   Accident damage to the wishbone may result in the camber angle being altered and rapid tyre wear. Check the underside for kinks and wrinkles and check that the front and profile sides are straight, using a straight-edge or an engineer's square.

5.8 Wheel bearing housing upper retaining bolt, showing eccentric for adjusting camber angle

Fig. 8.7 Checking the wishbone for accident damage (Sec 8)

4   Although the wishbone may be removed with the roadwheel in-situ it is easier and safer to support the vehicle on axle stands and remove the front wheel. Support the wheel hub with a jack. Undo the clamp bolt holding the steering balljoint to the wheel bearing housing and lower the wishbone as far as possible. Remove the nuts holding the U-clip and rear pivot, hold the wishbone level and undo and extract the front hinge bolt (photo). Remove the wishbone from the vehicle.

5   The rubber bush at the rear may be pressed off and after the pivot

8.4 Suspension lower wishbone front pivot bolt

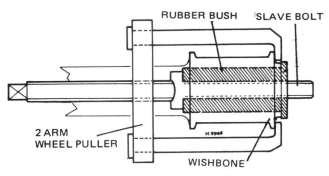

Fig. 8.8 Method of removing the front wishbone bush (Sec 8)

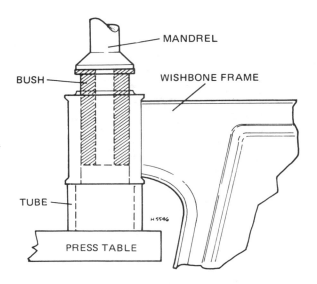

Fig. 8.9 Method of fitting the front wishbone bush (Sec. 8)

has been cleaned up a new one tapped into place with a hammer.

6   The front bush is a little more difficult. The simple way to press out the bush is to use a two arm puller. Fit a 10 mm bolt through the bush from the inside surface and push on the bolt with the puller centre bolt as shown in the diagram (Fig. 8.8) so that the bush is driven out from the wishbone. Smear the bore with a little brake grease and push a new bush in from the outside. When fully home, the bush protrudes past the bore of the wishbone so that the wishbone must be supported with a piece of tube large enough to allow the bush to slide inside it. A diagram shows this arrangement (Fig. 8.9).

7   When renewing the balljoint it is possible to drill out the rivets without removing the wishbone from the car, but it is possible that the drill may run out and enlarge the hole in the wishbone as well as removing the rivets. Therefore it is recommended that the wishbone is removed and the drilling carried out under a pillar drill with the wishbone clamped in position on the drilling machine table. Fit the new balljoint as described in paragraph 1.

8   When refitting the wishbone to the vehicle great care must be taken not to destroy the thread of the nut which holds the front hinge bolt in position. The bolt must be tightened to the specified torque. If this torque is not attainable then a new nut must be fitted and as the nut is welded **inside** the front crossmember its renewal is a major task only possible in a fully equipped workshop by professionals who have the right equipment. It involves opening up of the front crossmember – you have been warned! VW recommend the use of a new bolt the thread of which should be coated with D6 locking fluid (ask the VW storeman) and stress that lockwasher part no 411 399 267 must be fitted under the head of the bolt.

9   Before refitting the wishbone try the new bolt in the nut. Make sure it screws in easily. Remove it and position the wishbone in the correct place. Fit the U-clip for the back hinge but do not tighten it. Next try the front bolt and ease the wishbone until the bolt engages the thread in the nut easily. Keep the wishbone in that position, remove the bolt, fit the washer and coat the thread with D6 and install the bolt. Tighten to 1 kgf m (7 lbf ft) and then adjust the back bearing again. Check that the wishbone moves easily about the hinge bolts and then tighten the front one to the correct torque. Then tighten the rear hinge clip securing bolt. Check that the wishbone moves easily about the hinge bolts with no tight spots. If it does not, readjust the rear clip.

10   Finally refit the steering balljoint to the wheel bearing housing. Remove the jack from under the housing, refit the wheel and lower the vehicle to the ground.

9   Steering balljoints – inspection and renewal

1   A simple way to measure the vertical play of the balljoint is to fit a vernier caliper between the bottom of the wishbone and a convenient surface on the wheel bearing housing or brake caliper while the car is on its wheels (Fig. 8.10). Note the measurement. Jack-up the car so that the wheel is clear of the ground and recheck the measurement. Force the wheel down while measuring this distance. If the two measurements differ by more than 2.5 mm (0.10 in) then the joint

Fig. 8.10 Checking the steering balljoint for wear (Sec 9)

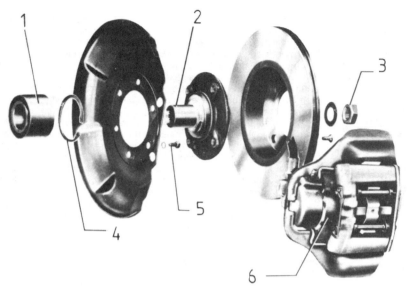

Fig. 8.11 Front hub and wheel bearing components (Sec 11)

1 *Wheel bearing*
2 *Hub*
3 *Axle nut*
4 *Circlip*
5 *Bolt*
6 *Brake caliper*

requires renewal. However it will be best to have this rechecked by the agent with special tools before proceeding further.

2   The method of removal and refitting is described in Section 8, paragraphs 1 and 7.

10 Wheel bearing housing – removal and refitting

1   With the vehicle standing on all four wheels undo the axle nut and slacken the wheel studs. Jack-up the front wheels and support the vehicle on axle stands. Remove the front wheel.

2   Remove the nut from the tie-rod balljoint and break the joint using a wheel puller.

3   Undo the clamp bolt and remove the steering balljoint from the wheel bearing housing. Push the wishbone down out of the way.

4   Remove the brake caliper, refer to Chapter 6, and tie it up out of the way with a piece of wire or cord. Do not allow it to hang by the brake hose.

5   Undo the crosshead screw securing the brake disc to the hub and remove the disc.

6   At this point there is a choice in procedure. Either remove the strut complete by undoing the nuts securing it to the frame in the engine compartment or remove the wheel bearing housing from the strut. The second method involves marking the camber adjustment bolt, so that it may be reassembled with the same camber adjustment, removing it and the lower bolt and then drawing the housing off the bottom of the strut and at the same time pulling it off the driveshaft splines. We found it easier to remove the wheel bearing housing from the strut. Whichever way you do it the bearing housing may now be removed from the car.

7   Assembly is the reverse of removal. If you have disturbed the camber angle set it as near as you can and have it checked when you go to the VW agent to have a **new** axle nut fitted to the correct torque.

11 Wheel bearing (front) – removal and refitting

1   The removal of a wheel bearing is a lengthy job so it is as well to be sure that it is actually necessary before doing the job. A defective bearing will make a rumbling noise under load. Jack-up the suspect wheel and test the rim rock. Spin the wheel and listen for noise indicating wear. A good bearing will make little or no noise. If you are not sure consult someone with experience because a defective race could cause a lot of trouble and, if it collapses, a nasty accident.

2   Having decided that it is necessary, remove the wheel bearing housing as described in Section 10. The next job is to press the hub out of the bearing race and for this job a press is necessary with the correct sized mandrels. **Do not** try to hammer it out. Using a feeler gauge measure the clearance between the hub and the wheel bearing housing to give you an idea of how much clearance to leave when refitting the hub in the housing. Once the hub is removed the splash

plate may be removed. The task will not present much difficulty if the wheel bearing housing has been separated from the strut but if it is still attached to the strut suitable provision must be made to support the strut during pressing operations.

3   The inner bearing race will come away on the hub and must be pulled off with a wheel puller. Hold the flange of the hub in soft jaws in a vice so that there is room for the inner race to be removed. Ideally a plug VW 431 which fits in the bore of the hub should be used on which the screw of the wheel puller can push. If such a plug is not available, then put a piece of plate behind the hub in the vice and, using a suitable piece of packing in the bore, push against that.

4   The outer bearing is held in the wheel bearing housing bore by two large circlips. Remove these and press the bearing out using a press and suitable mandrel. Again, do not use a hammer. Refit the outer circlip and press the new bearing into the housing from the inside pushing on the outer race only until it rests on the circlip. Now refit the inner circlip.

5   Refit the splash plate and then press the bearing housing on to the hub. This may sound the wrong way round but actually it is much easier to support the hub and press the housing on by pushing on the

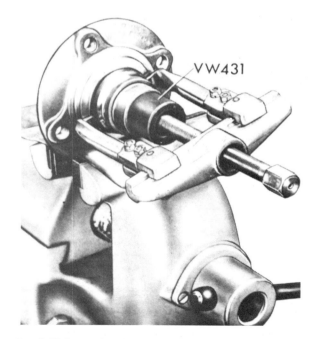

Fig. 8.12 Removing the wheel bearing inner race (Sec 11)

inner bearing race. **On no account** push on the outer race. If you measured the clearance between the hub and the housing before removing the hub then you know how much room to leave.

6 A word of caution. You will have gathered that the old race has been destroyed and a new one has to be bought. Unless you have a press and experience at this job we recommend you to ask the VW agent from whom you buy the race to fit it. It is very easy to damage the race and possibly the bore of the hub if you do not have the correct tools. This will mean a new hub and another race.

7 When the hub is in position reassemble the wheel bearing housing, strut and wishbone. Refit the brake caliper, refer to Chapter 6. If the camber angle has been disturbed, have it checked when you go to have the new axle nut tightened to the specified torque.

12 Tie-rods – removal and refitting

1 Refer to Fig. 8.15. On new vehicles the left-hand tie-rod is made in one piece and is not adjustable. The right-hand tie-rod consists of two pieces screwed together so that its length may be altered to adjust toe-in.

2 When a new tie-rod is required on the left-hand side the solid type is not supplied, an adjustable one is provided which must be adjusted to the same length as the original solid rod.

3 When setting the tie-rods in position the steering rack must protrude equally from each side of the casing, see Fig. 8.13. Note that the right-hand datum is the back (inside) of the flange.

4 When the rack is correctly set the tie-rods should be screwed on to the dimensions given in paragraph 8 below (Fig. 8.14). Once the rods are set to the correct dimension the locknuts should be tightened and the rubber cover fitted in position.

5 The outer ends of the tie-rods are attached to the steering arms by balljoints. These joints are pre-packed with lubricant. If the rubber seal perishes and the balljoint becomes worn a new tie-rod end must be fitted (on original left-hand side rods the complete rod must be renewed).

6 To renew a tie-rod end, mark the position of the locknut and then slacken the locknut. Remove the split-pin and castellated nut attaching the balljoint to the steering arm. Use a balljoint separator to disconnect the balljoint from the steering arm. Screw the new tie-rod end onto the same position on the tie-rod and tighten the locknut. Fit the balljoint to the steering arm, then tighten the securing nut to the specified torque and fit the split-pin.

7 Toe-in must always be adjusted on the right-hand tie-rod. Whenever the tie-rods or tie-rod ends have been disturbed, have the wheel alignment checked at your local VW garage.

8 Tie-rod dimensions are as follows:

Tie-rod length – LHS	379 mm (14.92 in)
Adjustable tie-rod length – RHS (Fig. 8.16)	379 mm (14.92 in)
Protrusion of rack (dimension [a] in Fig. 8.13)	Equal
Dimension (a) in Fig. 8.14 – LHS	69 mm (2.716 in)
Dimension (b) in Fig. 8.14 – RHS	69 mm (2.716 in)

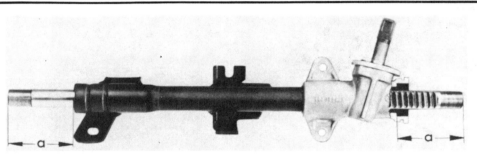

Fig. 8.13 Steering rack in central position – a = a (Sec 12)

Fig. 8.14 Tie-rod setting dimensions (Sec 12) *For a and b see text*

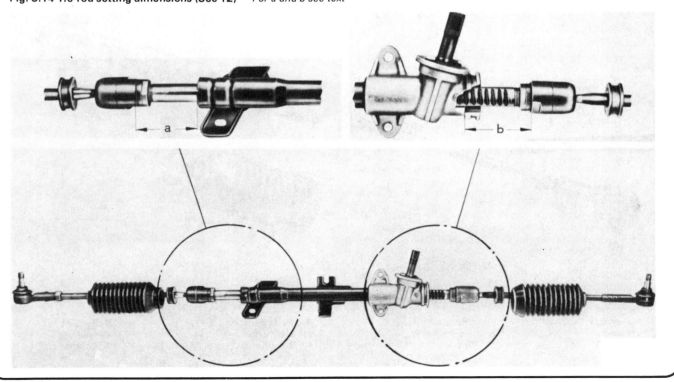

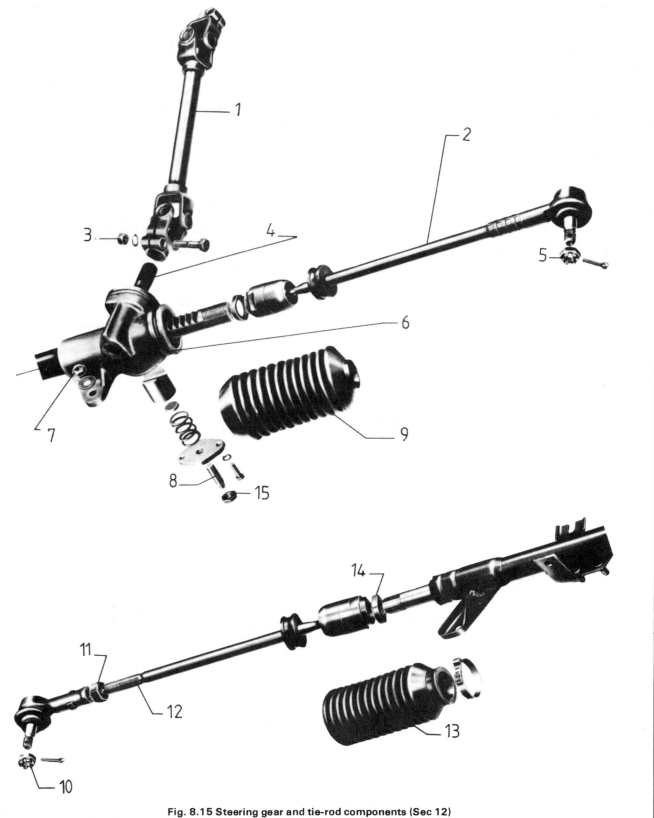

Fig. 8.15 Steering gear and tie-rod components (Sec 12)

1	Lower steering shaft	5	Castle nut	9	Bellows	13	Bellows
2	LH tie-rod	6	Steering gear	10	Castle nut	14	Lockring
3	Nut	7	Nut	11	Locknut	15	Locknut
4	Pinion	8	Adjusting screw	12	RH tie-rod		

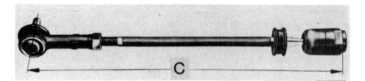

Fig. 8.16 Basic tie-rod adjustment dimension C (Sec 12)

13 Steering gear – removal and refitting

1   Refer to Fig. 8.15. The steering gear is located in the engine compartment behind the engine. Push back the rubber boot from the universal shaft joint and remove the clamp bolt from the lower universal joint (photo). Push the universal joint up the pinion shaft splines as far as possible. It will not come off the pinion shaft at this stage.

2   Working underneath the car, disconnect the bracket which attaches the gearchange linkage to the steering gear.

3   Refer to Section 12 and remove the tie-rods. There is no need to disconnect the outer joints. Slacken the locknuts and unscrew the balljoints from each end of the rack.

4   Undo the nuts securing the U-clamps which attach the steering gear to the body (Fig. 8.17), then remove the clamps and at the same time lift away the steering gear, which will now come away from the

13.1 Steering column to steering gear universal joint bellows

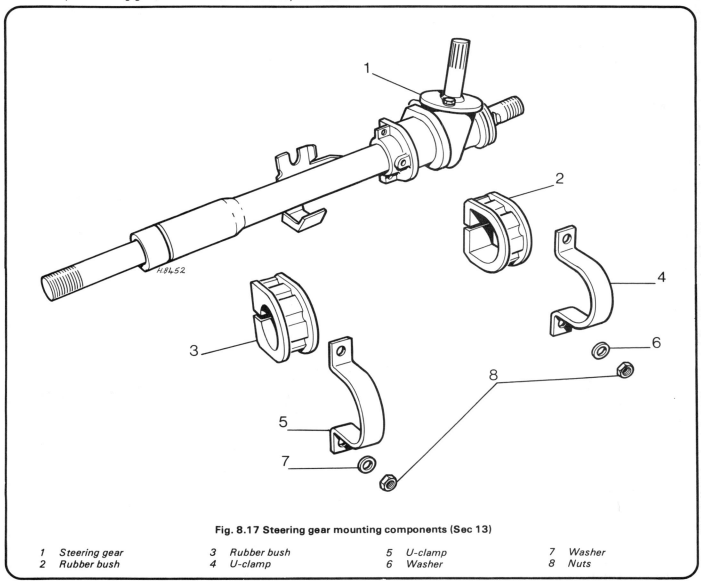

Fig. 8.17 Steering gear mounting components (Sec 13)

1	Steering gear	3	Rubber bush	5	U-clamp	7	Washer
2	Rubber bush	4	U-clamp	6	Washer	8	Nuts

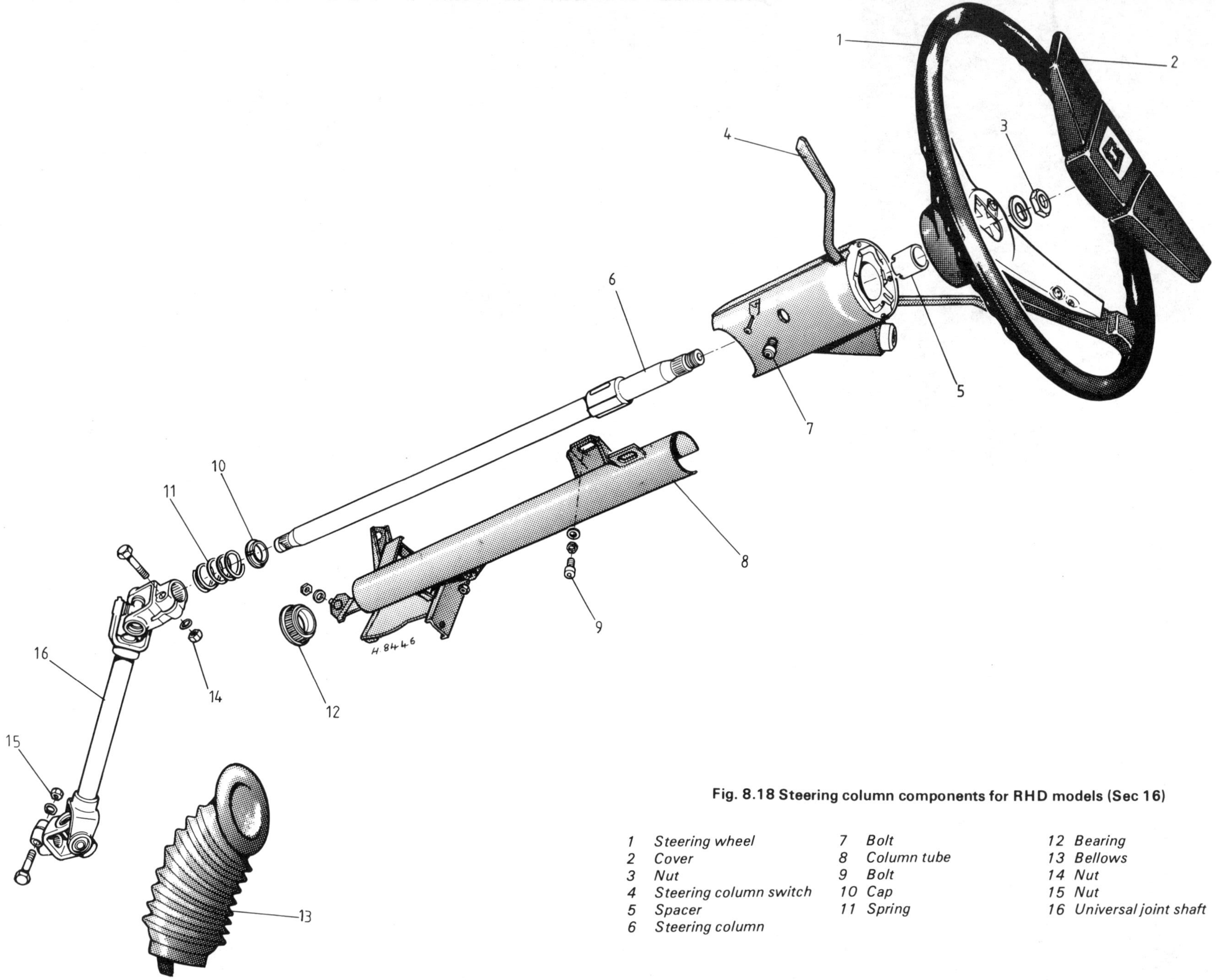

Fig. 8.18 Steering column components for RHD models (Sec 16)

1	Steering wheel	7	Bolt	12	Bearing
2	Cover	8	Column tube	13	Bellows
3	Nut	9	Bolt	14	Nut
4	Steering column switch	10	Cap	15	Nut
5	Spacer	11	Spring	16	Universal joint shaft
6	Steering column				

H 8446

universal joint shaft. The steering gear can now be removed through the right-hand wheel arch. It may be necessary to remove the roadwheel to pull the gear clear.

5   Refitting is the reverse of the removal procedure. Ensure that the rubber mounting bushes on the gear casing are in good condition. When fitting the universal joint shaft take care that the flat on the pinion shaft lines up with the clamp bolt hole. Fit the clamp bolt loosely, then tighten the U-clamp to the body. Tighten all the nuts to the specified torque.

6   Refit the tie-rods, refer to Section 12. Adjust the gearchange linkage, refer to Chapter 5. Have the front wheel alignment checked and adjusted as necessary.

14   Steering gear – adjustment

1   The steering gear is not repairable: if it is damaged or worn beyond adjustment, a complete new assembly must be fitted.

2   The only adjustment is the pressure on the engagement between the rack and pinion. This is adjusted by a screw which is screwed in to increase the pressure and out to reduce the pressure.

3   The adjustment screw is located behind the gear assembly and it is difficult to gain access to adjust the steering.

4   If rattling noises are heard coming from the steering gear when the vehicle goes over rough surfaces then the pinion is loose in the rack and must be adjusted. To do this first jack-up the front of the car and set it on axle stands. Undo the adjuster locknut and back off the adjuster a little. Now tighten it until it touches the thrust washer, you will note more resistance at this point. Hold the adjuster in this position and tighten the locknut.

5   A creaking sound from the rack and pinion denotes lack of lubrication. Move the steering to full lock and pull back the rubber rack cover on the extended side, wipe the grease away and spray on Molykote 321 R. Allow this to dry for ten minutes and then apply a thin film of lithium based grease and refit the rubber cover.

6   When correctly adjusted there should be a natural self-centring force when cornering. If this is absent and the steering is stiff then the pinion is binding on the rack and must be adjusted.

15   Steering wheel – removal and refitting

1   Disconnect the battery earth lead to avoid accidental short circuits. The horn pad pulls off, after a struggle, to expose the steering column nut. Disconnect the lead, undo the nut and pull the wheel off the splines (photos).

2   When refitting the wheel be careful to install the wheel in the central position.

3   Do not forget to reconnect the battery earth lead.

16   Steering column (RHD models) – removal and refitting

1   Disconnect the battery earth strap and remove the steering wheel (Section 15).

2   Refer to Fig. 8.18. Remove the steering column switches as described in Chapter 7 and then prise out the spacer sleeve.

3   At the bottom of the column tube there is a cross bracket which supports the pedals. Remove the pedal connections (for the clutch refer to Chapter 4 and for the brake pedal refer to Chapter 6).

4   Remove the nuts securing the bottom bracket to the body. Remove the screws securing the upper column bracket to the dashboard.

5   Undo the nut and remove the bolt clamping the universal joint to the steering column. Remove the steering column and tube from the car.

6   Remove the column shaft from the tube. At the bottom of the tube there is a spring and spring seat: take care not to lose these. If the steering column bearing has to be renewed it can be pushed out and a new bearing pressed in.

7   Assembly is the reverse of removal. Fit the spring seat and spring, insert the column and reconnect the UJ shaft at the bottom. Refit the nuts and bolts holding the steering column to the body and reconnect the brake pedal and clutch pedal. Refit the column switch and the multipin plugs and now press in the spacer sleeve until the distance

15.1A The steering wheel retaining nut

15.1B Steering wheel horn lead connection

from the top of the column to the top of the spacer sleeve is 41.5 mm (1.63 in). This will set the gap between the steering wheel and the column switch at 2 to 4 mm (0.08 to 0.16 in). Fig. 8.19 shows the measurement. Now refit the steering wheel and the covers. Check the clutch and brake pedal movement.

17   Steering column (LHD models) – removal and refitting

1   Refer to Fig. 8.23 and it will be seen that the steering column lower attachment is different from that on RHD models. Otherwise the removal and refitting procedure is the same as described in Section 16.

2   Instead of the column being fixed rigidly to the pedal bracket, which is bolted to the frame, the column is attached to the bracket by a leaf spring. The bracket is reshaped so that the column may be inserted from the left-hand side and then the leaf spring fitted across the open end of the bracket.

3   In the event of a collision the shaft will be pushed sideways, removing the spring. In this event the complete steering gear should be dismantled and thoroughly inspected for damage before using the car again.

4   When removing the steering column, the leaf spring is removed by using a screwdriver to press down on the spring to release it from the retaining clip, see Fig. 8.20, and then withdrawing it from the slot in

the bracket.

5   To refit the leaf spring, insert one end of the spring in the bracket slot (arrow A in Fig. 8.21) and then press down on the other end of the spring until it locates in the retaining clip.

6   Note that the mounting ring shown in Fig. 8.23 has been modified and a split bush fitted instead. To remove the bush, pry it open and slide it from the column tube. When fitting a new bush, ensure that the lug enages with the slot in the column tube (see Fig. 8.22).

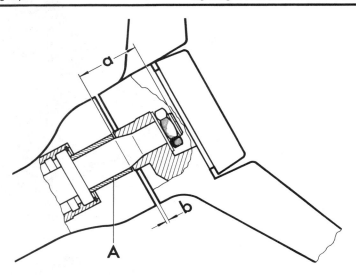

Fig. 8.19 Steering column spacer sleeve A adjustment dimensions
(Sec 16)

a = 41.5 mm (1.63 in)
b = 2.0 to 4.0 mm (0.08 to 0.16 in)

Fig. 8.20 Removing the steering column retaining leaf spring on
LHD models (Sec 17)

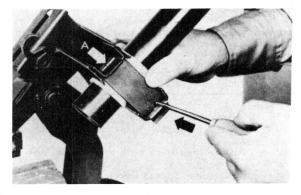

Fig. 8.21 Refitting the steering column retaining leaf spring on LHD
models (Sec 17)

A ∙ Spring end in bracket slot

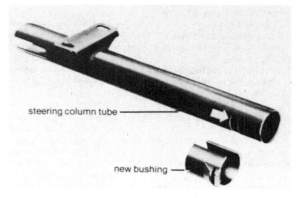

steering column tube

new bushing

Fig. 8.22 Modified mounting ring location slot – arrowed
(Sec 17)

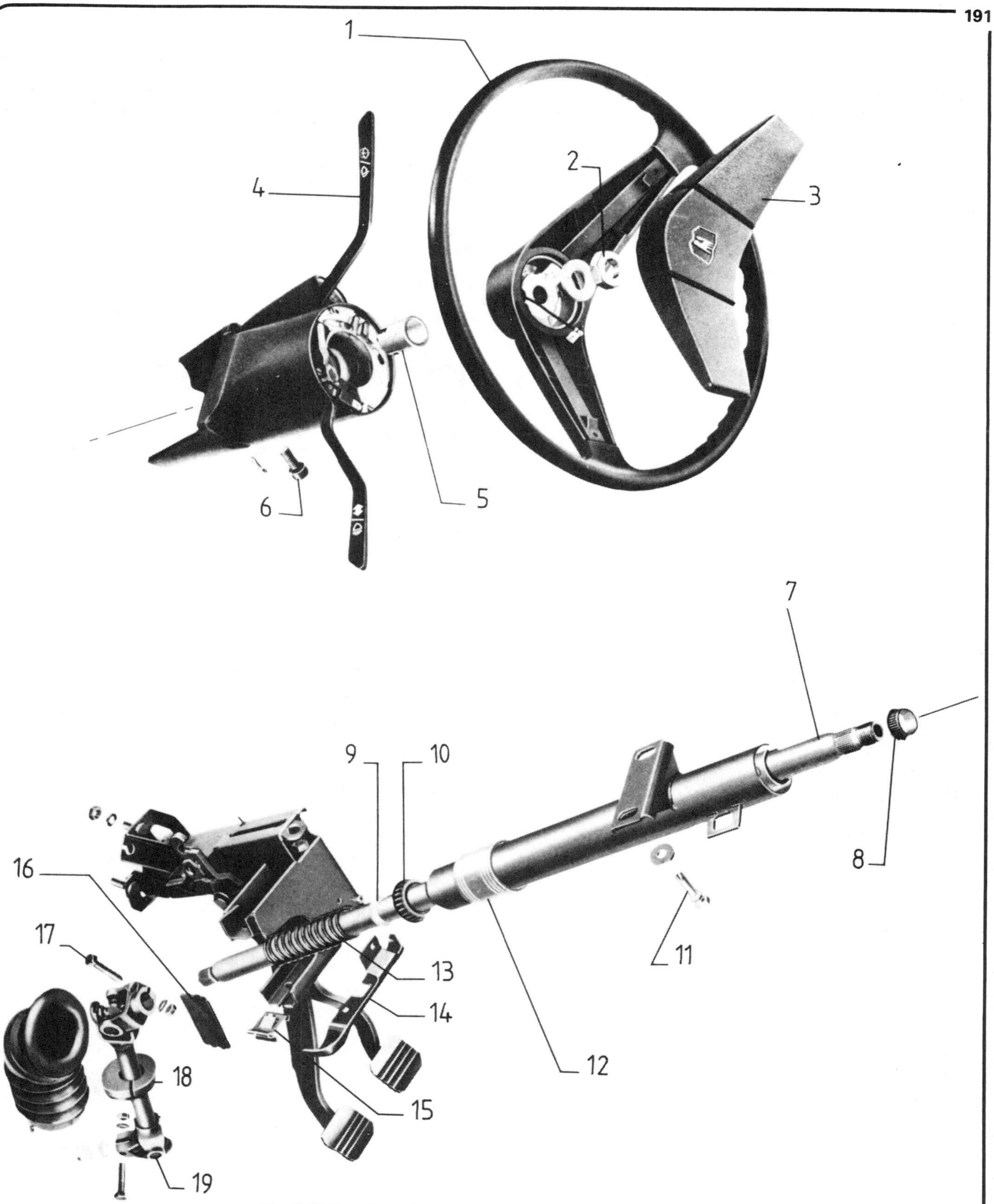

Fig. 8.23 Steering column components for LHD models (Sec 17)

1	Steering wheel	6	Bolt
2	Retaining nut	7	Steering column
3	Cover	8	Bearing support ring
4	Steering column switch	9	Support ring
5	Spacer sleeve	10	Steering column bearing

11	Shear bolt	16	Leaf spring
12	Mounting ring	17	Clamp bolt
13	Spring	18	Damping grommet
14	Cover plate	19	Lower steering shaft
15	Retaining spring		

18 Fault diagnosis – front suspension, steering and driveshafts

Symptom	Reason/s
Noise from front suspension	Coil springs bottoming Shock absorber defective Brake pads require renewal Front wheel bearing defective
Tyres wearing excessively on inner or outer edges of the tread	Steering geometry incorrect Wishbone damaged or bushes worn Steering balljoint worn Tie-rod balljoints worn
Steering wanders and is unstable	Front tyres soft Check all items from fault 2, (excessive tyre wear) Shock absorbers defective Wheel bearing defective Steering gear loose UJ shaft bolts not tight
Steering stiff and does not centre correctly	Steering wheel hard on spacer sleeve Steering gear requires adjustment or lubrication Steering balljoints damaged Wishbones damaged Steering geometry incorrect (this will be a first sign before tyre wear occurs)
Wheel wobble or 'shimmy'	Wheels or tyres out of balance Steering linkages worn or loose Tyre pressures incorrect Wear in suspension

Chapter 9 Rear axle and rear suspension

Contents

Specifications

Type .... Torsion axle beam with trailing arms. MacPherson type struts with coil spring and co-axial shock absorber. Wheels carried on stub axles bolted to trailing arms

Coil springs .... Initial fitting: three grades with 1, 2 or 3 paint marks. New springs available only with two green paint marks

Shock absorbers .... Hydraulic, telescopic, double-acting

Geometry

Adjustment .... All angles fixed – non-adjustable
Camber .... – 1° 15′ ± 5′
Maximum difference between sides .... 40′
Wheel alignment (total toe-in) .... + 20′ ± 30′
Maximum deviation from driving direction .... 30′
Track .... 1358 mm (53·4 in)

Hub bearings .... Taper roller, adjustable

Torque wrench settings

	kgf m	lbf ft
Axle beam to mounting bracket	6·0	43
Mounting bracket to body	4·5	32
Shock absorber to trailing arm	4·5	32
Shock absorber to body	3·5	25
Shock absorber piston rod nut	2·0	14
Stub axle to trailing arm	6·0	43

1 General description

1   A fabricated axle beam is located across the vehicle body held on either side in mounting brackets which are bolted to the underside of the body. The axle is held in the mounting by a hinge bolt which passes through a bonded rubber bush. The cross beam is a T-section.
2   Welded to the beam and supported by gusset plates are trailing arms of circular section. These terminate in fabricated brackets which serve as lower anchors for the shock absorbers and as mounting pads for the stub axles and rear brake backplates.
3   The stub axle carries the rear hub, brake drum and wheel on two taper roller bearings. The movement of the wheel is thus a radial one in the vertical plane. The weight of the body and its contents is supported by a suspension strut on each side which is secured to the body at its upper end and the axle at the lower end. The strut consists of a coil spring and shock absorber mounted co-axially. The shock absorbers are of hydraulic telescopic construction. Approximately half way up the outer casing of the shock absorber is welded a spring platform which houses the lower end of the spring (photo). The upper end is housed in spring cup which is kept in place by a slotted nut fitted to the piston

rod of the shock absorber. A rubber buffer is fitted on the piston rod to stop the spring being compressed until its coils are solid.
4   The suspension strut is assembled complete away from the vehicle and then fitted, first to the body by a nut removable from inside the vehicle body and at the lower end by a hinge bolt to the bracket at the end of the trailing arm.
5   The different types of spring fitted are discussed in Section 8.
6   The camber angle and toe-in are fixed. Details are given in the Specifications for checking, should distortion be suspected.
7   The suspension struts may be removed without dismantling the axle, and once the brake hoses and the handbrake cables are disconnected the whole assembly may be removed from the car by removing six nuts.
8   If the axle beam or the stub axles are distorted or otherwise damaged they must be renewed. Repair by straightening or welding is not permitted.

2 Rear wheel bearings – adjustment

1   The rear wheel bearings are normal taper bearings. To adjust

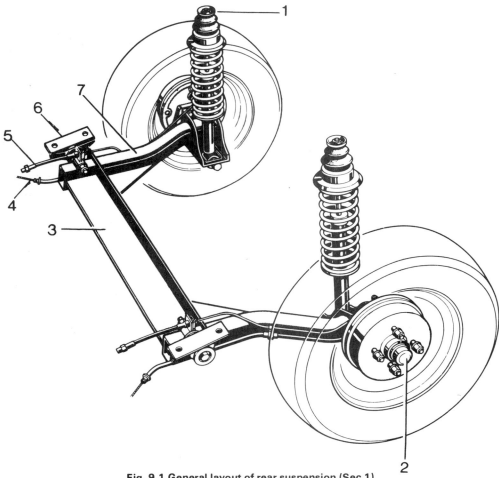

Fig. 9.1 General layout of rear suspension (Sec 1)

1 Suspension strut
2 Wheel bearing hub
3 Axle beam
4 Handbrake cable

5 Hydraulic brake pipe
6 Mounting
7 Trailing arm

1.3 Rear suspension strut and coil spring

2.1 Checking the rear wheel bearing for wear. Rocking movement indicates the need for adjustment

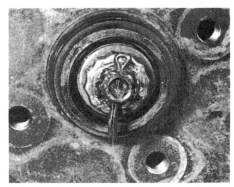

2.2 Rear wheel bearing nut locking ring and retaining split-pin

them, first raise the rear of the car and support it on axle stands or other suitable supports (photo).
2   Remove the dust cap with a suitable lever, remove the split-pin and withdraw the nut locking ring (photo).
3   Slacken off the hub nut and then tighten it while turning the wheel to settle the bearings.
4   Now slacken off the hub nut again, then tighten it until the thrust

washer can be moved (rotated) slightly with a screwdriver (or similar tool) as shown in Fig. 9.2. Do not twist or lever the screwdriver to obtain movement.
5   Refit the nut locking ring and a new split-pin.
6   Fill the dust cap with multi-purpose grease and tap it into position on the hub.
7   Remove the axle stands and lower the car to the ground.

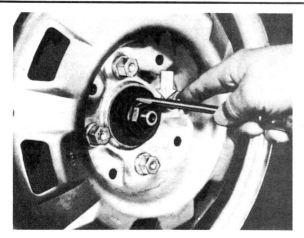

Fig. 9.2 Checking the rear wheel bearing adjustment (Sec 2)

3.2 Removing the rear wheel bearing adjusting nut

3 Rear wheel bearings – removal and refitting

1   Slacken the wheel nuts, jack-up the rear wheel, support the vehicle on an axle stand and remove the wheel. Refer to Fig. 9.3.

2   Remove the hub grease cap, remove the split-pin and locking ring. Remove the adjusting nut (photo). Slacken the brake adjusters (Chapter 6), and remove the brake drum. The thrust washer and the outer bearing complete will come away with the drum, together with the oil seal and the outer race of the inner bearing. The inner race of the inner bearing will remain on the stub axle.

3   Remove the oil seal and tap the bearings out of the brake drum with a brass drift (photo). Clean the drum and stub axle and oil them lightly. Wash the bearings in clean paraffin and then swill out all residue with more clean paraffin. Dry them carefully with a non-fluffy rag.

4   Examine the tracks of the races for scoring or signs of overheating. If these are present then the complete bearing should be renewed.

Inspect the roller bearings carefully, there should be no flats or burrs. Lubricate the race with a light oil and spin the inner race in the outer race. Any roughness indicates undue wear and the bearing should be renewed. Once a bearing begins to wear the wear accelerates rapidly and may be the cause of damage to the stub axle or drum so if you are in doubt get an expert opinion.

5   Examine the oil seal. Ideally it should be renewed; if there is any damage or sign of hardening renew it anyway. Failure of an oil seal will mean contamination of the brake shoes and the minimum penalty will be new shoes on **both** rear wheels.

6   If all the items are correct and the stub axle bearing surfaces and brake drum bore are in good order then proceed to assemble the hub.

7   Pack the taper bearings with a lithium based grease, and smear the stub axle with a light film of grease. Fit the inner race, the inner bearing and the oil seal into the brake drum. Press the seal into place,

Fig. 9.3 Exploded view of the rear wheel bearings (Sec 3)

1	Dust cap	4	Nut	7	Brake drum and hub
2	Split-pin	5	Thrust washer	8	Inner bearing
3	Nut locking ring	6	Outer bearing	9	Oil seal

3.3 Rear wheel hub oil seal location

tap it home with a rubber hammer taking care that it is squarely seated.

8   Fit the drum to the stub axle then the outer race and finally the thrust washer. Fit the nut and adjust the bearing as in Section 2. Fit the nut locking ring and a new split-pin. Refit the dust cap and the road-wheel and test the bearing by spinning the wheel. Lower the vehicle to the ground.

4   Stub axles – removal, inspection and refitting

1   Apart from scoring on the bearing surfaces or ovality due to excessive bearing wear the only other defect to check on the the stub axle is distortion due to bending. This could happen if the vehicle has been in an accident or has been driven heavily laden at excessive speed over rough ground.

2   The effect of a bent stub axle will be excessive tyre wear due to the wrong camber angle and possibly incorrect toe-in. The angles are small with fine limits and, in our opinion, not measurable without the proper equipment. If irregular wear occurs the owner is advised to have these angles checked right away. Before deciding that the stub axle is bent read Section 5.

3   Alternatively the stub axle may be removed, bolted to a lathe face plate and checked for alignment with a dial gauge. The allowable run out is 0.25 mm (0.010 in).

4   To remove the stub axle proceed as in Section 3 and remove the

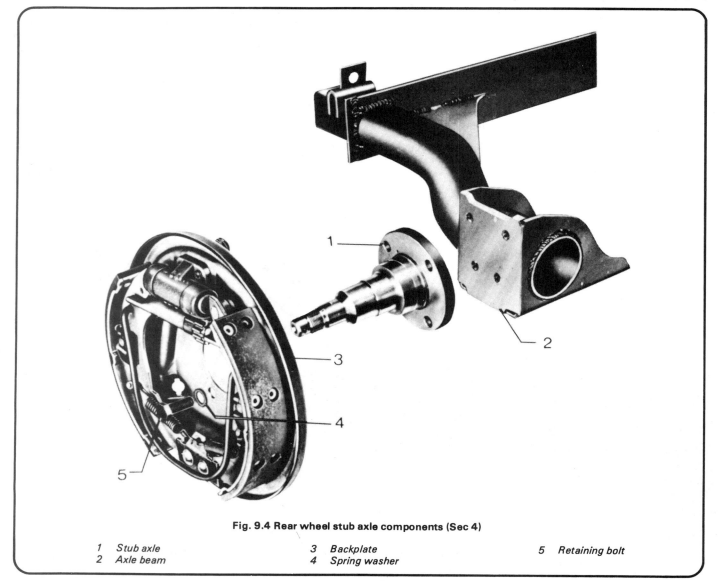

Fig. 9.4 Rear wheel stub axle components (Sec 4)

| 1 | Stub axle | 3 | Backplate | 5 | Retaining bolt |
| 2 | Axle beam | 4 | Spring washer | | |

brake drum and bearings. The brake backplate and stub axle are held to the axle beam by four bolts. Unfortunately these are only accessible after the brake shoes have been removed (see Chapter 6). Remove the shoes and then the four bolts. The backplate and wheel cylinder may be moved out of the way to extract the stub axle.

5   Refitting is the reverse of removal. Make sure the joint faces of the stub axle and axle beam are clean and free from burrs before assembly.

5   Axle beam – visual check for distortion

1   If irregular wear of the rear tyres is observed the reason will probably be incorrect camber angle. Before dismantling the stub axle check that the gusset plate of the axle beam is not distorted. If this fault is present the axle beam will be out of alignment. This will require a new axle beam. The removal and refitting of the complete rear axle is discussed in Section 10. Before deciding to renew the axle beam we suggest that the camber angle should be checked by the VW agent and your diagnosis confirmed.

6   Suspension strut – removal and refitting

1   Open the tailgate and lift the parcel shelf. On each side of the body on top of the wheel arches are plastic caps which cover the rear suspension strut upper mounting. Remove the plastic cap (photo).

2   Slacken the wheel nuts, raise the rear of the car and support the body on axle stands. The best place for this is the recommended jacking point, just forward of the wheel, which is a narrow flat surface with a hole in it. Remove the roadwheel.

3   Remove the nut from the bolt securing the shock absorber to the trailing arm and tap out the bolt (photo). It may be necessary to take the weight of the hub when removing this bolt. If the bolt fouls the brake drum then the brake backplate must be removed, refer to Section 4.

4   Once the lower anchorage is clear remove the nut securing the upper mounting of the shock absorber piston inside the body, and lift off the special washer (photo). This operation needs two people: one to

undo the nut and one to hold the strut. Remove the strut from the car.

5   Refitting is the reverse of the removal procedure. Tighten the upper and lower mounting nuts to the specified torque. On models from July 1978 ensure that the protective tube, see Fig. 9.6, is

Fig. 9.6 Suspension strut components fitted to later models (Sec 6)

1	Plastic cap	6	Alternative hexagon nut
2	Plate	7	Spring cap
3	Upper bush	8	Protective tube
4	Lower bush	9	Coil spring
5	Spacer sleeve		

Fig. 9.5 Rear axle gusset plate – arrowed (Sec 5)

6.1 Removing a rear suspension strut upper mounting cap

6.3 Rear suspension strut lower mounting

6.4 Rear suspension strut upper mounting

Fig. 9.7 Exploded view of the rear suspension strut (Sec 6)

1 Nut
2 Slotted nut
3 Spring cap
4 Coil spring
5 Flat washer
6 Nut
7 Rear axle
8 Shock absorber
9 Nut
10 Handbrake cable holder
11 Mounting pivot bolt
12 Concave washer
13 Mounting bracket
14 Piston rod
15 Buffer

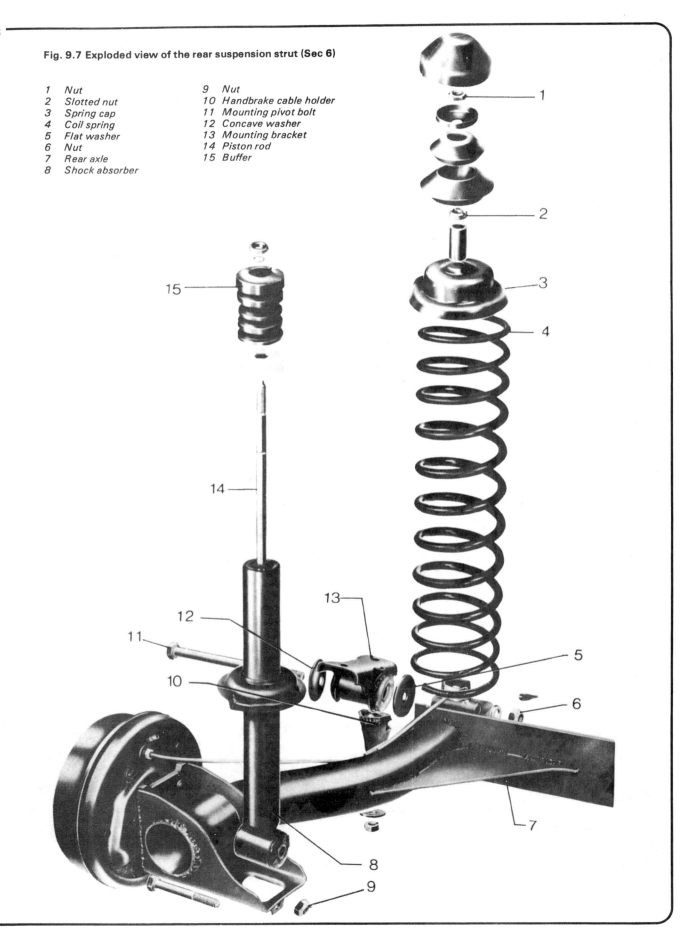

correctly fitted to prevent the entry of dirt and water which would result in premature failure of the shock absorber.

7 Suspension strut – dismantling and reassembly

1   Refer to Fig. 9.7. The spring is held in compression by a special slotted nut (an ordinary nut may be found instead on some models). It is not necessary to clamp the spring with a spring compressing tool as described for the front springs (Chapter 8). Mount the strut assembly in a vice as shown in Fig. 9.8.

2   If the special slotted nut is fitted, VW tool No. 50-200 will be required to unscrew the nut while holding the shock absorber piston rod with a suitable spanner, to prevent the rod from turning.

3   Remove the slotted nut and separate the spring from the shock absorber.

4   To assemble the strut fit the protective cap and the rubber buffer on the shock absorber piston rod, followed by the circlip and washer.

5   Fit the spring, spring retainer and spacer sleeve. Fit the retaining nut on the piston rod and tighten it to the specified torque. The spring may have to be compressed a little to get the nut started.

6   The remaining parts of the upper mounting are fitted when the strut assembly is fitted on the car.

8 Coil springs – inspection

1   Three faults may occur; either the spring is broken, which is very rare, or more often a rattling noise coming from the region of the back axle when the vehicle is driven over rough surfaces. The latter fault may be due to the end coil of the spring at the top coming into contact with the next coil. Finally the spring may just have got tired and distorted. In any case the suspension strut must be removed and dismantled as in Sections 6 and 7.

2   If the spring is broken then a careful examination of the fracture is indicated. Should the surface of the fracture show a crystalline form plus a smaller portion of clean metal then the spring was probably faulty when assembled. It would be worthwhile pointing this out to the agent. Anyway renewal is indicated.

3   If the metal shows a clean break with no flaws, then a careful examination of the rest of the suspension is indicated for the force required for such a fracture will be of very large proportions indeed.

4   If the top coil has been knocking on the next coil there will be evidence in the form of marking. In this case a piece of damping sleeve may be fitted (Part No 321 511 123) over the top two coils. This is plastic tube. There is enough for top and bottom so cut it in half. The spring must be cleaned and the upper part of the coil spring and the inside of the plastic tube coated with petroleum jelly. Slide one half of the tube over the upper coils of the spring. If necessary, fit the other half of the tube on the bottom coils of the spring.

5   Once the plastic tube is in position the spring may be put back on the strut. The coils will still bottom but the noise will stop, for a while at least.

6   If the spring has distorted, then it has just got tired and it must be renewed. The cause could be one of several: incorrect material, wrong

heat treatment, or even the wrong spring. These occasions are mercifully rare and distortion is usually brought on by continuous overloading.

7   When the springs are fitted they are selected for the purpose. Three grades are used, denoted by one, two or three paint stripes. When renewal is required VW state that only the spring with two stripes is available. They further say that it is not necessary to renew both springs if only one is faulty. So fit a spring with two green paint stripes.

9 Shock absorbers – testing

1   A defective shock absorber usually makes a rumbling noise as the car goes over rough surfaces. A quick test to confirm this suspicion is to press the rear of the car down on the suspected side and release it sharply. The car should rise and settle at once, if it oscillates at all the shock absorber is not working correctly. A small seepage of fluid round the piston seal is normal and need cause no worry, but a large leakage indicates that the shock absorber must be changed. There is no repair possible.

2   Remove and dismantle the suspension strut as in Sections 6 and 7. Hold the lower portion of the shock absorber in a vice with the piston rod in a vertical position. Pull the rod right up and press it down again. The force required in each direction should be even and equal. Repeat this test several times. If the stroke is uneven or jerky then the unit must be renewed.

3   Examine the lower anchorage. The bush must be a good fit on the locating bolt, and the rubber mounting in good condition. If either of these are faulty enquire whether a new bush and mounting are available from the VW store. Should this be so get a new locating bolt at the same time. Press the bush out of the eye with the mounting and press both of them into the eye. Lubricate the eye with a little rubber grease or soap before pressing the mounting home and be careful to enter it squarely. This must be done on a flypress or in a large vice, do not attempt to hammer it in. Alternatively an arrangement of a draw bolt with a nut and two large washers may be used.

10 Rear axle – removal and refitting

1   If the rear axle beam is distorted the entire rear suspension must be removed. It is not possible to remove the pivot bolts from the mountings as the bolts foul the body.

2   Support the vehicle body on axle stands (Section 6) and remove the wheels. Remove the brake drums and dismantle the brake shoes to free the handbrake cables (Chapter 6). Unclip the handbrake outer cables from the trailing arms (Fig. 9.9).

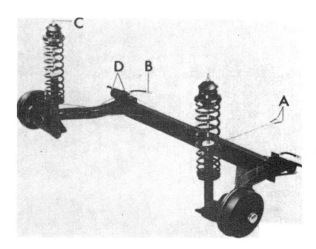

Fig. 9.9 Rear axle assembly removal (Sec 10)

A	Handbrake cables	C	Suspension strut upper
B	Brake hydraulic hose		mounting
		D	Pivot bolt

Fig. 9.8 Rear suspension strut mounted in a vice, showing holding flats (arrowed) and special tool (Sec 7)

3   Disconnect the hydraulic brake lines and plug the hoses to prevent dirt or grease entering the system.
4   It may be necessary to remove parts of the exhaust system of the Rabbit before proceeding further.
5   Each mounting is held by two studs and nuts. These must now be slackened off. Be careful not to shear off the studs. If you do, refer to Section 11.
6   From inside the body remove the caps from the suspension struts and slacken off the nuts holding the shock absorber pistons to the body.
7   Support the axle and remove all the retaining nuts. It will be best to have three people to do this job. The axle beam and suspension struts may now be lowered to the ground and removed.
8   Separate the mountings by removing the hinge bolts. Note how the large washer is situated between the axle beam and the mounting. The dished washer is fitted with the bolt.
9   When assembling, lubricate the dished washer to prevent squeaks.
10   Refitting is the reverse of the removal procedure. Remember to adjust the handbrake and bleed the hydraulic system as described in Chapter 6.
11   When the car is back on its wheels, check that the hinge bolt nuts are tightened to the specified torque.

11 Rear axle mountings – removal and refitting

1   If you have the misfortune to shear one of the studs then the stud must be drilled out and the resultant hole tapped for a 10 mm thread.

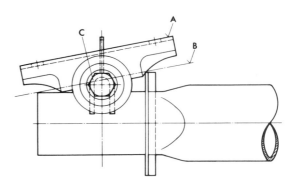

Fig. 9.10 Rear axle pivot bush tightening diagram (Sec 11)

Raise axle until line B is approximately parallel to upper face of mounting bracket A, then tighten nut C

Use an 8 mm drill and be careful to drill exactly in the centre of the stud. We advise caution. Unless you have experience in this type of work get a trained mechanic to do it for you. If you drill in the wrong place, the result will be very expensive. After tapping the hole fit a 10 mm bolt x 40, tensile class 10.9.
2   When refitting the mounting align it as shown in Fig. 9.10.

12 Fault diagnosis – rear axle and rear suspension

Symptom	Reason/s
Excessive or uneven tyre wear	Stub axle bent, check camber Axle beam distorted Wheel bearings defective Shock absorber defective Brake binding
Rumbling noise from rear axle	Shock absorber defective Wheel bearing defective
Chattering or knocking from rear axle	Top coil spring knocking on lower coil Lower mount of shock absorber worn Broken spring
Squeak from rear axle	Disc washer on hinge bolt rubbing on the bonded rubber bush Guide sleeve of handbrake cable requires lubrication

Chapter 10 Bodywork and fittings

For modifications, and information applicable to later models, see Supplement at end of manual

Contents

1 General description

The body is of all-steel unit construction with impact-absorbing front and rear crumple zones which take the brunt of any accident, leaving the passenger compartment with minimum distortion. The front crumple zones take the form of two corrugated box sections in the scuttle and firewall.

There are two-door and four-door models. All models have a large tailgate hinged at the top, which is propped open by a gas-filled telescopic strut.

The front wings are bolted on to the body and can easily be renewed in the event of damage.

The type of bumpers fitted varies. In the USA and certain other territories, shock absorbing bumpers are mandatory. Where this is not a legal requirement normal bolt-on bumpers are fitted.

All models have individual fully reclining front bucket seats that can be adjusted to any position.

2 Maintenance – bodywork and underframe

The general condition of a vehicle's bodywork is the one thing that significantly affects its value. Maintenance is easy but needs to be regular. Neglect, particularly after minor damage, can lead quickly to further deterioration and costly repair bills. It is important also to keep watch on those parts of the vehicle not immediately visible, for instance the underside, inside all the wheel arches and the lower part of the engine compartment.

The basic maintenance routine for the bodywork is washing – preferably with a lot of water, from a hose. This will remove all the loose solids which may have stuck to the vehicle. It is important to flush these off in such a way as to prevent grit from scratching the finish. The wheel arches and underframe need washing in the same way to remove any accumulated mud which will retain moisture and tend to encourage rust. Paradoxically enough, the best time to clean the underframe and wheel arches is in wet weather when the mud is thoroughly wet and soft. In very wet weather the underframe is usually cleaned of large accumulations automatically and this is a good time for inspection.

Periodically, except on vehicles with a wax-based underbody protective coat, it is a good idea to have the whole of the underframe of the vehicle steam cleaned, engine compartment included, so that a thorough inspection can be carried out to see what minor repairs and renovations are necessary. Steam cleaning is available at many garages and is necessary for removal of the accumulation of oily grime which sometimes is allowed to become thick in certain areas. If steam cleaning facilities are not available, there are one or two excellent grease solvents available which can be brush applied. The dirt can then

be simply hosed off. Note that these methods should not be used on vehicles with wax-based underbody protective coating or the coating will be removed. Such vehicles should be inspected annually, preferably just prior to winter, when the underbody should be washed down and any damage to the wax coating repaired. Ideally, a completely fresh coat should be applied. It would also be worth considering the use of such wax-based protection for injection into door panels, sills, box sections etc, as an additional safeguard against rust damage.

After washing paintwork, wipe off with a chamois leather to give an unspotted clear finish. A coat of clear protective wax polish will give added protection against chemical pollutants in the air. If the paintwork sheen has dulled or oxidised, use a cleaner/polisher combination to restore the brilliance of the shine. This requires a little effort, but such dulling is usually caused because regular washing has been neglected. Care needs to be taken with metallic paintwork, as special non-abrasive cleaner/polisher is required to avoid damage to the finish. Always check that the door and ventilator opening drain holes and pipes are completely clear so that water can be drained out. Bright work should be treated in the same way as paintwork. Windscreens and windows can be kept clear of the smeary film which often appears by the use of a proprietary glass cleaner. Never use any form of wax or other body or chromium polish on glass.

2.4 Bulkhead rubber grommet type water drain

This photographic sequence shows the steps taken to repair the dent and paintwork damage shown above. In general, the procedure for repairing a hole will be similar; where there are substantial differences, the procedure is clearly described and shown in a separate photograph.

First remove any trim around the dent, then hammer out the dent where access is possible. This will minimise filling. Here, after the large dent has been hammered out, the damaged area is being made slightly concave.

Next, remove all paint from the damaged area by rubbing with coarse abrasive paper or using a power drill fitted with a wire brush or abrasive pad. 'Feather' the edge of the boundary with good paintwork using a finer grade of abrasive paper.

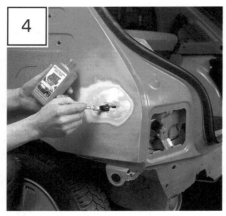

Where there are holes or other damage, the sheet metal should be cut away before proceeding further. The damaged area and any signs of rust should be treated with Turtle Wax Hi-Tech Rust Eater, which will also inhibit further rust formation.

For a large dent or hole mix Holts Body Plus Resin and Hardener according to the manufacturer's instructions and apply around the edge of the repair. Press Glass Fibre Matting over the repair area and leave for 20-30 minutes to harden. Then ...

... brush more Holts Body Plus Resin and Hardener onto the matting and leave to harden. Repeat the sequence with two or three layers of matting, checking that the final layer is lower than the surrounding area. Apply Holts Body Plus Filler Paste as shown in Step 5B.

For a medium dent, mix Holts Body Plus Filler Paste and Hardener according to the manufacturer's instructions and apply it with a flexible applicator. Apply thin layers of filler at 20-minute intervals, until the filler surface is slightly proud of the surrounding bodywork.

For small dents and scratches use Holts No Mix Filler Paste straight from the tube. Apply it according to the instructions in thin layers, using the spatula provided. It will harden in minutes if applied outdoors and may then be used as its own knifing putty.

Use a plane or file for initial shaping. Then, using progressively finer grades of wet-and-dry paper, wrapped round a sanding block, and copious amounts of clean water, rub down the filler until glass smooth. 'Feather' the edges of adjoining paintwork.

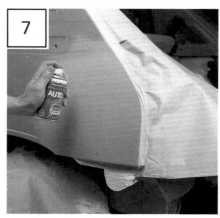

Protect adjoining areas before spraying the whole repair area and at least one inch of the surrounding sound paintwork with Holts Dupli-Color primer.

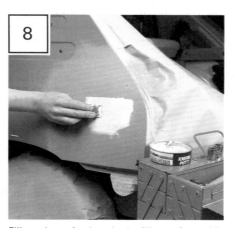

Fill any imperfections in the filler surface with a small amount of Holts Body Plus Knifing Putty. Using plenty of clean water, rub down the surface with a fine grade wet-and-dry paper – 400 grade is recommended – until it is really smooth.

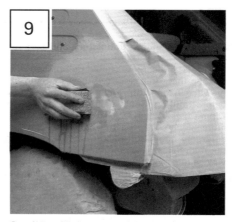

Carefully fill any remaining imperfections with knifing putty before applying the last coat of primer. Then rub down the surface with Holts Body Plus Rubbing Compound to ensure a really smooth surface.

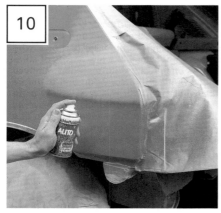

Protect surrounding areas from overspray before applying the topcoat in several thin layers. Agitate Holts Dupli-Color aerosol thoroughly. Start at the repair centre, spraying outwards with a side-to-side motion.

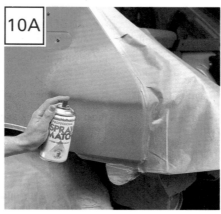

If the exact colour is not available off the shelf, local Holts Professional Spraymatch Centres will custom fill an aerosol to match perfectly.

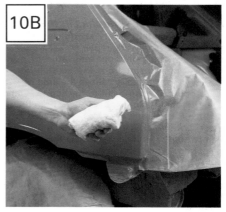

To identify whether a lacquer finish is required, rub a painted unrepaired part of the body with wax and a clean cloth.

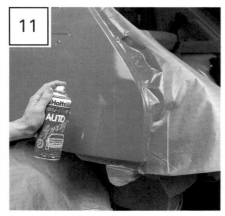

If *no* traces of paint appear on the cloth, spray Holts Dupli-Color clear lacquer over the repaired area to achieve the correct gloss level.

The paint will take about two weeks to harden fully. After this time it can be 'cut' with a mild cutting compound such as Turtle Wax Minute Cut prior to polishing with a final coating of Turtle Wax Extra.

When carrying out bodywork repairs, remember that the quality of the finished job is proportional to the time and effort expended.

3   Maintenance – upholstery and carpets

Mats and carpets should be brushed or vacuum cleaned regularly to keep them free of grit. If they are badly stained remove them from the vehicle for scrubbing or sponging and make quite sure they are dry before refitting. Seats and interior trim panels can be kept clean by wiping with a damp cloth. If they do become stained (which can be more apparent on light coloured upholstery) use a little liquid detergent and a soft nail brush to scour the grime out of the grain of the material. Do not forget to keep the headlining clean in the same way as the upholstery. When using liquid cleaners inside the vehicle do not over-wet the surfaces being cleaned. Excessive damp could get into the seams and padded interior causing stains, offensive odours or even rot. If the inside of the vehicle gets wet accidentally it is worthwhile taking some trouble to dry it out properly, particularly where carpets are involved. *Do not leave oil or electric heaters inside the vehicle for this purpose.*

4   Minor body damage – repair

The photographic sequences on pages 202 and 203 illustrate the operations detailed in the following sub-sections.

Repair of minor scratches in the car's bodywork

If the scratch is very superficial, and does not penetrate to the metal of the bodywork, repair is very simple. Lightly rub the area of the scratch with a paintwork renovator, or a very fine cutting paste, to remove loose paint from the scratch and to clear the surrounding bodywork of wax polish. Rinse the area with clean water.

Apply touch-up paint to the scratch using a thin paint brush; continue to apply thin layers of paint until the surface of the paint in the scratch is level with the surrounding paintwork. Allow the new paint at least two weeks to harden: then blend it into the surrounding paintwork by rubbing the paintwork in the scratch area with a paintwork renovator or a very fine cutting paste. Finally, apply wax polish.

If the car is painted with a two-coat metallic finish an entirely different technique is required. The materials may be obtained from the official agent. Two types of repair are possible, the 80°C drying method and the Air-drying method. A 'wet-on-wet' procedure for the topcoat and clear varnish is used. The repair can be done satisfactorily only if the specified top coat and varnish are used with the specially developed synthetic thinner. After filling with Filler L145, if required, sand down with 400-500 wet and dry paper. Apply the first top coat using synthetic metallic paint LKL of spraying viscosity 15-17 seconds (DIN cup 4 mm). Let the paint flash off for 25 minutes, then apply the second layer of Air-drying L100 clear varnish with hardener L101 mixed in proportion 8:1. This becomes unusable after six hours. The repair is dust dry after 30 minutes but requires up to 8 days for complete drying. As can be seen it is a complicated process and you are advised to go to the official agent for advice if you have not done the job before. If you have other than a metallic finish then proceed as follows.

Where the scratch has penetrated right through to the metal of the bodywork, causing the metal to rust, a different repair technique is required. Remove any loose rust from the bottom of the scratch with a penknife, then apply rust inhibiting paint to prevent the formation of rust in the future. Using a rubber or nylon applicator fill the scratch with bodystopper paste. If required, this paste can be mixed with cellulose thinners to provide a very thin paste which is ideal for filling narrow scratches. Before the stopper-paste in the scratch hardens, wrap a piece of smooth cotton rag around the top of a finger. Dip the finger in cellulose thinners and then quickly sweep it across the surface of the stopper paste in the scratch; this will ensure that the surface of the stopper paste is slightly hollowed. The scratch can now be painted over as described earlier in this Section.

Repair of dents in the bodywork

When deep denting of the car's bodywork has taken place, the first task is to pull the dent out, until the affected bodywork almost attains its original shape. There is little point in trying to restore the original shape completely, as the metal in the damaged area will have stretched on impact and cannot be reshaped fully to its original contour. It is better to bring the level of the dent up to a point which is

about (3 mm) $\frac{1}{8}$ in below the level of the surrounding bodywork. In cases where the dent is very shallow anyway, it is not worth trying to pull it out at all.

If the underside of the dent is accessible, it can be hammered out gently from behind, using a mallet with a wooden or plastic head. Whilst doing this, hold a suitable block of wood firmly against the impact from the hammer blows and thus prevent a large area of the bodywork from being 'belled-out'.

Should the dent be in a section of the bodywork which has double skin or some other factor making it inaccessible from behind, a different technique is called for. Drill several small holes through the metal inside the area – particularly in the deeper section. Then screw long self-tapping screws into the holes just sufficiently for them to gain a good purchase in the metal. Now the dent can be pulled out by pulling on the protruding heads of the screws with a pair of pliers.

The next stage of the repair is the removal of the paint from the damaged area, and from an inch or so of the surrounding 'sound' bodywork. This is accomplished most easily by using a wire brush or abrasive pad on a power drill, although it can be done just as effectively by hand using sheets of abrasive paper. To complete the preparation for filling, score the surface of the bare metal with a screwdriver or the tang of a file, or alternatively, drill small holes in the affected area. This will provide a really good key for the filler paste.

To complete the repair see the Section on filling and respraying.

Repair of rust holes or gashes in the bodywork

Remove all paint from the affected area and from an inch or so of the surrounding 'sound' bodywork, using an abrasive pad or a wire brush on a power drill. If these are not available a few sheets of abrasive paper will do the job just as effectively. With the paint removed you will be able to gauge the severity of the corrosion and therefore decide whether to renew the whole panel (if this is possible) or to repair the affected area. New body panels are not as expensive as most people think and it is often quicker and more satisfactory to fit a new panel than to attempt to repair large areas of corrosion.

Remove all fittings from the affected areas except those which will act as a guide to the original shape of the damaged bodywork (eg headlamp shells etc). Then, using tin snips or a hacksaw blade, remove all loose metal and any other metal badly affected by corrosion. Hammer the edges of the hole inwards in order to create a slight depression for the filler paste.

Wire brush the affected area to remove the powdery rust from the surface of the remaining metal. Paint the affected area with rust inhibiting paint; if the back of the rusted area is accessible treat this also.

Before filling can take place it will be necessary to block the hole in some way. This can be achieved by the use of one of the following materials: Zinc gauze, Aluminium tape or Polyurethane foam.

Aluminium or plastic mesh is probably the best material to use for a large hole. Cut a piece to the approximate size and shape of the hole to be filled, then position it in the hole so that its edges are below the level of the surrounding bodywork. It can be retained in position by several blobs of filler paste around its periphery.

Aluminium tape should be used for small or very narrow holes. Pull a piece off the roll and trim it to the approximate size and shape required, then pull off the backing paper (if used) and stick the tape over the hole; it can be overlapped if the thickness of one piece is insufficient. Burnish down the edges of the tape with the handle of a screwdriver or similar, to ensure that the tape is securely attached to the metal underneath.

Bodywork repairs – filling and respraying

Before using this Section, see the Sections on dent, deep scratch, rust holes and gash repairs.

Many types of bodyfiller are available, but generally speaking those proprietary kits which contain a tin of filler paste and a tube of resin hardener are best for this type of repair. A wide, flexible plastic or nylon applicator will be found invaluable for imparting a smooth and well contoured finish to the surface of the filler.

Mix up a little filler on a clean piece of card or board – use the hardener sparingly (follow the maker's instructions on the packet) otherwise the filler will set very rapidly.

Using the applicator, apply the filler paste to the prepared area: draw the applicator across the surface of the filler to achieve the correct contour and to level the filler surface. As soon as a contour that approximates the correct one is achieved, stop working the paste – if you carry on too long the paste will become sticky and begin to 'pick up' on the applicator. Continue to add thin layers of filler paste at twenty-minute intervals until the level of the filler is just proud of the surrounding bodywork.

Once the filler has hardened, excess can be removed using a metal plane or file. From then on, progressively finer grades of abrasive paper should be used, starting with a 40 grade production paper and finishing with 400 grade wet-and-dry paper. Always wrap the abrasive paper around a flat rubber, cork, or wooden block – otherwise the surface of the filler will not be completely flat. During the smoothing of the filler surface the wet-and-dry paper should be periodically rinsed in water. This will ensure that a very smooth finish is imparted to the filler at the final stage.

At this stage the 'dent' should be surrounded by a ring of bare metal, which in turn should be encircled by the finely 'feathered' edge of the good paintwork. Rinse the repair area with clean water, until all of the dust produced by the rubbing-down operation has gone.

Spray the whole repair area with a light coat of grey primer – this will show up any imperfections in the surface of the filler. Repair these imperfections with fresh filler paste or bodystopper, and once more smooth the surface with abrasive paper. If bodystopper is used, it can be mixed with cellulose thinners to form a really thin paste which is ideal for filling small holes. Repeat this spray and repair procedure until you are satisfied that the surface of the filler, and the feathered edge of the paintwork are perfect. Clean the repair area with clean water and allow to dry fully.

The repair area is now ready for final spraying. Paint spraying must be carried out in a warm, dry, windless and dust free atmosphere. This condition can be created artificially if you have access to a large indoor working area, but if you are forced to work in the open, you will have to pick your day very carefully. If you are working indoors, dousing the floor in the work area with water will help settle the dust which would otherwise be in the atmosphere. If the repair area is confined to one body panel, mask off the surrounding panels; this will help to minimise the effects of a slight mis-match in paint colours. Bodywork fittings (eg chrome strips, door handles etc) will also need to be masked off. Use genuine masking tape and several thicknesses of newspaper for the masking operations.

Before commencing to spray, agitate the aerosol can thoroughly, then spray a test area (an old tin, or similar) until the technique is mastered. Cover the repair area with a thick coat of primer; the thickness should be built up using several thin layers of paint rather than one thick one. Using 400 grade wet-and-dry paper, rub down the surface of the primer until it is really smooth. While doing this, the work area should be thoroughly doused with water, and the wet-and-dry paper periodically rinsed in water. Allow to dry before spraying on more paint.

Spray on the top coat, again building up the thickness by using several thin layers of paint. Start spraying in the centre of the repair area and then using a circular motion, work outwards until the whole repair area and about 2 inches of the surrounding original paintwork is covered. Remove all masking material 10 to 15 minutes after spraying on the final coat of paint.

Allow the new paint at least two weeks to harden, then, using a paintwork renovator or a very fine cutting paste, blend the edges of the paint into the existing paintwork. Finally, apply wax polish.

5 Major body damage – repair

Where serious damage has occurred or large areas need renewal due to neglect it means certainly that completely new sections or panels will need welding in and this is best left to professionals. If the damage is due to impact it will also be necessary to check the alignment of the body structure. In such instances the services of an agent with specialist checking jigs are essential. If a body is left misaligned it is first of all dangerous as the car will not handle properly – and secondly, uneven stresses will be imposed on the steering, engine and transmission, causing abnormal wear or complete failure. Tyre wear will also be excessive.

6 Front wings – removal and refitting

1 A badly damaged front wing may be removed complete and a new one fitted. The wing is secured with 10 fixing screws. Refer to Fig. 10.2 in which the locations of the screws are shown. Those marked 'A1' are under the wing and not easily accessible.
2 It will be necessary to remove the side bumper before removing the wing. The screws fastening the wing are fitted very tightly and may not come out without considerable force. Do not use an impact screwdriver or you will distort the frame. It may be necessary to grind off the heads and drill out the shanks.
3 Once all the screws are out, the wing may be levered away pulling it out of the guides. If it does not come out easily it may be necessary to warm the line of the joint with a blow lamp to melt the adhesive underseal. Be careful how you do this, for apart from the fire risk to the car the adhesive is also inflammable.
4 When removing, lever the wing away from the wheel housing and the door pillar, work it to-and-fro, pulling it forwards to the front of the car a little.
5 Clean up the frame and paint with inhibitor if any rust is present. Use a good sealing tape along the line of the bolts before installing the wing, and once the wing is securely in place treat the underside with underseal compound. Refer to Section 4 for respraying techniques.

7 Radiator grille – removal and refitting

The grille is held in position by eight screws. There are four along the top., visible when the bonnet is opened. There are two more by each headlamp. Fig. 10.1 refers. Note that some later models have plastic clips instead of screws (photo).

8 Tailgate, strut and lock – removal and refitting

1 Disconnect the battery earth strap.
2 Open the tailgate and remove the straps which support the rear shelf. Disconnect the gas-filled support strut from the tailgate.
3 Ease the headlining back to uncover the hinge securing bolts. Take care not to tear the lining. Now slacken the hinge bolts. This will

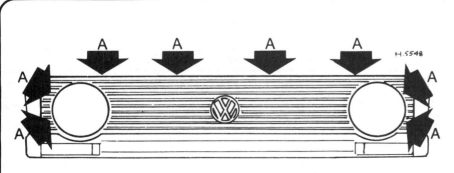

Fig. 10.1 Radiator grille fixing screw locations (A) (Sec 7)

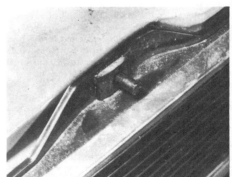

7.1 Radiator grille retaining clip

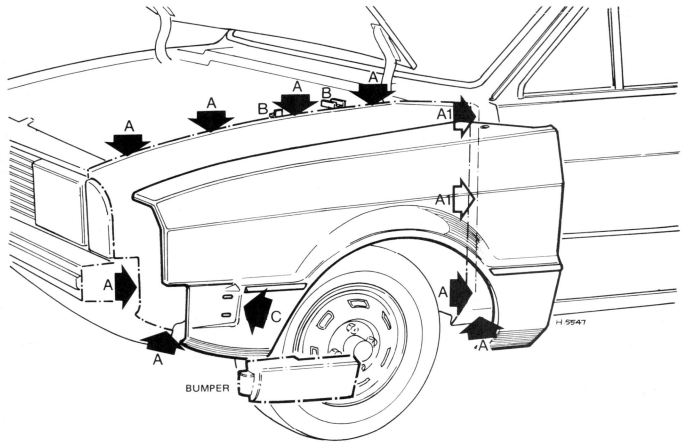

Fig. 10.2 Front wing fixing screw locations (Sec 6)

Note: Wing is shown in continuous line, car frame in broken line

A1 *Two screws beneath wing*
A   *Eight screws along top, front and rear of wing*

B   *Guides*
C   *Bumper fixing location*

require an impact screwdriver with a special bit.
4   Disconnect the electrical wiring to the heated rear window at the connector.
5   With the help of an assistant remove the hinge bolts and lift away the tailgate.
6   When refitting the tailgate, insert the hinge bolts and tighten them hand-tight. Close the tailgate and check that there is an even gap all round and that the lock works correctly. If it does not, adjust the hinge position until it does. Tighten the hinge bolts fully and refit the headlining in position over them.
7   Refit the tailgate support strut.
8   If the support strut is to be renewed, it is important to get the correct one. There are two kinds, type A has one groove around the body of the strut at the top. This type of strut has the tube attached to the tailgate and the piston rod to the car body. The other type, B, has two grooves and the tube is attached to the body while the piston rod is attached to the tailgate. Both struts have the same part number (171 827 550A) but if you try to fit one in place of the other, the tailgate will not function properly. Make sure you get the same type as the one taken off.
9   The lock is secured to the bottom edge of the tailgate by three crosshead screws (photo). No repair to the lock is possible. If it is faulty remove it and fit a new one.

9 Bumpers – removal and refitting

1   The front bumper consists of a crossmember and two side pieces on early Golf models, and the sections are fitted to each other and the wings by studs and nuts. To remove the bumper, first disconnect the bumper lamp wires and unscrew the stud nuts. Withdraw the side pieces then unbolt the centre section from the underframe.
2   Later Golf models are fitted with a similar centre section to which is attached a single plastic covering. To remove this type, use a screwdriver to prise the side covering from each wing, disconnect the bumper lamp wires and headlamp washer tubing where fitted, and unbolt the centre section from the underframe. The plastic covering is obtainable as a separate item but a press will be required to attach it to the centre section (Fig. 10.6).
3   The front bumper fitted to Rabbit models is removed in a similar manner but bolts holding the recuperators to the underframe must be removed first.
4   Removal of the rear bumper is similar to the procedure for the front except that there are no lighting or washer connections.
5   Refitting is a reversal of removal.

10 Bonnet – removal and refitting

1   The bonnet, or engine compartment cover, is hinged at the rear and held shut by a lock operated from inside the vehicle. It is held to the hinge by two bolts on each side (photo). Remove these, and it may be lifted off and taken away. Two people are needed to lift it, not because it is heavy but to avoid scratching the paint.
2   Refitting is a reversal of removal procedure.

11 Bonnet cable and lock – removal, refitting and adjustment

1   Working inside the car, unscrew the two crosshead retaining screws and release the bonnet lock handle from the left-hand side panel.

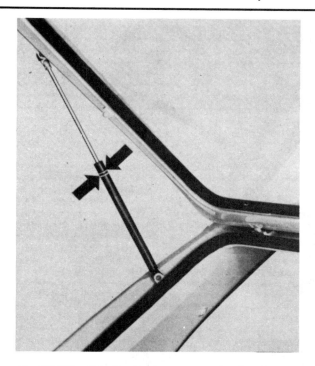

Fig. 10.3 Type B tailgate support strut showing the two identification rings (arrowed)(Sec 8)

2 Disconnect the cable at the lock end after removing trhe radiator grille.
3 Bend the clamping plate in the operating handle outwards, and remove the handle from the cable.
4 Remove the cable from the car.
5 Refitting is a reversal of removal, but make sure that the cable is routed free of strain without any sharp curves. To adjust the cable, pull it through the clamp on the lock as far as possible then, with the lever fully released, tighten the clamp screw and bend the excess cable over.

8.9 The tailgate lock

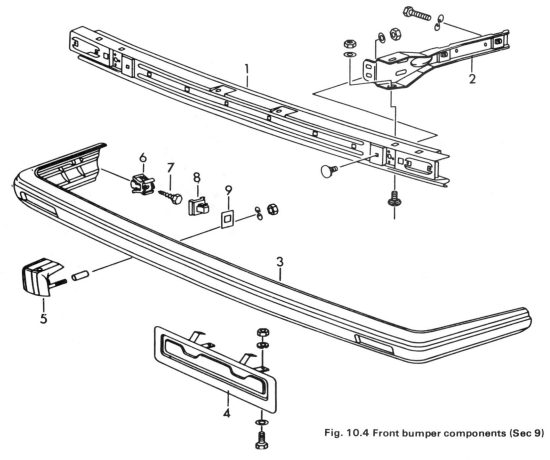

Fig. 10.4 Front bumper components (Sec 9)

1	Centre section	4	Number plate backing	7	Bolt
2	Bracket	5	Overrider	8	Clip
3	Plastic cover	6	Clamp	9	Seal

Fig. 10.5 Bumper location hole in front wings — arrowed (Sec 9)

Fig. 10.6 Using a press to fit the plastic cover to the bumper (Sec 9)

Arrows A indicate direction of pressure, and remaining arrows location lugs

10.1 Bonnet hinge and retaining bolts

6   To remove the bonnet lock, first withdraw the radiator grille and disconnect the cable.
7   Unscrew the two retaining bolts and lift the lock assembly from the crossmember.
8   Refitting is a reversal of removal but it will be necessary to adjust the cable as described in paragraph 5.

12 Door interior trim — removal and refitting

1   Using a screwdriver, prise the plastic cover from the window regulator handle (photo).
2   With the window shut, note the position of the handle, then remove the retaining screw and slide the handle from the shaft (photo).
3   Unscrew and remove the two crosshead retaining screws and withdraw the door pull (photo).

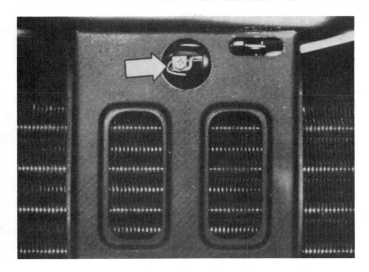

Fig. 10.7 Bonnet lock cable adjusting screw – arrowed (Sec 11)

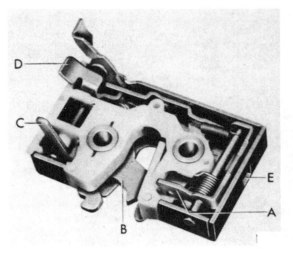

Fig. 10.8 Door lock components (Sec 13)

A   Remote control lever   D   Locking lever
B   Latch   E   Access hole
C   Locking lever

4   Prise the recessed cover from the door interior handle assembly. Unscrew the retaining screw and withdraw the handle cover (photos).
5   Where fitted, prise off the cover and remove the mirror adjusting knob and escutcheon.
6   Using a wide blade screwdriver inserted between the trim and the door, prise the retaining clips out of the holes. Lever as near to the clips as possible to avoid tearing them from the trim panel (photo).
7   Refitting is a reversal of removal, but make sure that the plastic sheeting is correctly positioned before mounting the trim on the door.

13 Door lock – removal and refitting

Note: *It is not necessary to remove the door interior trim in order to remove the door lock.*
1   Open the door and set the lock in the locked position, either by moving the interior knob or by turning the exterior key.
2   Using a hexagon key, unscrew and remove the two retaining screws, then withdraw the lock approximately 12 mm (0·5 in) to

12.1 Removing the window regulator handle cover

12.2 Removing the window regulator handle

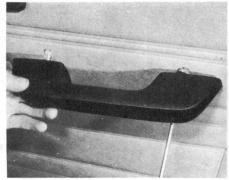

12.3 Removing the door pull/armrest

12.4A Removing the door interior handle recessed cover

12.4B Door interior handle cover retaining screw

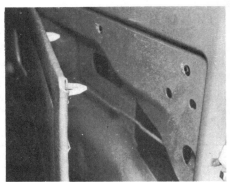

12.6 Removing the door interior trim panel

13.2 The door lock assembly

14.3 Door interior lock remote control handle

Fig. 10.9 Removing the door lock (Sec 13)

A   Lever
C   Locking lever
G   Remote control rod
H   Sleeve

expose the operating lever (photo) (Figs. 10.8 and 10.9).
3   Retain the lower lock lever in the extended position by inserting a screwdriver through the hole in the bottom of the lock.
4   Unhook the lower lever from the remote control rod and pull the upper lever from the sleeve. Remove the lock from the door.
5   Refitting is a reversal of removal, but remember to set the lock in the locked position first.

14 Door lock remote control – removal and refitting

1   Remove the door lock as described in Section 13.
2   Remove the door interior trim as described in Section 12.
3   Unbolt the remote control handle from the door and remove it (photo).

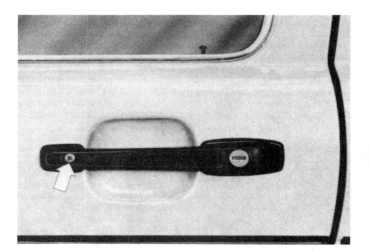

Fig. 10.10 Door exterior handle outer retaining screw – arrowed
(Sec 15)

4   Refitting is a reversal of removal, but make sure that any sound deadening foam is positioned correctly on the control rod.

15 Door exterior handle – removal and refitting

1   Open the door and remove the retaining screw located above the door lock.
2   Prise the plastic insert from the handle and remove the second crosshead retaining screw. Note that some early models may not have this screw.
3   If the driver's side handle is being removed, make sure that it is unlocked.
4   Withdraw the handle from the door.
5   Refitting is a reversal of removal.

16 Window regulator – removal and refitting

1   Remove the interior trim as described in Section 12, after fully opening the window, then pull back the plastic sheeting (photo).
2   Remove the bolts securing the winding gear to the door, and the bolts securing the lifting plate to the window channel (photos).
3   Unclip the regulator tube from the door and remove it through the aperture.

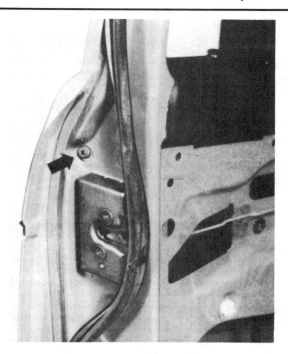

Fig. 10.11 Door exterior handle side retaining screw – arrowed (Sec 15)

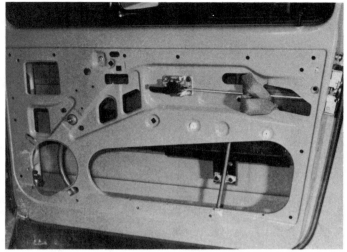

16.1 View of door inner panel with plastic sheeting removed

4   Refitting is a reversal of removal, but ensure that the cable is adequately lubricated with grease, and if necessary adjust the position of the regulator tube so that the window moves smoothly.

17 Door window glass – removal and refitting

1   Remove the window regulator as described in Section 16.
2   Remove the chrome moulding from the window aperture.
3   Remove the front window channel by unscrewing the upper retaining screw and drilling out the lower rivet (Fig. 10.12).
4   Unclip the window seals from the door.
5   Withdraw the window from the door.
6   If necessary, the triangular vent window can also be removed from the door at this stage.
7   Refitting is a reversal of removal, but a rivet inserting tool will be required.

16.2A Window regulator gear

18 Doors (front) – removal and refitting

1   The hinges on the Golf/Rabbit are secured to the pillar with shallow socket headed bolts which are very difficult to undo unless the special tools are available. They are also in awkward position. If the socket heads are damaged and the hexagon hole is converted into a round one then you are in serious trouble, as it will be necessary to drill the bolt and extract it with a special bolt extractor. For this reason we recommend that door hinges should be undone by professionals with the correct equipment. However, if you can undo these bolts the door is easily removed.
2   Take the pin out of the check strap, slacken the hinge bolts, have someone hold the door while you remove the bolts, and lift the door away (photo). Check the weather strip and fit a new one, if necessary.
3   When refitting the door first remove the striker bolt from the frame. You cannot adjust the hinge while this is in place. Fit the door to the pillar and tighten the hinge bolts enough to hold the door in place. Close the door and check that the gap all round the edge is symmetrical. Adjust the hinge until it is correct then tighten the hinge bolts fully. Refit the striker bolt.
4   Note that on late models, self-locking M8 x 18 hinge bolts are fitted, and those must always be renewed when the door is removed. They should be tightened to 5 kgf m (37 lbf ft).

16.2B Window regulator lifting plate and window channel

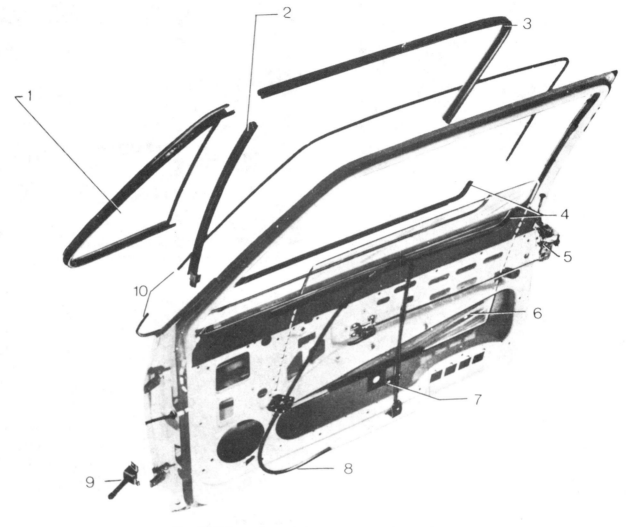

Fig. 10.12 Front door window components (Sec 17)

1	Vent window	4	Seals	7	Lifting plate	9	Check strap
2	Front window channel	5	Lock	8	Regulator	10	Trim moulding
3	Guide	6	Glass				

18.2 The door check strap

19 Remote controlled exterior mirror – removal and refitting

1   Remove the door interior trim panel as described in Section 12.

2   Unscrew the countersunk screws securing the mirror to the door exterior and lift it out together with the reinforcement plate.

3   From the door interior panel, unscrew the three retaining bolts, and withdraw the remote control lever and bracket together with the anti-rattle foam.

4   Refitting is a reversal of removal.

20 Front seats – removal and refitting

Removal of the front seat from the car is done in the following manner. At the back of the runners are small caps, lever these off the runners. Now look under the seat. There is an extra clip which must be removed and then the seat can be pushed towards the rear. When refitting fit the spring clips in the upper slide, install the seat from the rear, guiding the adjusting lever into the latch bolt mountings. Refit the covers on the runners.

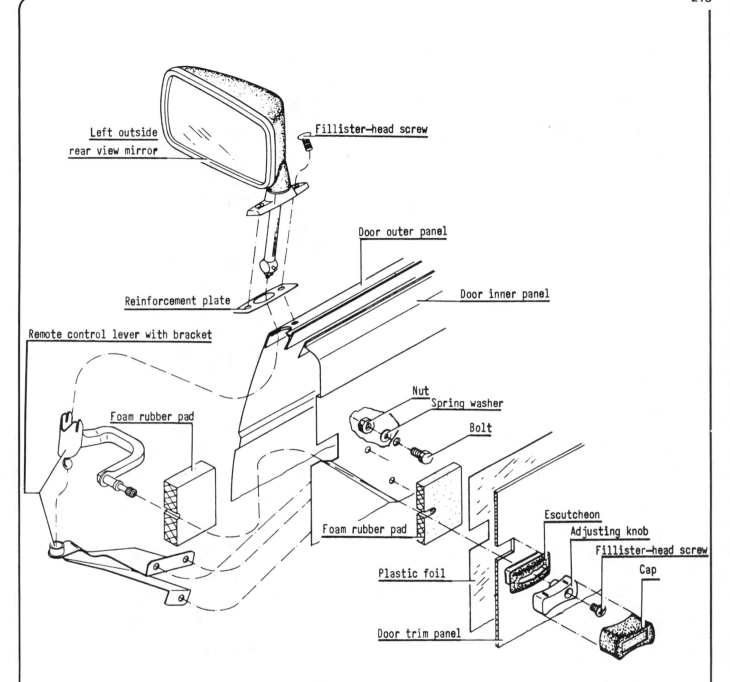

Fig. 10.13 Remotely controlled exterior mirror components (Sec 19)

VW Diesel Jetta

Chapter 11 Supplement:
Revisions and information on later models

Contents

1 Introduction

Since its introduction in 1978 the VW Golf diesel has had a number of modifications and improvements made in order to keep pace with current technological and servicing innovations. The major improvements being the introduction of the 1588 cc diesel engine and the 5-speed gearbox.

To increase the appeal of the Golf range the Jetta became available with a diesel power unit in 1981. Being identical to the Golf in virtually all mechanical respects, the notchback Jetta and Hatchback Golf now offered the same family car package in both diesel and petrol engine versions.

Information applicable to later models, and modifications made to early models since the original publication of this manual, are included in this Supplement where servicing and/or repair procedures are affected.

In order to use the supplement to the best advantage it is suggested that it is referred to before the main Chapters of the manual: this will ensure that any relevant information can be noted and incorporated within the procedures given in Chapters 1 to 10. Time and cost will therefore be saved and the particular job will be completed correctly.

2 Specifications

The specifications listed below are revisions of, or supplementary to, the main specifications given at the beginning of each Chapter

Engine – 1588 cc
The engine is identical to the 1471 cc unit except for the differences listed below

General

Stroke	86.4 mm (3.404 in)
Capacity	1588 cc (96.86 cu in)
Compression ratio	23.0 : 1
Maximum output (DIN)	40 kw (54 bhp) at 4800 rpm
Maximum torque (DIN)	100 Nm (73.8 lbf ft) at 2300 rpm

Cylinder block and pistons

Piston sizes:

	Piston diameter: mm (in)	Cylinder bore diameter: mm (in)
Standard	76.48 (3.013)	76.51 (3.015)
1st oversize	76.73 (3.023)	76.76 (3.024)
2nd oversize	76.98 (3.033)	77.01 (3.034)
3rd oversize	77.48 (3.053)	77.51 (3.054)

Crankshaft

Connecting rod journals:

Standard	47.80 mm (1.883 in)
1st undersize	47.55 mm (1.873 in)
2nd undersize	47.30 mm (1.863 in)
3rd undersize	47.05 mm (1.853 in)

Torque wrench settings (all engines)

	kgf m	lbf ft
Connecting rod caps:		
Rigid bolt	4.5	33
Stretch bolt:		
Stage 1	3.0	22
Stage 2	Tighten further through 180°	
Cylinder head bolts:		
M11 hexagon socket head:		
Stage 1	5.1	37
Stage 2	7.2	52
Stage 3	9.1	66
Stage 4 (engine hot)	9.1	66
M12 12 point socket head:		
Stage 1	4.1	30
Stage 2	6.1	44
Stage 3	7.6	55
Stage 4	Tighten further through 180°	
Stage 5 (engine hot)	Tighten further through 90°	
Crankshaft sprocket:		
M12 bolt (with thread locking agent)	8.1	59
Durlock bolt (threads oiled)	15.2	110
M14 bolt (threads oiled)	18.4	133
Engine to transmission:		
M10 bolts	4.5	33
M12 bolts	7.6	55
Toothed belt tensioner locknut	4.5	33

Cooling system

Thermostat (August 1978 onward)

Starts to open	87°C (189°F) approx
Fully extended	102°C (215°F) approx
Minimum stroke	7.0 mm (0.27 in)

Fuel system

Idle speed (Bosch system)

Models with injection pump identification 068 130 107J*	920 to 970 rpm
All other models	800 to 850 rpm

Identification number stamped on a plate on the pump body

Maximum speed without load (Bosch system)

1471 cc models	5500 to 5600 rpm
1588 cc models	5300 to 5400 rpm

Idle speed (CAV system)

Models with hydraulic pump governor	760 to 860 rpm
Models with mechanical pump governor	920 to 980 rpm

Maximum speed without load (CAV system)
1471 cc models	5500 to 5600 rpm
1588 cc models	5300 to 5400 rpm

Clutch
Driven plate (friction disc)
Diameter:
Up to approximately December 1980	190 mm (7.5 in)
From approximately December 1980	200 mm (7.9 in)

Transmission
Gear ratios (4-speed gearbox)
1471 cc models up to August 1980:
1st	3.45 : 1
2nd	1.94 : 1
3rd	1.29 : 1
4th	0.969 : 1
Reverse	3.17 : 1
Final drive	3.89 : 1

1471 cc and 1588 cc models from September 1980 onward:
1st	3.45 : 1
2nd	1.94 : 1
3rd	1.29 : 1
4th	0.909 : 1
Reverse	3.17 : 1
Final drive	3.89 : 1

Gear ratios (5-speed gearbox)
1st	3.45 : 1
2nd	1.94 : 1
3rd	1.29 : 1
4th	0.909 : 1
5th	0.711 : 1
Reverse	3.17 : 1
Final drive	3.89 : 1

Overhaul data (5-speed gearbox)
3rd gear axial movement	0 to 0.20 mm (0 to 0.008 in)
Axial movement adjustment	Selected circlips
Minimum baulk ring-to-gear clearance:	
1st and 2nd gear	0.60 mm (0.023 in)
3rd gear	0.65 mm (0.026 in)
4th and 5th gear	0.80 mm (0.031 in)
Oil capacity (5-speed gearbox)	2.0 litres (3.5 Imp pints, 4.2 US pints)

Torque wrench settings (5-speed gearbox)
	kgf m	lbf ft
End cover bolts	2.5	18
5th gear synchro-hub screw	15.1	110
Mainshaft bearing retainer	1.5	11
Reverse shaft retaining bolt	3.0	22
Casing-to-housing bolts	2.5	18
Pinion bearing retainer	4.1	30
Drain and filler plugs	2.5	18
Relay lever pillar retaining bolts	2.5	18
Gearbox to engine:		
M12 bolts	7.6	55
M10 bolts	4.5	33

Braking system, wheels and tyres
Front brakes (disc)
Disc thickness (new):
With servo	12 mm (0.47 in)
Without servo	10 mm (0.39 in)
Disc thickness (minimum) after refinishing:	
With servo	10 mm (0.39 in)
Without servo	8 mm (0.31 in)
Maximum disc run-out	0.06 mm (0.002 in)
Pad thickness (new):	
With servo	14 mm (0.55 in)
Without servo	10 mm (0.39 in)
Pad thickness (minimum) including backing	7 mm (0.28 in)
Master cylinder bore diameter:	
With servo	20.64 mm (0.81 in)
Without servo	17.46 mm (0.69 in)

Torque wrench settings

	kgf m	lbf ft
Caliper to wheel bearing housing (modified type M10 x 30 flanged locking bolt)	7.2	52

---

3   Engine

1588 cc engine – description

1   From approximately August 1980, all Golf and Jetta models covered by this manual were fitted with a larger 1588 cc diesel engine. The unit is virtually identical to the 1471 cc engine, apart from the stroke, which was lengthened to provide the increase in capacity, and the other minor changes, as shown in the Specifications.

2   Repair and overhaul procedures for the 1588 cc engine are therefore identical to the 1471 cc unit and are as described in this Supplement and in Chapter 1.

Engine – removal and refitting

3   Using the procedure described in Chapter 1 it is also possible to remove the engine/transmission assembly by lifting it upwards and out of the vehicle if this method is preferred.

4   On cars manufactured from approximately August 1979 the exhaust system front pipe has been modified and its method of attachment to the manifold changed. The pipe on these models is now retained by two spring clips instead of the nuts used on early versions. A VW special tool is available for removal and refitting of the clips, but if care is taken they can be levered off with a stout screwdriver. When refitting the clips take care to avoid distorting them, or their tension will be lost.

Fig. 11.1 VW special tool for removing exhaust front pipe retaining clips (Sec 3)

Turn in direction of arrow

Separating the transmission from the engine

5   From approximately November 1978 the method of securing the transmission to the engine has been changed, from studs and nuts, to bolts. Consequently it is not necessary to turn the flywheel to a certain position before separating the engine and transmission.

Modified connecting rod cap retaining bolts

6   On later engines modified bolts and nuts are used to secure the connecting rod cap to the rod.

7   The modified bolts are termed 'stretch' bolts and replace the previously used 'rigid' bolts. The stretch bolts have obvious visual differences and can be easily identified.

8   When refitting the retaining nuts to the stretch type bolts, note that a revised torque wrench setting and tightening procedure are used, as given in the Specifications at the beginning of this Supplement. The contact surfaces of the retaining nuts should be lightly oiled before fitting. This applies to **both types** of bolts.

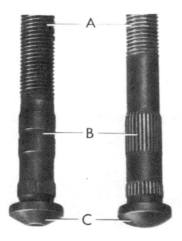

Fig. 11.2 Connecting rod retaining bolt identification (Sec 3)

Left – Stretch bolt   A   *Modified thread length*
Right – Rigid bolt   B   *Smooth centre section*
                             C   *Revised head shape*

Modified inlet and exhaust valves

9   Valves with three grooves on their stem are fitted to later engines. Modified split collets and a spring retainer having chamfers on its inner and outer circumferences are also used with the modified valves.

10   New valves to the later pattern may be fitted to cylinder heads having the early type valves, but the new split collets and spring retainer must be used as well.

Cylinder head bolts – revised tightening procedure

11   Modified retaining bolts are fitted to later engines to secure the cylinder head to the block. The new bolts are 12 point socket head M12 type which supersede the M11 hexagon socket head type.

12   The tightening procedure for both types has been revised and is now as follows:

M11 hexagon socket head

13   Tighten the bolts in the sequence shown in Fig. 11.5 to the Stage 1 torque setting given in the Specifications.

14   Repeat the tightening procedure, in the sequence shown, to the Stage 2 setting, then once more to the Stage 3 setting.

15   After the engine has been started and warmed-up to its normal operating temperature, switch it off, remove the valve cover and tighten the bolts again to the Stage 4 setting. Make sure that they are tightened in the correct sequence and **do not** slacken them first before tightening.

16   After approximately 600 miles (1000 km) the bolts should be tightened finally. To do this slacken each bolt individually by 30°, working in the sequence given in Fig. 11.5, then immediately tighten it to the Stage 4 setting before going on to the next bolt. The engine may be hot or cold for this final tightening operation.

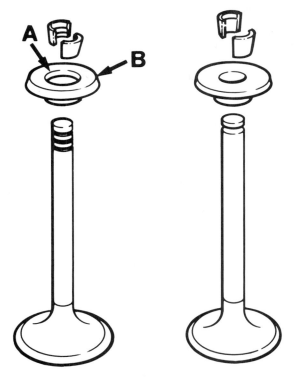

Fig. 11.3 Modified inlet and exhaust valve identification (Sec 3)

Left – Modified valve
Right – Early type valve

A   Chamfer on spring
    retainer inner
    circumference
B   Wider outer chamfer

Fig. 11.4 Cylinder head bolt identification (Sec 3)

Left – M12 12 point
socket head

Right – M11 hexagon
socket head

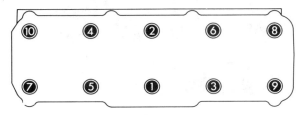

Fig. 11.5 Cylinder head bolt tightening sequence (Sec 3)

M12 12 point socket head

17   These bolts should **always** be renewed when refitting the cylinder head.

18   Tighten the bolts in the sequence shown in Fig. 11.5 to the Stage 1 torque setting given in the Specifications.

19   Repeat the tightening procedure, in the sequence shown, to the Stage 2 setting, then once more to the Stage 3 setting.

20   Now tighten all the bolts, in the correct sequence by a further 180° (half a turn).

21   After the engine has been started and warmed-up to its normal operating temperature, switch it off and remove the valve cover. Again working in the correct sequence, tightening each bolt by a further 90° (quarter turn). **Do not** slacken the bolts first before tightening.

22   After approximately 600 miles (1000 km) the bolts should be tightened finally . To do this tighten each bolt by a further 90° (quarter turn) in the correct sequence. **Do not** slacken the bolts first before tightening. The engine may be hot or cold for this final tightening operation.

Piston projection (1588 cc engine) – checking

23   The method of checking piston projection to determine the necessary cylinder head gasket thickness is the same as described in Chapter 1, Section 42, but for 1588 cc engines the projection dimensions are different as follows:

Piston projection in mm (in)	Gasket identification (no of notches)
0.67 to 0.80 (0.026 to 0.031)	1
0.81 to 0.90 (0.032 to 0.035)	2
0.91 to 1.02 (0.003 to 0.040)	3

Note that, on these engines, only three different thicknesses of cylinder head gasket are available.

4   Cooling system

Hose clips – modifications

1   Spring clips are now fitted in place of screw type clips to secure the cooling and heating system hoses.

2   Where spring clips are used the factory supplied hoses and engine outlets have been modified accordingly. Hoses for use with spring clips are marked near their end with a spring clip symbol and have a different structure and finish compared to those designed for use with screw type clips. Also the outlet to which the hose is secured is longer, smoother and has higher ridges at the end of the connection zone.

3   Consequently, screw type hose clips may only be used in an emergency and should be replaced by the spring type as soon as possible. Spring type clips must be installed with their matching hoses and outlets.

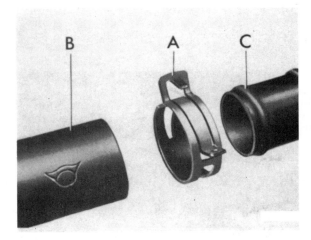

Fig. 11.6 Cooling system spring clip details (Sec 4)

A   Spring clip
B   Hose with spring clip identification symbol
C   Modified outlet size, shape and surface finish

Radiator mountings — modifications

4   From approximately January 1981 the method of securing the radiator in the engine compartment has been altered.

5   The radiator bottom mounting now consists of 2 pins which engage in conical adaptors. The top mounting comprises 2 brackets secured with screws.

6   Removal and refitting procedures are unchanged, apart from the mounting modifications.

---

5   Fuel and exhaust systems

Injection pump timing (Bosch system) — alterations

1   When checking and adjusting the injection pump timing using the procedure described in Chapter 3, Section 8, proceed as described in paragraphs 1 to 4 inclusive, but note that the value shown on the dial gauge should be in the range 0.83 to 0.97 mm. If the lift recorded is outside this tolerance, adjust by turning the pump to obtain a value of 0.88 to 0.92 mm. These figures apply in retrospect to **all** diesel engines fitted with Bosch injection equipment.

2   The remainder of the checking and adjusting procedure is as described in Chapter 3, Section 8.

Injection pump timing (CAV system) — checking and adjusting

3   The information contained in Chapter 3, Section 9 is applicable to CAV injection pumps with hydraulic governor control. Injection pumps with mechanical governors are fitted to later engines and a different method is used to check and adjust the timing on these pumps, as follows.

4   Checking and adjusting should be carried out with the engine in the car and with No 1 piston at TDC on compression. Refer to Chapter 3, Section 8, paragraph 1.

5   Clean the area around the plug on the side of the pump body then unscrew and remove the plug.

6   Pull the cold start control fully out.

7   Screw the adaptor (VW tool No 3071) into a dial gauge then back off the adaptor by half a turn.

8   Screw the adaptor and dial gauge into the side of the pump body (Fig. 11.7) so that there is approximately 2 mm preload on the gauge.

9   Slowly turn the crankshaft anti-clockwise approximately 20 to 30 mm.

10   Now slowly turn the crankshaft clockwise until the dial gauge needle indicates the lowest value. This will occur when the adaptor pin locates in the timing notch in the pump (Fig. 11.8). The engine should now be at the TDC position with an allowable tolerance of 2 mm either side.

11   If adjustment is necessary, return the engine to TDC for No 1 piston, slacken the pump mounting bolts and rotate the pump body

until the lowest value is shown on the dial gauge. Tighten the pump mounting bolts in this position and recheck the adjustment.

12   When the adjustment is correct, remove the dial gauge and refit the plug to the pump body.

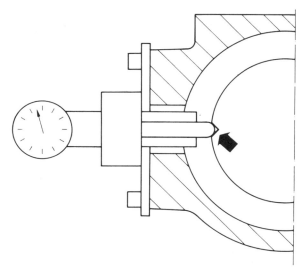

Fig. 11.8 Dial gauge adaptor pin engaged with injection pump timing notch — arrowed (Sec 5)

Accelerator cable — adjustment

13   On later models the cable adjusting nuts have been superseded by a spring clip which engages with grooves in the outer cable. The adjustment procedure is the same as described in Chapter 3, but instead of altering the adjusting nut positions, release the spring clip and move it to one of the other grooves in the outer cable as necessary (Fig. 11.9).

Idle speed and maximum speed — checking and adjusting

Bosch system

14   The procedure for checking and adjusting remains unchanged, but the setting values have altered and are now as given in the Specifications at the beginning of this Supplement.

CAV system

15   The procedure described in Chapter 3, Section 12 is applicable to CAV systems with hydraulically governed injection pumps. The procedures and setting values remain unchanged.

16   The following procedure is applicable to models equipped with mechanically governed CAV injection pumps.

Fig. 11.7 Checking injection pump timing on CAV system with mechanical governor (Sec 5)

Fig. 11.9 Accelerator cable with spring clip adjustment — arrowed (Sec 5)

Idle speed

17 Check that the idle speed is as given in the Specifications at the beginning of this Supplement. If not, slacken the locknut on the idle speed adjusting screw then turn the screw as necessary (Fig. 11.10). When the speed is correct, hold the screw and tighten the locknut.

Maximum speed

18 Open the throttle fully and check that the speed is as given in the Specifications. If not, slacken the locknut on the stop screw then turn the screw as necessary (Fig. 11.11). When the speed is correct, hold the screw and tighten the locknut.

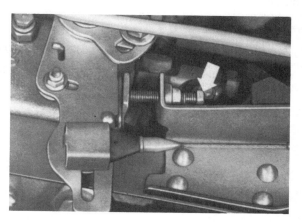

Fig. 11.11 Maximum speed adjustment screw (arrowed) – CAV system with mechanical governor (Sec 5)

Fig. 11.10 Idle speed adjustment – CAV system with mechanical governor (Sec 5)

1   *Locknut*
2   *Idle speed adjusting screw*
3   *Governor lever stop screw* – **Do not alter setting**

Manifold and exhaust system – general

19 Various changes have taken place to the exhaust system during the course of production and the current system is shown in Fig. 11.12. There may be minor differences to the systems fitted to certain models according to year or export territory.

20 The information given in Chapter 3, Section 18 is still applicable apart from the method of connecting the front pipe to the manifold. Two spring clips are used to secure the flange joint and a friction ring is incorporated to ensure a gas-tight seal. VW tool No 3049A is provided to remove and refit the spring clips, but a stout screwdriver can be used instead if care is taken. When fitting the clips, engage their ends with the slots in the manifold first, push up on the front pipe and engage the other end of the clips into the front pipe slots. Ensure that the clips are properly seated.

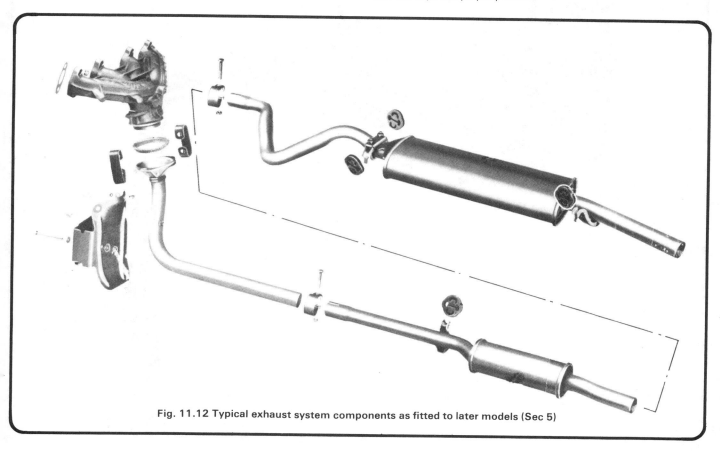

Fig. 11.12 Typical exhaust system components as fitted to later models (Sec 5)

6   Clutch

Clutch — modifications

1   From approximately December 1980 a larger 200 mm (7.9 in) clutch has been fitted to cater for the increased power of the 1588 cc engine.

2   The removal, refitting and inspection procedures described in Chapter 4 are also applicable to the larger unit with the exception of the release plate and retaining ring fittings. These have been modified so that the ring ends bend inward and locate in one of the holes in the release plate (photo).

3   When reassembling **all** clutches, ensure that the centering pins in the flywheel engage with the centering holes or slots in the pressure plate. If care is not taken here the flywheel TDC mark will no longer be accurate.

Clutch release mechanism (5-speed gearbox) — removal and refitting

4   The release mechanism is located in the gearbox end housing and is accessible after removal of the endplate.

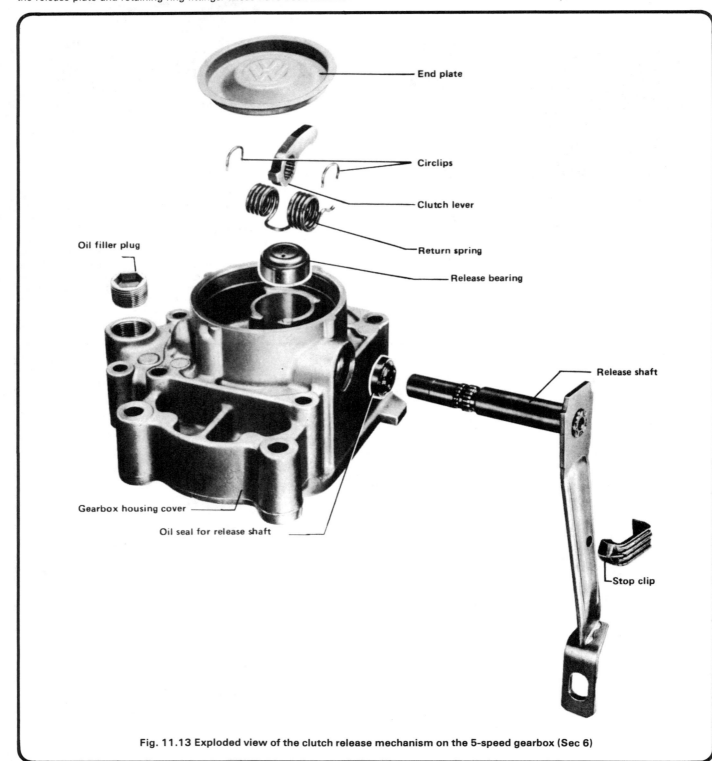

Fig. 11.13 Exploded view of the clutch release mechanism on the 5-speed gearbox (Sec 6)

6.2 Correct fitting of later release plate retaining ring. Ring must locate under lugs (arrowed) with ends in hole

5   Support the engine/gearbox unit with a trolley jack then remove the engine front mounting and gearbox mounting. Lower the jack slightly to provide access to the endplate.
6   Using a sharp instrument, pierce the endplate and lever it out from the gearbox. Have a container handy as there may be some oil spillage. A new endplate must be obtained before refitting.
7   Two circlips secure the clutch lever to the shaft (one on early models) and these can now be removed.
8   With the clutch cable disconnected, as described in Chapter 4, withdraw the release shaft, lift out the lever then remove the release bearing. Renew the release bearing if there is any sign of wear or roughness when it is spun.
9   Refitting is the reverse sequence to removal. Note that the clutch lever and shaft have a master spline, and when fitting the return spring ensure that the bent ends bear against the casing with the centre part hooked over the clutch lever. Use a suitable block of wood to tap on a new endplate and check the gearbox oil level after refitting.

---

7   Transmission

Gearbox (4-speed) – pinion shaft bearing modifications
1   From approximately October 1979 the method of retaining the pinion shaft needle roller bearing in the gear carrier housing has been changed.
2   The bearing is secured by a countersunk screw which must be undone before removal. The bearing can then be withdrawn using the procedure described in Chapter 5, Section 8. If the bearing is excessively tight, warm the housing to 80°C (176°F) first.

Gearbox (4-speed) – deletion of shift fork shaft circlips
3   The method of retaining the shift fork shaft in the shift fork set has been changed from positive location by two circlips to fully floating with a small spring at each end of the shaft.
4   The overhaul details given in Chapter 5 remain unchanged apart from the reference to the two circlips.

Gearbox (4-speed) – gear linkage modifications
5   Various modifications have been made to the gear linkage to improve gear selection on later models.
6   From August 1980 the bearing supporting the shift rod has been changed from a multipart assembly to a simplified one-piece design. From April 1981 a cap was incorporated in the rubber boot at the base of the gear lever so that adjustments can be made by removing the cap only, not the entire boot. From February 1982 the relay lever

incorporates a larger rubber ball to give more positive gear engagement.
7   Apart from the changes mentioned, removal, refitting and adjustment procedures are still as described in Chapter 5.

Gearbox (5-speed) – description
8   Apart from the additional 5th gear and obvious changes to the gear selector mechanism, the 5-speed gearbox is essentially the same, both internally and externally, as the 4-speed unit. The general information and removal and refitting procedures given in Chapter 5 are therefore also applicable to the 5-speed gearbox.

Gearbox (5-speed) – separating the housings
9   Remove the clutch pushrod from the centre of the mainshaft.
10   Undo and remove the retaining bolts and withdraw the main casing end cover. Remove the clutch release bearing and the gasket.
11   Move the selector shaft lever to the neutral position.
12   Unscrew the selector shaft detent plunger, the 5th gear detent plunger and the reversing lamp switch.
13   Undo and remove the nut securing the selector shaft lever to the shaft. Withdraw the lever and the rubber boot.
14   Using a suitable box spanner, such as a spark plug spanner, undo and remove the selector shaft end cap and lift out the spring. Carefully slide out the selector shaft assembly.
15   Undo and remove the reverse idler shaft lockbolt.
16   Using a screwdriver inserted through the selector shaft opening, engage 5th and reverse gears simultaneously by moving the front and rear selector forks towards the clutch housing (photo).
17   Using a Torx drive socket bit, unscrew the 5th gear synchro-hub retaining screw. **Note:** *this screw is extremely tight and is also retained with a thread locking compound.* It will be necessary to engage the help of an assistant to hold the gearbox as the screw is undone. Remove the washer from under the screw head.
18   Prise out the locking plate securing the selector tube to the fork.
19   Using a pair of right-angle circlip pliers, or a similar tool engaged in the slots of the selector tube, turn the tube anti-clockwise to unscrew it from the selector fork.
20   When the fork is released, lift off the synchro-hub assembly complete with 5th gear, thrust washer, needle roller bearing and selector fork. *Do not pull the selector rod out of the selector tube, otherwise the selector fork assembly will fall apart inside the gearbox.*
21   Extract the circlip and withdraw the thrust washer and 5th gear from the pinion shaft. Lever the gear up carefully, using two screwdrivers if it is tight.
22   Prise the plastic cap from the centre of the left-hand side drive flange, extract the circlip and washer, and withdraw the flange using a two-legged puller.

7.16 Using a screwdriver to engage two gears simultaneously

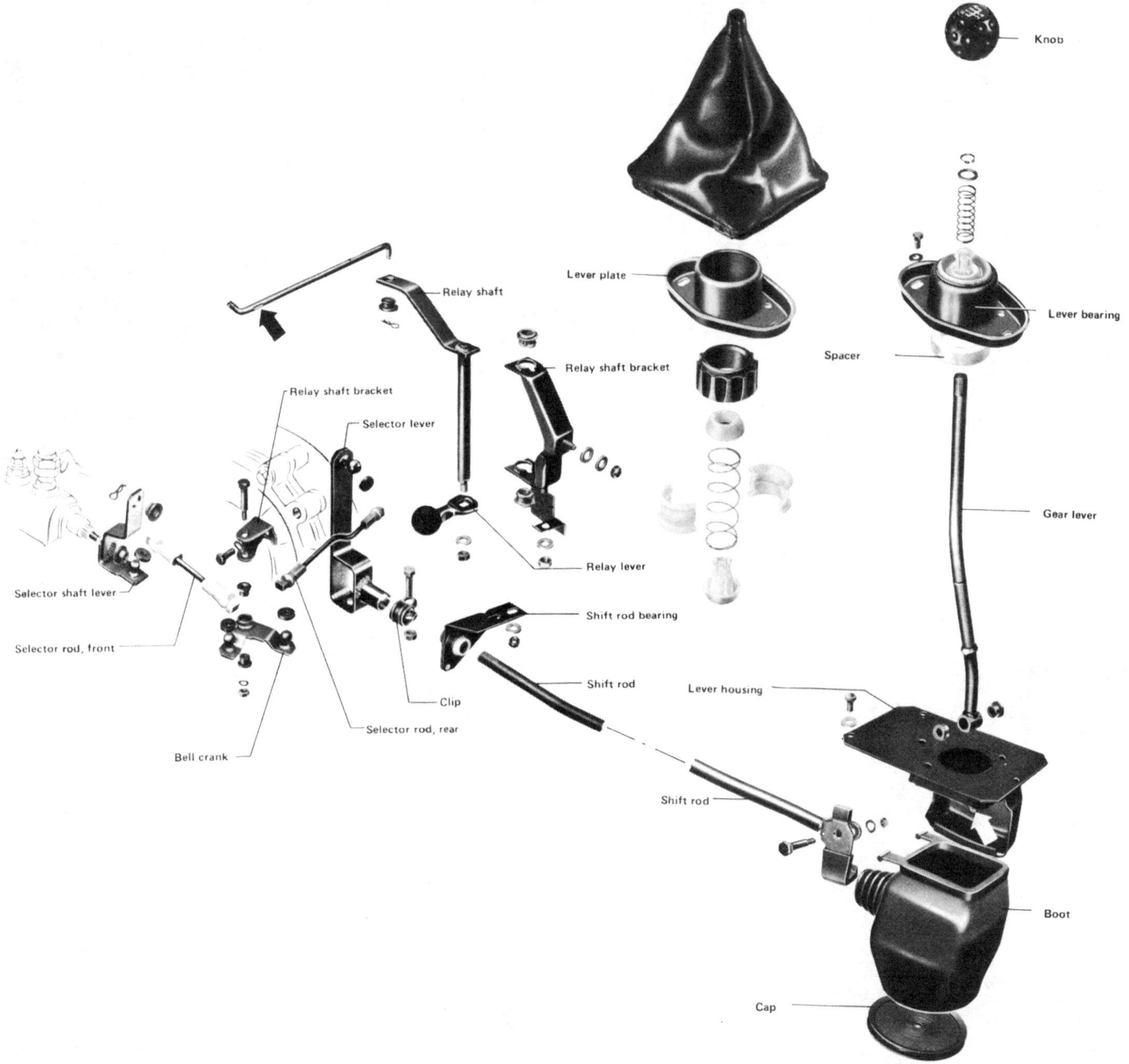

Knob

Lever bearing

Gear lever

Boot

Spacer

Cap

Lever housing

Lever plate

Relay shaft bracket

Relay lever

Shift rod bearing

Shift rod

Shift rod

Relay shaft

Selector lever

Clip

Selector rod, rear

Relay shaft bracket

Bell crank

Selector shaft lever

Selector rod, front

Fig. 11.14 Exploded view of the gearchange linkage fitted to later models with 4 or 5-speed gearbox (Sec 7)

23 Using a Torx driver bit and ratchet or bar, undo and remove the four bolts securing the mainshaft bearing retainer to the gearbox housing.

24 Undo and remove the bolts securing the main casing to the gear carrier housing. Using strips of angle iron, or suitable alternatives, make up a removal bracket to enable the casing to be drawn off the mainshaft (photo). Fasten a bar or piece of angle iron across the clutch housing in such a manner as to support the end of the mainshaft. Tighten the centre screw of the casing separator tool until it touches a suitable thrust pad placed over the end of the mainshaft (or a steel ball placed in the hollow centre) and then continue tightening until the casing is pulled away (photo), leaving the mainshaft bearing complete on the mainshaft.

25 Lift the casing off and recover the shim located against the bearing outer race (where fitted). Remove the gasket and the magnet from the gear carrier housing, and disconnect the removal brackets.

Gearbox (5-speed) mainshaft, pinion shaft and differential – removal

26 Withdraw the selector fork rod from the gear carrier housing, disengage the forks from the synchro sleeves and remove the fork set sideways as a complete assembly.

27 Undo and remove the two bolts securing the reverse gear relay lever pillars to the housing and lift off the pillars and relay lever.

28 Withdraw the reverse idler shaft and remove the shaft and gear from the gear carrier housing.

29 Extract the circlip from the end of the pinion shaft, then lift the mainshaft assembly out of the gear carrier while at the same time sliding 4th gear off the pinion shaft.

30 Extract the remaining circlip from the pinion shaft and then, using a suitable long two-legged puller, pull the 3rd and 2nd gears off the pinion shaft together.

31 Withdraw the 2nd gear needle roller bearing.

32 Position the legs of the puller beneath 1st gear and pull off the needle roller bearing inner race, 1st/2nd synchro unit and 1st gear together as an assembly.

33 Withdraw the 1st gear needle roller bearing and thrust washer.

34 Undo and remove the four bolts securing the bearing retaining plate, then remove the plate and the pinion shaft from the gear carrier housing. Note that the retaining plate incorporates the reverse gear stop which locates beneath the reverse gear.

35 Remove the remaining differential flange, as described in paragraph 22, then lift out the differential assembly.

Gearbox (5-speed) main casing – overhaul

36 The three oil seals in the main casing should be renewed by prising them out, noting their fitted direction, and fitting new seals using a block of wood, large socket or tube to drive them in. Fill the lips of the seals with multi-purpose grease before fitting.

37 The needle roller bearing for the pinion shaft is retained by a screw and can be withdrawn for renewal after removal of the screw.

38 If the differential bearing outer race requires renewal, this should be left to a VW dealer, as the bearings also require accurate setting up using jigs and fixtures.

39 If the mainshaft has been dismantled, or if the mainshaft bearing has been removed, it should now be fitted to the main casing.

7.24A Suitable apparatus for main casing removal – in position

7.24B Removing the main casing

40 Position the bearing on the casing with the plastic side facing outward. If there were any shims recovered during dismantling, these should be fitted between the bearing and casing.

41 Drive the bearing into position and then refit the bearing retaining plate (photos). Secure the plate with the four Torx screws (photo).

7.41A Refit the mainshaft bearing ...

7.41B ... fit the retaining plate ...

7.41C ... and secure the plate with the Torx screws

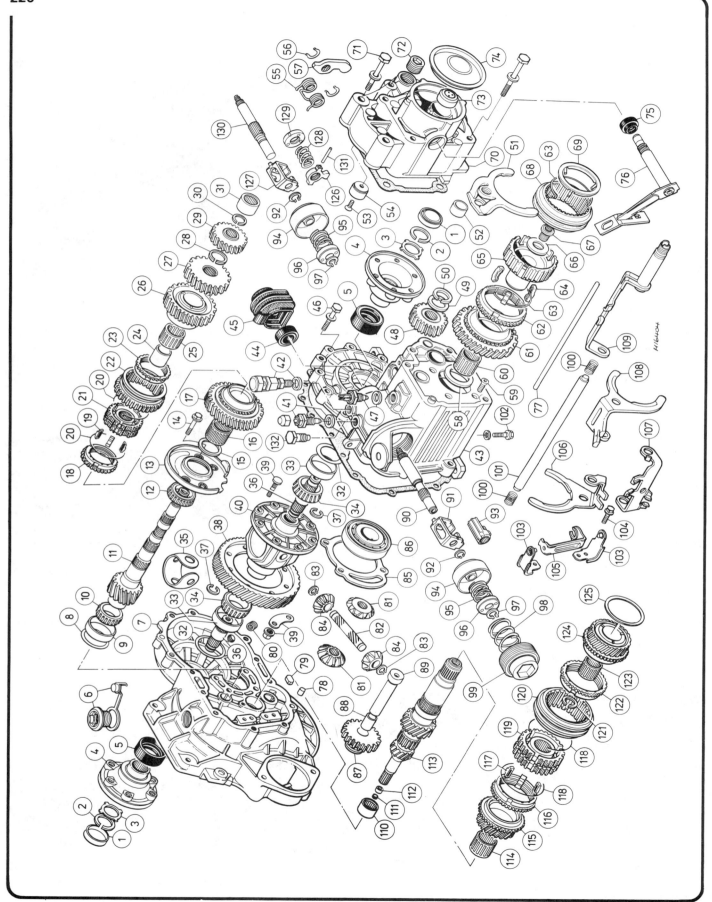

Fig. 11.15 Exploded view of the 5-speed gearbox (Sec 7)

1 Plastic cap
2 Circlip
3 Spring washer
4 Drive coupling
5 Differential oil seal
6 Blanking plug
7 Gear carrier housing
8 Shim
9 Bearing outer race
10 Pinion shaft bearing
11 Pinion shaft
12 Pinion shaft bearing
13 Bearing outer race and retaining plate assembly
14 Retaining plate bolt
15 Thrust washer
16 Needle roller bearing
17 1st gear
18 1st gear baulk ring
19 Synchro key
20 Spring
21 1st/2nd gear synchroniser hub
22 1st/2nd gear synchroniser sleeve and reverse gear
23 Baulk ring
24 Needle roller bearing inner race
25 Needle roller bearing
26 2nd gear
27 3rd gear
28 Selected circlip
29 4th gear
30 Circlip
31 Needle roller bearing
32 Shim
33 Bearing outer race
34 Taper roller bearing

35 Thrust washer
36 Differential shaft
37 Circlip
38 Final drive gear
39 Bolt, lock plate and nut
40 Differential cage
41 Selector shaft detent plunger and washer
42 5th gear detent plunger and washer
43 Main casing
44 Selector shaft oil seal
45 Selector shaft boot
46 Casing retaining bolt
47 Reverse lamp switch and washer
48 5th gear
49 Thrust washer
50 Circlip
51 5th gear selector fork
52 Spacer bush (early models only)
53 Bearing retainer screw
54 Needle roller bearing
55 Clutch return spring
56 Circlip
57 Clutch lever
58 Thrust washer
59 Bearing retaining plate screw
60 Needle roller bearing
61 5th gear
62 5th baulk ring
63 Spring
64 Synchro key
65 5th gear synchroniser hub

66 Washer
67 Synchroniser hub screw
68 5th gear synchroniser sleeve
69 Stop plate
70 End cover
71 End cover bolt
72 Filler/level plug
73 Clutch release bearing
74 End cap
75 Operating shaft oil seal
76 Clutch release shaft
77 Clutch pushrod
78 Dowel
79 Magnet
80 Drain plug
81 Differential gear
82 Pinion pin
83 Circlip
84 Differential pinion
85 Mainshaft bearing retaining plate
86 Mainshaft bearing
87 Reverse idler gear
88 Bush
89 Reverse idler shaft
90 Selector shaft
91 Yoke
92 Circlip
93 Selector finger
94 Sleeve
95 Spring
96 Spring plate
97 Circlip
98 Spring
99 End cover
100 Spring

101 Selector rod
102 Reverse idler shaft bolt
103 Relay lever pillar
104 Pillar bolt
105 Reverse gear relay lever
106 1st/2nd selector fork
107 Reverse selector fork
108 3rd/4th selector fork
109 5th gear selector link and tube
110 Needle roller bearing
111 Clutch pushrod oil seal
112 Clutch pushrod bush
113 Mainshaft
114 Needle roller bearing
115 3rd gear
116 Baulk ring
117 Synchro key
118 Spring
119 3rd/4th synchroniser
120 3rd/4th synchroniser sleeve
121 Circlip
122 Baulk ring
123 Needle roller bearing
124 4th gear
125 Shim (if fitted)
126 Selector finger*
127 Yoke*
128 Spring*
129 Detent plate*
130 Shaft*
131 Roll pin*
132 Peg bolt*
*Alternatives to items 41, 90, 91 and 93 (where applicable)

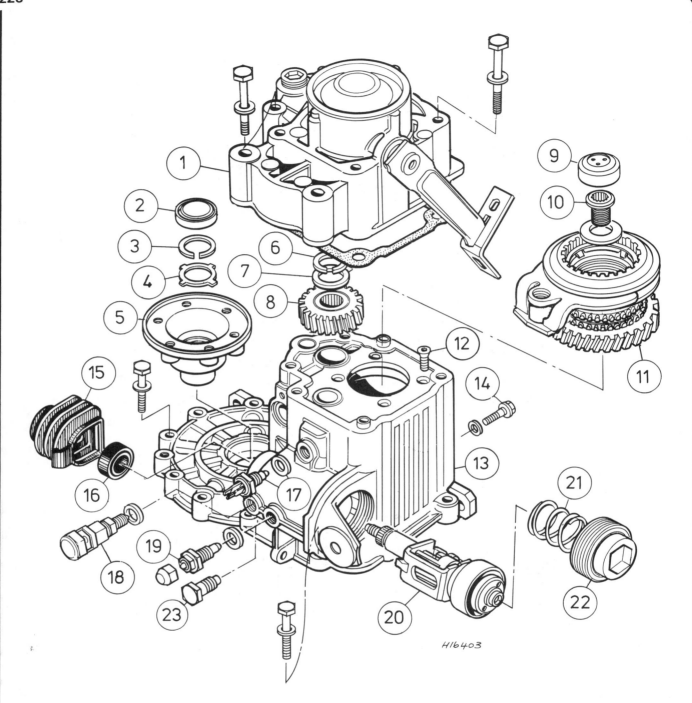

Fig. 11.16 Main casing components – 5-speed gearbox (Sec 7)

1	Main casing end cover	10	5th gear synchro-hub retaining screw	17	Reverse lamp switch
2	Plastic cap	11	5th speed gear, selector fork and synchroniser assembly	18	5th gear detent plunger
3	Circlip	12	Main shaft bearing retainer screws	19	Selector shaft detent plunger
4	Spring washer	13	Main casing	20	Selector shaft assembly
5	Drive coupling	14	Reverse idler shaft bolt	21	Spring
6	Circlip	15	Selector shaft rubber boot	22	End cap
7	Thrust washer	16	Selector shaft seal	23	Selector shaft peg bolt – alternative to item 19 (where applicable)
8	5th gear				
9	Clutch release bearing				

42 Removal and refitting procedures for the clutch release mechanism are covered earlier in this Supplement.

Gearbox (5-speed) gear carrier housing — overhaul

43 Prise or drift out the oil seals and fit new seals using a socket or tube and hammer to drive them in (photos). Fill the space between the seal lips with a multi-purpose grease before fitting.

Fig. 11.17 Prising out the selector tube locking plate — 5-speed gearbox (Sec 7)

7.43A Fit a new differential drive flange oil seal ...

7.43B ... and drive it fully into place

44 The mainshaft needle roller bearing may be removed, if necessary, using a suitable extractor. Do not remove the bearing unless it is defective as it is likely to be damaged during removal.

45 If the outer races of the differential bearings are in need of renewal, then this, and the renewal of the corresponding inner races and bearings on the differential, should be left to a VW dealer, as a complicated setting up procedure is involved.

46 The fit of the starter motor armature should be tried in the starter bush. If undue wear is apparent, renew the bush.

Gearbox (5-speed) pinion shaft bearings — renewal

47 The large and small bearings accurately locate the pinion shaft gear with the crownwheel of the differential. If either bearing is defective then both must be renewed. In the removal process the bearings are destroyed. New ones have to be shrunk on and the shim under the smaller bearing changed for one of the correct size.

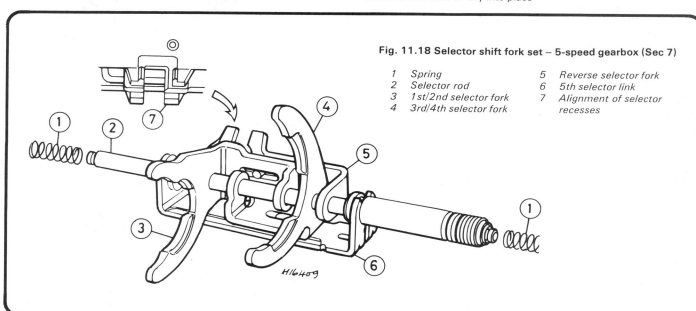

Fig. 11.18 Selector shift fork set — 5-speed gearbox (Sec 7)

1	Spring	5	Reverse selector fork
2	Selector rod	6	5th selector link
3	1st/2nd selector fork	7	Alignment of selector
4	3rd/4th selector fork		recesses

48 This operation is quite complicated and requires special equipment for preloading of the shaft and measurement of the torque required to rotate the new bearings. In addition the shim at the top of the mainshaft and the axial play at the circlip of the 3rd gear on the pinion shaft will be affected. This will mean selection of a new shim and circlip. There are six different thicknesses of circlip. Therefore it is recommended that if these bearings require renewal, the work should be left to your VW agent.

Gearbox (5-speed) mainshaft – dismantling and re-assembly

49 Extract the circlip securing the ball-bearing to the mainshaft.
50 Using a press, or a hydraulic puller with its legs positioned beneath 4th gear, draw the gear and bearing off the mainshaft.
51 Remove the 4th gear needle roller bearing and extract the circlip securing the 3rd/4th gear synchro-hub to the shaft.
52 Again using a press or hydraulic puller remove 3rd gear and the 3rd/4th synchro-hub from the mainshaft as an assembly.
53 Withdraw the 3rd gear needle roller bearing.

54 Begin reassembly by sliding the 3rd gear needle roller bearing and 3rd gear onto the mainshaft (photos). Place the baulk ring onto 3rd gear (photo).
55 Heat the 3rd/4th synchro-hub in an oven to approximately 120°C (248°F). Place the hub on the mainshaft with the identifying groove in the hub boss towards 3rd gear, and drive the synchro-hub assembly into position using a hammer and suitable tube. Make sure that the slots in the baulk ring engage with the keys in the synchro-hub assembly as it is fitted.
56 Secure the synchro-hub in position using the circlip (photo).
57 Place the baulk ring against the synchro-hub assembly with the slots aligned with the keys (photo).
58 Slide the needle roller bearing onto the mainshaft and refit 4th gear (photos).

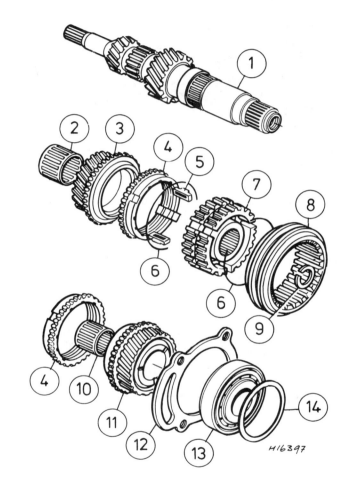

Fig. 11.20 Mainshaft components – 5-speed gearbox (Sec 7)

1	Mainshaft	8	Synchro sleeve
2	Needle roller bearing	9	Circlip
3	3rd gear	10	Needle roller bearing
4	Baulk ring	11	4th gear
5	Synchro-hub	12	Bearing retaining plate
6	Retaining spring	13	Mainshaft bearing
7	Synchro-hub	14	Shim (where fitted)

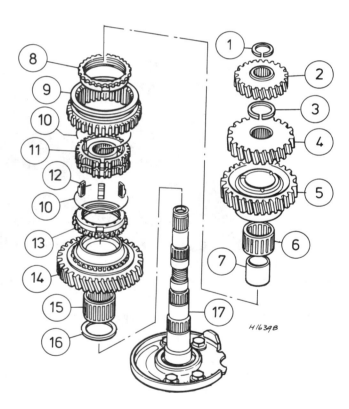

Fig. 11.19 Pinion shaft components – 5-speed gearbox (Sec 7)

1	Circlip	9	1st/2nd synchro sleeve
2	4th gear	10	Retaining spring
3	Selected circlip	11	1st/2nd synchro-hub
4	3rd gear	12	Synchro key
5	2nd gear	13	1st gear baulk ring
6	Needle roller bearing	14	1st gear
7	Needle roller bearing inner race	15	Needle roller bearing
		16	Thrust washer
8	Baulk ring	17	Pinion shaft

Gearbox (5-speed) synchroniser units – inspection

59 The synchroniser unit hubs and sleeves are supplied as a matched set and must not be interchanged. Before dismantling the units, mark the sleeve and hub in relation to each other.

7.54A Slide the 3rd gear needle roller bearing ...

7.54B ... and 3rd gear onto the mainshaft

7.54C Place the baulk ring on the gear

7.56 Refit the 3rd/4th synchro unit and secure with the circlip

7.57 Fit the baulk ring to the synchro-hub

7.58A Slide the needle roller bearing onto the mainshaft ...

7.58B ... and fit 4th gear

7.60 Checking baulk ring wear

60 When renewing the synchro baulk rings it is advisable to fit new sliding keys and retaining springs. When examining the units for wear bear in mind the following:

   (a) *With the keys removed, the hub and sleeve should slide easily with minimum backlash or axial rock*

   (b) *With the baulk rings in position the clearance from the face of the baulk ring to the face of the gear, measured with feeler gauges (photo), must not be less than the dimension given in the Specifications at the beginning of this Supplement*

   (c) *Check for excess movement between the selector forks and their groove in the sleeve. If in doubt compare the clearance with that of new components*

61 To reassemble the synchroniser units lay them out on the bench with the identifying marks made during removal uppermost (photo).
62 Slide the synchro sleeve over the hub, with the slots in the sleeve splines (photo) aligned with the cutaways in the hub. Note also that the selector fork groove on the 1st/2nd synchro unit must be fitted away from the side of the hub having the identifying grooves (photo).
63 Fit the keys into the hub and sleeve grooves (photo) and then place one of the retaining springs in position with its hooked end engaged with a key (photo).
64 Turn the synchro unit over and fit the other retaining spring, in the opposite direction to the first, and with its end engaged in a different key.

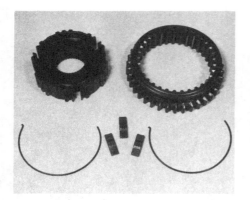

7.61 Synchroniser unit components prior to reassembly

7.62A The slots in the synchro sleeve must align with the cutaways in the hub

7.62B Identifying grooves (arrowed) in synchro-hub

7.63A Fit the keys ...

7.63B ... and secure them with the retaining springs with their hooked ends (arrowed) engaged with the keys

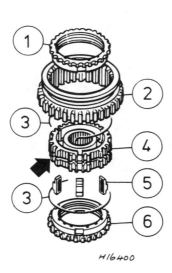

Fig. 11.21 Exploded view of the 1st/2nd synchroniser unit – 5-speed gearbox (Sec 7)

1	2nd gear baulk ring	4	Synchro-hub
2	Synchro sleeve	5	Synchro key
3	Retaining spring	6	1st gear baulk ring

Arrow indicates identification grooves in synchro-hub

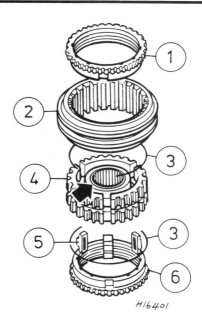

Fig. 11.22 View of the 3rd/4th synchroniser unit – 5-speed gearbox (Sec 7)

1	4th gear baulk ring	4	Synchro-hub
2	Synchro sleeve	5	Synchro key
3	Retaining spring	6	Baulk ring

Arrow indicates identification groove on hub boss

65 Note that when assembling the 5th gear synchroniser, the chamfer on the sleeve splines must face toward the hub boss.

Gearbox (5-speed) differential unit — inspection

66 Dismantling and overhaul of the differential are considered to be beyond the scope of the home mechanic. If the differential assembly is obviously in need of renewal it will be necessary to obtain a complete unit and entrust the work to a VW dealer, as critical adjustments are required.

67 If the problem with the differential is purely one of noise, and if the noise is more of a whine than a rumble, the unit may continue working for some considerable time without getting any worse. Again, the help or advice of a dealer is recommended for deciding the course of action to be taken.

Gearbox (5-speed) differential, pinion shaft and mainshaft — reassembly

68 Refit the differential unit in the gear carrier housing (photo).

69 Fit the right-hand drive flange and drive it fully into position using a hammer and a suitable tube.

70 Refit the spring washer, retaining circlip and a new plastic cap.

71 With the bearings in position on the pinion shaft (photo), place the shaft in the gear carrier housing and mesh it with the differential gear (photo).

72 Fit the bearing retaining plate and tighten the bolts to the specified torque (photos).

73 Place the thrust washer over the pinion shaft with the shoulder on its internal diameter towards the pinion (photo).

74 Slide on the 1st gear needle roller bearing followed by 1st gear and the baulk ring (photos).

75 Heat the assembled 1st/2nd synchro unit in an oven to approximately 120°C (248°F) and then, with the identifying groove in the hub circumference towards 1st gear, drive the unit onto the pinion shaft using a hammer and a suitable tube or press. As the unit is fitted align the slots in the 1st gear baulk ring so that they engage with the keys of the synchro unit.

76 Heat the 2nd gear needle roller bearing inner race and slide it over the pinion shaft and position it in contact with the shoulder on the shaft (photo).

77 Position the needle roller bearing over the inner race (photo) and then refit the baulk ring and 2nd gear (photos).

78 Place the 3rd gear on the pinion shaft with its boss facing 2nd gear (photo), and drive or press it onto the shaft (photo).

79 Fit the circlip to the pinion shaft groove above 3rd gear and then, using feeler gauges, measure the clearance between the gear and circlip (3rd gear axial movement) (photo). If the clearance is in excess of the specified amount, an oversize circlip must be fitted. Circlips are available in a range of thicknesses from 2.5 mm (0.098 in) to 3.0 mm (0.118 in), in 0.1 mm (0.004 in) increments.

80 At this stage the mainshaft must be fitted in position on the gear carrier housing (photo). Engage its end into the needle roller bearing and bring the gears into mesh.

81 Place 4th gear, boss upwards, on the pinion shaft (photo) and secure with the retaining circlip (photo).

82 Ensure that the reverse gear stop is in place on the pinion shaft bearing retaining plate and then refit the reverse idler gear and shaft (photo).

83 Locate the magnet in its location in the gear carrier housing (photo).

84 Engage the selector forks with their respective gears and position the forks and selector rod in the housing (photo).

85 Engage the forked end of the reverse gear relay lever with the reverse idler gear, and secure the relay lever pillars with the two retaining bolts (photo).

7.68 Refit the differential

7.71A With the pinion bearings in position ...

7.71B ... place the pinion shaft in the gear carrier housing

7.72A Refit the bearing retaining plate ...

7.72B ... and tighten the bolts to the specified torque

7.73 Fit the thrust washer

7.74A Slide on 1st gear needle roller bearing ...

7.74B ... followed by 1st gear ...

7.74C ... and the baulk ring

7.76 Fit the needle roller bearing inner race

7.77A Place the bearing over the inner race

7.77B Fit the baulk ring ...

7.77C ... and slide on 2nd gear

7.78A Place 3rd gear on the pinion shaft ...

7.78B ... and drive it fully home

7.79 Checking the 3rd gear axial movement

7.80 Position the assembled mainshaft on the gear carrier housing

7.81A Fit 4th gear to the pinion shaft ...

7.81B ... and secure with the retaining circlip

7.82 Fit the reverse idler gear and shaft

7.83 Place the magnet in its location

7.84 Refit the selector forks and rod

7.85 Refit the relay lever and pillars

Gearbox (5-speed) – reassembling the housings

86 Check that the reverse idler shaft is positioned correctly, as shown in Fig. 11.23, and set the geartrain by moving the selector forks to neutral.

87 Fit a new gasket on the gear carrier flange and then carefully lower the main casing over the gears, shafts and selector rod (photo).

88 Support the clutch housing end of the mainshaft with an angle iron bracket and thrust screw, as described during removal, or on a block of wood. Using a tube against the mainshaft bearing inner race in the main casing, drive the bearing and the casing fully into position (photo).

89 Refit and tighten the reverse idler shaft lockbolt (photo), and then secure the gear carrier housing and main casing together – with the

retaining bolts tightened to the specified torque.

90 Heat the 5th gear to 120°C (248°F) and fit it to the pinion shaft with the groove near its centre facing away from the main casing (photo).

91 Secure 5th gear with the thrust washer and circlip (photo).

92 Place the needle roller bearing and thrust washer in the mainshaft 5th gear, and place the locking plate in the selector fork. With the fork engaged with the synchroniser fit this assembly over the mainshaft and engage the selector fork and locking plate over the selector rod.

93 Hold the selector rod and, using right-angled circlip pliers or another suitable tool, turn the selector tube clockwise to engage the fork. Screw the tube into the fork until the upper edge of the tube protrudes above the fork face by 5.0 mm (0.197 in) (Fig. 11.24).

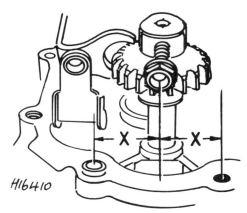

Fig. 11.23 Correct positioning of reverse idler shaft – 5-speed gearbox (Sec 7)

Dimensions X must be equal

Fig. 11.24 Selector tube protrusion dimension X – 5-speed gearbox (Sec 7)

7.87 Lower the main casing onto the gear carrier housing

7.90 Fit the 5th gear to the pinion shaft

7.88 Drive the bearing onto the mainshaft

7.91 Secure the gear with the thrust washer and circlip

94 Engage 5th and reverse gears simultaneously, as described in the removal procedure.

95 Apply a thin smear of thread locking compound to the threads of a new 5th gear synchroniser retaining screw and refit the screw and washer (photo). Tighten the screw to the specified torque.

96 Move the selector forks back to the neutral position and refit the selector shaft assembly, spring and end cover (photos). Apply a thin smear of thread locking compound to the threads of the end cover and tighten it using a spark plug box spanner or a suitable bolt with two nuts locked together on the bolt thread.

97 Refit the selector shaft detent plunger. The detent plunger should only be adjusted if the housing, selector shaft or detent plunger have been renewed.

(a) *Refer to Fig. 11.25. Slacken the locknut and screw in the adjusting sleeve until the lockring lifts off the adjusting sleeve*

(b) *Screw the adjusting sleeve out until the lockring just contacts the sleeve*

(c) *Check that the lockring lifts as soon as the shaft is turned, tighten the locknut and refit the plastic cap*

98 Refit the 5th gear detent plunger and adjust it as follows if the casing, selector shaft or detent plunger have been renewed, or if too little or too much force is needed to overcome the 5th gear detent.

(a) *Select neutral and remove the plunger plastic cap*

7.89 Refit the reverse idler shaft lockbolt

7.95 Secure the 5th gear synchroniser with the retaining screw

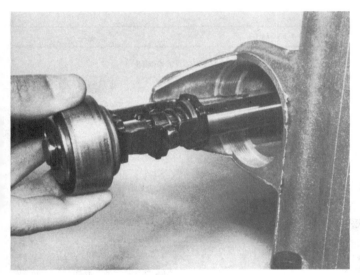

7.96A Refit the selector shaft assembly ...

7.96B ... followed by the spring and end cover

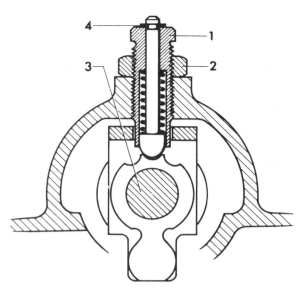

Fig. 11.25 Sectional view of the selector shaft detent plunger — 5-speed gearbox (Sec 7)

1	Adjusting sleeve	3	Selector shaft
2	Locknut	4	Lockring

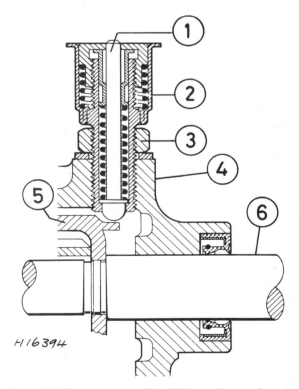

H16394

Fig. 11.26 Sectional view of the 5th gear detent plunger — 5-speed gearbox (Sec 7)

1	Centre pin	4	Main casing
2	Plunger	5	Selector shaft yoke
3	Locknut	6	Selector shaft

(b) Slacken the locknut and screw in the plunger until the centre
     pin starts to lift
(c) Slacken the plunger $\frac{1}{3}$ of a turn and tighten the locknut

99 Refit the reversing lamp switch.
100 Make sure that the selector tube protrusion is still as described in
paragraph 93 and then engage 5th gear. Check that, with 5th gear
engaged and the selector fork held away from the gearbox to take up
any free play, the synchro sleeve overlaps the hub teeth by at least 1.0
mm (0.040 in).
101 Using pliers, clamp the locking plate, as shown in Fig. 11.27.
102 Place the clutch release bearing in its housing (photo) and, with
a new gasket in place, refit the end cover to the main casing (photo).
103 Refit and tighten the end cover retaining bolts, noting that the two
short bolts are fitted either side of the oil level/filler plug.
104 Refit the remaining differential drive flange, spring washer, circlip
and plastic cap (photos).
105 Refit the selector shaft rubber boot, position the selector shaft
lever on the shaft and secure with the retaining nut.
106 Attach the linkage support bracket to the main casing retaining
bolt.
107 Finally slide the clutch operating pushrod into the mainshaft.

*Gearbox (5-speed) gearshift linkage and lever —
adjustment, removal and refitting*
108 The gearshift linkage and lever assembly used on the 5-speed
gearbox is the same as for 4-speed units described in Chapter 5, but
incorporating the modifications detailed earlier in this Supplement.
The procedures described for the 4-speed unit are therefore applicable,
but note that the gearshift rod adjusting dimension a (see Fig. 5.22) is
15 mm (0.6 in) on the 5-speed gearbox.

Fig. 11.27 Clamping the locking plate – 5-speed gearbox (Sec 7)

8 Braking system

Modified brake caliper retaining bolts
1 From October 1981 the two bolts used to secure the brake caliper to
the wheel bearing housing (stub axle) have been changed from

7.102A Fit the clutch release bearing to the
end cover ...

7.102B ... and fit the cover to the main
casing

7.104A Fit the remaining differential drive
flange ...

7.104B ... spring washer ...

7.104C ... retaining circlip ...

7.104D ... and plastic cap

conventional hexagon head bolts to flanged locking bolts (Fig. 11.28). To suit the modified bolt the two holes in the caliper have been provided with a chamfer (Fig. 11.29). Only the flanged locking bolts will be supplied as replacement parts.

2   If the new flanged locking bolts are being used to secure an old type caliper, a 45° chamfer of 1 mm width must be made in the caliper bolt holes. This can be done with a scraper or countersunk drill bit. The early type hexagon head bolts **must not** be used to secure a modified caliper with chamfered bolt holes.

3   The torque wrench setting for the flanged locking bolt has been increased to the figure given in the Specifications at the beginning of this Supplement.

9   Electrical system

Starter motor – modifications

1   Certain later models are equipped with a Bosch starter motor of the type shown in Fig. 11.30. Overhaul procedures are virtually the same as

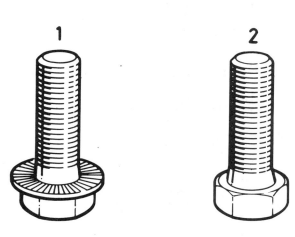

Fig. 11.28 Modified brake caliper retaining bolts (1) and early type bolts (2) (Sec 8)

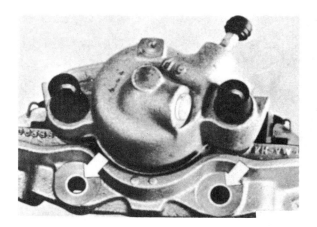

Fig. 11.29 Brake caliper bolt hole chamfers (arrowed) for use with flanged retaining bolts (Sec 8)

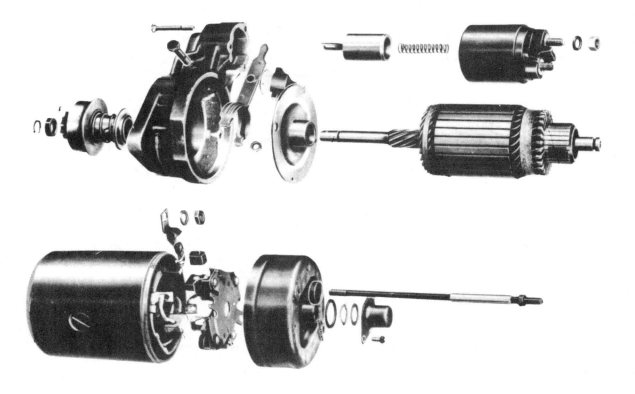

Fig. 11.30 Alternative starter motor fitted to later models (Sec 9)

for other Bosch versions, and the information contained in Chapter 7 is still applicable, but with reference to the illustration in this supplement.

Front turn signal lamp (Jetta models) – bulb renewal

2　Open the bonnet and pull off the rubber cap on the rear of the bulb holder.

3　Press the plastic lug on the bulb holder and withdraw the bulb (Fig. 11.31).

4　Turn the bulb anti-clockwise and remove it from the holder.

5　Refitting is the reverse sequence to removal.

Fig. 11.31 Turn signal bulb holder lug (arrowed) – Jetta models (Sec 9)

Fuses and relays – modifications

6　From 1983 onwards a new fuse and relay panel has been fitted, providing 22 fuse positions and up to 17 relay positions. The fuses, their current rating and the circuits they protect are given in the following table. The relay locations are shown in Fig. 11.32. Note that the fuse and relay information given is typical, and slight variations may occur according to territory or model.

Fuse	Amps	Circuit
1	30	Radiator fan
2	10	Stop-lights
3	10	Cigarette lighter, clock, interior light
4	15	Hazard flashers
5	15	Not used
6	15	Foglights
7	10	Side and tail lights, left
8	10	Side and tail lights, right
9	10	Main beam, right and main beam warning light
10	10	Main beam, left
11	15	Windscreen wipers, washers
12	15	Not used
13	15	Heated rear window
14	20	Fresh air fan
15	10	Reversing lights
16	15	Horn
17	10	Not used
18	10	Brake warning lamp
19	10	Direction indicators
20	10	Number plate light, glovebox light, foglights
21	10	Low beam, left
22	10	Low beam, right

Additional fuse in a separate holder above the fusebox:

	10	Rear foglights

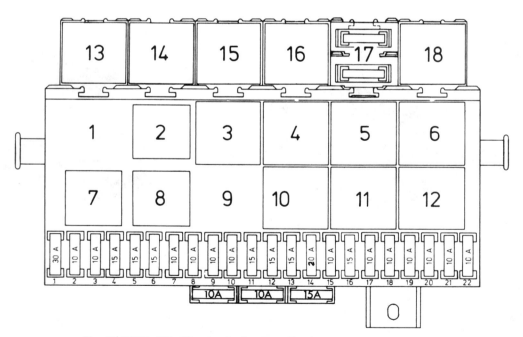

Fig. 11.32 Modified fuse and relay plate fitted to 1983 models (Sec 9)

Relay	Relay designation	Relay	Relay designation	Relay	Relay designation	Relay	Relay designation
1	Vacant	7	Fog and rear foglight relay	11	Rear window wiper and washer relay (Golf only)	16	Vacant
2	Glow plug relay	8	Ignition X contact relief relay	12	Hazard flasher relay	17	Rear foglight fuse
3	Vacant			13	Vacant	18	Coolant shortage indicator switch unit (where applicable)
4	Vacant	9	Vacant	14	Vacant		
5	Vacant	10	Intermittent windscreen wash/wipe relay	15	Headlight washer relay (where applicable)		
6	Vacant						

7 The information contained in Chapter 7 and applicable to the fuses and relays on early models remained basically unchanged up to the end of 1982. The only major change being the deletion of the heated rear window relay and the addition of a relay for the glow plug system. More detailed information relating to components and their connections is shown in the wiring diagrams at the end of Chapter 7 and this Supplement.

Instrument panel (Jetta and later Golf models) – removal and refitting

8 Disconnect the battery negative terminal.
9 Remove the steering wheel, as described in Chapter 8.
10 Pull off the heater and fresh air control knobs and lever off the trim surround.
11 If a radio is not fitted, withdraw the oddments tray. On models with a radio, prise off the control knobs, remove the surrounds, then reach under the radio and depress the two side clips. Ease the radio out and disconnect its wiring at the rear.
12 Undo the instrument panel trim retaining screws (Fig. 11.33) and ease the trim off slightly.
13 Detach the switches and warning lamps from the trim by pulling forward then withdraw the trim.
14 Unscrew the instrument panel retaining screws (Fig. 11.34). Ease the panel forward, disconnect the speedometer cable and wiring multi-plugs then withdraw the panel.
15 Refitting is the reverse sequence to removal.

Instrument panel printed circuit connections

16 The instrument panel 14 point multi-plug terminals have been revised on later models. Fig. 11.35 shows the later type and its terminal connections.

Fig. 11.34 Instrument panel retaining screws (arrowed) (Sec 9)

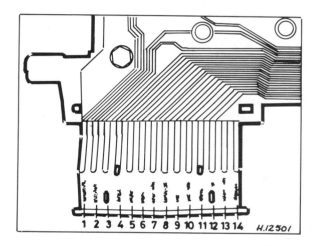

Fig. 11.35 Instrument panel 14 point multi-plug terminal (1981 models) (Sec 9)

1 Instrument lighting	8 Vacant
2 Earth	9 Oil pressure warning lamp
3 Fuel gauge sender	10 Glow plug warning lamp
4 Coolant temperature sender	11 Vacant
5 Vacant	12 Alternator warning lamp
6 Clock	13 Turn signal warning lamp
7 Main beam warning lamp	14 Live (+) wire

Fig. 11.33 Instrument panel trim retaining screws (arrowed) (Sec 9)

Wiring diagrams overleaf

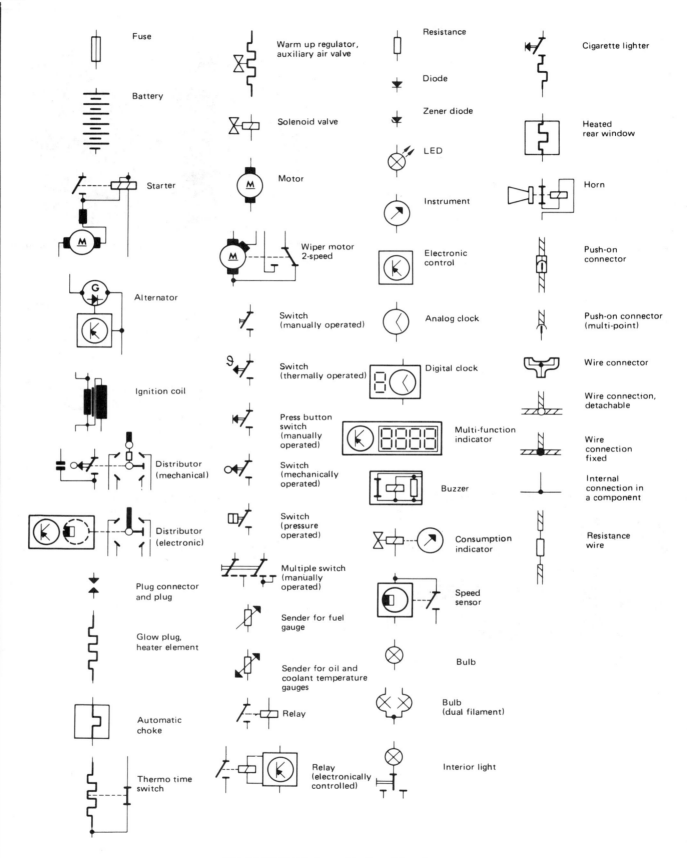

Fig. 11.36 Symbols used in the wiring diagrams

Key to wiring diagram for Golf D and LD models August 1978 to August 1979

Designation		In current track
A	Battery	4
B	Starter	5, 6
C	Alternator	3
C1	Voltage regulator	3
D	Ignition/starter switch	7 to 11
E1	Lighting switch	61 to 65
E2	Turn signal switch	45
E3	Emergency light switch	42 to 47
E4	Headlight dimmer/flasher switch	75 to 77
E9	Fresh air blower switch	26, 27
E15	Heated rear window switch	29, 30
E19	Sidelight switch (contact in turn signal switch E2 – not available – without function)	8, 9
E22	Intermittent wiper switch	36 to 40
F	Brake light switch	52
F1	Oil pressure switch	24
F2	Door contact switch, front left	86
F3	Door contact switch, front right	85
F14	Coolant temperature indicator switch	14
F18	Radiator from thermo-switch	88
G	Fuel gauge sender	25
G1	Fuel gauge	12
G27	Engine temperature sender	18
H	Horn button	58
H1	Horn	57
J2	Emergency light relay	44 to 46
J6	Voltage stabilizer	12
J31	Wash/wipe intermittent relay (L model only)	34 to 37
J52	Glow plug relay	18 to 21
J59	Relief relay for X contact	59, 60
K1	Main beam warning lamp	82
K2	Generator warning lamp	16
K3	Oil pressure warning lamp	15
K5	Turn signal warning lamp	17
K6	Emergency light warning lamp	47
K10	Heated rear window warning lamp	30
K28	Coolant temperature warning lamp	13
K29	Glow time warning lamp	19
L1	Headlight, left	78, 80
L2	Headlight, right	79, 81
L10	Instrument panel light	65 to 67
L22	Connection for foglights	83
M1	Sidelight, left	71
M2	Tail light, right	74
M3	Sidelight, right	73
M4	Tail light, left	72
M5	Turn signal, front left	48
M6	Turn signal, rear left	49
M7	Turn signal, front right	50
M8	Turn signal, rear right	51
M9	Brake light, left	54
M10	Brake light, right	53
M16	Connection for reversing light, left	55
M17	Connection for reversing light, right	56
N23	Fresh air blower series resistance	26
N23	Electro-magnetic cut-off	23
Q6	Glow plugs	21 to 22
R	Connection for radio, behind instrument panel insert	
S1 to S15	Fuses in fusebox	

Designation		In current track
S20	Glow plug fuse (50 amp) in engine compartment	21
T1	Connector, single, in engine compartment front left	
T1a	Connector, single, in engine compartment front left	
T1b	Connector, single, in engine compartment front right	
T1d	Connector, single, on brake light switch	
T1e	Connector, single, on brake light switch	
T1f	Connector, single, in engine compartment	
T1g	Connector, single, behind instrument panel	
T1h	Connector, single, behind instrument panel	
T1i	Connector, single, behind instrument panel	
T1j	Connector, single, behind instrument panel	
T1k	Connector, single, behind instrument panel (connection for clock – GL model only)	
T1l	Connector, single, behind instrument panel	
T1m	Connector, single, in boot left	
T1n	Connector, single, behind instrument panel (control wire connection for rear wiper/washer system)	
T1p	Connector, single, on brake light switch	
T2c	Connector, 2 point, behind instrument panel	
T2b	Connector, 2 point, behind instrument panel	
T3	Connector, 3 point, behind instrument panel	
T4	Connector, 4 point, behind instrument panel	
T14/	Connector, 14 point, on instrument panel insert	
V	Windscreen wiper motor	32 to 35
V2	Fresh air blower	27
V5	Windscreen washer pump	41
V7	Radiator fan	88
W	Interior light	86, 87
X	Number plate light	69, 70
Z1	Heated rear window	28

①	Earthing strap, battery/body/assembly mountings
②	Earthing wire – alternator/engine block
⑩	Earthing point, steering column strut
⑫	Earthing point, boot floor
⑬	Earthing point, on interior light
⑭	Earthing point, centre of rear roof crossmember
⑮	Earthing point, engine compartment front left
⑯	Earthing point, engine compartment front right
⑰	Earthing point, steering gear
⑱	Earthing point, rear apron, left
⑲	Earthing point, rear apron, right

Colour code

sw	–	black
bl	–	blue
br	–	brown
gn	–	green
gr	–	grey
ge	–	yellow
vi	–	violet
ro	–	red
we	–	white
or	–	orange
pi	–	pink

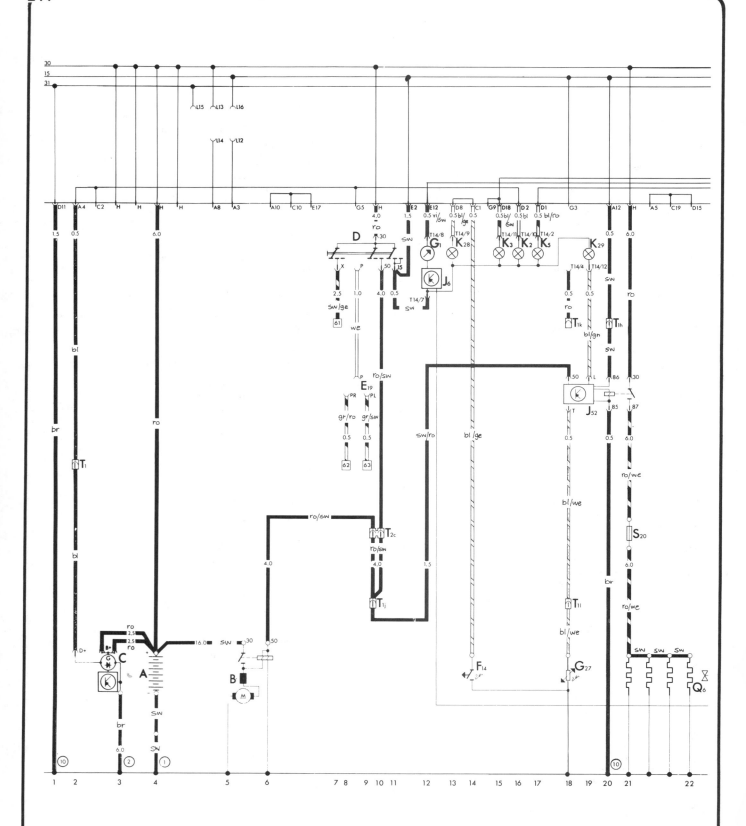

Fig. 11.37 Wiring diagram for Golf D and LD models, August 1978 to August 1979

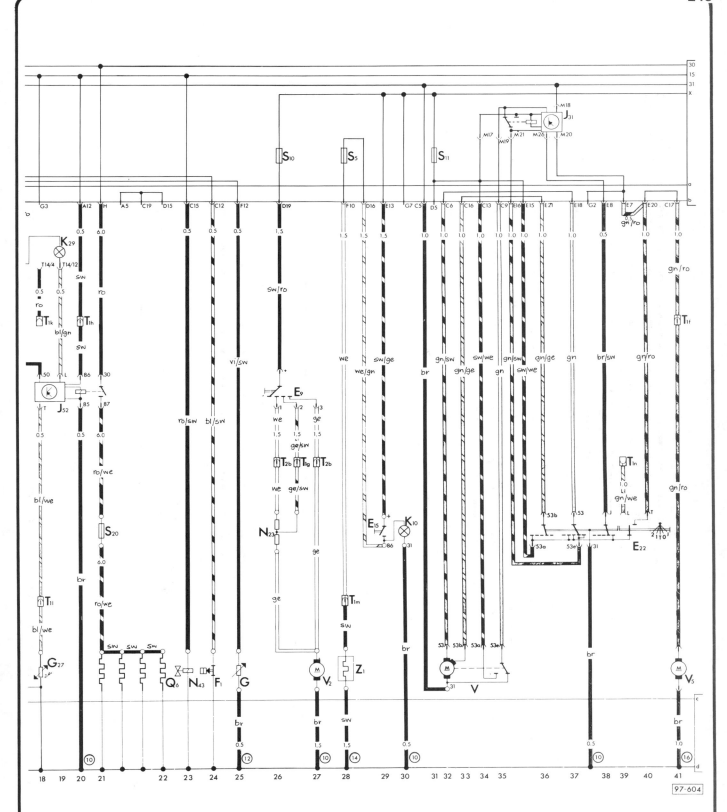

Fig. 11.37 Wiring diagram for Golf D and LD models, August 1978 to August 1979 (continued)

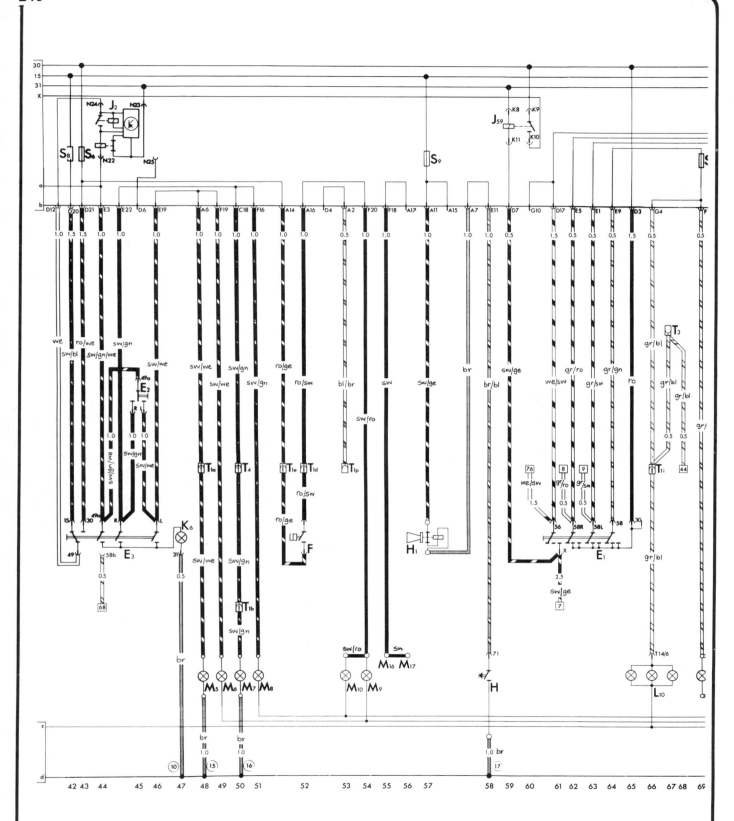

Fig. 11.37 Wiring diagram for Golf D and LD models, August 1978 to August 1979 (continued)

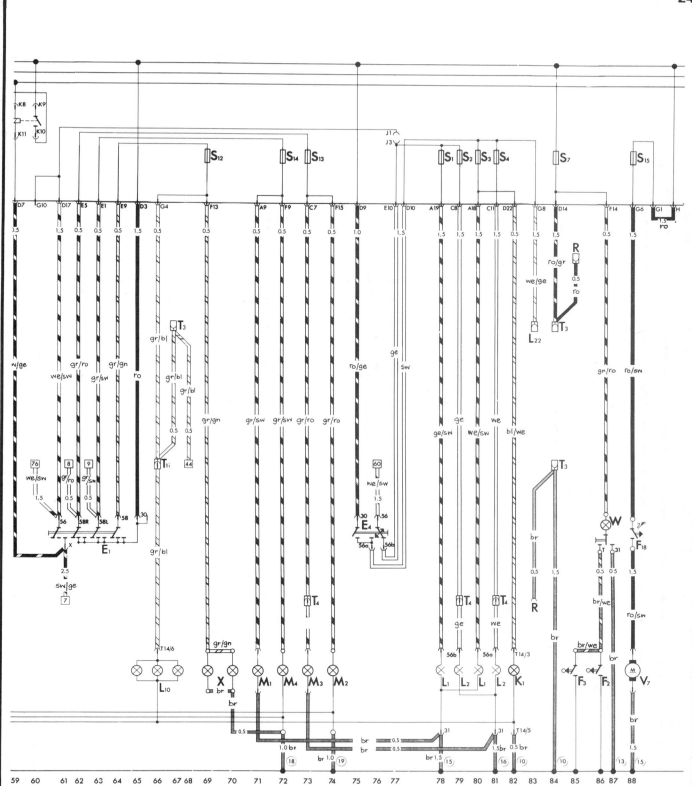

Fig. 11.37 Wiring diagram for Golf D and LD models, August 1978 to August 1979 (continued)

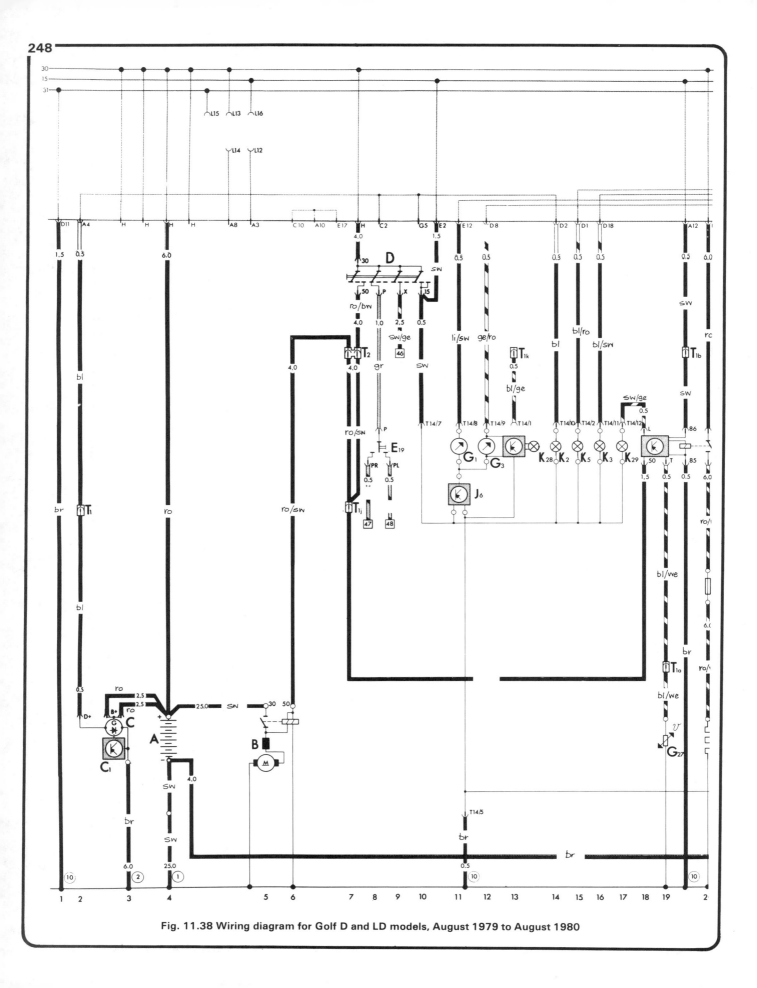

Fig. 11.38 Wiring diagram for Golf D and LD models, August 1979 to August 1980

Fig. 11.38 Wiring diagram for Golf D and LD models, August 1979 to August 1980 (continued)

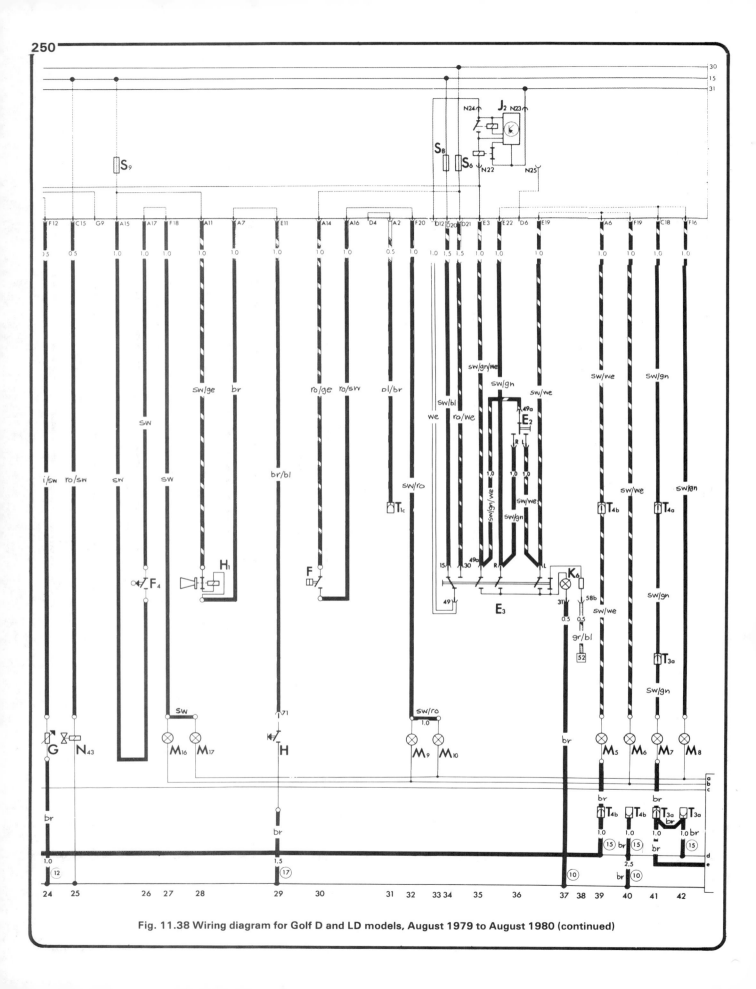

Fig. 11.38 Wiring diagram for Golf D and LD models, August 1979 to August 1980 (continued)

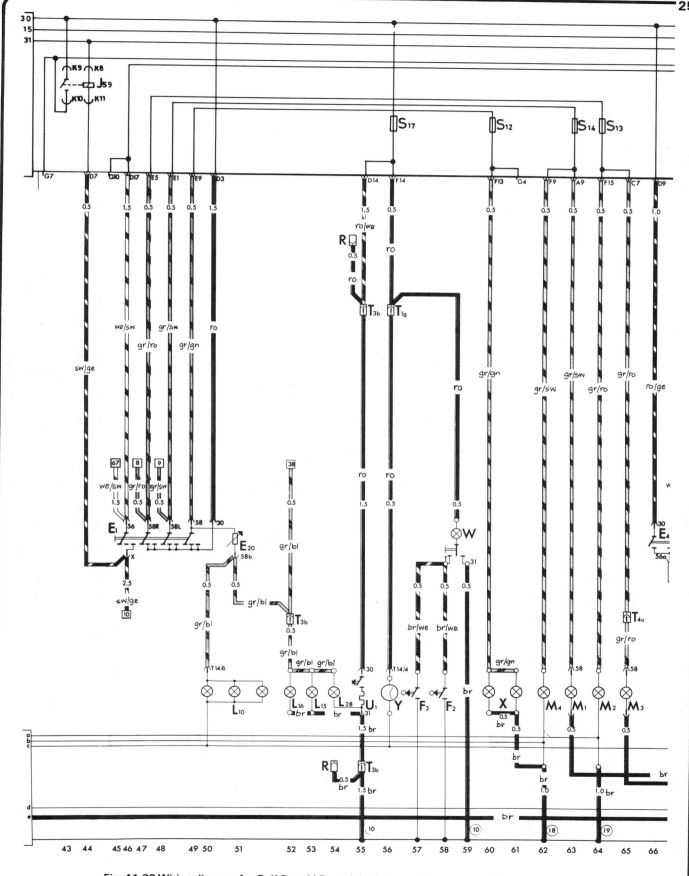

Fig. 11.38 Wiring diagram for Golf D and LD models, August 1979 to August 1980 (continued)

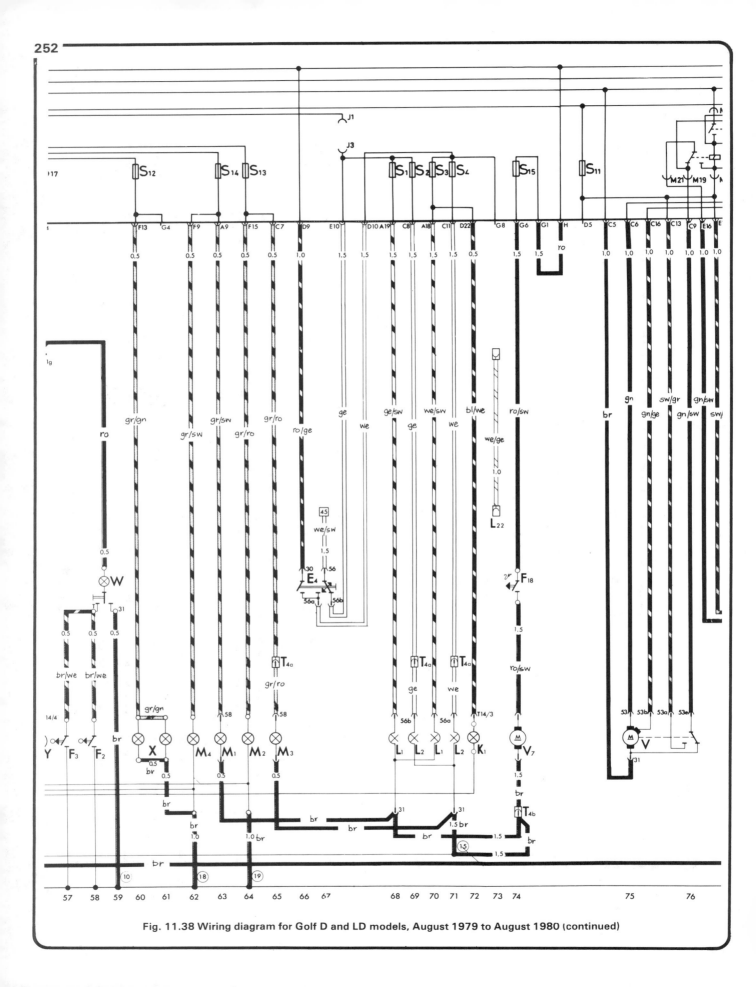

Fig. 11.38 Wiring diagram for Golf D and LD models, August 1979 to August 1980 (continued)

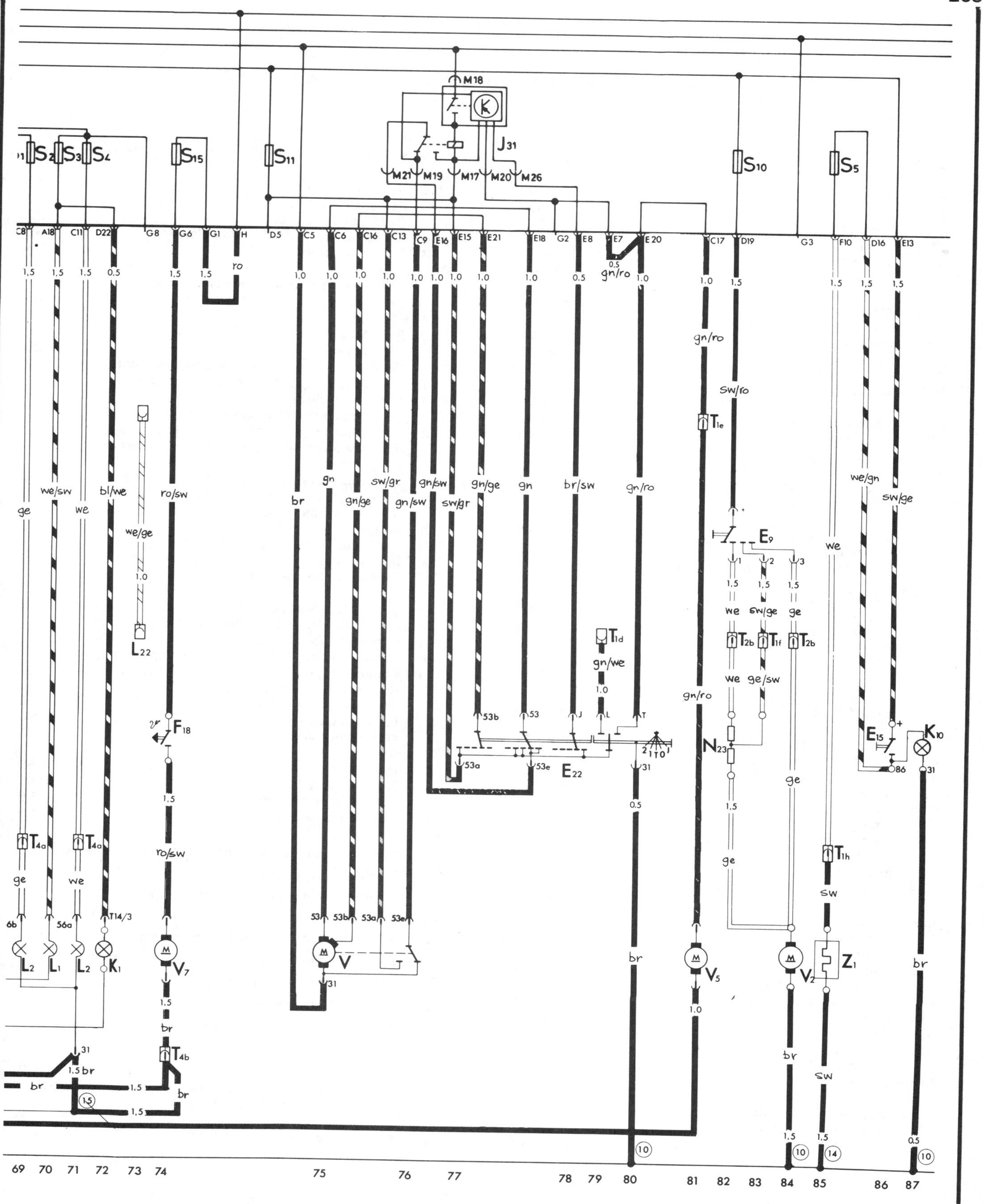

Fig. 11.38 Wiring diagram for Golf D and LD models, August 1979 to August 1980 (continued)

Key to wiring diagram for Golf D and LD models, August 1979 to August 1980

Designation		In current track
A	Battery	4
B	Starter	5,6
C	Alternator	3
C1	Voltage regulator	3
D	Ignition/starter switch	8 to 10
E1	Lighting switch	45 to 51
E2	Turn signal switch	36
E3	Emergency light switch	34 to 38
E4	Headlight dimmer/flasher switch	66,67
E9	Fresh air blower switch	82 to 84
E15	Heated rear window switch	86,87
E19	Sidelight switch (in turn signal switch)	8,9
E20	Instrument panel lighting control (GL models only)	51
E22	Intermittent wiper switch	77 to 80
F	Brake light switch	30
F1	Oil pressure switch	23
F2	Door contact switch, front left	58
F3	Door contact switch, front right	57
F4	Reversing light switch	26
F18	Thermo-switch for radiator fan	74
G	Fuel gauge sender	24
G1	Fuel gauge	11
G2	Coolant temperature gauge sender (GL model only)	22
G3	Coolant temperature gauge (GL model only)	12
G27	Engine temperature sender	19
H	Horn plate	29
H1	Horn	28
J2	Emergency light relay	35,36
J6	Voltage stabilizer	11
J31	Relay for intermittent wash/wipe facility	76 to 79
J52	Glow plug relay (automatic glow)	18 to 20
J59	Relief relay for X contact	43,44
K1	High beam warning lamp	72
K2	Generator warning lamp	14
K3	Oil pressure warning lamp	16
K5	Turn signal warning lamp	15
K6	Emergency light warning lamp	37
K10	Heated rear window warning lamp	87
K28	Coolant temperature warning lamp (overheating, red)	13
K29	Glow period warning lamp	17
L1	Headlight left	68,70
L2	Headlight right	69,71
L10	Instrument panel light	50,51
L15	Ashtray light (GL model only)	53
L16	Fresh air controls light (GL model only)	52
L22	Connection for foglights	73
L28	Cigarette lighter light	54
M1	Sidelight, left	63
M2	Tail light, right	64
M3	Sidelight, right	65
M4	Tail light, left	62
M5	Turn signal, front left	39
M6	Turn signal, rear left	40
M7	Turn signal, front right	41
M8	Turn signal, rear right	42
M9	Brake light, left	32

Designation		In current track
M10	Brake light, right	33
M16	Reversing light, left	27
M17	Reversing light, right	28
N23	Series resistance for fresh air blower	82
N43	Electro-magnetic cut-off	25
Q	Glow plugs	20,21
R	Connection for radio (behind instrument panel insert)	54,55
S1 to S15	Fuses in fusebox	
S20	Strip fuse (50 Amp) for glow plugs (in engine compartment)	20
T1	Connector, single, in engine compartment front left	
T1a	Connector, single, behind instrument panel	
T1b	Connector, single, near relay plate	
T1c	Connector, single, on brake light switch	
T1d	Connector, single, behind instrument panel (connection for rear window wiper/washer system control wire)	
T1e	Connector, single, behind instrument panel	
T1f	Connector, single, behind instrument panel	
T1g	Connector, single, behind instrument panel	
T1h	Connector, single, in boot left	
T1j	Connector, single, behind instrument panel	
T1k	Connector, single, behind instrument panel	
T2	Connector, two point, near relay plate	
T2b	Connector, two point, behind instrument panel	
T3a	Connector, three point, in engine compartment front right	
T3b	Connector, three point, behind instrument panel	
T4a	Connector, four point, behind instrument panel	
T4b	Connector, four point, in engine compartment front left	
T14/	Connector, fourteen point, on instrument panel insert	
U1	Cigarette lighter (GL model only)	55
V	Windscreen wiper motor	75,76
V2	Fresh air blower	84
V5	Windscreen washer pump	81
V7	Radiator fan	74
W	Interior light	58,59
X	Number plate lights	60,61
Y	Clock (GL model only)	56
Z1	Heated rear window	85

①	Earthing strap, battery – body, subframe assembly
②	Earthing wire, alternator – engine block
⑩	Earthing point, steering column support
⑫	Earthing point, boot rear (heel plate)
⑭	Earthing point, rear centre roof crossmember
⑮	Earthing point, in insulating hose of front wiring loom
⑰	Earthing wire, steering gear
⑱	Earthing point, rear apron, left
⑲	Earthing point, rear apron, right

The coolant temperature gauge and warning lamp circuit may be slightly different to that given here

For colour code see key to Fig. 11.37

Key to wiring diagram for Golf and Jetta D and LD models, August 1980 to August 1982

Designation		In current track
A	Battery	4
B	Starter	5,6
C	Alternator	2,3
C1	Voltage regulator	2,3
D	Ignition/starter switch	6 to 8
E1	Lighting switch	45 to 49
E2	Turn signal switch	36
E3	Emergency light switch	32 to 38
E4	Headlight dimmer/flasher switch	61,62
E9	Fresh air blower switch	76,77
E15	Heated rear window switch	79,80
E20	Instrument lighting brightness control	49
E22	Wiper switch for intermittent operation	72 to 74
F	Brake light switch	29
F1	Oil pressure switch	23
F2	Door contact switch front left	53
F3	Door contact switch front right	52
F18	Thermo-switch for radiator fan	69
F66	Switch for coolant shortage indicator	22
G	Fuel gauge sender	24
G1	Fuel gauge	9
G2	Coolant temperature gauge sender	21
G3	Coolant temperature gauge	10
G27	Engine temperature sender (glow plug system)	18
H	Horn control	28
H1	Horn	27
J2	Emergency flasher relay	34,35
J5	Voltage stabilizer	9
J31	Relay for wash/wipe intermittent operation (only LD)	71 to 73
J52	Relay for glow plugs	18,19
J59	Relief relay for X contact	43,44
K1	High beam warning lamp	14
K2	Alternator warning lamp	13
K3	Oil pressure warning lamp	16
K5	Turn signal warning lamp	15
K6	Emergency flasher system warning lamp	37
K10	Heated rear window warning lamp	80
K28	Coolant temperature warning lamp (too hot, red)	12
K29	Glow plug time warning lamp	17
L1	Headlight left	64,66
L2	Headlight right	65,67
L9	Lighting switch light	43
L10	Dash insert light	48 to 50
L22	Connection for foglights	68
M1	Sidelight left	58
M2	Tail light right	59
M3	Sidelight right	60
M4	Tail light left	57
M5	Turn signal front left	39
M6	Turn signal rear left	40
M7	Turn signal front right	41
M8	Turn signal rear right	42

Designation		In current track
M9	Brake light left	31
M10	Brake light right	32
N23	Ballast resistance for fresh air blower	76
N43	Electro-magnetic stop control	26
Q6	Glow plugs	19 to 20
R	Radio (positive)	33
R	Radio (negative)	50
S1 to S15	Fuses in fusebox	
S20	Fuse for glow plugs in engine compartment	
T1	Connector single, behind dash	
T1a	Connector single, in engine compartment front left	
T1b	Connector single, near relay plate	
T1c	Connector single, on brake light switch	
T1d	Connector single behind dash (connection of control wire for rear wiper and washer system)	
T1e	Connector single behind dash	
T1f	Connector single behind dash	
T1h	Connector single in boot rear right	
T1j	Connector single, behind dash	
T1k	Connector single, in engine compartment, near right headlight	
T2a	Connector two-point, on brake light switch	
T2b	Connector two-point, behind dash	
T2f	Connector two-point, in engine compartment, near left headlight	
T2g	Connector two-point, in engine compartment, near right headlight	
T2k	Connector two-point in engine compartment front left	
T3a	Connector three-point, behind dash	
T3b	Connector three-point, behind dash	
T4a	Connector four-point in engine compartment near right headlight	
T14/	Connector fourteen-point on dash insert	
V	Wiper motor	70,71
V2	Fresh air blower	77
V5	Windscreen washer pump	75
V7	Radiator fan	69
W	Interior light front	54
X	Number plate light	55,56
Y	Clock (only LD)	51
Z4	Heated rear window	78

(1) Earth strap, from battery via body to gearbox

(10) Earth point, on relay plate bracket

(11) Earth point, behind dash

(14) Earth wire, steering box

(15) Earth point, in insulating sleeve of front loom

(16) Earth point, bound with insulating cable, in dash loom

(18) Earth point cross panel rear left

(19) Earth point roof crossmember rear centre

For colour code see key to Fig. 11.37

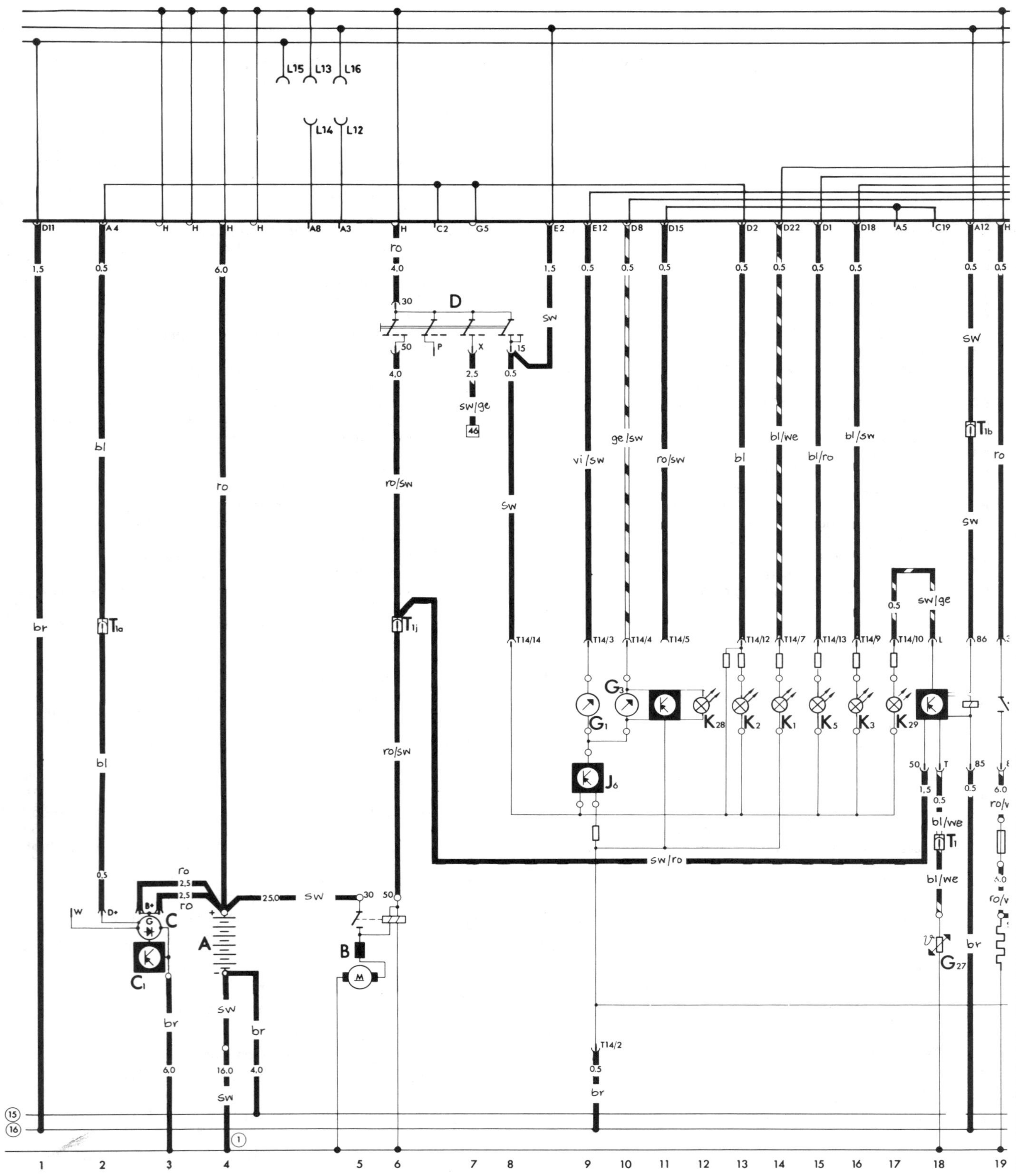

Fig. 11.39 Wiring diagram for Gold and Jetta D and LD models, August 1980 to August 1982

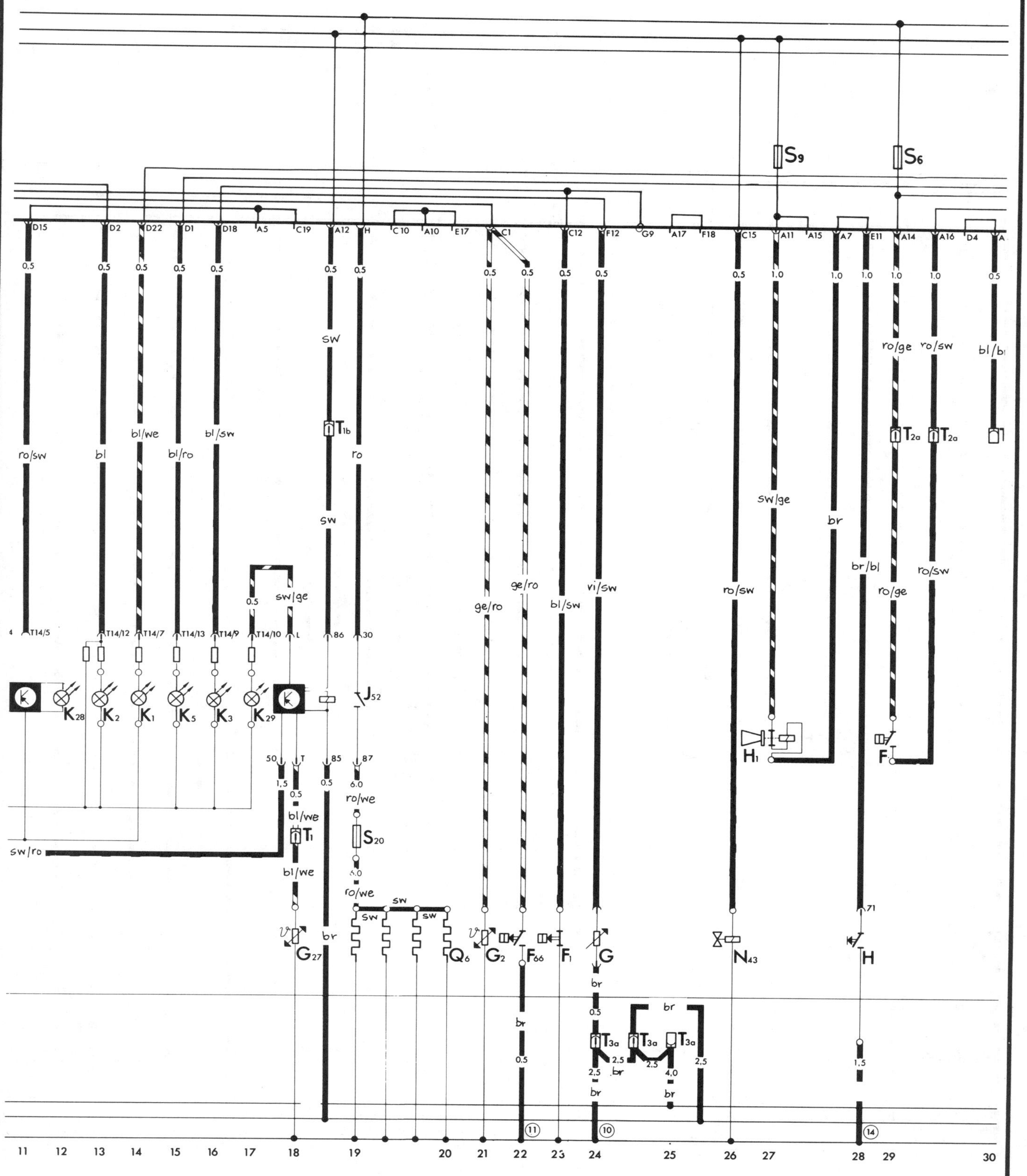

Fig. 11.39 Wiring diagram for Golf and Jetta D and LD models, August 1980 to August 1982 (continued)

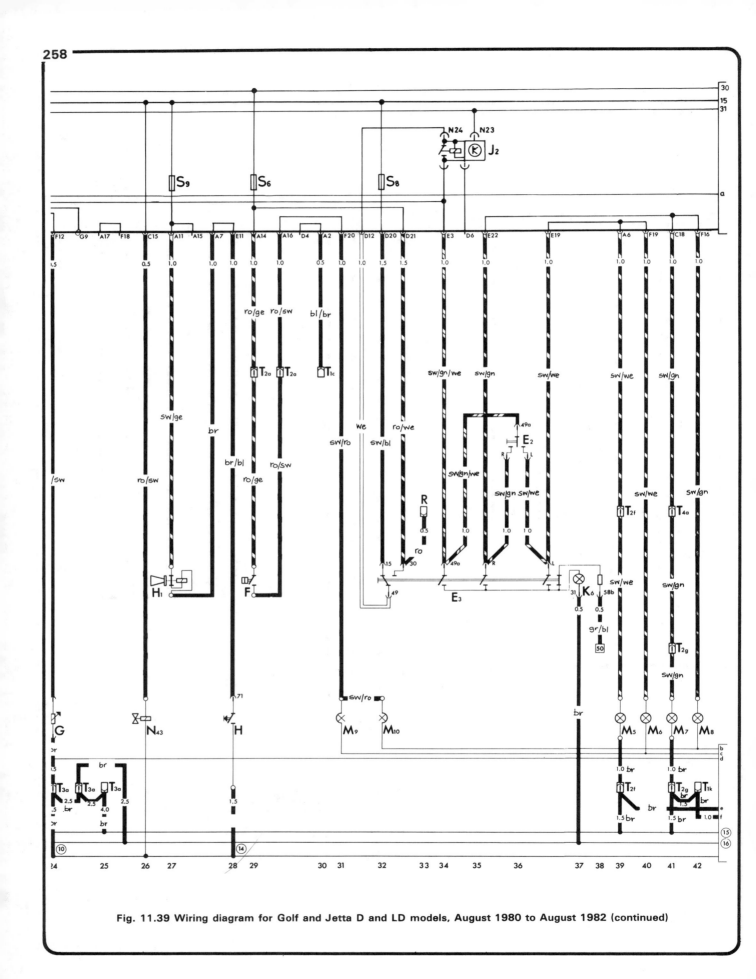

Fig. 11.39 Wiring diagram for Golf and Jetta D and LD models, August 1980 to August 1982 (continued)

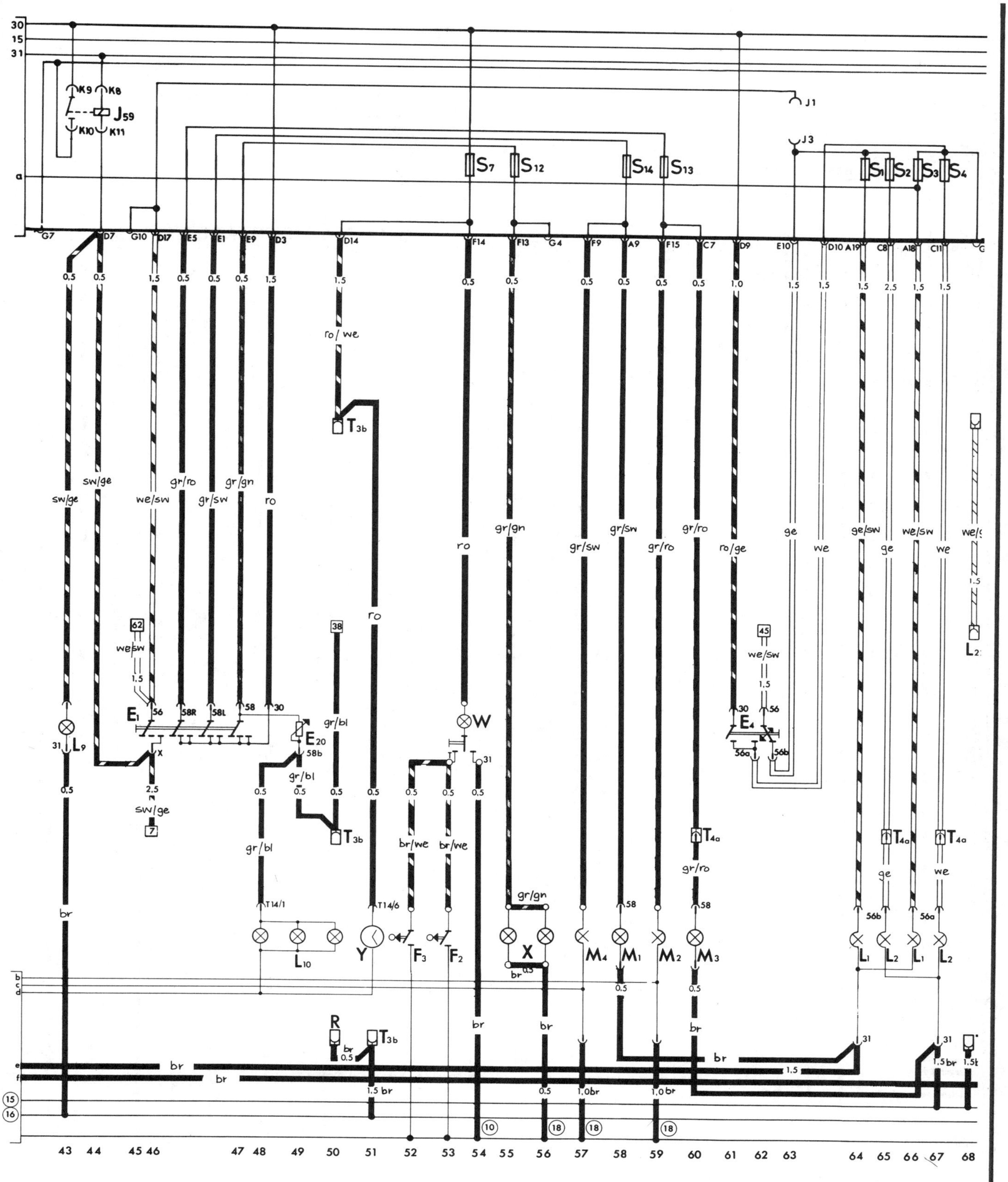

Fig. 11.39 Wiring diagram for Golf and Jetta D and LD models, August 1980 to August 1982 (continued)

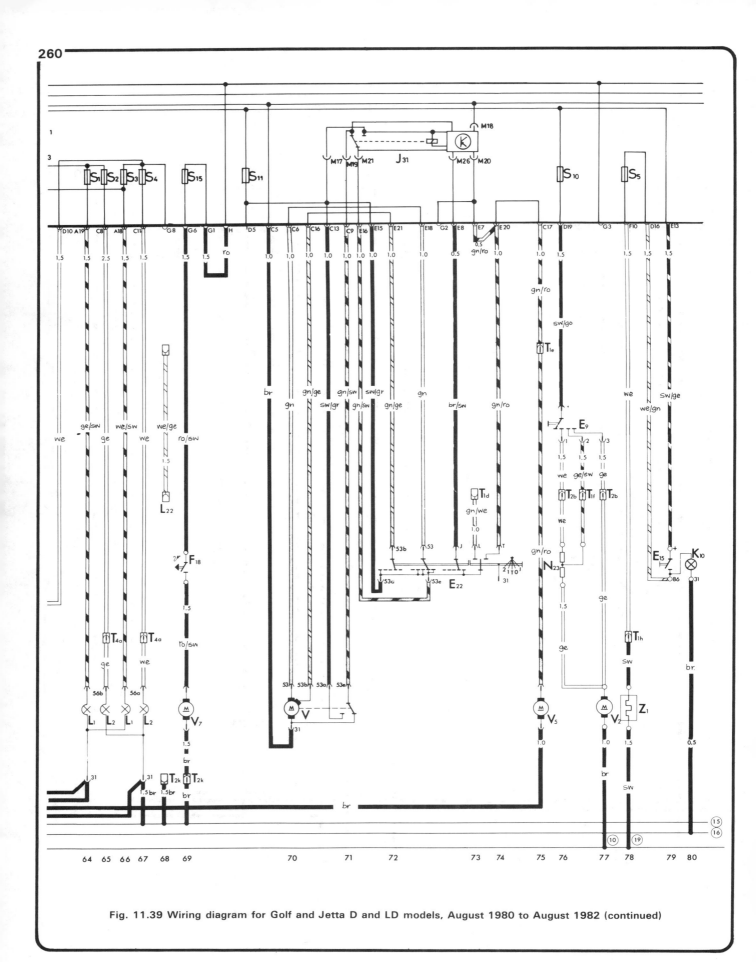

Fig. 11.39 Wiring diagram for Golf and Jetta D and LD models, August 1980 to August 1982 (continued)

Key to wiring diagram for Golf and Jetta C models, August 1982 onwards

Designation		In current track
A	Battery	6
B	Starter	7,8
C	Alternator	2,3
C1	Voltage regulator	2,3
D	Ignition/starter switch	19 to 22
E1	Lighting switch	83 to 90
E2	Turn signal switch	67,68
E3	Emergency light switch	63 to 71
E4	Headlight dimmer/flasher switch	98 to 100
E9	Fresh air blower switch	133 to 135
E15	Heated rear window switch	73 to 75
E19	Sidelight switch	19 to 21
E20	Instrument lighting control	90
E22	Intermittent wiper switch**	120 to 124
E23	Foglight and rear foglight switch	110 to 112
F	Brake light switch	56
F1	Oil pressure switch	37
F2	Front left door contact switch	43
F3	Front right door contact switch	42
F4	Reversing light switch	47
F9	Handbrake warning system switch	53
F18	Radiator fan thermo-switch	9
F34	Brake fluid level warning contact	55
F66	Coolant shortage indicator switch	35
G	Fuel gauge sender	13
G1	Fuel gauge	28
G2	Coolant temperature gauge sender	34
G3	Coolant temperature gauge	30
G27	Engine temperature (glow plug system) sender	15
H	Horn plate	51
H1	Horn	49
J2	Emergency light relay	64 to 68
J5	Fog and rear foglight relay	109,110
J6	Voltage stabilizer	28
J30	Rear window wiper/washer relay	125 to 127
J31	Intermittent wash/wipe relay	120 to 123
J39	Headlight washer system relay	129 to 131
J52	Glow plug relay	15
J59	Relief relay (for X contact)	81,82
J120	Switch unit for coolant shortage indicator	35,36
K1	Main beam warning lamp	27
K2	Generator warning lamp	25
K3	Oil pressure warning lamp	23
K5	Turn signal warning lamp	26
K6	Emergency light system warning lamp	70
K7	Dual circuit brake and handbrake warning lamp	53
K10	Heated rear window warning lamp	74
K17	Foglight warning lamp	111
K28	Coolant temp. warning lamp (overheating, red)	32
K29	Glow period warning lamp	24
L1	Twin filament bulb, left	103,105
L2	Twin filament bulb, right	104,106
L8	Clock light bulb	88
L9	Lighting switch light bulb	132
L10	Instrument panel insert light bulb	89,90
L16	Fresh air controls light bulb	38
L20	Rear foglight bulb	93
L22	Foglight bulb, left	107
L23	Foglight bulb, right	108
L28	Cigarette lighter light bulb	39
L39	Heated rear window switch bulb	73
L40	Front and rear foglight switch bulb	112
M1	Sidelight bulb, left	94
M2	Tail light bulb, right	97

Designation		In current track
M3	Sidelight bulb, right	96
M4	Tail light bulb, left	95
M5	Front left turn signal bulb	78
M6	Rear left turn signal bulb	79
M7	Front right turn signal bulb	80
M8	Rear right turn signal bulb	81
M9	Brake light bulb, left	59
M10	Brake light bulb, right	60
M16	Reversing light bulb, left	48
M17	Reversing light bulb, right	49
N23	Series resistance for fresh air blower	133,134
N43	Electro-magnetic cut-off	14
Q6	Glow plugs	16,17
R	Radio connection	39,41,73
S1 to S22	Fuses in fusebox	
S20	Fusible link for glow plugs – 50A	16
S27	Separate fuse for rear foglight	108
T	Junction box	
T1a	Connector, single near battery plus terminal	
T1b	Connector, single near battery plus terminal	
T1c	Connector, single behind relay plate	
T1d	Connector, single behind dash	
T1e	Connector, single behind dash	
T1g	Connector, single behind dash	
T1h	Connector, single behind dash	
T1i	Connector, single in boot on left	
T1m	Connector, single behind fusebox	
T2a	Connector, two point in engine compartment on left	
T2b	Connector, two point in engine compartment on right	
T2c	Connector, two point in engine compartment on left	
T2d	Connector, two point behind dash	
T2e	Connector, two point in engine compartment on left	
T2f	Connector, two point in engine compartment on left	
T2g	Connector, two point in engine compartment on right	
T2k	Connector, two point in boot	
T2n	Connector, two point behind fusebox	
T3b	Connector, three point behind dash	
T4a	Connector, four point behind dash	
T14/	Connector, fourteen point on dash insert	
U1	Cigarette lighter	40
V	Windscreen wiper motor	114 to 117
V2	Fresh air blower	135
V5	Windscreen washer pump	128
V7	Radiator fan	9
V11	Headlight washer pump*	131
V12	Rear wiper motor	126,127
V13	Rear washer pump motor	125
W	Interior light, front	43 to 45
X	Number plate light	91,92
Y	Clock	33
Z1	Heated rear window	77

①	Earth strap from battery via body to gearbox
⑩	Earth point on fusebox bracket
⑬	Earth wire, steering box
⑭	Earth point roof crossmember rear centre
⑮	Earth point in insulating sleeve of front loom
⑯	Earth point bound with insulating tape in dash loom
⑱	Earth point cross panel rear left

Standard on GL models only

**Optional on C models*

For colour code see key to Fig. 11.37

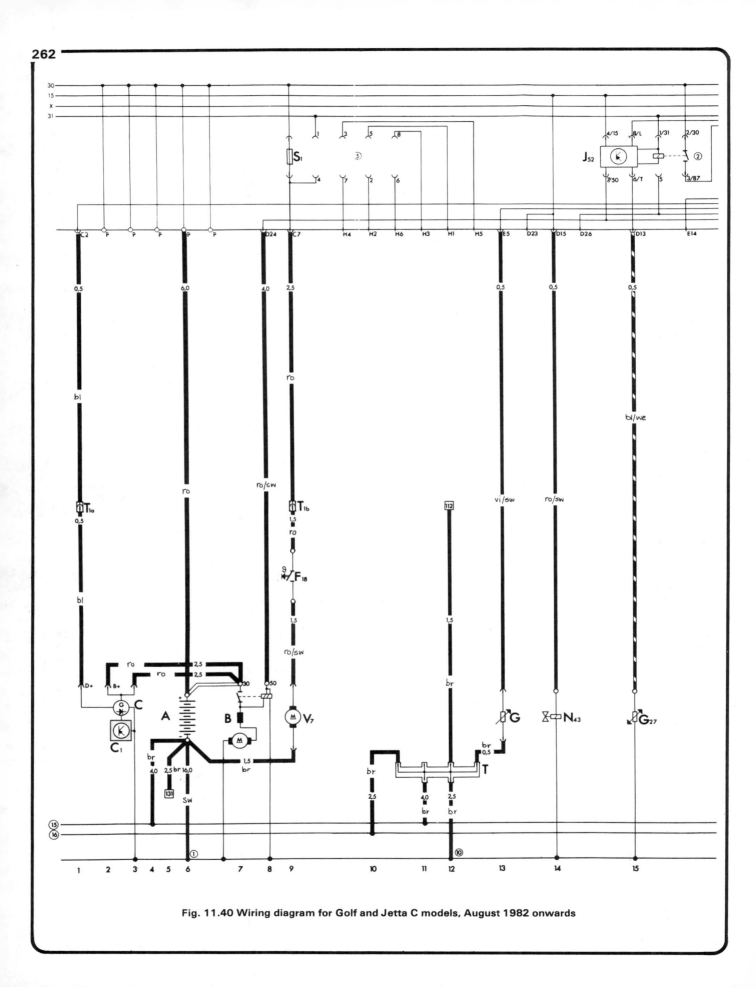

Fig. 11.40 Wiring diagram for Golf and Jetta C models, August 1982 onwards

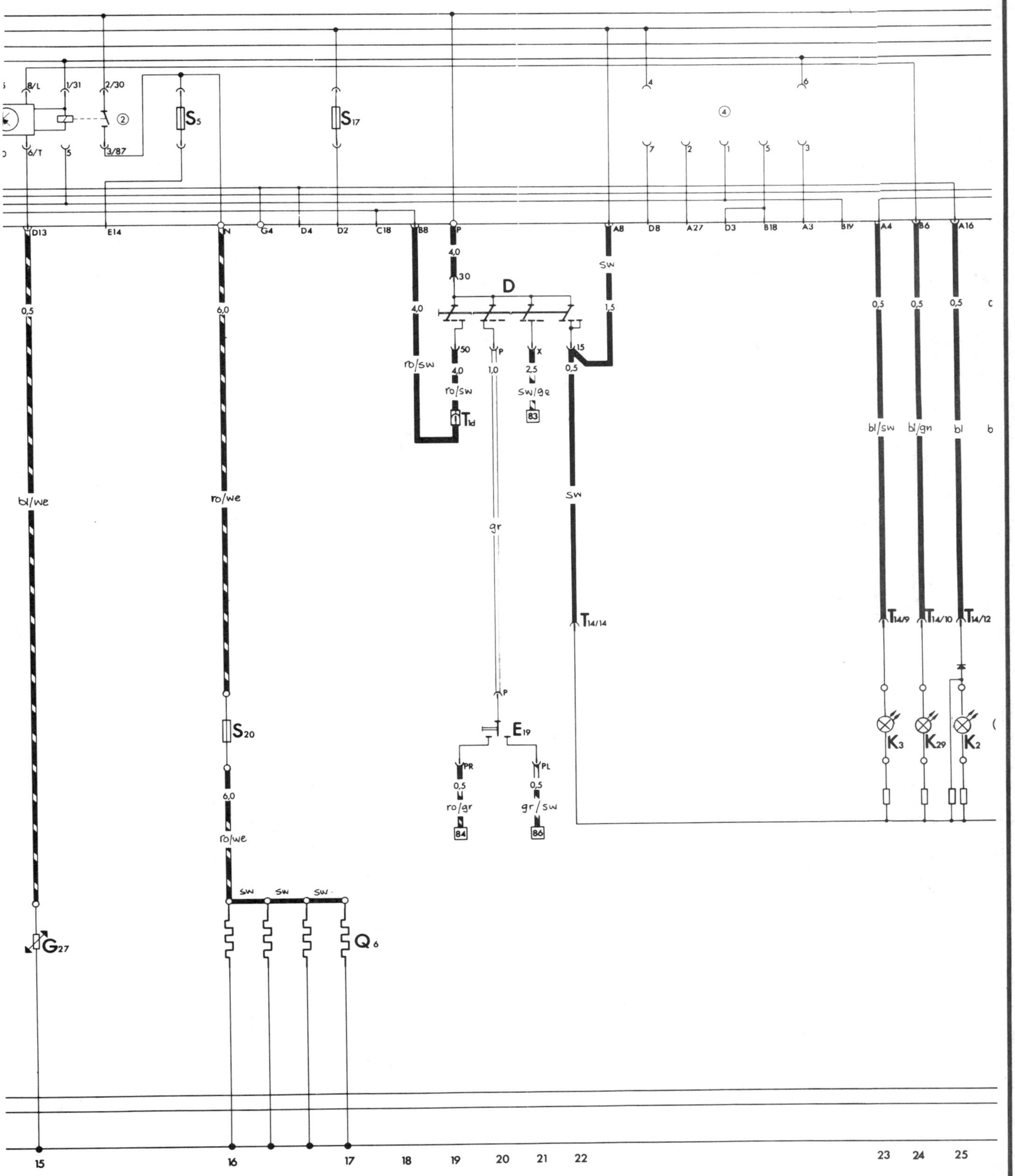

Fig. 11.40 Wiring diagram for Golf and Jetta C models, August 1982 onwards (continued)

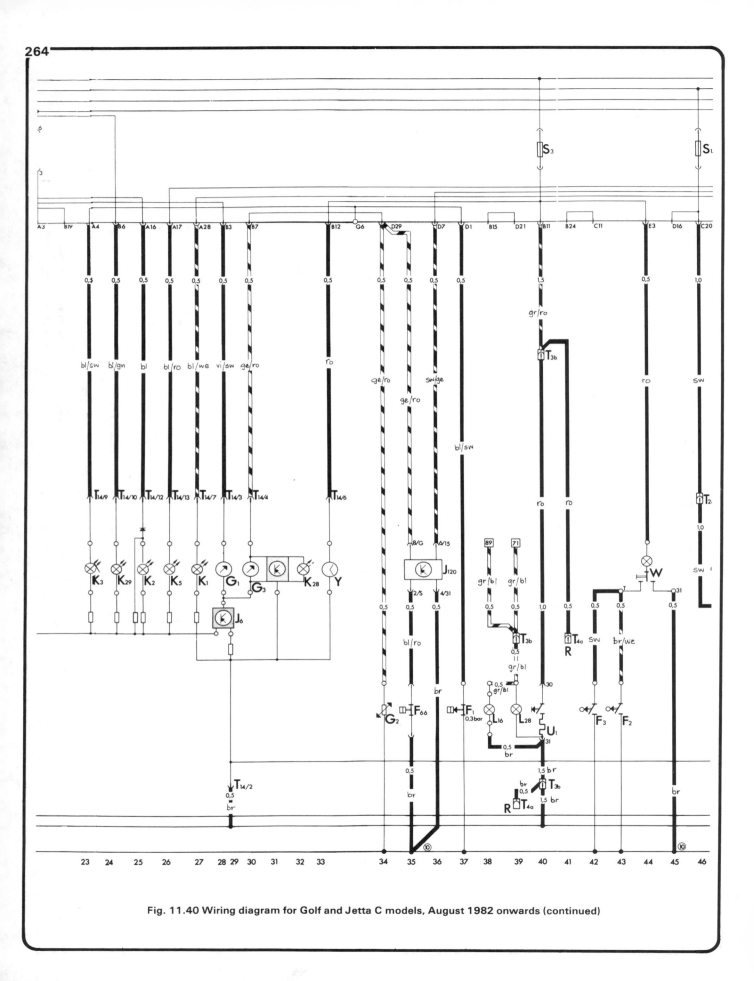

Fig. 11.40 Wiring diagram for Golf and Jetta C models, August 1982 onwards (continued)

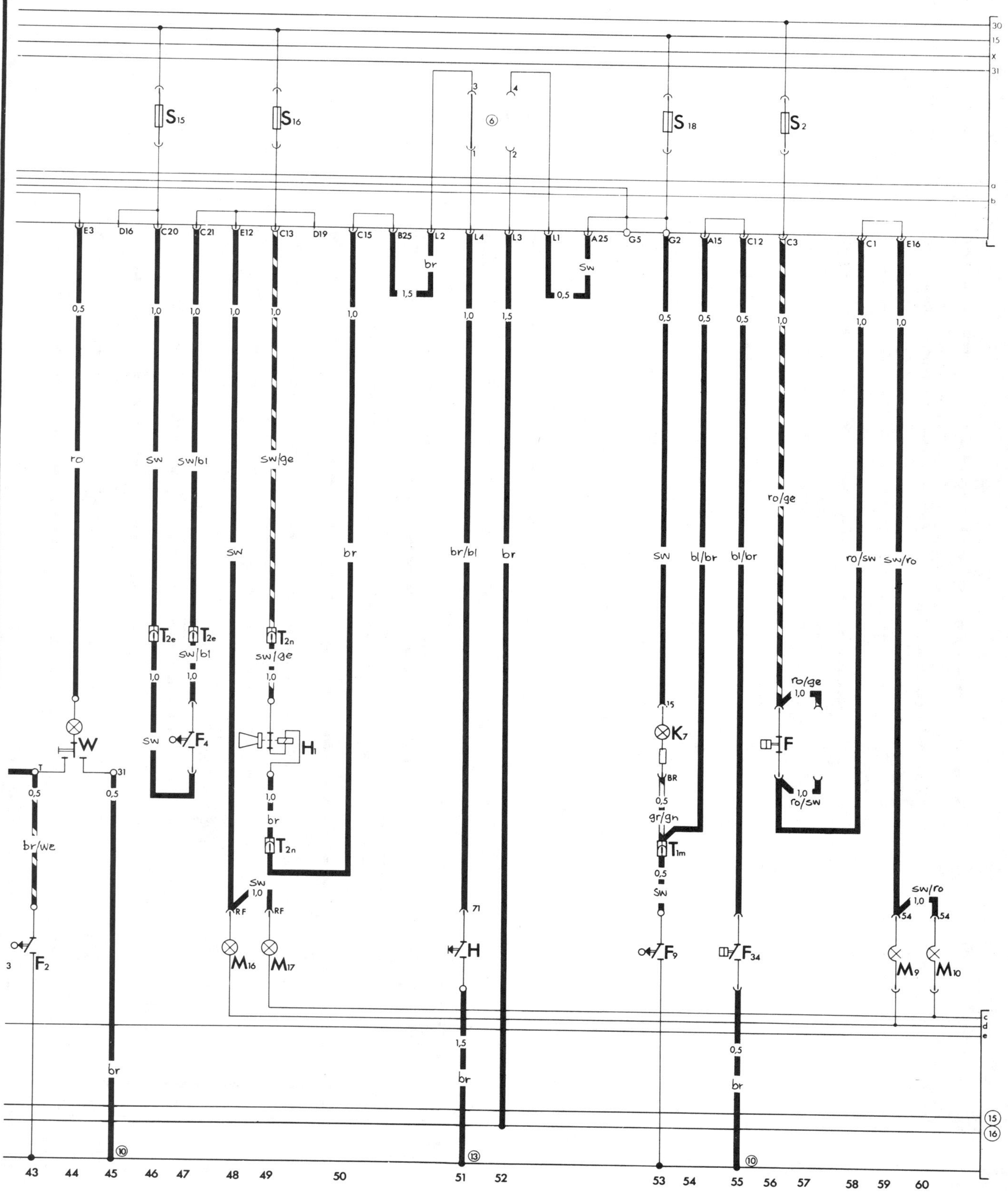

Fig. 11.40 Wiring diagram for Golf and Jetta C models, August 1982 onwards (continued)

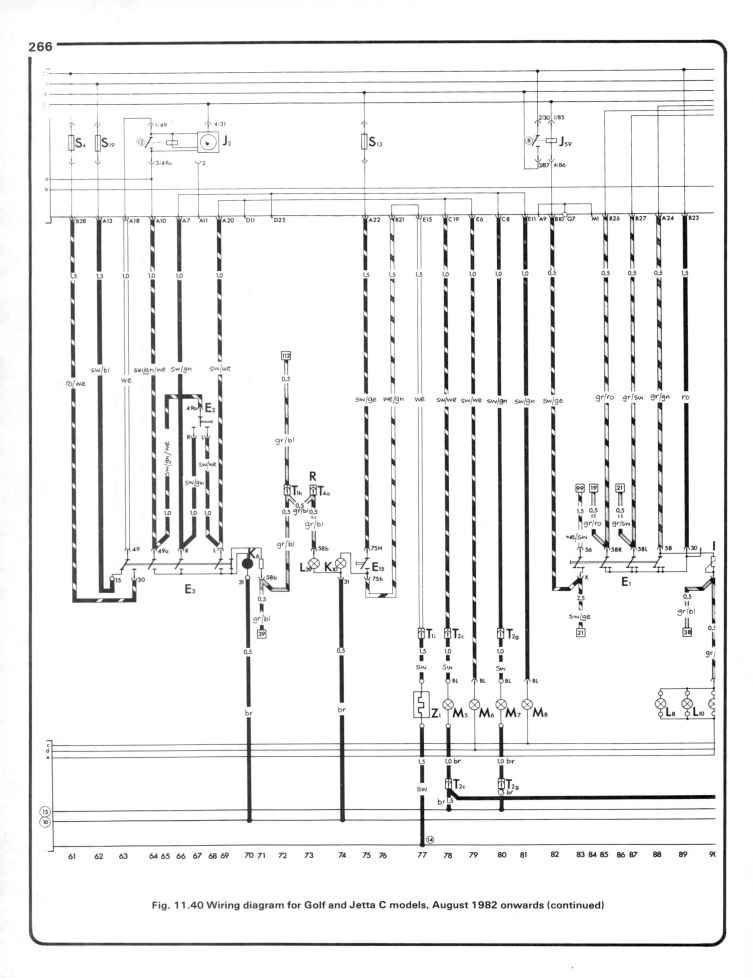

Fig. 11.40 Wiring diagram for Golf and Jetta C models, August 1982 onwards (continued)

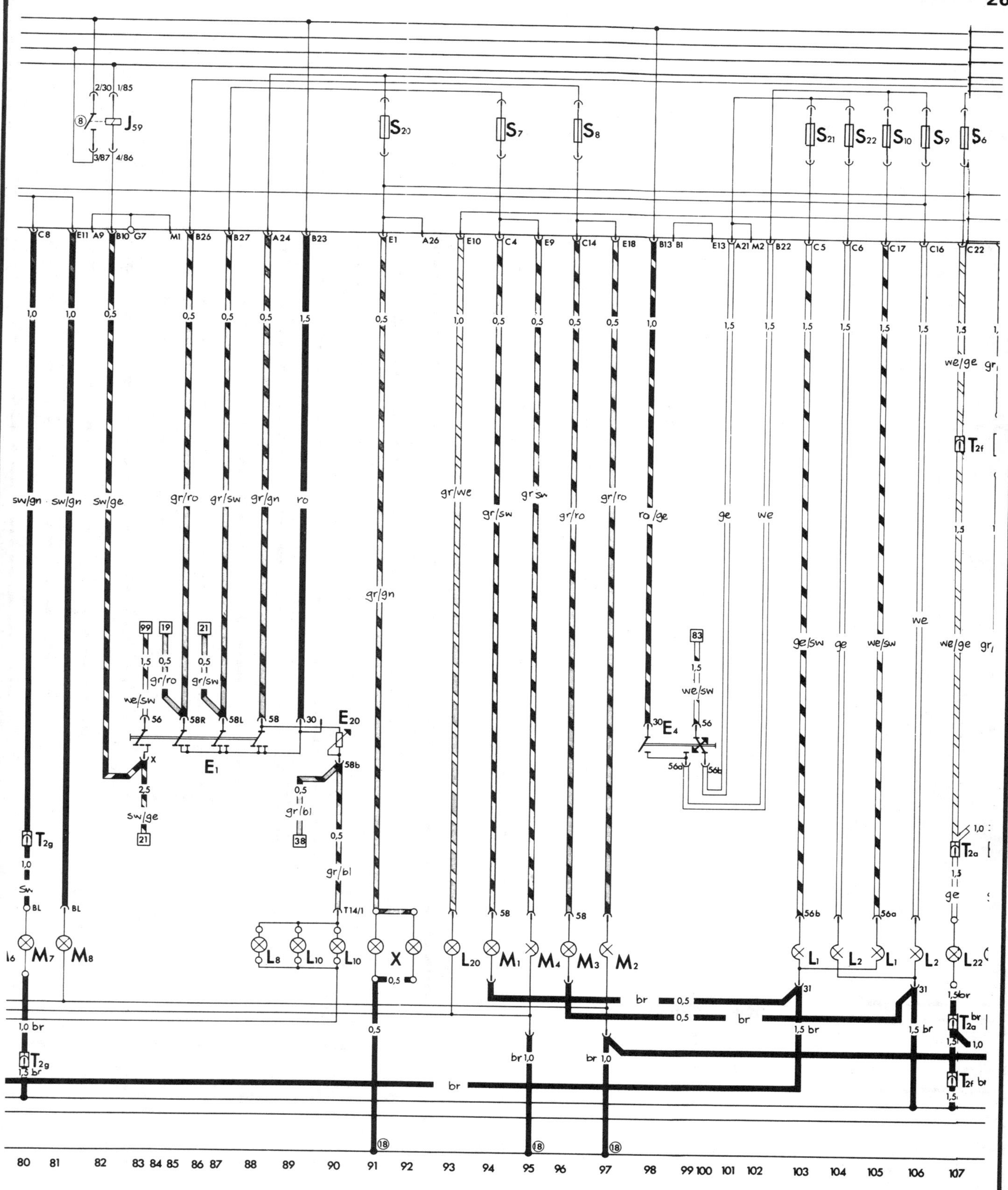

Fig. 11.40 Wiring diagram for Golf and Jetta C models, August 1982 onwards (continued)

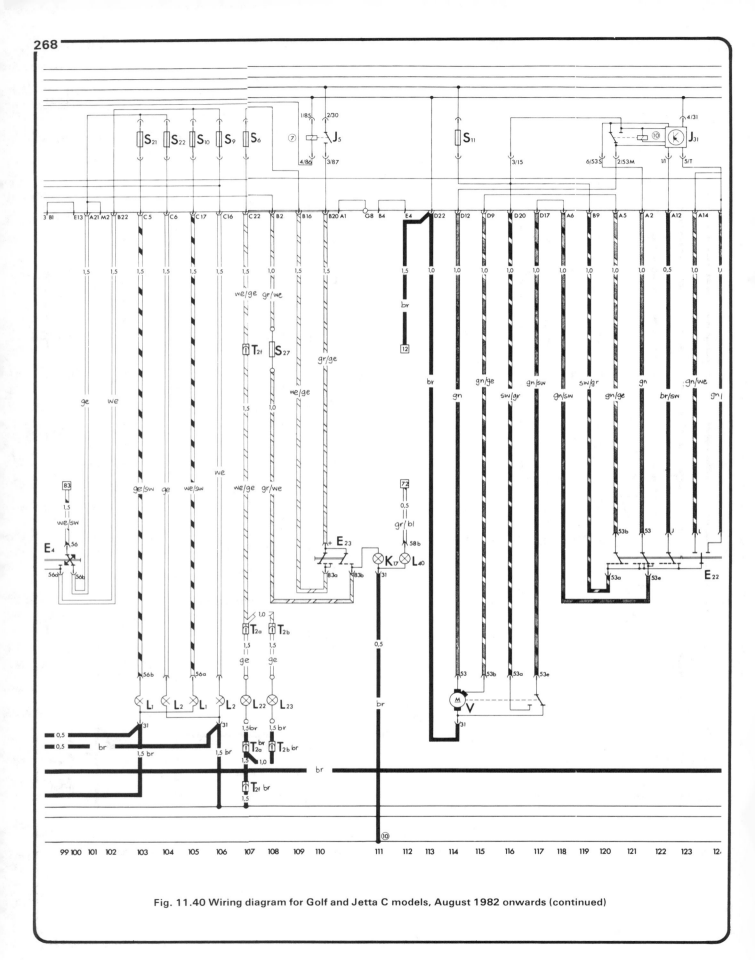

Fig. 11.40 Wiring diagram for Golf and Jetta C models, August 1982 onwards (continued)

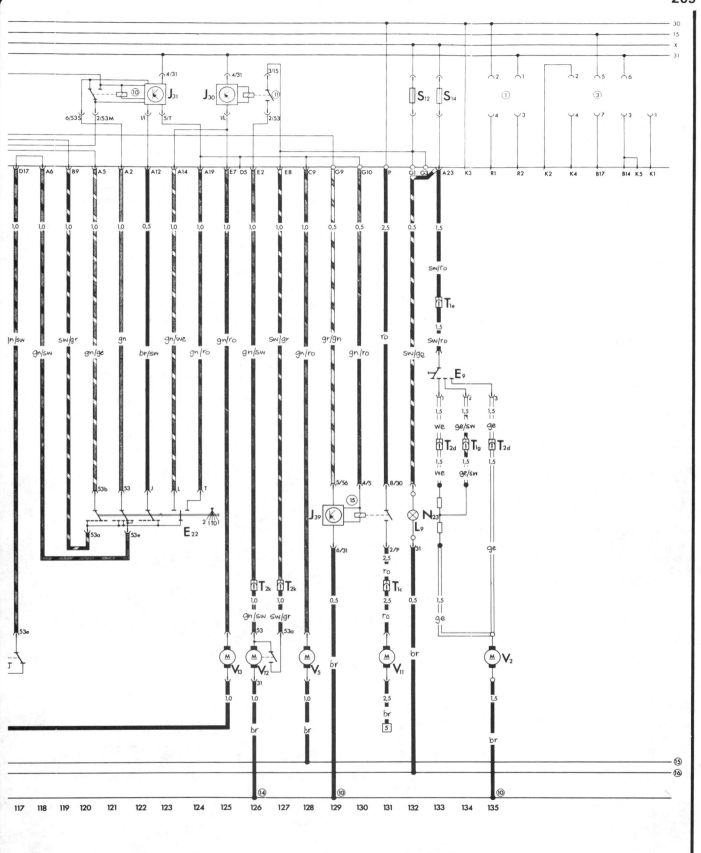

Fig. 11.40 Wiring diagram for Golf and Jetta C models, August 1982 onwards (continued)

10 Front suspension, steering and driveshafts

Driveshaft outer CV joint – modifications

1 From approximately December 1979 the circlip that secures the outer CV joint to the driveshaft is now located in a groove machined on the end of the shaft (Fig. 11.41).

2 To remove the CV joint with this method of retention, sharply strike the edge of the joint body using a soft-faced mallet, to knock it off the shaft. To refit the joint ensure that the circlip is located in its groove and sharply tap the joint back into place.

3 The overhaul instructions for the CV joint remain as described in Chapter 8.

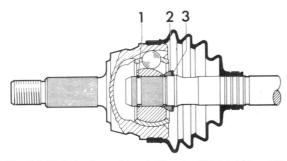

Fig. 11.41 Later type driveshaft outer CV joint (Sec 10)

1	Circlip	3	Dished washer
2	Spacer		

Suspension strut coil springs – modifications

4 From late 1979 onward, front coil springs with their last upper coil turned in and their last lower coil increased in diameter, have been fitted to all models.

5 To cater for the difference in the coils, modified upper and lower spring seats are also used and these must also be fitted if a modified spring is being fitted to an earlier vehicle.

11 Bodywork and fittings

Boot lid and lock (Jetta models) – removal and refitting

1 Disconnect the battery negative lead.

2 Disconnect the number plate lamp wiring at the connector.

3 Mark the position of the bolts securing the hinges to the boot lid.

4 With the help of an assistant, unscrew the bolts and withdraw the boot lid.

5 The boot lock and striker pin are each secured by two cross-head screws, but when removing the lock it will be necessary to unhook the connecting rod (photos).

6 Refitting is a reversal of removal, but make sure that the boot lid is central within the aperture and adjust its position on the hinge bolts if necessary. To adjust the boot lock striker, loosen the mounting screws, then tighten them sufficiently to hold the striker in position. Fully close the boot lid, then open it and fully tighten the screws. Adjust the stop rubbers if necessary.

Radiator grille (Jetta models) – removal and refitting

7 The grille is secured by screws and plastic clips located as shown in Fig. 11.42 (photo).

8 The headlamp surrounds should be removed first by undoing the retaining screws (photos). The screws and clips securing the grille in place can now be released and the grille removed.

9 Refitting is the reverse sequence to removal.

Door interior trim (Jetta models) – removal and refitting

10 Prise the plastic cover from the window regulator handle, then undo the retaining screw and slide the handle from the shaft.

11 Undo the door pull lower cross-head retaining screws, swivel the door pull upwards through 90° and lift it off (photos).

11.5A Boot lid lock ...

11.5B ... and striker pin (Jetta models)

11.7 Radiator grille plastic clip (Jetta models)

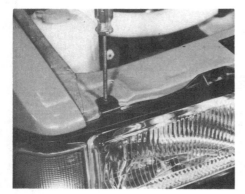

11.8A Remove the headlamp surround upper ...

11.8B ... and lower retaining screws ...

11.8C ... then withdraw the surround (Jetta models)

Fig. 11.42 Location of radiator grille retaining clips (1) and screws (2) on Jetta models (Sec 11)

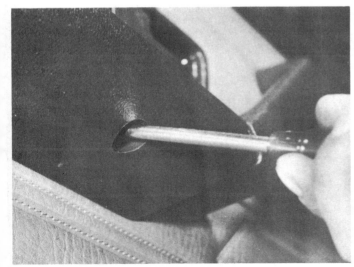

11.11A Undo the door pull screws ...

11.11B ... then rotate the pull through 90° to remove (Jetta models)

11.13A Prise out the door escutcheon recessed cover ...

11.13B ... undo the retaining screw and remove the escutcheon (Jetta models)

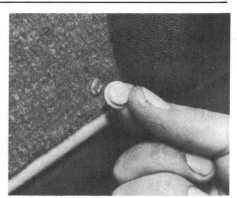

11.15A Prise off the caps ...

11.15B ... and undo the trim retaining screws ...

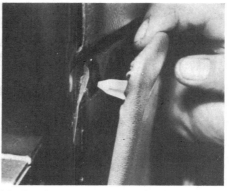

11.16 ... then remove the trim (Jetta models)

12 Unscrew and remove the locking knob where necessary.

13 Prise out the door escutcheon recessed cover, undo the retaining screw and remove the escutcheon (photos).

14 Where fitted, prise off the cover and remove the mirror, adjusting knobs and escutcheon.

15 Prise off the caps and undo the trim retaining screws (photos).

16 Using a wide-bladed screwdriver inserted between the trim and the door, prise out the retaining clips and lift away the trim (photo).

17 Refitting is the reverse sequence to removal, but make sure that the plastic sheeting is correctly positioned before mounting the trim on the door.

Cable type remote-controlled exterior mirror – removal and refitting

18 Remove the door interior trim, as described in Chapter 11 or earlier in this Supplement.

19 Unscrew the nut and press the adjusting knob through the hole into the door interior. Note that some models may have a retaining ring instead of a nut.

20 Remove the screws from the mirror head and withdraw the mirror and knob, together with the cable from the door.

21 Refitting is the reverse sequence to removal.

General repair procedures

Whenever servicing, repair or overhaul work is carried out on the car or its components, it is necessary to observe the following procedures and instructions. This will assist in carrying out the operation efficiently and to a professional standard of workmanship.

Joint mating faces and gaskets

Where a gasket is used between the mating faces of two components, ensure that it is renewed on reassembly, and fit it dry unless otherwise stated in the repair procedure. Make sure that the mating faces are clean and dry with all traces of old gasket removed. When cleaning a joint face, use a tool which is not likely to score or damage the face, and remove any burrs or nicks with an oilstone or fine file.

Make sure that tapped holes are cleaned with a pipe cleaner, and keep them free of jointing compound if this is being used unless specifically instructed otherwise.

Ensure that all orifices, channels or pipes are clear and blow through them, preferably using compressed air.

Oil seals

Whenever an oil seal is removed from its working location, either individually or as part of an assembly, it should be renewed.

The very fine sealing lip of the seal is easily damaged and will not seal if the surface it contacts is not completely clean and free from scratches, nicks or grooves. If the original sealing surface of the component cannot be restored, the component should be renewed.

Protect the lips of the seal from any surface which may damage them in the course of fitting. Use tape or a conical sleeve where possible. Lubricate the seal lips with oil before fitting and, on dual lipped seals, fill the space between the lips with grease.

Unless otherwise stated, oil seals must be fitted with their sealing lips toward the lubricant to be sealed.

Use a tubular drift or block of wood of the appropriate size to install the seal and, if the seal housing is shouldered, drive the seal down to the shoulder. If the seal housing is unshouldered, the seal should be fitted with its face flush with the housing top face.

Screw threads and fastenings

Always ensure that a blind tapped hole is completely free from oil, grease, water or other fluid before installing the bolt or stud. Failure to do this could cause the housing to crack due to the hydraulic action of the bolt or stud as it is screwed in.

When tightening a castellated nut to accept a split pin, tighten the nut to the specified torque, where applicable, and then tighten further to the next split pin hole. Never slacken the nut to align a split pin hole unless stated in the repair procedure.

When checking or retightening a nut or bolt to a specified torque setting, slacken the nut or bolt by a quarter of a turn, and then retighten to the specified setting.

Locknuts, locktabs and washers

Any fastening which will rotate against a component or housing in the course of tightening should always have a washer between it and the relevant component or housing.

Spring or split washers should always be renewed when they are used to lock a critical component such as a big-end bearing retaining nut or bolt.

Locktabs which are folded over to retain a nut or bolt should always be renewed.

Self-locking nuts can be reused in non-critical areas, providing resistance can be felt when the locking portion passes over the bolt or stud thread.

Split pins must always be replaced with new ones of the correct size for the hole.

Special tools

Some repair procedures in this manual entail the use of special tools such as a press, two or three-legged pullers, spring compressors etc. Wherever possible, suitable readily available alternatives to the manufacturer's special tools are described, and are shown in use. In some instances, where no alternative is possible, it has been necessary to resort to the use of a manufacturer's tool and this has been done for reasons of safety as well as the efficient completion of the repair operation. Unless you are highly skilled and have a thorough understanding of the procedure described, never attempt to bypass the use of any special tool when the procedure described specifies its use. Not only is there a very great risk of personal injury, but expensive damage could be caused to the components involved.

Safety first!

Professional motor mechanics are trained in safe working procedures. However enthusiastic you may be about getting on with the job in hand, do take the time to ensure that your safety is not put at risk. A moment's lack of attention can result in an accident, as can failure to observe certain elementary precautions.

There will always be new ways of having accidents, and the following points do not pretend to be a comprehensive list of all dangers; they are intended rather to make you aware of the risks and to encourage a safety-conscious approach to all work you carry out on your vehicle.

Essential DOs and DON'Ts

DON'T rely on a single jack when working underneath the vehicle. Always use reliable additional means of support, such as axle stands, securely placed under a part of the vehicle that you know will not give way.

DON'T attempt to loosen or tighten high-torque nuts (e.g. wheel hub nuts) while the vehicle is on a jack; it may be pulled off.

DON'T start the engine without first ascertaining that the transmission is in neutral (or 'Park' where applicable) and the parking brake applied.

DON'T suddenly remove the filler cap from a hot cooling system – cover it with a cloth and release the pressure gradually first, or you may get scalded by escaping coolant.

DON'T attempt to drain oil until you are sure it has cooled sufficiently to avoid scalding you.

DON'T grasp any part of the engine, exhaust or catalytic converter without first ascertaining that it is sufficiently cool to avoid burning you.

DON'T allow brake fluid or antifreeze to contact vehicle paintwork.

DON'T syphon toxic liquids such as fuel, brake fluid or antifreeze by mouth, or allow them to remain on your skin.

DON'T inhale dust – it may be injurious to health (see *Asbestos* below).

DON'T allow any spilt oil or grease to remain on the floor – wipe it up straight away, before someone slips on it.

DON'T use ill-fitting spanners or other tools which may slip and cause injury.

DON'T attempt to lift a heavy component which may be beyond your capability – get assistance.

DON'T rush to finish a job, or take unverified short cuts.

DON'T allow children or animals in or around an unattended vehicle.

DO wear eye protection when using power tools such as drill, sander, bench grinder etc, and when working under the vehicle.

DO use a barrier cream on your hands prior to undertaking dirty jobs – it will protect your skin from infection as well as making the dirt easier to remove afterwards; but make sure your hands aren't left slippery. Note that long-term contact with used engine oil can be a health hazard.

DO keep loose clothing (cuffs, tie etc) and long hair well out of the way of moving mechanical parts.

DO remove rings, wristwatch etc, before working on the vehicle – especially the electrical system.

DO ensure that any lifting tackle used has a safe working load rating adequate for the job.

DO keep your work area tidy – it is only too easy to fall over articles left lying around.

DO get someone to check periodically that all is well, when working alone on the vehicle.

DO carry out work in a logical sequence and check that everything is correctly assembled and tightened afterwards.

DO remember that your vehicle's safety affects that of yourself and others. If in doubt on any point, get specialist advice.

IF, in spite of following these precautions, you are unfortunate enough to injure yourself, seek medical attention as soon as possible.

Asbestos

Certain friction, insulating, sealing, and other products – such as brake linings, brake bands, clutch linings, torque converters, gaskets, etc – contain asbestos. *Extreme care must be taken to avoid inhalation of dust from such products since it is hazardous to health.* If in doubt, assume that they *do* contain asbestos.

Fire

Remember at all times that petrol (gasoline) is highly flammable. Never smoke, or have any kind of naked flame around, when working on the vehicle. But the risk does not end there – a spark caused by an electrical short-circuit, by two metal surfaces contacting each other, by careless use of tools, or even by static electricity built up in your body under certain conditions, can ignite petrol vapour, which in a confined space is highly explosive.

Always disconnect the battery earth (ground) terminal before working on any part of the fuel or electrical system, and never risk spilling fuel on to a hot engine or exhaust.

It is recommended that a fire extinguisher of a type suitable for fuel and electrical fires is kept handy in the garage or workplace at all times. Never try to extinguish a fuel or electrical fire with water.

Note: *Any reference to a 'torch' appearing in this manual should always be taken to mean a hand-held battery-operated electric lamp or flashlight. It does NOT mean a welding/gas torch or blowlamp.*

Fumes

Certain fumes are highly toxic and can quickly cause unconsciousness and even death if inhaled to any extent. Petrol (gasoline) vapour comes into this category, as do the vapours from certain solvents such as trichloroethylene. Any draining or pouring of such volatile fluids should be done in a well ventilated area.

When using cleaning fluids and solvents, read the instructions carefully. Never use materials from unmarked containers – they may give off poisonous vapours.

Never run the engine of a motor vehicle in an enclosed space such as a garage. Exhaust fumes contain carbon monoxide which is extremely poisonous; if you need to run the engine, always do so in the open air or at least have the rear of the vehicle outside the workplace.

If you are fortunate enough to have the use of an inspection pit, never drain or pour petrol, and never run the engine, while the vehicle is standing over it; the fumes, being heavier than air, will concentrate in the pit with possibly lethal results.

The battery

Never cause a spark, or allow a naked light, near the vehicle's battery. It will normally be giving off a certain amount of hydrogen gas, which is highly explosive.

Always disconnect the battery earth (ground) terminal before working on the fuel or electrical systems.

If possible, loosen the filler plugs or cover when charging the battery from an external source. Do not charge at an excessive rate or the battery may burst.

Take care when topping up and when carrying the battery. The acid electrolyte, even when diluted, is very corrosive and should not be allowed to contact the eyes or skin.

If you ever need to prepare electrolyte yourself, always add the acid slowly to the water, and never the other way round. Protect against splashes by wearing rubber gloves and goggles.

When jump starting a car using a booster battery, for negative earth (ground) vehicles, connect the jump leads in the following sequence: First connect one jump lead between the positive (+) terminals of the two batteries. Then connect the other jump lead first to the negative (–) terminal of the booster battery, and then to a good earthing (ground) point on the vehicle to be started, at least 18 in (45 cm) from the battery if possible. Ensure that hands and jump leads are clear of any moving parts, and that the two vehicles do not touch. Disconnect the leads in the reverse order.

Mains electricity and electrical equipment

When using an electric power tool, inspection light etc, always ensure that the appliance is correctly connected to its plug and that, where necessary, it is properly earthed (grounded). Do not use such appliances in damp conditions and, again, beware of creating a spark or applying excessive heat in the vicinity of fuel or fuel vapour. Also ensure that the appliances meet the relevant national safety standards.

Ignition HT voltage

A severe electric shock can result from touching certain parts of the ignition system, such as the HT leads, when the engine is running or being cranked, particularly if components are damp or the insulation is defective. Where an electronic ignition system is fitted, the HT voltage is much higher and could prove fatal.

Fault diagnosis

Introduction

The vehicle owner who does his or her own maintenance according to the recommended schedules should not have to use this section of the manual very often. Modern component reliability is such that, provided those items subject to wear or deterioration are inspected or renewed at the specified intervals, sudden failure is comparatively rare. Faults do not usually just happen as a result of sudden failure, but develop over a period of time. Major mechanical failures in particular are usually preceded by characteristic symptoms over hundreds or even thousands of miles. Those components which do occasionally fail without warning are often small and easily carried in the vehicle.

With any fault finding, the first step is to decide where to begin investigations. Sometimes this is obvious, but on other occasions a little detective work will be necessary. The owner who makes half a dozen haphazard adjustments or replacements may be successful in curing a fault (or its symptoms), but he will be none the wiser if the fault recurs and he may well have spent more time and money than was necessary. A calm and logical approach will be found to be more satisfactory in the long run. Always take into account any warning signs or abnormalities that may have been noticed in the period preceding the fault – power loss, high or low gauge readings, unusual noises or smells, etc – and remember that failure of components such as fuses may only be pointers to some underlying fault.

The pages which follow here are intended to help in cases of failure to start or breakdown on the road. There is also a Fault Diagnosis Section at the end of each Chapter which should be consulted if the preliminary checks prove unfruitful. Whatever the fault, certain basic principles apply. These are as follows:

Verify the fault. This is simply a matter of being sure that you know what the symptoms are before starting work. This is particularly important if you are investigating a fault for someone else who may not have described it very accurately.

Don't overlook the obvious. For example, if the vehicle won't start, is there fuel in the tank? (Don't take anyone else's word on this particular point, and don't trust the fuel gauge either!) If an electrical fault is indicated, look for loose or broken wires before digging out the test gear.

Cure the disease, not the symptom. Substituting a flat battery with a fully charged one will get you off the hard shoulder, but if the underlying cause is not attended to, the new battery will go the same way.

Don't take anything for granted. Particularly, don't forget that a 'new' component may itself be defective (especially if it's been rattling round in the boot for months), and don't leave components out of a fault diagnosis sequence just because they are new or recently fitted. When you do finally diagnose a difficult fault, you'll probably realise that all the evidence was there from the start.

Electrical faults

Electrical faults can be more puzzling than straightforward mechanical failures, but they are no less susceptible to logical analysis if the basic principles of operation are understood. Vehicle electrical wiring exists in extremely unfavourable conditions – heat, vibration and chemical attack – and the first things to look for are loose or corroded connections and broken or chafed wires, especially where the wires pass through holes in the bodywork or are subject to vibration.

All metal-bodied vehicles in current production have one pole of the battery 'earthed', ie connected to the vehicle bodywork, and in nearly all modern vehicles it is the negative (–) terminal. The various electrical components – motors, bulb holders etc – are also connected to earth, either by means of a lead or directly by their mountings. Electric current flows through the component and then back to the battery via the bodywork. If the component mounting is loose or corroded, or if a good path back to the battery is not available, the circuit will be incomplete and malfunction will result. The engine and/or gearbox are also earthed by means of flexible metal straps to the body or subframe; if these straps are loose or missing, starter motor, generator and ignition trouble may result.

Assuming the earth return to be satisfactory, electrical faults will be due either to component malfunction or to defects in the current supply. Individual components are dealt with in Chapter 7. If supply wires are broken or cracked internally this results in an open-circuit, and the easiest way to check for this is to bypass the suspect wire temporarily with a length of wire having a crocodile clip or suitable connector at each end. Alternatively, a 12V test lamp can be used to verify the presence of supply voltage at various points along the wire and the break can be thus isolated.

If a bare portion of a live wire touches the bodywork or other earthed metal part, the electricity will take the low-resistance path thus formed back to the battery: this is known as a short-circuit. Hopefully a short-circuit will blow a fuse, but otherwise it may cause burning of the insulation (and possibly further short-circuits) or even a fire. This is why it is inadvisable to bypass persistently blowing fuses with silver foil or wire.

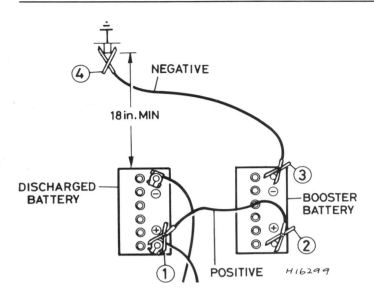

Jump start lead connections for negative earth – connect leads in order shown

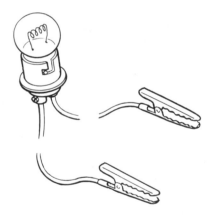

A simple test lamp is useful for checking electrical faults

Spares and tool kit

Most vehicles are supplied only with sufficient tools for wheel changing; the *Maintenance and minor repair* tool kit detailed in *Tools and working facilities,* with the addition of a hammer, is probably sufficient for those repairs that most motorists would consider attempting at the roadside. In addition a few items which can be fitted without too much trouble in the event of a breakdown should be carried. Experience and available space will modify the list below, but the following may save having to call on professional assistance:

 Drivebelt(s) – emergency type may suffice
 Spare fuses
 Set of principal light bulbs
 Tin of radiator sealer and hose bandage
 Exhaust bandage
 Roll of insulating tape
 Length of soft iron wire
 Length of electrical flex
 Torch or inspection lamp (can double as test lamp)
 Battery jump leads
 Tow-rope

 Litre of engine oil
 Sealed can of hydraulic fluid
 Emergency windscreen
 Worm drive clips
 Tube of filler paste

If spare fuel is carried, a can designed for the purpose should be used to minimise risks of leakage and collision damage. A first aid kit and a warning triangle, whilst not at present compulsory in the UK, are obviously sensible items to carry in addition to the above.

When touring abroad it may be advisable to carry additional spares which, even if you cannot fit them yourself, could save having to wait while parts are obtained. The items below may be worth considering:

 Clutch and throttle cables
 Cylinder head gasket
 Alternator brushes
 Fuel pump repair kit
 Tyre valve core

One of the motoring organisations will be able to advise on availability of fuel etc in foreign countries.

Engine will not start

Engine fails to turn when starter operated
 Flat battery (recharge, use jump leads, or push start)
 Battery terminals loose or corroded
 Battery earth to body defective
 Engine earth strap loose or broken
 Starter motor (or solenoid) wiring loose or broken
 Starter switch faulty
 Major mechanical failure (seizure)
 Starter or solenoid internal fault (see Chapter 7)

Starter motor turns engine slowly
 Partially discharged battery (recharge, use jump leads, or push start)
 Battery terminals loose or corroded
 Battery earth to body defective
 Engine earth strap loose
 Starter motor (or solenoid) wiring loose
 Starter motor internal fault (see Chapter 7)

Starter motor spins without turning engine
 Flat battery
 Starter motor pinion sticking on sleeve
 Flywheel gear teeth damaged or worn
 Starter motor mounting bolts loose

Engine turns normally but fails to start
 No fuel in tank (check for delivery)
 Other fuel system fault (see Chapter 3)
 Poor compression (see Chapter 1)
 Major mechanical failure (eg camshaft drive)

Engine fires but will not run
 Air leaks at inlet manifold
 Fuel starvation (see Chapter 3)

Engine cuts out and will not restart

Engine misfires before cutting out – fuel fault
 Fuel tank empty
 Fuel pump defective or filter blocked (check for delivery)
 Fuel tank filler vent blocked (suction will be evident on releasing cap)
 Other fuel system fault (see Chapter 3)

Engine cuts out – other causes
 Serious overheating
 Major mechanical failure (eg camshaft drive)

Engine overheats

Ignition (no-charge) warning light illuminated
Slack or broken drivebelt – retension or renew (Chapter 7)

Ignition warning light not illuminated
Coolant loss due to internal or external leakage (see Chapter 2)
Thermostat defective
Low oil level
Brakes binding
Radiator clogged externally or internally
Electric cooling fan not operating correctly
Engine waterways clogged

Note: *Do not add cold water to an overheated engine or damage may result*

Low engine oil pressure

Gauge reads low or warning light illuminated with engine running
Oil level low or incorrect grade
Defective gauge or sender unit
Wire to sender unit earthed
Engine overheating
Oil filter clogged or bypass valve defective
Oil pressure relief valve defective

Oil pick-up strainer clogged
Oil pump worn or mountings loose
Worn main or big-end bearings

Note: *Low oil pressure in a high-mileage engine at tickover is not necessarily a cause for concern. Sudden pressure loss at speed is far more significant. In any event, check the gauge or warning light sender before condemning the engine.*

Engine noises

Whistling or wheezing noises
Leaking manifold gasket
Blowing head gasket

Tapping or rattling
Incorrect valve clearances
Worn valve gear
Worn timing belt
Broken piston ring (ticking noise)

Knocking or thumping
Unintentional mechanical contact (eg fan blades)
Worn drivebelt
Peripheral component fault (generator, water pump etc)
Worn big-end bearings (regular heavy knocking, perhaps less under load)
Worn main bearings (rumbling and knocking, perhaps worsening under load)
Piston slap (most noticeable when cold)

Conversion factors

Length (distance)
Inches (in)	X	25.4	= Millimetres (mm)	X 0.0394	= Inches (in)
Feet (ft)	X	0.305	= Metres (m)	X 3.281	= Feet (ft)
Miles	X	1.609	= Kilometres (km)	X 0.621	= Miles

Volume (capacity)
Cubic inches (cu in; in^3)	X	16.387	= Cubic centimetres (cc; cm^3)	X 0.061	= Cubic inches (cu in; in^3)
Imperial pints (Imp pt)	X	0.568	= Litres (l)	X 1.76	= Imperial pints (Imp pt)
Imperial quarts (Imp qt)	X	1.137	= Litres (l)	X 0.88	= Imperial quarts (Imp qt)
Imperial quarts (Imp qt)	X	1.201	= US quarts (US qt)	X 0.833	= Imperial quarts (Imp qt)
US quarts (US qt)	X	0.946	= Litres (l)	X 1.057	= US quarts (US qt)
Imperial gallons (Imp gal)	X	4.546	= Litres (l)	X 0.22	= Imperial gallons (Imp gal)
Imperial gallons (Imp gal)	X	1.201	= US gallons (US gal)	X 0.833	= Imperial gallons (Imp gal)
US gallons (US gal)	X	3.785	= Litres (l)	X 0.264	= US gallons (US gal)

Mass (weight)
Ounces (oz)	X	28.35	= Grams (g)	X 0.035	= Ounces (oz)
Pounds (lb)	X	0.454	= Kilograms (kg)	X 2.205	= Pounds (lb)

Force
Ounces-force (ozf; oz)	X	0.278	= Newtons (N)	X 3.6	= Ounces-force (ozf; oz)
Pounds-force (lbf; lb)	X	4.448	= Newtons (N)	X 0.225	= Pounds-force (lbf; lb)
Newtons (N)	X	0.1	= Kilograms-force (kgf; kg)	X 9.81	= Newtons (N)

Pressure
Pounds-force per square inch (psi; lbf/in^2; lb/in^2)	X	0.070	= Kilograms-force per square centimetre (kgf/cm^2; kg/cm^2)	X 14.223	= Pounds-force per square inch (psi; lbf/in^2; lb/in^2)
Pounds-force per square inch (psi; lbf/in^2; lb/in^2)	X	0.068	= Atmospheres (atm)	X 14.696	= Pounds-force per square inch (psi; lbf/in^2; lb/in^2)
Pounds-force per square inch (psi; lbf/in^2; lb/in^2)	X	0.069	= Bars	X 14.5	= Pounds-force per square inch (psi; lbf/in^2; lb/in^2)
Pounds-force per square inch (psi; lbf/in^2; lb/in^2)	X	6.895	= Kilopascals (kPa)	X 0.145	= Pounds-force per square inch (psi; lbf/in^2; lb/in^2)
Kilopascals (kPa)	X	0.01	= Kilograms-force per square centimetre (kgf/cm^2; kg/cm^2)	X 98.1	= Kilopascals (kPa)

Torque (moment of force)
Pounds-force inches (lbf in; lb in)	X	1.152	= Kilograms-force centimetre (kgf cm; kg cm)	X 0.868	= Pounds-force inches (lbf in; lb in)
Pounds-force inches (lbf in; lb in)	X	0.113	= Newton metres (Nm)	X 8.85	= Pounds-force inches (lbf in; lb in)
Pounds-force inches (lbf in; lb in)	X	0.083	= Pounds-force feet (lbf ft; lb ft)	X 12	= Pounds-force inches (lbf in; lb in)
Pounds-force feet (lbf ft; lb ft)	X	0.138	= Kilograms-force metres (kgf m; kg m)	X 7.233	= Pounds-force feet (lbf ft; lb ft)
Pounds-force feet (lbf ft; lb ft)	X	1.356	= Newton metres (Nm)	X 0.738	= Pounds-force feet (lbf ft; lb ft)
Newton metres (Nm)	X	0.102	= Kilograms-force metres (kgf m; kg m)	X 9.804	= Newton metres (Nm)

Power
Horsepower (hp)	X	745.7	= Watts (W)	X 0.0013	= Horsepower (hp)

Velocity (speed)
Miles per hour (miles/hr; mph)	X	1.609	= Kilometres per hour (km/hr; kph)	X 0.621	= Miles per hour (miles/hr; mph)

Fuel consumption*
Miles per gallon, Imperial (mpg)	X	0.354	= Kilometres per litre (km/l)	X 2.825	= Miles per gallon, Imperial (mpg)
Miles per gallon, US (mpg)	X	0.425	= Kilometres per litre (km/l)	X 2.352	= Miles per gallon, US (mpg)

Temperature
Degrees Fahrenheit = ($^\circ$C x 1.8) + 32 Degrees Celsius (Degrees Centigrade; $^\circ$C) = ($^\circ$F - 32) x 0.56

*It is common practice to convert from miles per gallon (mpg) to litres/100 kilometres (l/100km),
where mpg (Imperial) x l/100 km = 282 and mpg (US) x l/100 km = 235*

Index

12N PLUG AND SOCKET NORMAL

INTERNATIONAL COLOUR CODE FOR 7 CORE CABLE TO BE FITTED TO 7 PIN PLUG AND SOCKET (NORMAL) FOR ROAD LIGHTING.

TERMINAL Nos.		CABLE COLOURS	APPLICATION	
1	L	YELLOW	L HAND DIRECTION INDICATOR LAMP	_Blue/Red_
2	54G	BLUE	REAR FOG LAMPS	
3	31	~~WHITE~~ BLACK	EARTH (COMMON RETURN)	_Blue/Black_
4	R	GREEN	R HAND DIRECTION INDICATOR LAMP	
5	58R	BROWN	R HAND TAIL, SIDE, NUMBER PLATE LAMP	_Grey/White_
6	54	RED	STOP LAMPS	_Green/Red_
7	58L	~~BLACK~~ WHITE	L HAND SIDE LAMP	_Grey/Yellow_

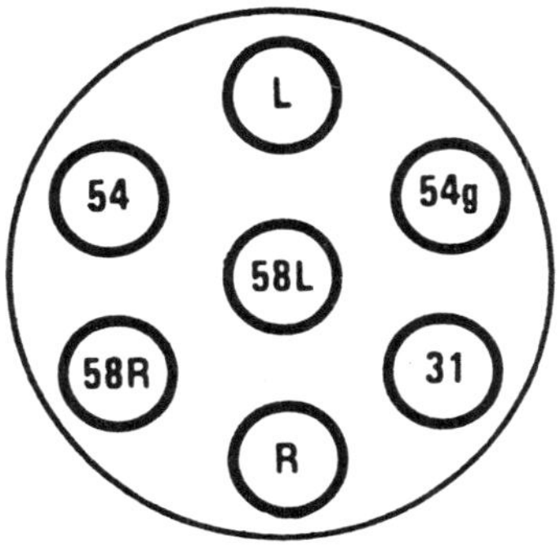

CONNECT AS ABOVE WHEN USING OUR:

Part No.	C109	7-Core Trailer Cable
Part No.	C109A	7-Core Trailer Cable Heavy Duty
Part No.	C110	7-Core Trailer Cable with Scotchlocks
Part No.	C110A	7-Core Trailer Cable Heavy Duty with Scotchlocks
Part No.	C107MN	7 Pin Metal Plug
Part No.	C107NN	7 Pin Nylon Plug
Part No.	C108MN	7 Pin Metal Socket
Part No.	C108NN	7 Pin Nylon Socket

TREND MOTOR ACCESSORIES LIMITED   Carr Lane, Low Moor, Bradford BD12 0QR. Tel: 0274 676272

Printed by
J H Haynes & Co Ltd
Sparkford Nr Yeovil
Somerset BA22 7JJ England